Learning to Learn

Learning to Learn provides a much needed overview and international guide to the field of learning to learn from a multidisciplinary lifelong and lifewide perspective. A wealth of research has been flourishing on this key educational goal in recent years. Internationally, it is considered to be one of the key competencies needed to compete in the global economy, but also a crucial factor for individual and social well-being. This book draws on leading international contributors to provide a cutting-edge overview of current thinking on learning to learn research, policy, and implementation in both formal and informal learning environments.

But what learning to learn is exactly, and what its constituting elements are, are much debated issues. These seem to be the crucial questions if assessment and development of this 'malleable side of intelligence' are to be accomplished. The approach of this volume is to consider a broad conception of learning to learn, not confined to only study strategies or metacognition, yet acknowledging the importance of such elements.

The book sets out to answer five main questions:

- What is learning to learn?
- What are its functions and how do we assess it?
- What does it promise to the individual and society at large?
- How is it conceived in national curricula internationally?
- How can it be developed in a variety of contexts?

The text is organized into two parts: the first addresses the core question of the nature of learning to learn from a theoretical and policy viewpoint, and the second presents recent research carried out in several educational systems, with special attention to assessment and curriculum. It gives an account of pedagogical practices of learning to learn and its role in individual empowerment from childhood to adulthood.

Contributors also highlight the potential use of learning to learn as an organizing concept for lifelong learning, school improvement, and teacher training along with potential conflicts with existing incentive practices and policies.

This book is a vital starting point and guide for any advanced student or researcher looking to understand this important area of research.

Ruth Deakin Crick, MEd, PhD, is Reader in Systems Learning and Leadership in the Graduate School of Education at the University of Bristol. She is one of the originators of the Effective Lifelong Learning Inventory, a self-assessment tool for developing learning power. Her research focuses on the implications of complexity and systems thinking for pedagogy. She co-directs the Learning Emergence network.

Cristina Stringher, PhD, is a researcher at the Italian Institute for the Educational Evaluation of Instruction and Training (INVALSI), and a lecturer at Roma Tre University. She currently serves as a member in the Project Advisory Committee of IEA's Early Childhood Education Study. Her interests focus on theoretical and empirical research in learning to learn development, with its lifelong and lifewide applications.

Kai Ren is a post-doctoral researcher at the School of Education, China Shaanxi Normal University. He is also a member of the learning power research team at the Graduate School of Education, Bristol University. Kai's research focuses on learning to learn and how it relates to people's identities and stories.

Learning to Learn

International perspectives from
theory and practice

Edited by Ruth Deakin Crick, Cristina Stringher and Kai Ren

Routledge
Taylor & Francis Group

LONDON AND NEW YORK

First published 2014
by Routledge
2 Park Square, Milton Park, Abingdon, Oxon OX14 4RN

and by Routledge
711 Third Avenue, New York, NY 10017

Routledge is an imprint of the Taylor & Francis Group, an informa business

British Library Cataloguing in Publication Data
A catalogue record for this book is available from the British Library

Library of Congress Cataloging in Publication Data
Learning to learn: international perspectives from theory and practice /
Edited by Ruth Deakin Crick, Cristina Stringher, Kai Ren.
      p. cm.
    Includes bibliographical references and index.
    ISBN 978-0-415-65623-8 (hardback)—ISBN 978-0-415-65624-5
    (pbk.)—ISBN 978-0-203-07804-4 (ebook) 1. Education. 2. Learning.
    3. Cognitive learning. 4. Learning, Psychology of. I. Deakin Crick,
    Ruth, 1955– II. Stringher, Cristina. III. Ren, Kai.
    LB1060.L43 2014
    370.15′23—dc23   2013039283

ISBN: 978-0-415-65623-8 (hbk)
ISBN: 978-0-415-65624-5 (pbk)
ISBN: 978-0-203-07804-4 (ebk)

Typeset in Galliard
by RefineCatch Ltd, Bungay, Suffolk

Printed and bound in the United States of America by Publishers Graphics,
LLC on sustainably sourced paper.

Contents

List of figures, tables, and boxes

Figures

Tables

Boxes

List of contributors

Editors

Ruth Deakin Crick is a Reader in Systems Learning and Leadership at the University of Bristol. She is one of the originators of a learning analytic tool designed to identify and strengthen an individual's learning dispositions, attitudes and values and provide a coaching framework for self-directed learning and teacher-led pedagogical change. Her research identified seven dimensions of 'Learning Power' which are both 'internal' and 'social' and influenced by a person's narrative, culture and tradition. Feedback from the learning analytic is in the form of an immediate visual image of an individual's learning 'profile' that forms a framework for a coaching conversation which moves between the coachee's identity as a learner and their learning goals and experiences.

Her research now focuses on processes of learning, adaptation and feedback in complex social systems. She has established a substantive research partnership with Engineers in the University of Bristol's Systems Centre, where she is a Co-Investigator in the International Centre for Infrastructure Futures which brings together stakeholders involved in renewing the UK's infrastructure systems. The Centre is developing a principled and generic learning journey framework for creating innovative, performance based business models to exploit infrastructure interdependencies. With colleagues at the Knowledge Media Institute of the Open University she has contributed to the creation of a new field of enquiry: dispositional analytics. www.learningemergence.net

Cristina Stringher is a researcher at the Italian Institute for the Educational Evaluation of Instruction and Training (INVALSI). She currently serves as a member in the OECD Early Childhood Education Network and in the Project Advisory Committee of IEA's Early Childhood Education Study. She is also a member of the European Association for Research on Learning and Instruction (EARLI). Since 2004 she has been a component of Cesmon, Centre for Montessori Studies, at University Roma Tre and a lecturer in Developmental Psychology on a master's degree course for coordinators of early childhood education services. Her research interests concern the theoretical definition of learning to learn and the application of techniques and didactic methodologies aimed at improving this malleable side of intelligence in a developmental and lifelong perspective. She is exploring the use of her learning to learn framework as the heart of her research and training activities in the areas of school improvement, teacher self-evaluation, adult learning and children's readiness for school and lifelong learning. Recently, she has been a contributor in the report to the Italian Parliament on the levels and quality of public education (CNEL, 2013) and to the IEA ICCS Encyclopedia (2013). Other publications include theoretical explorations on learning to learn (INVALSI, 2010; Franco Angeli, 2008), on initial training for teachers and coordinators of ECE services (AUFOP, 2012), and on the validation of experiential learning (Anicia, 2011, 2010).

Kai Ren is a post-doctoral researcher at the School of Education, China Shaanxi Normal University. He is also a member of the learning power research team at the Graduate School of Education, Bristol University, UK. Kai's research focuses on learning to learn and how it relates to people's identities and stories.

Contributors

Aureliana Alberici is Professor of Adult Education and President of the degree course in Human Resources Education and Development, University Roma Tre, and President of RUIAP (Italian University Network for Lifelong Learning). Her research interests include lifelong learning, qualitative methodologies, adult learning, and competenc.

Bronwen Cowie is Professor and Director of the Wilf Malcolm Institute of Educational Research, University of Waikato, New Zealand. Her research interests include formative assessment, science education, culturally responsive pedagogy, and curriculum implementation. Projects range from long-term national evaluations to in-depth classroom studies.

Andreas Demetriou is Professor of Psychology and President of the University of Nicosia Research Foundation and of the National Research Council of Cyprus. He is a fellow of Academia Europaea and the International Academy of Education, an Honorary Doctor of Middlesex University, UK and an Honorary Professor of the Northeastern Normal University, China. He developed a theory of intellectual development that integrates the developmental and the psychometric traditions in psychology.

Paolo Di Rienzo is Associate Professor of Pedagogy and of Adult Education in the Department of Education at the University of Roma Tre. His interests include adult education, lifelong learning, the theory of contructivism, and biographical methodologies in pedagogy.

Margot Foster, PSM, is the Director for Pedagogy and Leadership in the Department for Education and Child Development, Government of South

Australia. She leads innovative teams across the state to redesign teacher and leadership pedagogy for increased learner engagement and intellectual challenge.

Chris Goldspink, PhD, is a Director of Incept Labs, a social policy research company based in Sydney, New South Wales, Australia. His work focuses on building individual and collective capacity for learning, resilience, and innovation.

Jarkko Hautamäki is Professor of Special Education and Director, Centre for Educational Assessment, University of Helsinki, Finland, established in 1996 to develop tools for assessing learning to learn. He has participated in EU research on L2L, the PISA 2006 and 2015 Finnish teams, and in national and international evaluations of education.

Rosemary Hipkins, PhD, is Chief Researcher, New Zealand Council for Educational Research. Her research interests include ongoing development of New Zealand's curriculum and senior secondary qualifications, key competencies (as capabilities), and science education.

Paul Kloosterman is a Dutch freelance consultant based in Italy. He began as a youth worker with the European Youth in Action programme and has been a member of the European Network on Learning to Learn. In the past 20 years he has been active as a trainer, author, and expert in the field of European non-formal education.

Sirkku Kupiainen is Senior Fellow in the Centre for Educational Assessment, University of Helsinki, Finland, established in 1996 to develop tools for assessing learning to learn. She has coordinated the European Pilot Project on L2L, has participated in the PISA 2006 and 2015 Finnish teams, and is a member of the Finnish Education Evaluation Council.

Elena Martín is Full Professor in Educational Psychology at the Universidad Autónoma de Madrid, Spain. Her research interests are in the field of teacher's conceptions, curriculum, and assessment.

Barbara L. McCombs, PhD, is Senior Research Scientist and Director of the Human Motivation, Learning, and Development Centre at ARTI (Applied Research & Technology Institute) in the University of Denver's School of Engineering and Computer Science, Denver, Colorado, USA. Her interests focus on providing empirical and theoretical support for person and learner-centred approaches to the development of human potential.

Amparo Moreno is Associate Professor in Developmental and Educational Psychology at the Universidad Autónoma de Madrid, Spain. Her research area is related to cognitive (preschoolers' memory), educational (metacognitive skills development and learning to learn), and social (gender) development.

Nirmala Rao is Professor, Faculty of Education and Associate Dean, Graduate School, the University of Hong Kong. She is a Developmental and Chartered

(Educational) Psychologist, who has published widely on early childhood development and education in Asia.

Jin Sun is Assistant Professor, Department of Early Childhood Education, the Hong Kong Institute of Education, Hong Kong. Her research interests include early child development and education, interventions for economically disadvantaged children, and Chinese socialisation.

Julianne Willis, MEd, has worked in education for nearly 35 years, covering roles in primary through tertiary education in Australia. Over the last seven years, Julianne has been working as a consultant in public education, Catholic education, and independent schools. At the heart of her work is the search for ways in which learners can be empowered to learn to learn. 'Connectedness with the stream within' is a defining feature of her work.

Li Zhang is a lecturer in the School of Preschool and Special Education, East China Normal University, Shanghai. Her research focuses on the relationship between preschool experience and child development and early childhood education in rural China.

Foreword

Piero Cipollone

Being aware of one's own learning processes and preferences, together with ways to improve them, is a key educational objective for present and future citizens living in a constantly changing environment, not only to be more adaptive, but also to extrapolate one's own meaning out of life experiences. When I was a child, I used to live in a small village in southern Italy, where the local school was a place only for those who already had a well-educated family helping with homework. I had to develop a resilient attitude myself to go through the education system and take advantage of learning opportunities in higher education and beyond.

In 2010, I was appointed Executive Director of the World Bank Group to represent the constituency that includes Albania, Greece, Italy, Malta, Portugal, San Marino, and Timor-Leste. Before that, I was President at INVALSI, the Italian Institute for the Educational Evaluation of Instruction and Training. In this capacity, I met one of the editors of this book, Cristina Stringher, in late 2008 and entrusted her with the task to draft a comprehensive proposal to the Italian Ministry of Education contributing to the evaluation strategy of European Social Funds initiatives. She delivered the proposal and in early 2009 INVALSI eventually signed a convention with the Ministry to carry out projects in several areas to improve student learning and school accountability in deprived regions of southern Italy. Within this context, I encouraged Cristina to persist in her study of learning to learn with the ultimate scope to devise an assessment tool for this key competence for lifelong learning. This is how this book came about: Cristina presented her work at the EARLI Conference in 2011, Routledge editor Bruce Roberts found it of interest, and the book project was drafted.

We at the World Bank believe that education is a powerful driver of development. It is one of the strongest instruments for reducing poverty and improving health, gender equality, peace, and stability. Today, the World Bank is more committed than ever to expanding opportunities for children and youth and nations alike, through education. In 2011, the World Bank launched a new Education Sector Strategy 2020, 'Learning for All'. The strategy encourages countries to 'invest early' beginning in early childhood, 'invest smartly' in efforts proven to improve learning, and 'invest for all' focusing not only on privileged but on all students. The Bank is currently supporting countries to achieve the UN's Millennium Development Goals and to deliver the learning and skills necessary for all people to live healthy and productive lives. One of the key messages of the 2020 Strategy is that education should lead to more learning, especially during schooling: 'the period between birth and young adulthood is especially critical because the ability to learn that is developed during this period provides a foundation for lifelong learning' (World Bank, 2011: 25). Fostering learning and learning how to learn should thus be one of the primary objectives of today's education systems worldwide.

The aim of this book was to gather and reflect upon the most updated knowledge accumulated internationally in the field of learning to learn from a multidisciplinary lifelong and lifewide perspective. To achieve this ambitious aim, Cristina initially contacted Ruth Deakin Crick and Kai Ren as co-editors. This nucleus then aggregated a pool of the best international researchers and practitioners in the field. Some of the contributors have previous experience in the European Network on Learning to Learn, others come from three different continents to represent not only a Euro-centric view of learning to learn, but a wide array of research and practice traditions.

Within the wider discourse of lifelong learning, the European Lisbon and 2020 strategy placed learning to learn among the eight key competencies that are needed in the global economy not only for professional reasons but also for personal fulfilment and social well-being. Elsewhere, learning to learn is considered an organizing concept in education, serving multiple needs such as educational system improvement and learner empowerment for active citizenship. The volume addresses these themes in a lifelong and lifewide perspective, ranging from theoretical explorations of what learning to learn is, to several theoretical contributions from psychology, sociology, and education. Research and practice on learning to learn are also addressed with chapters covering how to foster learning to learn from the very early years throughout school years up to adult learning in informal and non-formal contexts.

Learning to learn seems to serve also social needs when it is used as an organizing concept for reflective communities of practice. The crucial issue, however, is to establish what learning to learn is so it can be assessed in a variety of contexts and across age-ranges, assessment being the baseline to start from for its development. How to endorse this primary objective of education is connected to its development in different contexts: in education, at work, and throughout one's own individual and social life.

In synthesis, the book covers broad theoretical aspects with a view to concrete applications of learning to learn in several contexts and in lifelong learning, including but not limited to all school levels. Most importantly, this volume is meant to shed light on learning to learn for all, in a way that should in particular appeal to researchers, scholars, and practitioners interested in this malleable side of intelligence. To develop citizens in all parts of the globe.

Piero Cipollone
Executive Director, World Bank
Washington DC, June 2013

Reference

World Bank (2011) *Learning for all: Investing in people's knowledge and skills to promote development*. Washington, DC: World Bank.

Acknowledgements

The editors wish to thank the two independent reviewers for their precious comments that helped shape this book.

Introduction

*Ruth Deakin Crick, Kai Ren,
and Cristina Stringher*

More than ever before, the development of learning to learn is seen as crucial for success in the complex, unpredictable, and data-drenched world we share. Learning to learn is both a process and an outcome of formal education, together with other trans-disciplinary and lifewide competences. It goes deep into pedagogy and practice and is influenced by culture and context. As an outcome, it is a competence we aspire to measure and celebrate.

There are four drivers for the production of this book. First, the most comprehensive volume to date on this topic was published more than 20 years ago (Smith et al., 1990), while a wealth of research, both theoretical and empirical, has been revitalizing this domain of knowledge and practice at the start of the new millennium.

Second, learning how to learn is a crucial competence for human flourishing in twenty-first-century conditions of risk and uncertainty. It is one of eight key competencies identified by the European Union in the Lisbon and the 2020 strategies (European Communities, 2006). The European Union maintains a keen interest in this topic, as demonstrated by the European network of policy-makers and several working groups on key competencies, including the creation of the European Network on Learning to Learn (Hoskins & Fredriksson, 2008). Internationally, learning to learn is emerging as a focus for school improvement and as a foundation for lifelong and lifewide learning. UNESCO (2013) has recently included approaches to learning as a key domain that should be an entitlement for all children, and one that needs to be assessed.

Third, language matters. There is a real need for serious debate about the term 'learning to learn', which is frequently used in different ways and in different contexts without clear definition. Often it is used within a conceptually narrow framework, limited to 'measurable' study strategies and learning styles (OECD, 2010) for which there is little evidence of success. There is an urgent need for a research validated foundation for learning to learn and what constitutes it.

Last, and by no means least, practitioners, university lecturers, teachers, and schools around the world encourage their students to take responsibility for their own learning and achievement – and for this they need to learn how to learn. Existing funds of knowledge are all 'out there on the Internet' and what matters is how individuals and teams make sense out of and utilize the mass of information that they are bombarded with every day. Dialogue between research and practice is crucial to underpin this movement, generating a discipline of research-informed practice that frames and informs both commercial and policy interests. In the absence of a *pensée unique* (see Chapter 4 by Alberici and Di Rienzo), the global community of scholarship in education provides an important voice that should make a healthy, collaborative contribution to the formation of policy and practice.

Assessment of competence in learning to learn is a critically important policy ideal – one that the European Union embraced and embarked upon with its Learning to Learn Network. After some serious effort, we came to the conclusion that there are so many different approaches to learning to learn from across the EU, that it was impossible in 2007 to arrive at a consensus for its measurement. Before we can ever effectively assess something, we need to know exactly what it is we are measuring – as a matter of professional ethics. We also need to know what measurement models are most suitable and what is the purpose of the assessment before we develop our assessment technologies. This book reports on attempts at measuring some aspects, precursors, and dimensions of learning to learn, although a systematic approach to assessment of this competence is yet to be developed.

The book addresses five basic questions:

- What is learning to learn?
- What are its functions and what does it promise to the individual and society at large?
- How is it implemented in national curricula?
- How can we assess it?
- How can we develop it in a variety of contexts?

The book is organized in two parts.

1. *Theory*: Theoretical reflections on the concept, internal structure, and relational factors of learning to learn and how it develops.
2. *International Research and Practice*: (a) empirical studies into how learning to learn is used in practice; and (b) practitioner stories about learning to learn.

In Part 1, the opening chapter by Stringher presents a view of what learning to learn is and an integrated model, drawing on an extensive review, which provides an organizing concept for lifelong learning. In Chapter 2, Demetriou analyses learning to learn in the context of the functioning and development of the human mind. Learning to think or reason and learning to learn are seen as complementary aspects of the same adaptive process of tuning the mind with the environment. Deakin Crick then explores how complexity and holistic systems thinking can contribute to our understanding of learning to learn and the pedagogical conditions necessary to support this crucial competence. In Chapter 4, Alberici and Di Rienzo explain why learning to learn is important for individuals, groups, and for society at large throughout the lifespan and why learning to learn is interpreted as a capacity for all, which eventually facilitates the development of democracy. In the closing chapter of the theoretical part of the volume, Ren addresses how the Confucian conceptualization of learning to learn as 'learning to be, to live and think, and to enjoy learning for life' has contributed to the lifelong learning culture in China and its implications for promoting competence in learning to learn worldwide.

Part 2 addresses international research and practice on learning to learn. In Chapter 6, Rao and colleagues discuss how attitudes and skills related to learning to learn are facilitated among Chinese learners in the home and preschool during early childhood. An account by Goldspink and Foster of an Australian learning to learn change initiative within the state education system in South Australia identifies complex lessons for school transformation and introduces the importance of learning-focused system reforms. Hautamäki and Kupiainen then consider how European regulations are affecting the conceptualization of learning to learn. Tensions between different epistemologies, different components to be assessed and ways to overcome them are discussed in this meta-reflection on the European pre-pilot study and on the Finnish learning to learn initiative. Moreno and Martín follow with a focus on how learning to learn has been developed in Spanish educational policy, research, and practice, including examples of a Spanish approach to the assessment of learning to learn. Stringher then describes a proposal for school improvement based upon learning to learn and argues that improvement actions should stem from clearly stated student, classroom, and school objectives, rather than from school effectiveness abstract reasoning or from mere statistical exercises. Linked to this theme of improvement is McCombs's chapter, which explains that less not more variables will get us where we need to be to support a whole learner model for school reform: what the students perceive as learning supports at school and classroom levels explains the most variance in a range of learning outcomes.

Three chapters conclude the volume, each with a unique practice experience related to learning to learn: Kloosterman reports on the European Learning to Learn research and practice project, with examples of activities for learners and trainers, and points to the need for an education system that can facilitate the generation and development of self-directed learners. Hipkins and Cowie, drawing on the New Zealand experience, maintain that learning to learn and lifelong learning, while obviously related, are differently focused, and each is deserving of explicit attention. In addition, lifewide learning recognizes that learners belong to, and that learning takes place in, multiple contexts and communities. The closing chapter by Willis portrays a professional learning journey which pursued strategies to support learning to learn capabilities in Indigenous Australian communities in the Northern Territory of Australia, offering a sensitive view of how disadvantaged learners can be empowered through learning to learn.

What becomes clear throughout all the contributions in this volume are two key themes: the complexity to be addressed in researching learning to learn and the value of international views and contributions.

Learning to learn is a complex process rather than either a simple or even a complicated one. In Chapter 2, Demetriou explores an architecture of mind that incorporates four interrelated systems, all of which may be relevant to learning to learn. Each contributor proposes a complex mix of processes that coalesce into learning to learn – including affective, cognitive, and dispositional factors. All agree that learning to learn is about the promotion of self-directed learning, the cultivation of intrinsic motivation for learning, and the development of intentional agency on the part of the learner. All agree that contextual factors – such as pedagogy, assessment regimes, quality of relationships, and socio-cultural factors – together interact and influence the ability of an individual to learn how to learn and to become an agent in their own learning journey.

The implications of this complexity are enormous. As Morin (2008) argues (and Carl Gustav Jung before him), Western thought has been dominated by the principles of disjunction, reduction, and abstraction. Engaging with learning to learn as a complex process requires a paradigm of distinction-conjunction, so that we can distinguish without disjoining and associate without identifying or reducing. In short, we need to develop new and more holistic ways of understanding, facilitating, and enabling learning to learn in our education communities, so that we can hold in tension the inner personal aspects of agency, purpose and desire and dispositions and the more measurable external and public manifestations of learning and performance and collaboration with others in learning to learn. We need measurement models that can account for quality of trust as a core resource, and story as a vehicle for agency as well as the more traditional and familiar measures of performance and problem-solving.

If learning to learn is about human beings becoming self-organizing agents of their own lives, as our contributors suggest, then it is clear that 'top-down', transmission-oriented approaches to learning, teaching, and school improvement are no longer enough. The challenge is how to create the conditions in which individual students are able to take responsibility for their own learning over time. By definition, this cannot be done for them. It has to be by invitation, allowing learning to learn to emerge and fuel agency and purpose.

The establishment of the framework for international comparison of educational achievement provided by the OECD through the Programme for International Student Assessment (PISA) and the means for regularly compiling the data is a considerable achievement. It has provided an evidence base for governments to inform domestic educational policy and against which to allocate priorities (Hanushek & Woessmann, 2011). What this data set is less effective at revealing are the reasons behind international and regional differences: we still understand too little about what drives these broad numbers. Furthermore, the numbers continue to reveal deep, intractable challenges in education such as embedded disadvantage linked to geography, economics, and ethnicity.

There is a pressing need to assemble an internationally comparable set of data which can better inform our understanding of factors such as learning how to learn and how this varies within and between different contexts. The academic and theoretical work that has been undertaken on these issues to date, while rich and deep, has focused on aspects of the problem, often failing to cross disciplinary boundaries. The real-world challenge of educational improvement, meanwhile, is relentlessly trans-disciplinary, involving a complex interplay between social, institutional, and individual factors. It presents a challenge both to theory and practice. The PISA data by comparison achieve comparability through the use of widely available proxy indicators but lack the depth and resolution needed to provide an understanding of the mechanisms driving the patterns that surface.

What is also clear from this volume is the value of different cultures in the debate about learning to learn. Two chapters are written explicitly from an Eastern perspective – demonstrating how Confucian philosophy can enrich our understanding of learning to learn and challenging some deeply held Western assumptions. Book contributors come from Australia, China, Cyprus, Finland, Hong Kong, Italy, the Netherlands, New Zealand, Spain, the UK, and USA. Uniquely, we report on a set of case studies from learning to learn projects in remote Indigenous communities where the cultural differences are enormous.

However comprehensive, this volume does not address a number of research and practice themes or leaves unanswered questions for further research. Among these, perhaps the most relevant is the road towards the assessment of learning to learn, although we provide a foundation for this through our contributions exploring what it is that should be assessed in learning to learn and why. Other open questions concern the deployment of learning to learn in school improvement; in the training of trainers, educators, and educational leaders; in personal development and empowerment. The connection of learning to learn with other key competencies, such as active citizenship and entrepreneurship, also requires further study.

This book draws on a rich, global tradition of research and practice. It is written by researchers and practitioners who care deeply about education and about learning how to learn in particular. Our purpose is to generate debate, to link learning communities, and to make a contribution to the ways in which societies worldwide are seeking to re-imagine their education systems. Our hope is that learning to learn will soon find a consistent place in educational policies worldwide.

References

European Communities (2006) 'Recommendation of the European Parliament and of the Council of 18 December 2006 on key competences for lifelong learning', *Official Journal of the European Union*. Retrieved from: http://eur-lex.europa.eu/LexUriServ/site/en/oj/2006/l_394/l_39420061230en00100018.pdf.

Hanushek, E., & Woessmann, V. (2011) 'The economics of international differences in educational achievement', in E. Hanushek, S. Machin, & L. Woessmann (Eds.) *Handbook of the economics of education*, Vol. 3. Amsterdam: North Holland.

Hoskins, B., & Fredriksson, U. (2008) *Learning to learn: What is it and can it be measured?* Luxembourg: European Communities.

Morin, E. (2008) *On complexity.* Cresskill, NJ: Hampton Press.

OECD (2010) *PISA 2009 results: Learning to learn – Student engagement, strategies and practices*, Vol. III. Paris: OECD.

Smith, R.M., and Associates (Eds.) (1990) *Learning to learn across the lifespan.* San Francisco, CA: Jossey-Bass.

UNESCO (2013) *Toward universal learning: What every child should learn.* Retrieved from: http://www.brookings.edu/~/media/Research/Files/Reports/2013/02/learning%20metrics/LMTFRpt1TowardUnivrslLearning.pdf.

Part 1

Theory

Chapter 1

What is learning to learn?
A learning to learn process and output model

Cristina Stringher

Abstract

Learning to learn has become a widely debated issue, both politically and among the international scientific community, yet confusion remains about the difference between learning and learning to learn. Furthermore, in the scientific literature there is little agreement concerning definitions of the latter concept. The aim of this chapter, therefore, is to describe learning to learn and identify its features through definitions taken from the literature. The ultimate goal is to provide a sound theoretical basis for the further study of learning to learn from an empirical perspective and for more precise use of this notion in diverse learning settings. The methodology is a literature review yielding 40 definitions from 90 studies examined. Other products of these analyses on learning to learn (including a concept map and a list of practical functions leading eventually to a meta-definition and a process and output model) are based upon subsequent elaboration of this material, and reference to international literature on learning to learn and to Maria Montessori's works.

Key words: learning to learn conceptual definition, components, functions.

Introduction

The first chapter in any scientific endeavour is generally devoted to defining the topic sharply and describing it according to a chosen perspective. In our case, this is not an easy task. It could be argued that learning to learn is not strictly a scientific concept, but rather involves politics and this is the first difficulty when trying to develop a definition. Second, confusion remains about the difference between learning and learning to learn. From a practitioner's and student's perspective (experts, primary school children, graduate students, and teachers), it is clear that learning to learn cannot be easily disentangled from the concept of learning. Some individuals appear unable to conceive of the two different concepts: this is especially true for school children, but not only them, and this is no coincidence, as I will explore here.

One aim of the chapter, therefore, is to describe learning to learn through definitions taken from the literature and to identify those characteristics that contribute to a meta-definition,[1] in an attempt to introduce the reader to concepts that will be analysed throughout this book. A more ambitious aim is to contribute some degree of order in learning to learn theory, avoiding reducing it to an umbrella term for all purposes: this reductionist position could take the scientific power away from a potentially powerful concept.[2] However, the complexity of this task is evident not only for the wide disparity of definitions to be found in the literature, but also considering that any meaning associated with learning to learn derives from how learning is conceptualized.

The scale of the challenge is evident in Moseley and colleagues' (2005) review, which incorporates 41 different frameworks or ways of understanding thinking and learning. However, learning to learn deserves an analysis of its own, since there seems to be little agreement about what it is and what it does. One way to achieve this discrete analysis is to present an account of learning to learn by identifying its features and providing a concept map, a list of its practical functions leading eventually to a definition and a conceptual model. The ultimate goal here is to provide a sound theoretical basis for the further study of learning to learn from an empirical perspective.

Let us start our journey with an overview of objectives attributed to learning to learn from different sources, some policy-led and others scientific. In 2010, the OECD published *PISA 2009 Results: Learning to learn – Student engagement, strategies and practices (Vol. III)*. The opening line of its foreword states that 'One of the ultimate goals of policy makers is to enable citizens to take advantage of a globalised world economy' (OECD, 2010: 3). The authors maintain that

> devising effective education policies will become ever more difficult as schools need to prepare students to deal with more rapid change than ever before, for jobs that have not yet been created, to use technologies that have not yet been invented and to solve economic and social challenges that we do not yet know will arise . . . Success will go to those individuals and countries that are swift to adapt, slow to complain and open to change.
>
> (OECD, 2010: 5)

In the same volume, the authors focus on those policies that may enhance students' reading competence and identify learning to learn as one of the keys to success. However, they do not define learning to learn and this phrase is used only in the title of the publication, with an attributed meaning ranging from learning 'motivation' and 'engagement', to 'study strategies' and 'approaches to learning'.[3]

It is widely accepted that empowering young people by creating favourable conditions for them to develop their skills so that they can work and participate actively in society is essential for the sound economic and social development of any country. In a context of globalization, knowledge-based economies, and ageing societies, every young person must be given the opportunity to fulfil his or her potential (European Commission, 2007: 1). Therefore, it is clear why learning to learn has been included among the eight key competences by the European Parliament (2006).

Political interest at the European level matches and follows worldwide scientific interest in the concept of learning to learn: dozens of researchers have variably defined and explored it, sometimes from very different epistemological backgrounds, accounting for the diversity of approaches and the resulting interdisciplinarity (Bateson, 1977; Hounsell, 1979; Candy, 1990; Collett, 1990; Gibbons, 1990; Smith, 1990; Boekaerts, 1999; Hautamäki et al., 2002; Deakin Crick et al., 2004). Jules Henry (cited in Smith, 1990) states that learning to learn has been and still is humans' essential evolutionary task. Similarly, Edgar Morin (2001) maintains that knowledge of one's knowledge is a prerequisite for clarity of mind. Moreover, knowledge of one's knowledge, which implies the integration of the knowers with their own knowledge, is a necessary principle for education. We need negotiation and reciprocal controls between our own mind and our own ideas in order to allow reflexivity and to avoid reasoning pitfalls (Morin, 2001: 11, 31–33).

According to Goleman (1999), the most basic knowledge of all is that of knowing how to learn. This opinion is shared by many scholars who refer to it as not only a concept, but an educational objective (Tuijnman & Van Der Kamp, 1992), the most secure foundation for lifelong learning (James et al., 2007: 29), a fundamental competence, just like numeracy or literacy (European Commission, 2003), the most urgent item on the agenda together with educational reform for the development of people (Candy, 1990), and even an ultimate life skill for the twenty-first century (Burgogne, 1998, cited in Carr & Claxton, 2002, 9). Candy (1990), however, warns the reader not to make learning to learn a slogan in danger of losing its power through overuse. Twelve years after Candy, Coffield adds to this warning, stating that for too long learning to learn remained an empty expression, a vacuum slogan especially when – notwithstanding its unanimous utility – there is no consensus on its definition (Coffield, 2002).

In this chapter, I present a detailed account of methodological choices guiding this research, the products of the analysis of learning to learn definitions and models, along with a meta-definition and a concept map of the components of learning to learn. Together, these contribute to the construction of a process and output model, also discussed here. Provisional conclusions point to the need to synthesize this knowledge in a coherent learning to learn theory, which, I will argue, is preliminary to any empirical study of this notion. This work on a definition of learning to learn and learning to learn modelling is the basis for improving the assessment of learning to learn and for more precise use of this notion in diverse learning settings.

Methodology

The Campaign for Learning initiative in the UK recently published a review on learning to learn (Amalathas, 2010). The author maintains that 'some components of learning to learn may be found outside learning to learn models'

(Amalathas, 2010: 6), rendering the concept partial or flawed. This is not the view of this chapter: the search for definitions and components of learning to learn can be made within learning to learn research and models, provided one searches for studies dealing with a 'wide concept'[4] of learning to learn. The methodology used here is a qualitative review of worldwide literature with a comparative analysis of four major learning to learn models and 40 definitions from 90 contributions examined, accounting for a diachronic representation of learning to learn studies to date.

The literature review was based on the University of London's EPPI Centre process for systematic reviews of evidence. Major sources include the EPPI Centre, the Eric Database, the British Educational Index and other Ebsco databanks, together with a number of university and research centre web sites, Italian resources, and international journals available electronically.[5] The study was organized around one key question: How exactly is learning to learn defined? Sub-questions were concerned with how it is described in the literature: (a) What words/locutions can be considered synonyms for learning to learn? (b) What are its features, dimensions, components, and functions? (c) Is it possible to model them?

The literature search was carried out using the following key words: learning to learn, learning competence/competency, learning how to learn, learning power, learning about learning, independent learning, understanding learning, improving own learning, learning strategies, metacognitive learning strategies, learning-to-learn skills, study skills, ability to learn, and self-regulated learning. The initial search of these key words produced a total of 37,064 documents, which were screened with finer searches. This selection was performed by combining key words, the reading of titles, verification of the occurrence in the title of the words 'learning to learn' and not just 'learning', and availability of studies. In this way, 212 documents were identified for further scrutiny.

The schema shown in Fig. 1.1 provides an overview of the initial literature search: in the large oval, key words used to interrogate search engines have been grouped. Literature that was of policy versus academic origin was examined. Psycho-sociological fields contributing to learning to learn are highlighted in the smaller ovals, while in the background or at the core of each field lies evaluation and assessment studies in formal education.

The 212 documents identified in the previous phase were further scrutinized through reading of abstracts. This resulted in 90 studies, mostly theoretical in nature, dealing specifically with the target topic. Of these, 40 were incorporated into the review based on the criterion of presenting a different definition of learning to learn.[6] All 40 definitions were integrally extracted with their bibliographic reference. They were then coded into categories and classified based on the following parameters: research background (political vs. academic), research paradigm, specific epistemic approach, components and functions of learning to learn. With the aid of cross-references, it seems reasonable to consider these studies as representative of major trends in international learning to learn research, summarized in Table 1.1 in the Appendix.

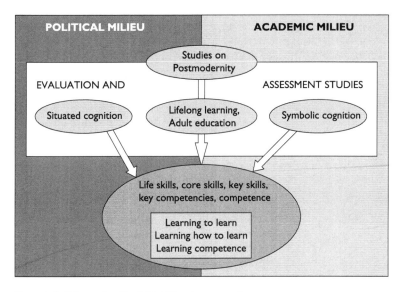

Figure 1.1 Schema for the initial literature search.

The disparity in approaches is one feature of this field of study. Definitions of learning to learn can be classified according to two main research paradigms[7] (lifelong learning and developmental psychology) and study approaches (cognitive, socio-cultural, historical, etc.). Of the 40 definitions collected, 32 can be classified as belonging to the lifelong learning paradigm and eight to developmental psychology. The cognitive and metacognitive approach[8] is equally distributed across learning to learn studies belonging to the two paradigms. Within paradigms, the socio-cultural approach prevails in lifelong learning, while the cognitive approach is exclusive to developmental psychology.[9]

Following this classification, a list of learning to learn components from all the 40 definitions was compiled,[10] together with a list of functions attributed to learning to learn. Other products of these analyses (including the concept map and the model) were based upon subsequent elaboration of this material, reference to international literature on learning to learn, and to Maria Montessori's works.

Results

The main objective of this study was to understand what learning to learn is in order to derive a meta-definition.[11] The analyses produced the following study outputs: two paradigmatic definitions of learning to learn (one per study approach, the cognitive and socio-constructivist); a selection of four full learning to learn models with functions; a list of 523 learning to learn components enabling a distinction to be made between this and related concepts, which helps to determine what learning to learn is not; key features of learning to learn with a concept map synthesizing the component list into 46 macro-components; a meta-definition with learning to learn functions; a synthesis and output model created from an aggregate of macro-components previously identified. The products of analysis are presented below.

Paradigmatic definitions

Two definitions are reported here so as to provide evidence of the different approaches to learning to learn (Box 1.1).

Models of learning to learn

A selection of learning to learn models was made based on their comprehensiveness, their capacity to explain learning to learn, and their significance for lifelong learning. The following models meet these criteria: the Alberta Project (Collett, 1990), Gibbon's Cube (Gibbons, 1990), the Learning to Learn Framework of the University of Helsinki (Hautamäki et al., 2002), and the ELLI Project (Deakin Crick et al., 2004). A description of each model can be found in the Appendix.

All of these authors share the idea that learning to learn can be attained throughout the life span, and that this has deep consequences for policies to foster its acquisition: if learning to learn were to be developed only during the school years, one consequence would be to avoid empowerment interventions for adult learners, while learning to learn is probably one of the most important drivers of change in adulthood. Although diverse epistemologies guided these research studies, similarities are evident among them. They all share the comprehensiveness of the concept of learning to learn, which is not confined to study strategies or to strictly cognitive or metacognitive variables, but includes the regulation of affective and motivational components. All models underline the importance of the social environment and of situated learning (and learning to learn), best displayed in interaction with others.

Learning to learn clearly lends itself to a competence adults could exploit in their working lives, but the abilities and competencies it mobilizes can be taught in all phases of education and independently of a concrete and immediate application to a certain working situation. The seven learning dimensions identified by the ELLI Project, for example, seem to be equally important during the school years and in adulthood, as a deep search for individual meaning, self-understanding, and self-construction.

The differences in these models relate to their intended recipients, to differential foci attributed to learning to learn components, and to diverse applications of this notion: for the Alberta study, the target group were low performing adults and the scope was a specific pedagogic intervention; for Gibbons, the intent was to systematize learning to learn in a theoretical frame with a developmental perspective, with application in three domains (technical, social, developmental); for the research team at Helsinki, the target groups were children, teenagers, and

Box 1.1 Paradigmatic definitions of learning to learn

Cognitive and socio-cultural approaches to learning to learn

An example of the cognitive and metacognitive approach to learning to learn:

> An efficient learner needs five elements: a) motivation to employ learning abilities and techniques; b) an organized knowledge base, providing a structure for new knowledge; c) skills for future learning; d) strategies for the optimal use of those learning skills; e) meta-cognitive strategies (planning and control in the first place).
>
> (McKeachie, 2000)

An example of the socio-cultural-historical approach to learning to learn:

> [Learning to learn] is a developmental process in which people's conceptions of learning evolve and become consciously available to systematic analysis and review. It involves the acquisition of a repertoire of attitudes, understandings, and skills that allow people to become more effective, flexible, and self-organized learners in a variety of contexts. It occurs both prior to, and coincidental with, learning endeavors. It may be enhanced through processes of formal schooling and the way in which the curriculum is constructed and is therefore a viable – perhaps crucial – objective for educational systems at all levels. It involves entering into the deep meaning structures of material to be learned and, in its most advanced forms, may lead to critical awareness of assumptions, rules, conventions, and social expectations that influence how people perceive knowledge and how they think, feel, and act when learning.
>
> It has both generic and context-specific components. It is a multidimensional entity whose meaning varies according to the meaning given to the word learning.
>
> (. . .) if learning means roughly 'an interpretative process aimed at the understanding of reality', then 'learning-how-to-learn' means something like 'an interpretative process aimed at understanding how to interpret and understand reality'.
>
> (Candy, 1990)

adults, while the objective was to develop indicators for school system evaluation;[12] for the Bristol group, the target was similar, while the scope was rather to elaborate an empowering pedagogical intervention.

This seems to be a major point for discussion: the Helsinki model is concentrated on the development of policy indicators and its definition of learning to learn seems to reflect the need to form a nation of 'good learners' but also of adaptive citizens, willing to adapt (and accept) novel tasks from others, such as business and other social players. The emphasis of Bristol's ELLI Project is instead on learning power contributing to lifelong personal development. The strategic strengthening of individuals is the core of the Bristol, Gibbons, and Alberta models, while from this perspective Helsinki's seems the most heterogeneous of the models analysed.

Learning to learn in its wider sense shares many similarities with such concepts as Gardner's intrapersonal, Sternberg's practical, and Goleman's emotional intelligence (Gardner, 1983; Sternberg et al., 1990; Goleman, 1999). In addition, it seems a candidate to fit Gardner's eight criteria for identifying a new intelligence.[13] Most of all, learning to learn is somehow transferrable, and thus teachable.

Learning to learn functions

Knowles anticipated current views on the functions of learning to learn when he warned against the 'catastrophe of human obsolescence', which can be contrasted with lifelong learning (Knowles, 1990). From his perspective, learning to learn is an indispensable human survival tool. For Smith (1990), learning to learn has its roots within the lifelong learning paradigm that emerged after the First World War. Exacerbating this trend after the Second World War, the acceleration of social change highlighted the need for lifelong learning and adult learning. Smith (1990) reports that in 1967 Bergevin already maintained that learning to learn was the primary objective for adult learning, and in 1971 Tough pointed out that participation in adult education programmes increased self-directed learning.

According to these models and the wider literature search, learning to learn comprises multiple functions, in at least two main areas: learner self-improvement and social improvement. Box 1.2 incorporates learning to learn functions classified in this way.

Box 1.2 Learning to learn functions

Learning to learn functions according to literature

Learner self-improvement, where the focus is:

- to contribute to general self-improvement and pursuit of Socratic examined life (Collett, 1990; Gibbons, 1990; Deakin Crick et al., 2004);
- to help learners feel more self-confident (Collett, 1990);

- to develop stronger problem-solving skills (Collett, 1990);
- to help learners improve their learning and become more strategic, responsible, autonomous, and collaborative rather than independent learners (Weinstein & Van Mater Stone, 1996; Deakin Crick et al., 2004; James et al., 2007);
- learner development (Diez & Moon, 1990);
- learner adaptability (Bateson, 1977; Hautamäki et al., 2002);
- to develop self-reflective power and awareness functional to individuals' learning and life needs (Hautamäki et al., 2002);
- to allow knowledge, skills, and attitudes to be transferred from one learning context to another and from learning situations in which this information has been acquired to a leisure and work context (Boekaerts, 1999);
- to aid in the search and development of (self-) meaning (Candy, 1990; Gibbons, 1990; Deakin Crick et al., 2004);
- to guide concrete learning and allow optimization and regulation of learning processes (Puustinen & Pulkkinen, 2001; Weinert, 2001);
- to allow the individual freedom of self-determination (in the developmental domain, the product being a well-functioning adulthood) with the possibility of individual change, self-construction, and empowerment (Gibbons, 1990; Alberici, 2008);
- to aid students with learning difficulties (Cornoldi et al., 2001);
- to manage one's own career path (European Commission, 2004c).

Social functioning of individuals and society, where the focus is:

- to maintain and update basic knowledge and competencies in times of socio-economic change (Eurydice, 2002);
- to enhance productivity (in the technical domain, the product being control over practical tasks) (Gibbons, 1990);
- to enable individuals to relate to others (in the social domain, the product being social integration) (Gibbons, 1990);
- to contribute to the creation of 'a nation of good learners' (Hautamäki et al., 2002);
- to cope with growing complexity, uncertainty, and individual responsibility (Carr & Claxton, 2002);
- to equip young people to learn from and for real-life situations (Carr & Claxton, 2002);
- to foster personal development and a well functioning society (European Commission, 2002):
- to be able to survive, to develop their full capacities, to live and work in dignity, to participate fully in development, to improve the quality of their lives, to make informed decisions, and to continue learning (World Conference on Education for All, 1990).

To summarize, learning to learn serves developmental, functional, and empowering functions: youth development is the primary learning to learn mission according to developmental research, while according to the lifelong learning paradigm, learning to learn serves the adaptation to working and domestic life, including the creation of balanced personalities and social well-being.

Learning to learn components and concept map

The qualitative analysis of the extracted definitions yielded 523 initial components of learning to learn. After removing duplications, 146 components, sub-components, and descriptors remained, which have been logically grouped into 46 macro-components. Both the resulting map and the model presented in the following pages have been systematized according to Montessori's (1993, 1999, 2000, 2009) work. The choice of Montessori as a pedagogic lens may not be without bias, but it was considered coherent for several reasons. The Montessori perspective is topical precisely because her method does not translate any theory into practice:[14] Montessori starts with an accurate observation of the child and derives protocols for intervention from there. It seems she deliberately privileged this grounded approach rather than an elegant theoretical systematization of her observations. In the first page of her book *The discovery of the child* (1999), Montessori states the purpose of her research, which is not to elaborate a treatise on the science of education, but rather to present the results of a teaching experience.

The teaching experience is her starting point, practical applications the end point, and scientific experiments the means, in a praxis-to-praxis model that is unique compared with other educational thinkers. As a result of her systematic observation of the learner within the prepared environment, Montessori maintains individuals are all motivated to learn from innate curiosity. A teacher's aim is thus to cultivate and respect this inherent desire to learn. Montessori's foundation for learning to learn can be traced in these basic educational principles and key concepts:[15]

- A science of education does not only have the task of observing children, but to transform them into better humans, into autonomous yet disciplined observers and researchers which may improve the future progress of mankind (Montessori, 1999: 33, 54, 103–104).
- Education is the active aid to the normal expansion of life (Montessori, 1999: 67).
- The individual has an innate desire to learn, which triggers intrinsic learning motivation, learning endeavours, and learning how to learn: no-one can concentrate by imitation (Montessori, 1999: 107–108).
- 'Psychological development is self-organized with the aid of external stimuli, which must be experimentally determined' (Montessori, 2000: 63).

- The learning environment should foster innate desire to learn, volition, and a learning autonomy that is socially mediated, in order to acquire 'social habits' necessary to cooperate with others (Montessori, 2000: 152).
- The active, applied learning experience of the learners within their own and broader social environment should foster the material control of the error, essential if the child is to develop the capacity to detect differences, to critique, and to reason (Montessori, 1999: 114).
- Self-discovery of the learners through their own self-directed learning endeavours and self-reflection is key for Montessori, who maintains that all human victories rest on an interior force that cannot be increased with prizes or punishments (Montessori, 1999: 17).
- Learner stages of development provide lifelong connectivity for increasingly deeper understanding and meaning-making (Montessori, 2009: 25).
- Teachers, as learning facilitators, should always aim to keep children's intelligence alive,[16] rather than leading children in every action, overlapping adults' *ability* and *will* to that of the child (Montessori, 2000: 113, 209; Montessori, 1999: 103–104).

The Montessori option seems coherent with learning to learn theory:[17] this pedagogy is grounded in practice and embraces a wide perspective on learning. Learning to learn originates from so many epistemological fields that it is necessary to find a unifying standpoint that embraces, not only cognition, self-regulation, affective and biological conceptions on learning, but also those social influences that nowadays seem so powerful yet obscure. In addition, the practical pedagogical approach is essential: if learning how to learn is what matters, and thus also teaching learning how to learn, we inevitably need to focus on pedagogy not just psychology or sociology. Montessori, a medical doctor herself, did precisely this: she observed the natural development of individuals within their historical, social, and physical environment. In so doing, she did not translate any psychological or sociological principles of learning into practice: she conceived of a pedagogy whose force is grounded in the learning actions of individuals in and on their environment in a search for meaning.[18] The Montessori approach should appeal in particular to all those concretely interested in fostering learning to learn, as 'practice' is the key word of her entire work. This is coherent with what James et al. (2007: 28–29) have found in their extensive study on learning how to learn: the emphasis on practice in fostering learning autonomy.

Montessori's pedagogic standpoint is also key to what Mezirow (2003) termed 'transformative learning' – that is, reflective and adult learning (very similar to learning to learn), which questions its own premises to make progress. Montessori herself strongly questioned both traditional top-down pedagogy and the scope of schooling: she proposed to form a nation of better humans, of observers and researchers needed for a rapidly changing world and to let the children unfold their learning curiosity with the support of a radically new type of teacher (a learning facilitator in Montessori's own words), who was capable of aiding the 'normal expansion of life', rather than simply imparting prescribed knowledge and lessons.

Last but not least, a Montessori approach is useful when trying to picture learning to learn components in some hierarchical order, although it must be underlined that individual differences in learning and learning to learn could affect this hierarchy in many ways. This classification seems necessary especially in an attempt to clarify key components for future measurement of learning to learn. The concept map in Fig. 1.2 is the result of this qualitative analysis.

Based on the literature search, the 46 macro-components were aggregated into two domains, the personal and the social, each with its own dimensions. Components are grouped under these headings and relationships among components according to the literature are indicated with arrows.[19] The proactive dimension (of learners acting upon or with their own learning) and the developmental dimension (of learning to learn evolving in a time/age trajectory according also to stages of development) are depicted as transversal to the personal and social dimensions.

At this stage, one way of synthesizing the process of learning to learn is through the explanations of the outlined ovals in Fig. 1.2: the innate desire to learn is characteristic of the human species, which faces the demands of the environment in a continuous search for meaning (Deakin Crick et al., 2004). These elements trigger learning activity (Diez & Moon, 1990; Hautamäki et al., 2002; Hautamäki & Kupiainen, 2002) and motivation (Smith, 1990; Weinstein & Van Mater Stone, 1996; Boekaerts, 1999; Hautamäki & Kupiainen, 2002; Deakin Crick et al., 2004), which produce knowledge and activate reflection (Smith, 1990, 1996; Weinert, 2001; Cornford, 2002), also yielding to self-awareness of the learner (Smith, 1990; Simons, 1992; Weinstein & Van Mater Stone, 1996; Eurydice, 2002; Deakin Crick et al., 2004). A provisional metaphor representing this complexity refers to developing neural networks, which, in the newborn child, evolve and grow in number and relationships with their progressive maturation. In spite of the complexity of this representation stemming from the literature, learning to learn seems to have a core in meaning-making (Diez & Moon, 1990; Smith, 1992; Deakin Crick et al., 2004) sustained by self-evaluation and reflection: while evolving in time, mental assets, both cognitive and socio-affective-motivational, seem to be activated through a combination of intrinsic and extrinsic needs, demands, and values; biological, psychological, and social drivers seem to be at the foundation of learning to learn and these are variably translated by learners into learning actions mediated by learning motivation. Learning actions seem to be successful for the individual when meaningful learning is produced; when reflection on one's own learning action takes place, those learning products are somehow internalized and can be used to enrich the repertoire of experiences that can be stored in memory for future transferability.

Affective-motivational (Collett, 1990; Simons, 1992; Boekaerts, 1999; Hautamäki & Kupiainen, 2002; Deakin Crick et al., 2004) and often uncon-scious tacit learning, though extremely important, is not sufficient for learners to develop learning to learn; similarly, cognitive learning strategies alone will not work, unless the affective-motivational side of learning to learn is properly addressed. This is why metacognition seems so important (Diez & Moon, 1990; Smith, 1992; Boekaerts, 1999; Weinert, 2001; Puustinen & Pulkkinen, 2001),

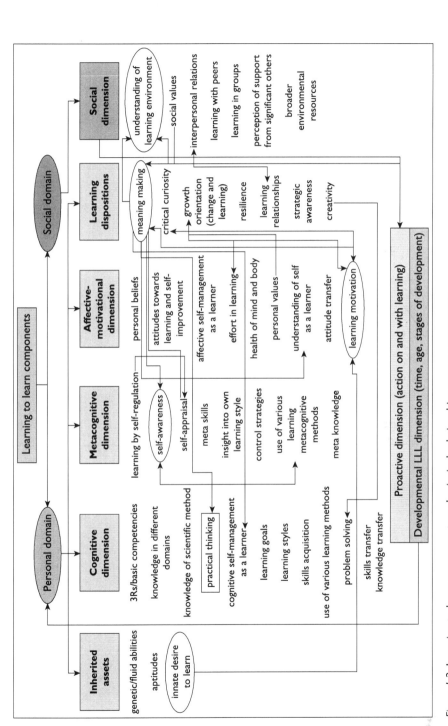

Figure 1.2 Learning to learn components and principal relationships among components.

its basis being the conscious evaluation of one's learning modes enabling a self-reflection upon learning. It seems that the more explicit this operation is, the more control learners will exert upon their own learning. Not only are experiences enhanced, but also the cognitive and socio-affective-motivational assets are empowered, in a sort of virtuous cycle triggered and sustained by reflective learning. During this process, self-awareness is both essential in order to act upon learning and to produce additional reflection for self-improvement in learning. Learning and learning to learn, as seems evident from this reconstruction, do not happen in a vacuum or alone in the individual's head, rather they are processes that are heavily influenced by the narrow or wider social environment in which learners operate (Candy, 1990; Collett, 1990; Gibbons, 1990; Nanzhao, 2000; Carr & Claxton, 2002; Deakin Crick et al., 2004).

The time trajectory is also relevant in learning to learn (Hautamäki & Kupiainen, 2002; Deakin Crick et al., 2004): one consideration is how children acquire the basics of this 'intelligence', another the complexity handled by adults. This aspect, well known to Piagetian theorists, could also be studied from a neurological standpoint, as cerebral development seems to qualitatively vary during ageing, with the two hemispheres 'dialoguing' more at later stages in life (Cohen, 2005).

A meta-definition of learning to learn

Based on the above discussion, I now present a working definition of learning to learn that summarizes the personal, pedagogical, and learning-trajectory elements highlighted in the literature so far. Learning to learn is the:

> *Executive process of control of learning, conceivable as a disposition to engage deeply in learning, which bestows individuals with increasingly higher command over modes, time, and spaces of their own learning. Such a process evolves in a developmental and lifelong trajectory, with the ultimate goal of making sense of reality.*

If the basic human psychological need to make sense of reality[20] is the aim, learning to learn seems to be a means to achieve that end. Such a management function in learning appears to mobilize different energies of the individual-in-context (the previously mapped learning to learn components) to produce knowledge and improvement in learning through variations in learning experiences and reflection upon them. Learning to learn lifetime functions are youth development, individual adaptability in working and domestic life, the development of balanced personalities, and social well-being. Inherited assets, self-regulated learning (cognitive and metacognitive), learning dispositions, the affective-motivational, social, and active dimensions of learning contribute to learning to learn in a lifelong trajectory.

Key features of this definition are:

1. Self-management of the learning process: learning to learn is a methodology rather than an outcome. It is the 'how to' more than the 'what' of learning.

It is a process as distinct from its product, which is the efficient learning of information or skills, or even meta-knowledge.

2. Learning to learn might contain productive elements if it is considered a process in which knowledge about learning is created by transforming experience. I introduce a distinction here between learning to learn (the lifelong process) and learning knowledge (its product).

3. Such knowledge about learning can be translated into learning improvement if the individual chooses so, the direction of the improvement being a function of motivation and individual and socially accepted or socially fostered values.

4. The social aspect of learning is emphasized not only to distinguish learning to learn from metacognition, but also because learning actually takes place throughout the life span in different social contexts. Some of these facilitate and some of them inhibit or thwart learning experiences. In either case, the environment acts as one of the drivers of learning motivation at least as much as the biological individual desire to learn.

In this definition, reference is made to metacognition (self-knowledge, self-regulation within the individual's dimension), self-determination theory, and the sociology of learning (different contexts and social dimension of lifewide learning). The developmental dimension throughout the lifetime seems to be equally crucial, as learning to learn improves, grows, and evolves well beyond concrete operations of the mandatory school years,[21] where the focus should be the acquisition of those technical aspects of learning and autonomy that constitute the basis for further developments in later years.

The theoretical implications of this definition are as follows:

1. Learning to learn is a meta-competence, in which a person orchestrates a range of abilities and competencies deployed with the ultimate goal of better learning. In any context, learning to learn contributes to learners' empowerment and enables them to adapt to their environment. Learning to learn as a 'meta-competence' includes the search for meaning, mobilizing emotions, and deep values of individuals for themselves and in relation to their social environment.

2. Learning to learn in this broad and deep sense is configured almost as an 'intelligence', which is indispensable for individual learners to create meaning, direction, and a sense of purpose for their own existence, through reflexivity, autonomy, and proactivity (Goleman, 1999; Alberici, 2008). Indeed, it seems to be the pivotal nucleus for the development of a balanced personality.

3. The emphasis on the environment is important, since a favourable milieu for learning and learning to learn can make a difference in individual and societal development (Montessori, 1999, 2000).

4. The assessment of learning to learn presupposes preliminary studies into intelligence appraisal and possibly into new roads to capture how individuals make use of their existing and established learning ability in facing new and diverse learning situations. The use of ICT to assess learning to learn is a

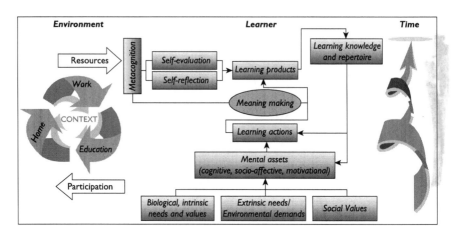

Figure 1.3 Learning to learn process and output model.

possibility, given the extensive development of learning technologies in recent years.

Learning to learn process and output model

The model presented in Fig. 1.3 is intended as a working hypothesis of how learning to learn works according to this definition and components previously analysed in the concept map. Thirteen of the 46 macro-components have been used to produce it. The model is thus a further elaboration of the map and its components have been aggregated according to self-determination theory (Deci & Ryan, 2000, 2002). The choice of this latter theoretical underpinning is consistent with Montessori principles and with responsible learning autonomy and agency in social environments, which seems a common denominator of paramount importance in the reviewed literature (Bereiter & Scardamalia, 1989; Collett, 1990; Resnik, 1996; Carr & Claxton, 2002; European Communities, 2006; James et al., 2007; OECD, 2010).

As Montessori stated, we are all born with an innate desire to learn that is functional to our development. Biological needs, intrinsic needs[22] and values, extrinsic needs and environmental demands, as well as social values seem to trigger learning and learning to learn processes in individuals. These drivers activate mental assets (socio-affective and motivational prior to cognitive ones), which lead to learning actions in a search for personal meaning for the individual. Up to this point, the learning process yields learning 'products' such as knowledge of facts. However, if metacognition, with self-evaluation and self-reflection, takes place and the learning process and products are analysed, knowledge about one's learning can be acquired and the individual will develop a repertoire of learning strategies and tactics that can be employed in different contexts and occasions for further activation of the learning process. A virtuous cycle of learning to learn is thus initiated in a time trajectory that varies at the individual level but can roughly follow the life stages of development we all experience.

As individuals do not function in a vacuum, this recursive process is both nurtured with environmental resources (from home, leisure, work, and education) and participated in by individuals contributing to their environment. The strength of learning to learn as a powerful tool for the individual can be extended to groups of individuals and whole settings, such as a school (James et al., 2007). The social aspects of learning to learn in this case are displayed, fostering social learning to learn and awareness of a group's drives, motives, and direction through shared reflection.

Conclusions

The learning to learn model provided here synthesizes this systematic review of research and offers the reader one way to grasp this very challenging concept, by providing an initial answer to the core question, 'What exactly is learning to learn', but at the same time the analysis is open to other conceptualizations that will be presented throughout this volume. Summarizing this chapter, learning to learn is not just learning, but learning of a higher order; it is not only cognition, metacognition or thought, but also includes affective and biological dimensions; it is not just school-related skills, but also lifelong and lifewide learning skills; it is not just study strategies, learning strategies or cognitive styles (cognitive dimension), no matter how important these components are; it is not only self-regulated individual learning, but also social aspects of learning and reflection are involved; it is not just cognitive problem-solving, but a reflective methodology useful to evaluate solutions also in affective-motivational and experiential learning domains.

This systematic review suggests that learning to learn is not just a mere instrument for survival in working life, but rather it calls into question the deep meaning structures of the individual for personal well-being. Learning to learn assists individuals in their search for meaning, mobilizing emotions and deep values for themselves and in relation to their social environment. The situated nature of learning to learn is not to be underestimated, as it is influenced by the historical and social milieu and cultural background of individuals, in addition to biological inherited traits. Learning to learn can be defined as the malleable side of intelligence, and thus subject to change over time with optimal pedagogic interventions. Though malleable, some aspects of learning to learn can be measured at a certain point in time, since they seem to be sufficiently stable to be captured by a qualitative and quantitative snapshot of its constituents. Measuring such aspects could be the starting point for empowering individuals with this essential emotional, mental, and social asset.

The theoretical representations of learning to learn, of its ultimate goals and of its components influence decisions on its measurement. The need to precisely define learning to learn and to agree on a set of core components is of utmost importance for the accurate measurement of this concept, in its processing as well as in its productive aspects. The recent European study on the measurement of learning to learn concluded that 'further research is needed to improve the theoretical and the conceptual development of this test . . . there is a need to find a broad consensus [between cognitive and social sciences] and this creates a situation where the concept of learning to learn has to be carefully elaborated' (Hoskins & Fredriksson, 2008: 38).

However, the few attempts made to measure this 'intelligence' have resulted in researchers' disagreement precisely on the construction of an instrument (Kupiainen et al., 2008). The attempt to capture that 'ecology of variables' – that is, 'the conglomerate of variables as they might operate in persons in particular social contexts, and in particular trajectories in time' (Deakin Crick et al., 2004) – is an endeavour that requires further work.

The aim of this chapter is to contribute to conceptualizing learning to learn for future measurement. It provides theoretical updates to our understanding of how leaning to learn operates and a list of aspects to start from for its operationalization. It must be underlined that there is no agreement on how to label each component and sub-component of learning to learn and thus a glossary of terms to be agreed upon by diverse research traditions would be of help in creating consensus. In spite of these shortcomings, the learning to learn model here delineated could be put to the test with empirical research in the future.

Learning to learn measurement and assessment at various life stages of individuals is one starting point to equip people with this 'intelligence' for their own lifelong benefits. People need to learn how to learn: in fact, there seems to be more than one analogy between the complexity pictured in Fig. 1.2 and those mental demands facing adults coping with modern life, as described by Kegan (1994) in *In over our heads*. His evolving ways of knowing, allowing adult development as an open-ended process, calls into question Bateson's deutero-learning and learning to learn growing complexity. As Kegan (1994: 272) puts it, 'to stretch one's mind, to better adjust to new demands in one's private life, to advance in one's job or career, to change jobs or re-enter the workforce after one's children are grown or one's marriage has ended, adults go to school'. And if they do, one might say, they need to know how to learn. However, according to Kegan, only 20 per cent of American adults are self-regulated learners (1994: 195–196). Learning to learn thus seems a high priority for democracies, as Chapter 5 will argue. As Gooler (1990: 321) maintains,

> societies that do not give all their people a chance at a relevant education, and also periodic opportunities to tune up their knowledge and their insights, will be left in the jetstream of history by those that do.

Notes

1 The author was involved in a European study to measure learning to learn. This chapter derives from contributions to the European Learning to Learn Network and from subsequent independent study.
2 Several studies dealing with this concept do not even define it explicitly. There are also commercial websites addressing learning to learn as a set of strategies to be taught.

3 The OECD considers learning strategies and approaches to learning to be roughly the same concept, composed of 'understanding and remembering', 'memorization strategies', 'control strategies' (considered synonymous with self-directed learning), 'elaboration strategies', and 'summarizing'. OECD experts tried to operationalize the concept of learning to learn and considered these constituents for accurate measurement. The issue of accuracy is extensively addressed in their publication: self-reported measures for these authors risk reducing the informative power of the concept. However, the experts do not explain their choice of those measures for memorization, elaboration, and control strategies.

4 In this exploration, a helpful distinction is Dai Hounsell's (1979) wide and narrow conception of learning to learn. It seems particularly useful when setting boundaries for learning to learn: the narrow notion concerns techniques and means, such as the acquisition of study strategies; the wider conception, in contrast, involves the ultimate scope of learning and the relation of the individual with that scope, thus mobilizing one's search for meaning. Both Hounsell's conceptions are useful, although their contributions for learners are quite different.

5 The review began on 26 May 2006 and ended on 21 February 2007. Updates were made in November 2010 and August 2012.

6 Inclusion criteria also considered the evaluation of sources: this has been done mainly with the aid of cross-references and journal ranking/reputation.

7 According to Knoer (1996), a paradigm is a theoretical framework within a given science, used for a certain period of time. The classification has been done considering the epistemologies explicitly referred to by the authors in their definitions or in their full text.

8 Includes symbolic cognition and metacognition.

9 Nine definitions can be classified as belonging to other study approaches, such as functionalist, pedagogic or market-driven/managerialist approaches. Sometimes the study approach was unclear and in this case the definition was classified as belonging to the 'other approaches' category.

10 All the definitions have been imported into QDA Miner, a computer program for quali-quantitative analysis. With the aid of the program, the components of learning to learn have been tagged and listed. The operation necessary to net duplicating concepts was done manually, since this implied identifying synonyms from the initial component list.

11 Elsewhere, I have also elaborated a distinction of learning to learn from other related concepts, so to answer the question 'what learning to learn is not' (Stringher, 2006).

12 This aspect seems particularly important for governments willing to place learning to learn at the core of their education systems. See chapters by Hautamaki and Kupiainen, Goldspink, and Stringher in this volume for learning to learn and school improvement.

13 These are: support from psychometric findings; support from experimental psychological tasks; potential isolation by brain damage; evolutionary plausibility; a core set of operations; susceptibility to encoding in a symbol system; a distinct developmental history; existence of exceptional individuals.

14 Although reference to Montessori is not scientifically neutral, so is the influence of other thinkers (such as Dewey) who inspired learning to learn studies. The important point is how learning is conceptualized and what functions and methods to enhance learning experiences are sustained by one or another epistemological stance.

15 For a deep understanding of Maria Montessori's work and learning principles, see Tornar (2007). Perhaps all pedagogues today should pay tribute to Montessori for founding a pedagogy of action and reflection that seems necessary these days: an OECD publication analyses Montessori's as a promising 'alternative' method (OECD, 2008).

16 With this expression Montessori means teachers are to cultivate intelligence, leaving children free to express their learning needs rather than constantly controlling them and imparting notions only.

17 See, for instance, Claxton's four generations of teaching learning (Claxton, cited in Wall et al., 2010), with an emphasis on the latest generation of teaching, promoting involvement of students in the learning process. One key feature of the fourth generation is that teachers/facilitators should aid students in helping themselves. 'Help me doing it by myself' is the motto of a little child Maria Montessori had been observing during painstaking work with sensorial materials (Montessori, 1999).

18 For a more articulated understanding of Maria Montessori's pioneering work in the field of learning to learn, see Stringher (2009).

19 The relationships identified among components here are only those explicitly or implicitly suggested in the literature I reviewed; yet they could well be but a few of many possible links.

20 According to Deci and Ryan (2000: 248), there are 'the innate tendencies of human beings to engage in interesting activities and to elaborate and refine their inner representation of themselves and their world'. I interpret this as a broad basic need of finding purpose and meaning in our daily life.

21 Research on the development of learning to learn seems to point to the need for the individual to acquire formal operation schemata prior to being able to conceptualize learning to learn as something different from pure learning (Stringher, 2007).

22 What Deci and Ryan (2000, 2002) termed psychological needs of autonomy, relatedness, and competence. Recent developments in SDT have pointed to the importance of differentiating motivation in terms of its quality (poor/external/controlled vs. good/internal/autonomous and amotivation) (Vansteenkiste et al., 2009).

Acknowledgements

I wish to thank Piero Cipollone for the possibility to work on this challenging yet fascinating topic. I also wish to thank Victor McNair and Geraldine Sutton for their reviews of the original manuscript. I dedicate this effort to all learners wishing to empower themselves, and especially to my beloved son, Francesco.

References

Alberici, A. (2008) *La possibilità di cambiare: apprendere ad apprendere come risorsa strategica per la vita*. Milano: Franco Angeli.

Amalathas, E. (2010) *Learning to learn in further education: A literature review of effective practice in England and abroad*. Reading: CfBT Education Trust. Retrieved from: http://www.campaign-for-learning.org.uk/cfl/assets/documents/Research/LearningToLearn_v5FINAL.pdf.

Bateson, G. (1977) *Verso un'ecologia della mente [Steps to an ecology of mind]*. Milano: Adelphi.

Bereiter, C., & Scardamalia, M. (1989) 'Intentional learning as a goal of instruction', in L.B. Resnick (Ed.) *Knowing, learning, and instruction: Essays in honor of Robert Glaser* (pp. 361–392). Hillsdale, NJ: Lawrence Erlbaum Associates.

Boekaerts, M. (1999) 'Self-regulated learning: where we are today', *International Journal of Educational Research, 31*(6), 445–457.

Candy, P. (1990) 'How people learn to learn', in R.M. Smith and Associates (Eds.) *Learning to learn across the lifespan* (pp. 30–73). San Francisco, CA: Jossey-Bass.

Carr, M., & Claxton, G. (2002) 'Tracking the development of learning dispositions', *Assessment in Education*, 9(1), 9–37.

Coffield, F. (2002) 'Skills for the future: I've got a little list', *Assessment in Education*, 9(1), 39–43.

Cohen, G. (2005) *The mature mind: The positive power of the ageing brain.* New York: Basic Books.

Collett, D. (1990) 'Learning to learn needs for adult basic education', in R.M. Smith and Associates (Eds.) *Learning to learn across the lifespan* (pp. 247–266). San Francisco, CA: Jossey-Bass.

Cornford, I.R. (2002) 'Learning-to-learn strategies as a basis for effective lifelong learning', *International Journal of Lifelong Education*, 21(4), 357–368.

Cornoldi, C., De Beni, R., & Gruppo, M.T. (2001) *Imparare a studiare 2 – Strategie, stili cognitivi, metacognizione e atteggiamenti nello studio.* Trento: Erickson.

Deakin Crick, R., Broadfoot, P., & Claxton, G. (2004) 'Developing an effective lifelong learning inventory: The ELLI Project', *Assessment in Education*, 11(3), 247–272.

Deci, E., & Ryan, R. (2000) 'The "what" and "why" of goal pursuits: Human needs and the self-determination of behavior', *Psychological Inquiry*, 11(4), 227–268.

Deci, E., & Ryan, R. (2002) *Handbook of self-determination research.* Rochester, NY: University of Rochester Press.

Diez, M.E., & Moon, C. J. (1990) 'Stimulating thought and learning in preschool and elementary years', in R.M. Smith and Associates (Eds.) *Learning to learn across the lifespan* (pp. 171–190). San Francisco, CA: Jossey-Bass.

European Commission – Directorate General for Education and Culture (2002) *Follow-up of the 'Report on the Concrete Future Objectives of the Education and Training Systems'.* Working Group on Basic Skills, Foreign Language Teaching and Entrepreneurship. Brussels: European Commission – Directorate General for Education and Culture.

European Commission – Directorate General for Education and Culture (2004c) *'Key Competencies', Implementation of "Education and Training 2010' Work Programme – Key competencies for lifelong learning – A European reference framework.* Working Group B. Brussels: European Commission – Directorate General for Education and Culture.

European Communities (2006) 'Recommendation of the European Parliament and of the Council of 18 December 2006 on key competences for lifelong learning', *Official Journal of the European Union.* Retrieved from: http://eur-lex.europa.eu/LexUriServ/site/en/oj/2006/l_394/l_39420061230en00100018.pdf.

European Communities (2007) *Key Competences for Lifelong Learning – European Reference Framework*, Annex of the Recommendation of the European Parliament and of the Council of 18 December 2006 on key competences for lifelong learning. Luxembourg: Office for Official Publications of the European Communities. Retrieved from: http://ec.europa.eu/dgs/education_culture/publ/pdf/ll-learning/keycomp_en.pdf.

European Council (2006) *Key competences for lifelong learning*, February 2006. Retrieved from: http://www.consilium.europa.eu/uedocs/cms_data/docs/pressdata/en/educ/88498.pdf.

Eurydice (2002) *Key competencies.* Brussels: Eurydice. Retrieved from: http://promitheas.iacm.forth.gr/i-curriculum/Assests/Docs/Key%20Competences%20Eurydice.pdf.

Gardner, H. (1983) *Frames of mind: The theory of multiple intelligences*. New York: Basic Books.

Gibbons, M. (1990) 'A working model of the Learning-How-to-Learn process', in R.M. Smith and Associates (Eds.) *Learning to learn across the lifespan* (pp. 63–97). San Francisco, CA: Jossey-Bass.

Goleman, D. (1999) *Intelligenza emotiva [Emotional intelligence]*. Milano: Rizzoli-Bur.

Gooler, D.D. (1990) 'Changing the way we live and learn in an information age', in R.M. Smith and Associates (Eds.) *Learning to learn across the lifespan* (pp. 307–326). San Francisco, CA: Jossey-Bass.

Hautamäki, J., Arinen, P., Eronen, S., Hautamäki, A., Kupiainen, S., Lindblom, B. et al. (2002) *Assessing Learning-to-Learn – A framework*. Helsinki: National Board of Education, Finland.

Hautamäki, J., & Kupiainen, S. (2002) *The Finnish Learning-to-Learn Assessment Project – A concise report with key results*. Helsinki: Centre for Educational Assessment.

Hoskins, B., & Fredriksson U. (2008) *Learning to learn: What is it and can it be measured?* Ispra: Centre for Research on Lifelong Learning (CRELL). Retrieved from:http://publications.jrc.ec.europa.eu/repository/bitstream/111111111/979/1/learning%20to%20learn%20what%20is%20it%20and%20can%20it%20be%20measured%20final.pdf.

Hounsell, D. (1979) 'Learning to learn: Research and development in student learning', *Higher Education*, 8(4), 453–469.

James, M., McCormick, R., Black, P., Carmichael, P., Drummond, M.J., Fox, A. et al. (2007) *Improving learning how to learn: Classrooms, schools and networks*. London: Routledge.

Kegan, R. (1994) *In over our heads: The mental demands of modern life*. Cambridge, MA: Harvard University Press.

Knoer, A. (1996) 'Paradigms in instructional psychology', in E. De Corte & F.E. Weinert (Eds.) *International encyclopedia of developmental and instructional psychology* (pp. 317–321). Oxford: Elsevier Science.

Knowles, M.S. (1990) 'Fostering competence in self-directed learning', in R.M. Smith and Associates (Eds.) *Learning to learn across the lifespan* (pp. 123–136). San Francisco, CA: Jossey-Bass.

Kupiainen, S., Hautamäki, J., & Rantanen, P. (2008) *EU Pre-pilot on Learning to Learn – Report on the compiled data*. Retrieved from: http://ec.europa.eu/education/lifelong-learning-policy/doc/pilot_survey/report_en.pdf.

McKeachie, W.J. (2000) *Helping students learn how to kearn*, Opinion paper. Retrieved from: http://www.eric.ed.gov/ERICWebPortal/custom/portlets/recordDetails/detailmini.jsp?_nfpb=true&_&ERICExtSearch_SearchValue_0=ED450864&ERICExtSearch_SearchType_0=no&accno=ED450864.

Mezirow, J. (2003) *Apprendimento e trasformazione [Transformative dimension of adult learning]*. Milano: Raffaello Cortina Editore.

Montessori, M. (1993) *La formazione dell'uomo [To educate the human potential]*. Milano: Garzanti.

Montessori, M. (1999) *La scoperta del bambino [The discovery of the child]*. Milano: Garzanti.

Montessori, M. (2000) *L'Autoeducazione [The advanced Montessori method, Vols. I & II]*. Milano: Garzanti.

Montessori, M. (2009) *Dall'infanzia all'adolescenza [From childhood to adolescence]*. Milano: Franco Angeli.

Morin, E. (2001) *I sette saperi necessari all'educazione del futuro.* Milano: Cortina Editore.

Moseley, D., Baumfield, V., Elliott, J., Gregson, M., Higgins, S., Miller, J. et al. (2005) *Frameworks for thinking: A handbook for teaching and learning.* Cambridge: Cambridge University Press.

Nanzhao, Z. (2000) *A reflection on 'Learning to Learn': The four pillars of learning and their implications for curriculum reforms.* Paris: International Bureau of Education, UNESCO.

OECD (2008) *Innovating to learn, learning to innovate.* Paris: OECD.

OECD (2010) *PISA 2009 results: Learning to learn – Student engagement, strategies and practices,* Vol. III. Paris: OECD.

Puustinen, M., & Pulkkinen, L. (2001) 'Models of self-regulated learning: a review', *Scandinavian Journal of Educational Research, 45*(3), 269–286.

Resnick, L. (1996) 'Situated learning', in E. De Corte & F.E. Weinert (Eds.) *International encyclopaedia of developmental and instructional psychology* (pp. 341–347). Oxford: Elsevier Science.

Simons, P. (1992) 'Theories and principles of learning to learn', in A. Tuijnman & M. Van Der Kamp (Eds.) *Learning across the lifespan: Theories, research, policies.* Oxford: Pergamon Press.

Smith, R.M. (1990) 'The promise of learning to learn', in R.M. Smith and Associates (Eds.) *Learning to learn across the lifespan* (pp. 3–29). San Francisco, CA: Jossey-Bass.

Smith, R.M. (1992) 'Implementing the learning to learn concept', in A. Tuijnman & M. Van Der Kamp (Eds.) *Learning across the lifespan: Theories, research, policies.* Oxford: Pergamon Press.

Smith, R.M. (1996) 'Learning to learn: Adult education', in E. De Corte & F.E. Weinert (Eds.) *International encyclopaedia of developmental and instructional psychology.* Oxford: Elsevier Science.

Sternberg, R.J., Okagaki, L., & Jackson, A.S. (1990) 'Practical intelligence for success in school', *Educational Leadership, 48,* 35–39.

Stringher, C. (2006) *Learning competence: An Italian exploratory research in elementary schools.* Paper presented at the 2nd Meeting of the Network on Learning to Learn, Ispra Joint Research Centre – European Commission. Retrieved from: http://crell.jrc.ec.europa.eu/.

Stringher, C. (2007) *Imparare ad apprendere e valutazione. Studio esplorativo in classi primarie tradizionali e Montessori [Learning to learn and assessment: Exploratory study in primary school traditional and Montessori classrooms].* Unpublished doctoral dissertation, University Roma Tre, Roma.

Stringher, C. (2009) *Apprendere ad apprendere: da Montessori una lezione attuale.* Paper presented at the International Conference on Infancy and Adolescence, 27 November, Rome. Retrieved from: http://www.montessori.uniroma3.it/.

Tornar, C. (2007). *La pedagogia di Maria Montessori tra teoria e azione.* Milano: Franco Angeli.

Tuijnman, A., & Van Der Kamp, M. (Eds.) (1992) *Learning across the lifespan: Theories, research, policies.* Oxford: Pergamon Press.

Vansteenkiste, M., Sierens, E., Soenens, B., Luyckx, K., & Lens, W. (2009) 'Motivational profiles from a self-determination perspective: The quality of motivation matters', *Journal of Educational Psychology, 101,* 674–688.

Wall, K., Hall, E., Baumfield, V., Higgins, S., Rafferty, V., Remedios, R., Thomas, U., Tiplady, L., Towler, C., & Woolner, P. (2010). *Learning to learn in schools phase 4 and Learning to learn in further education.* Newcastle: Newcastle University. Retrieved from: http://www.campaign-for-learning.org.uk/cfl/assets/documents/ Research/ Learning%20to%20Learn%20Report%20April%202010.pdf

Weinert, F. (2001) 'Concept of competence: A conceptual clarification', in D.S. Rychen & L.H. Salganik (Eds.) *Defining and selecting key competencies* (pp. 45–65). Göttingen: Hogrefe & Huber.

Weinstein, C.E., & Van Mater Stone, G. (1996) 'Learning strategies and learning to learn', in E. De Corte & F.E. Weinert (Eds.) *International encyclopaedia of developmental and instructional psychology.* Oxford: Elsevier Science.

World Conference on Education For All (WCEFA) (1990) *Meeting basic learning needs: A vision for the 1990s.* New York: WCEFA.

Learning to learn research trends and models

Table 1.1 Learning to learn research trends – classification of definitions

Paradigms	Approaches			
	Cognitive and metacognitive	Socio-cultural-historical	Others	Total
Lifelong learning	10	13	9	32
Developmental psychology	8	0	0	8
Total	18	13	9	40

Learning to learn models

The Alberta Project

Based on an inductive methodology, this model was developed in the early 1980s in Alberta, Canada, within a context of adult basic education (Collett, 1990). The study proposed a taxonomy of abilities in learning to learn as the core of an adult education curriculum. The point of departure has been the identification of a list of abilities and competences needed in adult life, coupled with learning needs expressed by adults with low functional literacy. Learning to learn emerged as one of the major categories in this analysis. The research group produced a catalogue of 946 basic competencies, abilities, and indicators, of which 150 are connected with learning to learn. A synthesized list of learning to learn components is reported in Table 1.2.

Table 1.2 Learning to learn components (Collett, 1990)

ADULT BASIC SKILLS – Category G: Learn how to learn (synthesis)

1. Understand self as a learner
2. Manage self as a learner
3. Understand the learning environment
4. Utilize other learning methods
5. Practical thinking
6. Recall and apply data to new situations
7. Apply problem-solving techniques to make rational and reasonable decisions

Gibbons' cube

This second model is the most comprehensive attempt to conceptualize learning to learn to date. The cube moves away from the inductive taxonomy described above, as it represents a deductive construction attributing high relevance to the developmental trajectory of this meta-competence (Table 1.3). Central to the argument is the search for and creation of meaning underpinning all learning to learn activities.

Gibbons maintains that in learning to learn, the 'natural', 'personal', and the 'formal' dimensions of learning are interwoven with the developmental dimension. For example, learning of a natural kind is interactive – the individual spontaneously interacts with the environment; learning of a formal kind is directed – the individual is directed through teaching/learning procedures; and learning of a personal kind is self-directed – the individual projects the desired learning procedure.

Table 1.3 Bidimensional matrix of Gibbons' cube (adapted from Gibbons, 1990)

Aspects	Kinds of learning		
	Natural	Formal	Personal
Type of learning	*Interactive:* the individual spontaneously interacts with the environment	*Directed:* the individual is directed through teaching/learning procedures	*Self-directed:* the individual projects the desired learning procedure
Source of content	*Available:* contents selected from the environment based on personal interest	*Assigned:* contents assigned by a teaching authority	*Selected:* contents selected and organized by the individual
Instruction method	*Transactional:* the process happens in an interaction between accidental influences and interior states	*Presented:* content is systematically presented to the learner	*Performed:* the individual performs and monitors own learning procedures
PROCESSES AND OPERATIONS	L2L from interactions with others	L2L from instruction (listening, questioning, observing, synthesizing, memorizing, visualizing, applying and revising content)	Learning to decide what to learn (using objectives, scopes, available options, choices, learning plans)

Aspects	Kinds of learning		
	Natural	*Formal*	*Personal*
	L2L from environmental stimuli	L2L to engage in and execute assigned learning tasks	Learning to manage one's learning time (using time and human resources, modulating one's efforts)
	L2L exploring the environment	L2L from an assigned learning task	L2L from experience (one's own and that of others)
	L2L from practice (repetition and rehearsal)	Learning basic learning skills and strategies (find information, read to comprehend, synthesize, organize, review, memorize, rehearse)	Learning to be an individual who learns intentionally (awareness, motivation, control, and reflection on one's learning)
	L2L from the "teacher within"	Learning to generalize learning activities (transfer)	Learning to act (evaluating alternatives, risks, unforeseen circumstances)
EDUCATIONAL OBJECTIVES	Ensure adequate stimulation during the individual's early years	Increase the ability and capacity of the individual to control formal learning	Equip the individual with the abilities needed for lifelong learning
EDUCATIONAL STRATEGIES	Parent training Rich and encouraging pre-school experiences	Transitional curriculum enhancing natural learning prior to more formal experiences	Teach functional equivalents of direct instruction so that individuals can do for themselves (setting objectives, plan learning sequences, find resources, evaluate progress, review programmes)

(Continued)

Table 1.3 (Continued)

Aspects	Kinds of learning		
	Natural	Formal	Personal
ASPECTS	**REASON** *Reasoning ability*	**EMOTIONS** *Engagement, trust, self-esteem, self-control, interpersonal relationships*	**ACTION**
	Perceive from the environment	Feel own emotions	Take decisions
	Analyse phenomena within the broader picture	Construct a vision of self in the world	Take the initiative
	Create propositions upon reality and its interpretation	Build self-confidence	Practise, do, act, try again
	Use imagination to find alternatives and solutions	Develop determination	Solve problems
	Reflect and evaluate	Trustfully respond to own unconscious forces	Influence the course of events
DOMAINS	**TECHNICAL-EXECUTIVE** *In this domain, doing is learning and learning to do is LHTL*	**SOCIAL** *In this domain, relating to others is learning and learning to relate is LHTL*	**DEVELOP-MENTAL** *In this domain, learning is becoming ourselves and empowering ourselves by learning is LHTL*
Focus	Productivity	Relating to others	Freedom of self-determination
Mode of inquiry	Logical analysis	Interaction and negotiation	Critical reflection
Means	Study, experiment, practice	Communication	Developmental changes to increase our capacity to pursue choices
Outcome	Control over practical tasks	Social integration	Fully functioning adulthood

In addition, it is not sufficient to take just cognitive elements into account, like metacognition often does, rather it is necessary to contemplate also emotional and intentional aspects, variously combined throughout the lifespan of the individual. For example, aspects of reasoning ability include the need to perceive from the environment, analyse phenomena within the broader picture, create propositions upon reality and its interpretation, use imagination to find alternatives and solutions, and reflect and evaluate. Aspects connected to emotions (engagement, trust, self-esteem, self-control, interpersonal relationships) include the need to feel one's own emotions, construct a vision of self in the world, build self-confidence, develop determination, and trustfully respond to one's own unconscious forces. Aspects connected to actions include the need to take decisions, and the initiative, to practise, do, act, try again, solve problems, and influence the course of events.

For the author, major endeavours in a person's life are interactions with the environment, with other individuals, and with oneself. Following Habermas, for Gibbons (1990) an individual learns to learn in many different ways, depending on the three major endeavours, which he calls respectively the technical, social, and developmental domains of learning how to learn. For example, in the technical-executive domain, doing is learning and learning to do is learning how to learn. In the social domain, relating to others is learning and learning to relate is learning how to learn. In the developmental domain, learning is becoming ourselves and empowering ourselves by learning is learning how to learn.

The principles implicit in the model serve as a guide for learners wishing to empower themselves to learn and to pursue the 'Socratic examined life', which may begin during the school years, but certainly goes well beyond adolescence to embrace all stages of human development.

The Learning to Learn Framework – University of Helsinki

This model stems from a documented analysis of existing literature and from the convergence of different research traditions and paradigms: the socio-historical approach, with its emphasis on the creation of 'a nation of good learners', and the socio-cultural approach of Claxon, underlining the need for individuals to develop self-reflective power and awareness functional to their learning and life needs.

The psychological basis of the model lies in the Piagetian stages of cognitive development and the indicator scales are standardized according to formal operations mastery. The authors maintain that this allows this construct to be distinguished from intelligence, since concrete and formal operations are malleable and thus teachable.

The theoretical perspectives are integrated through the Snow model, evaluating the following components in a subject: conceptual structures, procedural skills, learning strategies, self-regulating functions, and motivational orientations.

The definition of learning to learn conceived by the research group reflects its scope:

> Learning-to-learn can be conceived of as the adaptive and voluntary mastery of learning action. After initial task acceptance, learning action is seen to be maintained through affective and cognitive self-regulation. Learning-to-learn is the readiness and willingness to adapt to a novel task. It consists of a complex system of cognitive competencies and self- and context-related beliefs. Readiness, or cognitive competence, refers both to the knowledge of

relevant facts and to the use of thinking and reasoning . . . The affective component of learning-to-learn is seen to consist of several relatively independent subsystems, comprising both self- and context-related beliefs. Among these, learning motivation, action-control beliefs, school-subject-related beliefs, task acceptance, socio-moral commitment, self-evaluation, and the experienced support of significant others . . .

The model has been created to respond to assessment needs of learning to learn not only within a scholastic environment, but also within lifelong learning. It can thus be considered a developmental approach.

The main dimensions polled are: (a) beliefs pertaining to learning context; (b) self-beliefs; (c) specific learning competencies, as depicted in Table 1.4.

The ELLI Project

The University of Bristol's ELLI (Effective Lifelong Learning Inventory) Project originated from the convergence of two research fields: (a) motivation to learn and (b) assessment for learning within a socio-cultural and lifelong approach.

Carr and Claxton (2002) maintain that the central goal of education is moving towards the development of attitudes and aptitudes to enable new generations to cope with growing complexity, uncertainty, and individual responsibility. In other words, to equip young people to learn from and for real-life situations. For these authors, learning power in everyday life consists of two correlated elements: capacities and dispositions. For capacities, read 'tools' – such as techniques, strategies, and abilities, needed in learning. These tools, however, are in themselves insufficient: it is necessary to be inclined to learn, and this means to be ready and motivated to capture learning opportunities in the environment.

A disposition is neither unique to a specific situation nor generally manifested across all situations. It is a tendency to respond or learn in a certain way that

Table 1.4 Finnish learning to learn model (adapted and synthesized from Hautamäki et al., 2002)

Learning to learn = ability and willingness to adapt to novel tasks

Context-related beliefs	Self-related beliefs	Learning competences
Societal frames	Learning motivation	Learning domain
Perceived support for learning and studying	Action-control beliefs	Reasoning domain
	Academic selves at school	Management of learning
	Assignment/task acceptance	Affective self-regulation
	Self-evaluation	
	Future orientation	

is somewhat, but incompletely, 'disembedded' from particular constellations of personal, social and material detail.

(Carr & Claxton, 2002: 12)

Dispositions vary in 'robustness' (persistence in less familiar and favourable situations and generalization to different experiential domains) and 'sophistication' (degree of 'richness' and differentiation). Dispositions are neither personality traits that remain biologically unchangeable, nor components or measures of general intelligence. They are cumulative, discrete, and interrelated dimensions.

The ELLI Project thus derives from Carr and Claxton's analysis of dispositions, yet goes well beyond with its three priorities: (a) research on the characteristics of the lifelong learner; (b) the construction of an instrument allowing learners to be classified on the basis of these characteristics-dimensions measured in a particular moment in time and in a particular context; (c) use of the information obtained to aid learners develop their learning power or learning energy (Deakin Crick et al., 2004: 248). According to Deakin Crick et al. (2004: 247), what we as learners bring to a learning situation in terms of our previous experiences, knowledge, abilities, and dispositions is the most important quality to be measured.

The Bristol group then identified the core of their analysis in the concept of learning power or learning energy, which they define as:

> a complex mix of dispositions, lived experiences, social relations, values, attitudes and beliefs . . . [that] . . . coalesce to shape the nature of an individual's engagement with any particular learning opportunity.

(Deakin Crick et al., 2004: 247)

An initial literature review identified four categories that seem to be cumulative, discrete, and interrelated dimensions of learning energy: (a) the capacity to learn (dispositions, awareness, and ability); (b) the learner's identity (in terms of beliefs, values, attitudes towards self, learning and knowledge); (c) the socio-cultural development of the learner in time; (d) the learner's learning relationships (their quality and substance) (Deakin Crick et al., 2004: 249).

The learner's profile, deriving from these premises, is neither unchangeable like the construct of general intelligence, nor so unstable as to impair its measure in a given moment in time. A learner's profile is not a static picture, but rather a situation that can be modified with appropriate interventions. Needless to say, this aspect assumes central importance in empowerment policies of adults and youth alike in formal, non-formal, and informal educational contexts.

The four categories operate as conglomerates of variables pertaining to a person within specific social contexts and trajectories in time, and this constitutes what the researchers call the ecology of 'an individual's learning orientation'. Factors contributing to a person's situated capacity and motivation to learn are numerous and of a different nature: physiological, affective, conative, cognitive, social, cultural, and technical aspects concur to a learner's learning power, and many of these factors are often out of conscious control of the individual.

Table 1.5 ELLI dimensions (Deakin Crick et al., 2004)

Seven dimensions of learning power and their opposites	
Changing and learning	Being stuck and static
Meaning-making	Data accumulation
Critical curiosity	Passivity
Creativity	Being rule-bound
Learning relationships	Isolation and dependence
Strategic awareness	Being robotic
Resilience	Fragility and dependence

The point of departure is the innate desire to learn as an intrinsic human quality, upon which emotional and cognitive factors display their influence. All these individual factors are acting within a socio-historical context, which probably variably influences their potential combinations throughout the lifetime. This temporal dimension through life experiences is what the authors call 'lateral connectivity' (Deakin Crick et al., 2004: 250). Such lateral connectivity in adults seems to hold together the individual's inner meaning of his or her own experience, ultimately aiding the development of self and the unfolding of individual potential.

Following their theoretic exploration, the Bristol group elaborated an assessment tool to identify and measure learning dispositions, translated into learning power profiles. The learning dimensions are described Table 1.5. The seven dimensions share some constitutive elements with the previously described learning to learn models, yet pay particular attention to motivation and self-efficacy, self-regulation and self-evaluation, in a socially shaped learning dimension.

In summary, this is an articulated attempt of assessment for learning and also of individual empowerment, allowing one to grasp the concept of learning to learn as the energy and power available to anyone. The model's main feature seems to be its relative simplicity and ease of application at low cost. Limitations lie in the instrument itself, which allows self-evaluation, yet with no more 'objective' measures. However, this could also be interpreted as an opportunity: the projective nature of this instrument allows learners to 'possess' their own profiles and self-image, thus allowing them to become aware of the capacities they can develop. This aspect seems particularly significant when dealing with adults reflecting on their own improvement possibilities.

Interestingly, the ELLI research programme found that there is a trend for learning power to decline as individuals progress through schooling. Such a tendency would corroborate the view that schools are not able to help learners learn how to learn (Diez & Moon, 1990).

Chapter 2

Learning to learn, know, and reason

Andreas Demetriou

Abstract

This chapter first outlines a theory of the organization and development of the human mind. The theory postulates that the mind involves four types of systems: specialized structural systems dealing with different types of objects and relations in the world; representational capacity, enabling the representation of information for processing; inference, enabling the integration and evaluation of information; and consciousness, enabling awareness and control of all other processes. Learning to learn is one of the functions of consciousness, aiming to facilitate and enhance learning. Then, based on the theory, an instruction system is advanced with the goal of enhancing learning to learn, know, and reason. This system aims to enable students to understand the organization and functioning of their own mind and their own individual strengths and weaknesses, develop skills to facilitate the functioning of each of the four systems above according to developmental and individual possibilities during different periods of the life course, and become critical both for knowledge and knowledge production systems, such as science. Methods for teaching special skills for different types of reasoning are proposed.

Key words: development of human mind, function of consciousness, learning to learn, instructional system.

Introduction

This chapter rests on five fundamental assumptions that frame how the main theme of the book, learning to learn, is dealt with. First, learning is a primary process of adaptation that enables organisms to deal with changes and variations in their environment. Second, dealing with a changing environment involves the ability to acquire new information (or knowledge) and new patterns of behaviour (including the possibility to plan them in advance), augmenting or modifying existing knowledge or behaviour. Learning to learn is part of this process, whenever and however this was made possible by evolution.

Third, knowledge and behaviour are represented in the brain and learning is the process of changing these representations. Therefore, what learning is possible for an individual is completely dependent on the brain. To serve learning, the brain is an open system that is continuously modified to adapt its representations of the environment and related behaviours. Its possibilities for representations and its modifiability vary across species (reflecting phylogenetic time), developmental phases (reflecting ontogenetic time), and individuals within developmental phases (reflecting an interaction between phylogenesis and ontogenesis). These possibilities constrain the kind and complexity of learning that is possible at any moment. Worms, cats, chimpanzees, and humans all learn. But can they all learn to learn? Obviously, there is a ceiling to what each species can learn. Although there is recent evidence to show that Rhesus monkeys can monitor and adjust their learning according to the complexity of information they have to deal with (Couchman et al., 2010), only humans can learn to learn because they have a brain that was built for this kind of learning.

Fourth, the concept of learning has changed extensively in psychology and education since their scientific beginnings in the late nineteenth century, depending upon the dominant epistemological paradigm of the time or school of thought. In the heyday of behaviourism, learning was interpreted as conditional learning of various kinds and learning to learn was not even a legitimate object of study. Legitimization came with the cognitive revolution in the 1960s. In psychometric psychology, learning is a function of general intelligence. The more one has of it (for instance, as indicated by IQ), the more and better one can learn, including learning to learn (Jensen, 1998). In developmental psychology, it is associated with metacognition, which is knowledge of cognitive processes and the factors that may affect them. This line of research yielded programmes with the aim of facilitating the acquisition and use of cognitive strategies to boost learning in the classroom (Presley & Harris, 2006). However, it is not always explicitly associated with learning to learn.

Fifth, although a recent term, learning to learn rests on an old assumption: humans can take charge of their learning, with the obvious aim of making it better than if they were not in charge of it. Old methods, such as memorization methods (e.g. rehearsal or association) for memory improvement, or the Socratic method for deepening understanding, recognized that learning is a manoeuvrable process. Research suggests that learning to learn is indeed possible. However, what (e.g. are all cognitive processes amenable to awareness and self-regulation?), how (e.g. what methods are available?), and when learning is possible (e.g. can humans learn to learn at any age?) and by whom (e.g. can everyone learn to learn?) is not yet well specified. In this chapter, we first outline a model of the human mind that integrates modern research in cognitive, developmental, and differential psychology. The aim is to embed learning to learn in the context of the functioning and development of the human mind.

We assume that our epistemological stance is clear by now: learning to think or reason and learning to learn are complementary aspects of the same adaptive process of tuning the mind with the environment. Thus, improving any one of these aspects of learning would also affect the others. In this chapter, the emphasis is on learning to think and reason (i.e. the processes underlying inference, problem-solving, and decision-making) rather than on skills or strategies for learning as such (i.e. that rehearsal improves later recall, self-assessment enables one to identify gaps in knowledge, etc.). This is because we believe that beneficially modifying the possibilities of the central engine of learning would have a wider and longer lasting effect than simply imparting learning skills or strategies. In fact, teachers are among the most important agents of learning and learning to learn. Thus, if they themselves understand how this central engine works, they may be able to better direct their students to take control of their learning processes.

The architecture and development of the mind

Psychometric, cognitive, and developmental research converge on the assumption that the human mind involves four types of systems that carry out different tasks during learning or problem-solving: representational capacity, inference, consciousness, and specialized structural systems (for detailed discussion, see Demetriou et al., 2011). Figure 2.1 highlights this architecture. Each of these systems participates in learning to various degrees based on prior experience, developmental phase, and individual differences. Learning to learn may both depend on and be directed to each of them. Below, we first outline the processes, development, and interactions of these systems and then focus on learning to think and learn.

Representational capacity

Organization of representational capacity

Representational capacity is the work-space of the mind where information is analysed, connected, combined, and transformed, for the sake of interpretation,

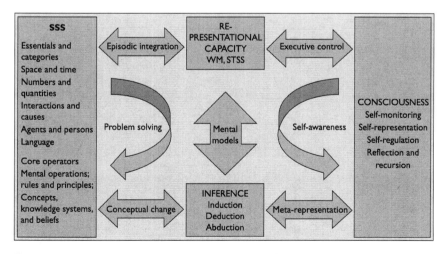

Figure 2.1 The general architecture of the human mind (based on Demetriou et al., 2011).

drawing of inferences, formation of action plans, and problem-solving (Cowan et al., 2007; Baddeley, 2012). Mental functioning at any moment occurs under the constraints of the available representational capacity. Technically, this capacity is defined as the maximum number of chunks or units of information (e.g. mental images, words, numbers) and mental operations (e.g. mental rotation, grammatical rules, arithmetic operations) that the mind can work on simultaneously. When active, representational capacity is transparent to consciousness. Thus, people are aware both of its content, which comes from the senses, such as hearing and vision, or from long-term memory, and of what they are doing on it. For example, if one is multiplying 24 × 31, one is aware of these numbers and the multiplication process. In the psycho-logical literature, terms such as working memory (executive control processes together with information represented), short-term storage (i.e. the number of chunks of information that one can hold, such as the number of words, numbers of visual images), and episodic memory (i.e. integration of information at a given moment so that a holistic representation of what is going on can be attained) stand for complementary aspects of representational capacity (Baddeley, 2012).

Development of representational capacity

Young infants do represent information coming to the senses. Impressively, iconic memory has a capacity of five objects at the age of 6 months, which is very close to the six-object capacity of adults (Blaser and Kaldy, 2010). However, it is only at the end of the second year that infants can focus processing on a small part of the content of their sensory storage and intentionally process it, which implies some control of attention at this age. This ability starts with one unit at the age of 2 years and it develops systematically until adolescence. Preschoolers are able to represent 1–2, primary school children 3–4, and adolescents and adults 5–7 chunks of information, respectively (Pascual-Leone, 1970; Case, 1985; Halford et al., 1998; Demetriou et al., 2002, 2008).

Inference

Organization of inference

Inference is probably the most active and powerful mechanism of integration of information. As such, it participates in every learning or knowledge change. It involves processes that enable the transfer of meaning from one representation to another. Transfer normally occurs on the basis of properties that are present in both the initial representation and the target representation. In inference, these common properties are used as an intermediary between two representations such that properties characterizing the initial representation (apart from common properties) are also ascribed to the target representation. There are several types of reasoning. The most frequently studied forms of inference are inductive (e.g. 'It is raining, we should get an umbrella'), analogical (e.g. 'You are big, you have a big brain; I am small, I have a small brain'), and deductive reasoning (e.g. 'You said I can go to the park if I eat my food; I ate my food, so I am going to the park'; all examples come from real conversations with my 3-year-old grandson) (Holland et al., 1986; Moshman, 1994; Rips, 1994; Ricco, 2010).

Development of inference

Inductive inference is probably present at birth. Initially, inductive inference is based on perceptual similarity, which enables infants to construct concepts by extracting general characteristics from overlapping perceptual features that appear across objects and by selectively attending to relevant features while ignoring irrelevant ones (e.g. round vs. square objects, self-moving vs. steady objects) (Gelman & Coley, 1990; Sloutsky & Fisher, 2011). Children are able to recognize similarity from birth, and are able to grasp second-order generalizations before they are 1 year old. For example, 9-month-olds capture the pattern underlying the characteristics of objects in different boxes (i.e. all round in this box, all square in this box, etc.) and generalize to a second-order relation that generates expectations about new objects (i.e. all objects in a box are similar in shape, so if there is a star-like object in a new box, all other objects in this box must be star-like) (Téglás et al., 2011). At preschool, children can identify patterns and create dimensions that span a recurrent relation; also, they can grasp analogical relations if the objects involved are familiar and related by personally meaningful relations. At 6–8 years, they can handle hidden or implied relations and align dimensions (e.g. table is to eating as bed is to sleep). Later, at 9–11 years, generalizations are compacted into concepts that can themselves be interrelated (e.g. 'speaking is to silence as water is to fire' is acceptable – they are opposites). In adolescence, analogical reasoning can structure third- or higher-order relationships involving abstract relations (e.g. children are to parents in the family as students are to teachers in education) (Mouyi, 2008; Demetriou et al., 2010). Many tests of intelligence, such as the Wechsler's test or the Raven's test, include tasks that require this kind of abstraction.

The development of deductive reasoning appears to follow a similar path. Some scholars have suggested that the basic patterns of logical relations exist in reality and thus pre-logical inferential schemas emerge very early in development that are antecedent to deductive forms of reasoning proper. For example, joint iteration, which refers to repetitions of elements, is the basis of conjuction (e.g. 'it has legs and eyes and it is moving on its own; it has eyes, so it has legs and it is moving on its own'). Permission rules or contingencies (e.g. 'if you do this, I will do this') may function as the basis for implication (Rosch, 1975; Braine, 1990).

However, these pre-logical schemas become deductive schemas only when integrated across occasions and contexts and used as such. This is not possible before language and awareness of mental processing. In fact, Moshman (1994, 2011) noted that the development of deductive reasoning goes hand in hand with the development of awareness of the elements and processes involved.

During the preschool years, children correctly use most of the connectives and conditionals involved in inference schemas but they have no understanding of the inferential process and they are not aware that the premises constrain the conclusion (e.g. 'there is a cat; there is an apple; so there is a cat and an apple'). Thus, inferences are integral parts of the relations between the elements included in undifferentiated representational blocks.

This awareness appears for the first time by about the age of 5 or 6 years, when inference becomes explicit but logic is implicit. Children at this phase can grasp modus ponens arguments (e.g. 'if there is a either a cow or a goat, then there is a pear; there is a cow, therefore there is a pear'). However, logic as such is still implicit in their reasoning and does not function as a frame explicitly guiding reasoning. Thus, they fail on problems in which the logical form of the argument must be explicitly differentiated from its content (e.g. 'birds fly; cats are birds; therefore cats fly'). During the next phase, at the age of about 9–10 years, children can deal with modus tollens inferences (e.g. 'if there is a cow, there is an apple; there is no cow; therefore, there is no apple'). Compared with modus ponens, modus tollens requires a model construction process that takes the modus ponens argument as a basis and then constructs alternative models which are compared with each other (IF P THEN Q, P, THUS Q, SO IF NO P THEN ALSO NO Q).

At 11–12 years of age, logic becomes explicit but metalogic is still implicit. Pre-adolescents understand that 'an argument is valid if, regardless of the empirical truth of its premises and conclusions, it has a logical form such that, if the premises were true, the conclusion would have to be true as well' (Moshman, 1990: 212). Thus, at this phase, they can deal with simple denying the antecedent and affirming the consequent fallacies (e.g. 'if there is a cow, there is a pear; there is a pear; we cannot be sure if there is a cow'). Fallacies place high demands on the mind, because a series of alternatives must be constructed and contrasted (Barrouillet et al., 2011). Moreover, the thinker at this level accepts that uncertainty may be part of the reasoning process itself because it is not always possible to derive a conclusion. Finally, at the stage of explicit metalogic, adolescents can function as theorists of reasoning. As a result, they can specify all implications of an argument, determinate or indeterminate, based on all possible logical forms involved.

Consciousness

Organization of consciousness

Obviously, not all cognitive functioning reaches consciousness. Perception, for example, rarely reaches consciousness, although its products do (e.g. that the object I see is blue). In fact, in evolution, consciousness arose as a mechanism to be called upon when things go wrong or when no ready-made or automated action schemas are available. Novel, conflicting or incongruent information relative to a specific goal causes uncertainty as to what to do. Thus, to meet their goals, individuals must be able to focus attention and process goal-relevant information efficiently, filter out goal-irrelevant information, and assemble a response or decision based on what is needed. Therefore, consciousness involves (i) awareness of the content of working memory, (ii) executive control processes enabling the regulation of attention according to the needs of the moment (Zelazo & Frye, 1998; Atkinson et al., 2000; Zelazo et al., 2005), and (iii) metarepresentation that enables the construction of new representations. Thus, consciousness is a mechanism for the integration of separate mental constructs or brain networks and thus a mechanism for cognitive and behavioural control and flexibility (Cleeremans et al., 2007). Obviously, representational capacity is the functional field of consciousness and inference its primary tool of action.

Metarepresentation looks for, typifies, and encodes similarities between mental experiences and between representations, thereby generating new mental operations, new higher-order rules integrating different operations, and new representations to stand for these new operations and rules are created. Thus, it broadens the basis for understanding and problem-solving in the future. During this ideoplastic process, metarepresentation gradually builds maps of mental functions that are continuously updated. These maps are generally accurate representations of the actual organization of cognitive processes (Demetriou & Kazi, 2001, 2006). Thus, when needed, these models may be called upon to guide problem-solving and understanding. We will explicate this process below.

Development of consciousness

All aspects of consciousness develop systematically from birth to maturity. In the first year of life, there is implicit awareness of one's own actions and bodily sensations (Kopp, 2011), while in the second year infants recognize themselves in the mirror. This enables infants to execute means–end actions, such as using a stick to pull an object within reach. At 2 years, children can plan action based on a single rule (e.g. 'If it is red it goes here'). However, it is only in the third year that infants can operate with a contrastive relation (e.g. 'If it is red it goes here, if it is blue it goes here'), which indicates reflective planning of action. At the age of 5 years, children can integrate two rules into a higher-order rule that specifies when each of them is to be used (e.g. 'If we were playing colour, then if it is red it goes here and if it is blue it goes here, but if we were playing shape, then if it is a red car it goes here and if it is a blue flower it goes here') (Zelazo and Frye, 1998; Zelazo, 2004). This indicates an analytic awareness of the contents of working memory.

The development of awareness of cognitive processes is more complicated and it lags behind awareness of action and executive control. At the age of 3–5 years, children base their judgements on perceptual similarity of the objects involved rather than what they are required to do with them (e.g. objects that look the same are thought to be processed by the same processes rather than according to what one is doing with them, such as counting or naming them). However, they have an intuitive understanding that cognitive processes are affected by the environment; for instance, they stare at the point where an object disappeared to remember its possible location later (Hupp & Sloutsky, 2011). At the age of

6–7 years, children recognize that pairs of tasks belonging to a different domain require different mental processes and they can recognize the mental operation required (e.g. classification or counting) regardless of external object characteristics. In adolescence, individuals start to be sensitive to delicate variations between mental operations according to their complexity and the special requirements of the problem concerned. Thus, self-evaluation of cognitive performance starts to be accurate in adolescence. The mental self-concept follows the same trend (Demetriou & Kazi, 2001, 2006). Overall, with development, cognitive processes and mental operations are increasingly differentiated from each other and this differentiation guides intellectual development because it allows the generation of increasingly interconnected, abstract, and flexible inferential processes and knowledge structures (Demetriou & Kazi, 2001, 2006; Zelazo, 2004; Kazi et al., 2012; Demetriou et al., 2013b).

Specialized structural systems

Organization of specialized structural systems

Specialized structural systems are responsible for the representation and processing of different types of relations in the environment. Five specialized structural systems have been identified by researchers:

1. *Categorical thought* forms concepts and relations between concepts to model the organizational and functional structure of the world. Our representations about physical objects and living beings, types of objects and beings belong to this system.
2. *Quantitative thought* deals with quantitative variations and relations in the environment. Mathematical concepts and operations are examples of this system.
3. *Causal thought* deals with cause–effect relations. Representations about causal relations between objects and persons and operations related to causality, such as trial-and-error or isolation of variables, that enable one to decipher causal relations belong to this system.
4. *Spatial thought* deals with orientation in space and the imaginal representation of the environment. Mental maps of places or mental images of familiar persons and objects and operations on them, such as mental rotation, belong to this system.
5. *Social thought* deals with social relationships and interactions. Mechanisms for monitoring non-verbal communication or skills for dealing with social interactions belong to this system (Case et al., 2001; Demetriou & Kazi, 2001, 2006).

Specialized structural systems involve three types of processes. First, *core processes* are foundational meaning-making devices that impose their ready-made meaning on objects. For instance, in colour perception a particular range of light wavelength is perceived as a particular colour; in subitization, the numerocity of small sets from 1 to 4 elements is automatically recognized if they are close to each other. Second, *mental operations* are mental processes that emerge from core processes, such as sorting or classifying objects by colour or counting and numerical operations. Third, *knowledge and beliefs* accumulate over the years as a result of the interactions of each specialized structural system with its respective domain. Knowledge in both its informal everyday version and its more formal version produced by science or other institutionalized systems of knowledge production is always a mixture of elements coming from different specialized structural systems. In short, specialized structural systems are the source of mental models about the world. That is, integrated systems of representations that may be evoked to stand for particular entities and relations in the world, when needed.

Development of specialized structural systems

All systems are present at birth. There is strong evidence that the core processes of categorical, quantitative, causal, spatial, and social thought are present in the first weeks of life (Carey, 2009; Demetriou et al., 2011). For instance, infants a few weeks old differentiate between objects according to their similarities, meaning that they have concepts about them. They can also recognize numerical changes if they are applied on sets of fewer than four objects. They can locate objects in three-dimensional space. They also recognize the causal constraints in the relations between objects, such as that if they are solid, they cannot pass through each other, and they can exert pressure on each other (Carey, 2009). Early in life, the core processes generate representations that provide the behavioural or mental analogues of the basic laws of physics, biology, and psychology. These enable the infant to interact with increasing efficiency with physical objects, animals, and other humans. Mental operations and knowledge emerge from the interactions between core processes and their respective domains.

With development, each of the specialized structural systems moves along three dimensions: complexity, abstraction, and flexibility. From one point of view, this is a continuous process of emergence, differentiation, and integration of new representations. From another, some changes at some periods alter how the developing individual views the world. These changes create milestones that are important both from the point of view of the person's own subjective experience and his or her relations with the world. There seem to be three such milestones.

Differentiation of representations.   With language and other forms of arbitrary representation at about the age of 2 years, children start to turn inwards and elaborate on their own and other people's experiences of the environment. An important milestone in this process of differentiation of representations is *dual representation*, which appears at the age of 3–4 years. It signifies the differentiation between representations and their referents, allowing children to intentionally focus mental processing on representations as tokens of the world. According to DeLoache (1995), in order to use a symbol one must represent both the object to be represented and the symbol itself and connect them by a relation.

At the age of 7–8 years, *reducent representation* takes the representations of the previous phase as its inputs and reduces them into generic representations within and across specialized structural systems. This allows the construction of systems of concepts, such as classes, numbers, and causes. For example, in the domain of categorical thought, systematic classification becomes possible because a set of criteria may be preselected and applied in order to specify the identity of objects and their similarity relations (e.g. colour, shape). Emergent logical necessity in this phase is an index that representations are cohesively interconnected and reduced to general concepts.

A third milestone comes at the beginning of adolescence, when representations become conditional. *Conditional representation* enables thinkers to view representations from the point of view of each other. The meaning of each component representation in conditional representations emerges from the relations of each representation with all other representations in the system. For example, adolescents can specify when $A + B + C = A + Y + C$ is true, fully grasp proportionality, and formulate and test alternative hypotheses. Logical necessity is fully established at this phase and it is used as a gauge of the fit of each representation in a system. Therefore, empirically non-true or counterintuitive representations may be logically valid and thus acceptable if they can be derived from the logical relations involved.

Relations between structures and processes

The processes above are in constant interaction. On the one hand, there indeed seems to be a gross correspondence between the capacity of working memory and the complexity of representations attained in the successive levels of development in the various specialized structural systems, inference, and consciousness. Based on this correspondence, developmental researchers assumed that changes in working memory cause changes in problem-solving and reasoning (Pascual-Leone, 1970; Case, 1985; Halford et al., 1998) and differential researchers assumed that individual differences in working memory cause individual differences in IQ. However, reality is more complicated than it appears. We showed recently that working memory does predict individual differences in intelligence within the same developmental phase (accounting for about 60–90% of the variance) but it contributes very little to changes in intelligence across developmental phases (accounting for about 3–4% of the variance) (Demetriou et al., 2013b). The crucial factor for change is metacognitive awareness of the processes involved in reasoning and practice in the production and use of mental models in order to draw valid inferences (Demetriou et al., 2013a). That is, change to a higher level of inference occurs when children become aware of the core aspects of inferential processes. For example, that the relations between propositions ('if . . . then', 'either . . . or') allow some conclusions and prohibit others. It seems that working memory and inferential ability development are alternative aspects of the state of mind at a given time. Working memory reflects the resolution of representations at a given moment and inference reflects their relations. Thus, changes in one of them are automatically transferred to the other, but change in them in the first place must be initiated from another source. This comes from an important component of consciousness, the abstraction-metarepresentation process, which produces inference patterns and associates each with its relevant problems (Demetriou et al., 2011, 2013a, 2013b).

This interpretation is consistent with the dual-process theory of reasoning and reasoning development. This theory postulates two very different but developmentally related types of reasoning: System 1 reasoning is highly dependent on context – it is more intuitive rather than systematic, and it is fast and effortless but it may be deceived by context; System 2 reasoning is analytic and systematic – thus it is context-free and resistant to deception, but it is effortful and slow (Ricco & Overton, 2011). In terms of the theory proposed here, System 2 reasoning emerges from the operation of System 1 reasoning through awareness of similarities and differences between heuristic processes and the construction of representations that unify and represent these heuristic processes. That is, the key components of reasoning are gradually decoupled from their context, fused with each other, and metarepresented as logically necessary reasoning schemas that are gradually interconnected with each other as reasoning rules. That is, achievements in inductive and analogical reasoning are reproduced in deductive reasoning with a time delay of several years, which are needed for metarepresentation to reconstruct inductively grasped relations into deductive inference models. This process is important for learning to learn because it transfers control of understanding from external sources of information to the individual, making him or her more critical about the value and consistency of information.

Natural language and other forms of symbolism are instrumental in the elevation of System 1 into System 2 reasoning. For example, children first construct meaning-based representations based on thematic context and then abstract logical form, when processing verbal information that is to be interpreted logically. For example, a common name for objects that do not appear completely identical directs infants to look for, represent, and tag similarities. Thus, object-naming by adults guides the induction of similarity relations between objects (Fisher, 2010). Conversations in which the linguistic and the actual structure of events are in direct correspondence contribute to the formation of deductive schemas, such as the modus tolens inference: 'If you drop it, it will break into pieces, you see' (Demetriou et al., 2011). Therefore, the symbolization process partakes in inferential processes by guiding the transfer of meaning across representations, as explicated above.

Learning to reason and learning to learn

The model of mind outlined here frames how learning to learn is to be interpreted. First, learning to learn is a function of the relation between consciousness and all other mental processes. As such, it requires awareness and control of the learning process so that it takes place at the right pace, it is geared to the demands of the task at hand, it can bypass possible processing and representational limitations by properly arranging the material to be learned, it judiciously uses relevant prior knowledge to enhance new learning, and it ensures that learning will endure.

Second, therefore, learning to learn requires an understanding of the organization and functioning of the mind and the role of the fundamental knowledge extraction and processing mechanisms. For example, that control of attention is crucial for the intake of relevant information, rehearsal and association are crucial to establish the necessary connections and protect them from forgetting, inference is crucial to build economical and efficient concepts and validate their relations or connections to reality, and self-testing is important to check if learning did occur.

Finally, learning to learn varies with age. Its kind, scope, and quality depend upon development. With increasing resolution of awareness about mental processes, individuals become increasingly able to regulate them so that the knowledge and skills acquired are more accurate, refined, properly intertwined, and on target. Below we outline a programme for learning to reason and learn that focuses on each of the main systems of the architecture of the mind and the mind's major developmental milestones.

Improving representational capacity

Representational capacity is crucial in learning because it is the interface between new and old knowledge. To strengthen the role of representational capacity in both learning as such and learning to reason and learn, education must have three main goals: (1) familiarize children with general and personal representational limits; (2) familiarize children with the role of representational capacity in learning; (3) increase children's personal control over representational capacity.

Familiarization with capacity limits requires involvement with activities where the volume and complexity of information are systematically manipulated. Specifically, recalling number digits or words of an increasing volume and recording the cut-off point between success and failure externalizes what one can store and recall. Recalling information under different organization (e.g. one-by-one, integrated into meaningful sentences) or recall strategies (e.g. in presentation order or backwards) shows that different executive plans influence how much information can be stored. Alternatively, recalling the output of the same mental operation on information of increasing complexity – for example, multiply numbers of increasing complexity, such as one- (e.g. 8×9), two- (e.g. 27×46), and three-digit (e.g. 464×639) numbers – demonstrates that mental processing generates information that needs to be represented together with the initial information and mental operations. Recalling a set of objects presented visually and verbally demonstrates that there may be different limits according to the type of information. Further rehearsal may be needed to process and remember verbal representations as compared to mental images.

Familiarization with capacity functions in learning requires learning activities in which capacity is systematically manipulated. For example, destruction (e.g. irrelevant sounds coming from a TV) while children are trying to understand a demanding problem in mathematics or a passage of text demonstrates that representational capacity is crucial at important stages of meaning-making. When target material is out of representational focus (because attention is attracted by what is on the TV screen), relations cannot be worked out and related to previous knowledge in order to become meaningful. As a result, understanding and later recall will suffer.

Increased personal control of representational capacity would first of all require sensitivity to variations in its content. Specifying variations in performance in the examples above would be helpful. Second, children must be trained to manage more than one task simultaneously by alternating between blocks or types of information and binding items according to type and time of presentation. Presenting visual information on the one side of a screen and a verbal description on the other side and asking children to integrate these to formulate a complete representation and story is one example. Third, they need practice in inhibiting irrelevant items. A relevant strategy here is practice in checking the compatibility between items and the current goal with ensuing deactivation or displacement of irrelevant items away from attention. Finally, practice in reorganization and re-chunking would enable children to trade-off an increasing volume of infor-mation with increasing semantic density of representations to be held in focus. For example, using the category name (e.g. animals) rather than object names (e.g. a cow and a cat and a dog) would reduce the volume of information to be stored.

There is research to show that interventions of this kind do improve attention and working memory. Moreover, researchers have claimed that improved control of these processes raises general intelligence (e.g. Buschkuehl & Jaeggi, 2010). Although this is disputed (Shipstead et al., 2012), it is clear that working memory is strongly involved in learning to reason, even if change in working memory alone is not sufficient to change reasoning (Demetriou et al., 2013a). Below we focus on methods that directly address the enhancement of reasoning ability.

Enhancing reasoning and critical thinking

Reasoning is a means to several important ends. Here we focus only on command of the inferential process so that information is validly interpreted, used, evaluated, and integrated into extant knowledge. Later, we focus on the role of inference in good decision-making and problem-solving. Targeting the first end would enhance control of the technical-procedural aspects of reasoning. Targeting the second end would improve its use in the actual world.

Commanding reasoning.   Instruction to enhance control of reasoning must aim to do the following: (1) Individuals must become aware of the dual nature of reasoning and acquire the necessary knowledge and flexibility to move between System 1 and System 2. (2) They must take control of the processes underlying production of System 2 reasoning from System 1 functioning. (3) As far as possible, they must be able to use the processes discussed above in concert with the representational capacity available to overcome the representational cost of employing System 2 reasoning. That is, they must be aware that System 2 reasoning taxes representational capacity because it requires one to keep in focus all premises or mental representations needed to draw a valid conclusion.

Technically, instruction must attain the following:

1. Demonstrate the difference between automatic (System 1) and analytic (System 2) inference.
2. Decontextualize inference.
3. Differentiate between inferential processes and logical forms, such as inductive, analogical, and deductive reasoning.
4. Make use of mental models for the sake of inference and reasoning.
5. Make use of metarepresentation to automate inference and reasoning.

We show how these aims may be attained using the examples presented in Table 2.1.

The first set of examples addresses inductive reasoning. They refer to the very familiar condition of flying birds. They aim to show that participating in a class allows one to generalize class properties (e.g. they have wings; they fly) from the class to novel class members (e.g. imaginary nigles) or that of having one class property (nappows fly) to class membership (are they birds?) or other class properties (e.g. do they fly?). At preschool, instruction should prioritize elaboration on object comparison and similarity identification. That is, instruction should elaborate on the reduction of individual elements into a class through a common crucial property present in each of them. Symbols standing for the class may be used to symbolize the connection between reality and representation. At primary school, the emphasis may shift to class specification through multiple properties and relations between classes. At secondary school, the emphasis may shift to the nature of inductive generalization as such; that is, that it is likely but never necessary. Thus belief in inductive generalizations must always remain open to future falsification.

The second set of examples addresses analogical reasoning. The emphasis of instruction here shifts from object similarity to relational similarity. Examples horizontally involve analogical relations of the same order, namely between specific elements (1), classes (2), and general functions (3). Thus, children may be instructed to pinpoint and elaborate on the relations within and across pairs within and across analogies. In preschool, teaching may start from studying actual animals and objects and specifying their relations within and across pairs within each analogy (or their toy representation). For example, that they both have parts enabling them to move. Observations may then be encoded into verbal statements with the explicit aim of showing how one kind of representation may be expressed as another kind of representation. In this way, observations or their action or visual models are metarepresented into language. At primary school, the relations may be elaborated across analogies with the aim of showing the relations between relations (i.e. that flying and walking are forms of motion). At the end of primary school or the beginning of adolescence, relations may be formalized in abstract representations as above. Eventually, during high school, the relations may be discussed from the context of different knowledge domains,

Table 2.1 Examples of tasks that can be used in learning to reason programmes

Inductive reasoning

Pigeons are birds, they have wings, and they fly
Sparrows are birds, they have wings, and they fly
Hawks are birds, they have wings, and they fly
Nigles are birds: Do they have wings? Do they fly?
Nappows fly: Are they birds? Do they have wings?

Analogical reasoning

Wings are to pigeons as feet are to cats
Wings are to birds as feet are to animals
Flying is to birds as walking is to animals

Wings are to aeroplanes as wheels are to cars
Wings are to flying machines as wheels are to rolling machines
Flying is to flying machines as rolling is to rolling machines

Flying, walking, and rolling enable motion, given the constraints of each living being or vehicle
A (flying) : B (birds) :: C (walking) : D (animals) ::: E (flying) : F (aeroplanes) :: G (rolling) : H (cars) → motion

Deductive reasoning

Birds fly	Birds fly,	Birds fly	Animals and birds either walk or fly
Nigles are birds	Cats are birds,	Nappows fly	Cats are animals
Nigles fly	Cats fly	Nappows are birds	Cats walk
P and Q		P and Q	P and Q R or S
P		Q	pl
Q		?P	?R

Note: The symbol ? stands for undecidable conclusions.

such as biology (motion is needed for survival), physics (wings and feet make use of similar principles to ensure animal motion), and technology (artificial parts such as wheels make use of the same physical principles). The aim would be to move from a learning exercise in reasoning to embedding reasoning into different knowledge domains, and to evaluate it from the point of view of different theories with the aim of bridging reasoning with epistemological awareness about the nature and limitations of both knowledge extraction and handling mechanisms and knowledge validation itself (Gentner, 2005).

The third set of examples addresses deductive reasoning. The aim of the examples here is to show the difference between induction (actual information is relevant and essential in induction), analogical reasoning (a general property, such as motion, constrains relations between apparently differing elements or properties), and deductive reasoning (form constrains inference, knowledge about properties is irrelevant to inference, truth may remain an open question).

The first two examples stand for classical and straightforward modus tollens. Given the premises, the conclusion is valid in both cases, although it is not true in the second example. The last two examples are inconclusive. Nappows may or may not be birds and cats may or may not walk, given the premises. These arguments may be compared with each other and with the inductive and analogical problems presented above from a number of respects. Overall, children would have to grasp the difference between a true statement and a statement taken as true. In inductive reasoning, inference is based on similarity and similarity of relations as suggested by information in the premises. In deductive reasoning, emphasis shifts from similarities of element properties or relations to relations imposed by the structure of the argument. For this to be possible, children must focus on the meaning of each sentence as given in the argument and ignore any other previous knowledge or information related to the words in the sentences. Also, they must understand that an argument involves a network of relationships systematically arranged which can be used as a basis for decoding the relationships. Thus, to grasp the logical relationships implied by a logical argument, one must break down or analyse the argument into the premises involved and focus on their logical relationships independently of content. Attention should be drawn to the role of connectives such as 'is', 'are', 'and', 'if . . . then', 'either . . . or', etc., as indexes of logical relations.

At preschool, children can be taught to realize that the information in the premises is connected by inference. Actual models of the organisms involved and visual representations of the line of inference going from the one to the other are obviously useful. At primary school, directed comparisons across the various arguments would enable children to differentiate form from content and understand that logic constrains inference. That is, when children understand that the conclusion 'cats fly' necessarily follows from the premises, given that we accept that 'cats are birds' and that 'birds fly', they already know that logical structure underlies inference and that content is irrelevant to the conclusion. In adolescence, they must be introduced to the conditional and suppositional nature of reasoning and the role of form in constraining inference.

Finally, instruction would have to reveal the similarities and differences between inductive, analogical, and deductive inference. That is, that the first structures information about realities, the second structures these structures, and the third generates processes that may help one to go beyond realities.

Educating self-awareness

Students must understand that it is better for future performance and learning to metarepresent the processes activated or the solutions reached. To support metarepresentation and facilitate the emergence of general reasoning patterns from domain-specific processing, teaching must continuously raise awareness of what may be abstracted from any particular domain-specific learning. Specifically, children must become aware of the underlying relations that surpass content differences and of the very mental processes used while handling them. For instance, the same core inference schemas may operate differently in different domains. Joint iteration (i.e. and, and, and) in the categorical specialized structural system does not change a class property (e.g. 'animal'), only its extension (e.g. 'cats and dogs and mice are animals'). However, it does change the cardinal value of a set (e.g. a cat (1 animal) and a dog (2 animals) and a mouse (3 animals), etc.). Moreover, the student must be facilitated to tag the new constructs by explicit new representations that will enable him or her to mentally recall, manipulate, and relate the new representations with others that already exist (Dixon et al., 2010).

Educating self-awareness and metarepresentation is limited by the lag of language and other symbolic means of representation. It must start from there though, focusing on the core operations. For example, classification skills and induction of relations must be based on perceptual similarity that generates concepts in the categorical system. There may be special markers that can direct attention to particular features of the objects, such as shape or colour. Moreover, there may be special effects that provide feedback about acceptable and unacceptable sorting actions, such as special sounds for successful and unsuccessful actions. These conditions may direct the infant to explore the form, size, shape, and relations between objects, which may generate mental representations of the objects and their categorical and visuo-spatial relations. Objects can be arranged variably within the subitization limit, so that they can be counted, numbered, and tagged visually so that representations about number can be constructed. In the causal domain, particular objects or components of objects may be associated with special effects, such as sounds or colours. The actions of the infants on these objects may enable them to build causal connections between their behaviour, objects, and effects. Mapping variations of actions with corresponding variations of effects is conducive to the construction of a mental space of causality.

At the edge between infancy and toddlerhood, with the emergence of language, education must enable the infant to connect core operators with representations and advance them into the respective mental operations of the specialized domains concerned. That is, the infant must be facilitated to recognize how different words, symbols, and the grammatical and syntactical structures of language are connected to realities related to each of the core operators mentioned above. In the preschool years, children must be systematically instructed to explore how the appearance of objects may change without affecting the identity of objects (e.g. changing the dressing of a doll, playing with transformers and other toys where variation in appearance is an integral part of their construction). They must be assisted to alternate between one's own point of view and another's point of view by systematically exchanging and comparing positions. Moreover, in these contexts, they must be helped to realize that different perspectives or different appearances may induce in different persons different representations and different beliefs about the realities concerned.

This is also a good context to make children aware of dual or multiple representations, their symbolic expressions, and their mapping onto their reality referents. For instance, tagging photographs to the objects they represent, and then varying the perceptual similarity between an object and its photograph until the photograph is transformed into an abstract representation of the object is a method for training toddlers in the nature of representation in the categorical domain (DeLoache, 1991). Tagging numbers onto sets of objects may have the same function in the quantitative domain. Tagging written words to expressions may have the same function in the domain of language. Moreover, associating alternative representations with the same reality (e.g. number digits and number words) may be helpful in enabling the child to dissociate representation from thought as such. Finally, tagging photographs of the different perspectives from which an object may be viewed and associating it with different persons is good practice in perspective-taking and theory of mind.

In the early primary school years, children start to be aware of mental activity and of the differences between cognitive functions. Therefore, at primary school, education must build awareness of the differences between mental functions and of their differential impact on learning. Moreover, it must focus on bridging activities with different mental functions and aspects of learning. For instance, children must realize that recall of information from memory and its connection with what is in front of their eyes facilitates understanding of new information. In turn, they must learn that rehearsal facilitates storage of new information in long-term memory for later use and that this may be tested by asking questions of themselves (Dehn, 2008). That association and relating with prior knowledge helps learning but variation and differentiation helps originality in problem-solving (Siegler, 1996; Simonton, 2000; Glassner & Schwarz, 2007). Also, that going too fast may be harmful for storing information in long-term memory but going too slow may be harmful for storing information in working memory, thus impoverishing problem-solving (Demetriou et al., 2013b).

In adolescence, self-awareness gradually becomes process-driven, the self-concept becomes dimensionalized and generally accurate, and problem-solving becomes planfull and systematic. For instance, by middle adolescence, students begin to be able to differentiate between the cognitive processes involved in different kinds of knowledge and activities, such as mathematics vs. physics, they know where they are strong and where they are weak, and they can plan their problem-solving activities from the start so that they can seek information when and where it is needed and integrate it into their current problem-solving endeavours (Demetriou, 2000; Demetriou & Kazi, 2001, 2006). Therefore, education at this phase should focus on awareness of the differences between cognitive domains in the mental processes they involve and in how they relate to their world domains. Also, education in early adolescence should enhance the 'if . . . then' stance approach to problem-solving and build epistemological awareness about the characteristics, possibilities, and limitations of different knowledge domains vis-à-vis their methods, functions, and priorities as elaborated above in relation to critical thinking.

Assessment for learning and learning to learn

Assessment in education is crucial for learning because it informs the learner of possible divergences between learning goals and outcomes. It is beyond the scope of the present chapter to embark on the vast literature on assessment in education. It is to be noted, however, that the model of mind proposed here offers a complete framework for assessment that would be very useful for learning in the school so that students (i) enhance their knowledge of their own mind, (ii) sharpen their self-monitoring, self-representation, and self-regulation skills, and (iii) become aware of their cognitive strengths and weakness and their facility with different domains of knowledge. In terms of the present theory, assessment must first of all enable the student to recognize the sources of difficulty in understanding a concept or solving a problem and assist them to develop strategies for overcoming these difficulties. The ultimate aim is to make assessment a powerful tool of metarepresentation. These provisions are in line with the aims of formative assessment or assessment for learning (e.g. Black & Wiliam, 2009).

Difficulty may arise from any component of the architecture of mind proposed here. For example, students consider problems or concepts difficult if they cannot make sense of them in reference to prior relevant knowledge or if they are inconsistent with each other. Assessment here must highlight what is lacking and direct the student to search for necessary knowledge and use it for the sake of the problem at hand. That search must be both self-directed (e.g. 'Do I know something similar?', 'Have I solved problems like this in the past?') and directed externally, if needed (e.g. turning to the teacher or other sources of knowledge for help). In the case of conflict or inconsistency between concepts, assessment must direct the student to notice the superiority of the new concepts to explicate the phenomena of interest. For example, why is the heliocentric model of our planetary system superior to the geocentric model?

Problems are also difficult for students if the amount or rate of presentation of information exceeds the available representational or processing resources. Assessment here must make the students sensitive to their 'personal point of command'. The discussion above about monitoring and regulation of representational capacity is relevant. Finally, inferential processes may be a source of difficulty. That is, if the concept or problem to be dealt with involves relations that require inferential schemes that are not available, the crucial relations will not be worked out. Assessment here must highlight the inferential schemeas missing and train the student in their use.

From core processes and specialized structural systems to critical thinking

Conceptual change, reasoning development, learning to learn, and critical thinking are complementary aspects of cognitive development and learning. Specifically, the very process of constructing and evaluating mental models for the sake of grasping target concepts and problem-solving skills may become a powerful field for the development of critical thinking. Envisaging, comparing, substantiating, debating, and choosing among alternative models, if properly directed, may enhance awareness of the role of evidence and logical and conceptual substantiation for alternative models.

Critical thinking includes the ability to (i) identify central issues and assumptions, (ii) envisage alternative models, (iii) associate each with its own supportive evidence and logical substantiation, (iv) embed it into its own conceptual or belief system, and (v) adopt an informed preference based on evidence or argumentation (e.g. Watson & Glaser, 1980; Ennis, 1996). Moreover, critical thinkers tolerate ambiguity and remain open to the possibility of change in conclusions and interpretations based on new evidence or analysis. Therefore, command of the processes and constraints of reasoning outlined above is important because valid reasoning is the one of the main tools of critical thinking, together with the ability to collect information and evaluate its relevance. At the same time, however, to be critical, thinking must be embedded in a context of epistemological understanding. Specifying what is truth, what is evidence, and what is more important, reason or evidence (Siegel, 1989).

Education in critical thinking would lead the developing individual to realize the knowledge, understanding, and decision-making limitations of their age. Also, they would need to understand the difference between reasoning and rationality. That is, that reasoning is a tool for analysis, evaluation, and selection of solutions, whereas rationality is integrative judgement that bridges multiple frames and points of view. Thus, attending to the formal prescriptions of reasoning ensures that valid conclusions may be derived. At the same time, valid conclusions may be useless or even harmful if they are not relevant to the situation at hand. For example, the statements 'the cat was flying when chasing the mouse' and 'Peter was so good, he was flying' cannot be induced or deduced from any of the example arguments given above. They could, however, if embedded in a metaphorical context where the meaning of flying is symbolic of something else, such as high speed and momentum in the case of the cat or success in the case of Peter. Thus, to become critical, children must learn how to evaluate or choose the relevant spaces in which logical analysis may be deployed. This education must capitalize on the worldview that prevails during each developmental milestone. In preschool, children must overcome the absolutist stance of this age phase that knowledge is either right or wrong. For example, they must come to realize that the knowledge of different children about an object (e.g. that it is red, and green, and blue) is right, depending on each child's perspective (i.e. because each of the three sides of the object is differently coloured and each child has access only to one side). In primary school, children must realize that the representations associated with each perspective are integrated by inference which gives them coherence and logicality, given the initial assumptions. Moreover, they must be gradually introduced to an epistemological approach to knowledge that enables them to understand that the knowledge generated by different knowledge extraction mechanisms, such as observation and experimentation, may differ in accuracy and validity, depending upon how well confounding factors are controlled by each. The adolescent must recognize that alternative approaches to knowledge, such as those associated with humanities versus science, may be equally acceptable depending upon the person's original stance to knowledge. For example, the humanities base their knowledge on argument and the subjectivity of experience and science on systematic observation and control. Distance from truth is only a matter of appropriateness and precision of methods and ingenuity of controls, which they improve with accretion of knowledge over time (Chandler et al., 2002). Moreover, critical thinking includes the skills necessary for the students to know themselves so that they orient themselves to the directions that are most suitable to them but also for their group. Critical thinkers are the citizens who can make choices for their own benefit and the benefit of society.

Conclusions

The main implications of this chapter may be summarized as follows:

1. Developmental milestones can direct the formulation of educational priorities in relation to crucial epistemological questions about the origins, nature, and change of knowledge and learning. Representational capacity may be a guide to the control of instructional complexity children encounter at different phases of their school life.
2. The development of consciousness can inform programmes focused on learning to learn, self-development, and self-guidance in knowledge-relevant life choices.
3. Specialized domains can direct the training of the various specialized mental mechanisms for the sake of better handling of different types of relations in the environment and different types of knowledge.
4. At any phase, education must lead the student to develop and refine the following cognitive skills: focus on relevant information; scan, compare, and choose according to goal; ignore irrelevant information; represent what is chosen and associate with extant knowledge; bind into models and rehearse if necessary; evaluate models in reference to evidence; reason by deduction to evaluate truth and validity of models and conclusions; estimate consistency with beliefs, extant theories, dominant views, etc.; encode, symbolize, and embed into the system.

5. Teachers operate in a vast field of intra- and inter-individual differences. Therefore, the curriculum, instruction methods, and moment-to-moment teaching must adapt to different students and to different subject matters. Students weak in processing efficiency may need more help and support to learn. The implications of this postulate for the development and use of appropriate diagnostic tools and the education of teachers are enormous. After all, democratic education must lead each student to reach, as close as possible, his or her potential across the board at successive developmental phases.

6. With reference to general issues about educational policies and orientations, the model suggests that plain constructivism, which has dominated discussions about educational priorities since the 1980s is not enough for efficient education. In addition to self-directed activity and discovery, guided abstraction and metarepresentation are very important for stable learning and learning transfer.

7. Education in epistemological issues concerning the similarities and differences between disciplines is an important part of education for critical thinking.

8. Finally, it is clear that the dominant theories of the various traditions that studied the mind since the late nineteenth century do not suffice to explicate or direct education for learning to learn. In psychometric theories, the assumption of a powerful general intelligence mechanism controlling everything (Jensen, 1998) is not enough to account for learning to learn because this mechanism involves only a part of the necessary processes, namely the inferential part (Carroll, 1993). The multiple intelligences (Gardner, 1983) theory is also inadequate to account for learning to learn. Postulating another domain-specific intelligence to account for self-awareness and self-regulation cannot explain how this intelligence exerts its effects in a fragmented mind of autonomous intelligences. The model summarized here maintains the balance between general and specialized processes and relegates ability for self-development to the dynamic relations between all of the processes because in this system the ability to know oneself and learn to learn is part of the evolutionary endowment underlying our ability to face the uncertain and the unexpected and to respond profitably to it.

References

Atkinson, A.P., Thomas, M.S.C., & Cleeremans, A. (2000) 'Consciousness: Mapping the theoretical landscale', *Trends in Cognitive Sciences*, *4*, 372–382.

Baddeley, A. (2012) 'Working memory: Theories, models, and controversies', *Annual Review of Psychology*, *63*, 1–29.

Barouillet, P., Portrat, S., & Camos, V. (2011) 'On the law relating processing to storage in working memory', *Psychological Review*, *118*, 175–192.

Black, P., & Wiliam, D. (2009) 'Developing the theory of formative assessment', *Educational Assessment, Evaluation, and Accountability*, *21*, 5–13.

Blaser, E., & Kaldy, Z. (2010) 'Infants get five starts on iconic memory: A partial-report test of 6-month-old infants' iconic memory capacity', *Psychological Science*, *21*, 1643–1645.

Braine, M.D.S. (1990) 'The "natural logic" approach to reasoning', in W.F. Overton (Ed.) *Reasoning, necessity, and logic: Developmental perspectives* (pp. 133–157). Hillsdale, NJ: Erlbaum.

Buschkuehl, M., & Jaeggi, S.M. (2010) 'Improving intelligence: A literature review', *Swiss Medical Weekly, 140*(19/20), 266–272.

Carey, S. (2009) *The origins of concepts.* Oxford: Oxford University Press.

Carroll, J.B. (1993) *Human cognitive abilities: A survey of factor-analytic studies.* New York: Cambridge University Press.

Case, R. (1985) *Intellectual development: Birth to adulthood.* New York: Academic Press.

Case, R., Demetriou, A., Platsidou, M., & Kazi, S. (2001) Integrating concepts and tests of intelligence from the differential and the developmental traditions, *Intelligence, 29*, 307–336.

Chandler, M.J., Hallett, D., & Sokol, B.W. (2002) Competing claims about competing knowledge domains, in B.K. Hofer & P.R. Pintrich (Eds.) *Personal epistemology: The psychology of beliefs about knowledge and knowing* (pp. 145–168). Mahwah, NJ: Erlbaum.

Cleeremans, A., Timmermans, B., & Pasquali, A. (2007) 'Consciousness and meta-representation: A computational sketch', *Neural Networks, 20*(9), 1032–1039.

Couchman, J.J., Coutino, M.V.C., Beran, M.J., & Smith, J.D. (2010) 'Beyond stimulus cues and reinforcement signals: A new approach to animal metacognition', *Journal of Comparative Psychology, 124*, 356–368.

Cowan, N., Morey, C.C., Chen, Z., & Bunting, M.F. (2007) 'What do estimates of working memory capacity tell us?', in N. Osaka, R. Logie, & M. D'Esposito (Eds.) *The cognitive neuroscience of working memory* (pp. 43–58). Oxford: Oxford University Press.

Dehn, M.J. (2008) *Working memory and academic learning: Assessment and intervention.* Hoboken, NJ: Wiley.

DeLoache, J.S. (1991) Symbolic functioning in very young children: Understanding of pictures and models, *Child Development, 62*, 736–752.

DeLoache, J.S. (1995) 'Early understanding of the use of symbols', *Current Directions in Psychological Science, 4*, 109–113.

Demetriou, A. (2000) 'Organization and development of self-understanding and self-regulation: Toward a general theory', in M. Boekaerts, P.R. Pintrich, & M. Zeidner (Eds.) *Handbook of self-regulation* (pp. 209–251). San Diego, CA: Academic Press.

Demetriou, A., Christou, C., Spanoudis, G., & Platsidou, M. (2002) 'The development of mental processing: Efficiency, working memory, and thinking', *Monographs of the Society of Research in Child Development, 67* (Serial No. 268).

Demetriou, A., & Kazi, S. (2001) *Unity and modularity in the mind and the self: Studies on the relationships between self-awareness, personality, and intellectual development from childhood to adolescence.* London: Routledge.

Demetriou, A., & Kazi, S. (2006) 'Self-awareness in g (with processing efficiency and reasoning)', *Intelligence, 34*, 297–317.

Demetriou, A., Mouyi, A., & Spanoudis, G. (2008) 'Modeling the structure and development of g', *Intelligence, 5*, 437–454.

Demetriou, A., Mouyi, A., & Spanoudis, G. (2010) 'The development of mental processing', in W.F. Overton (Ed.) *Biology, cognition and methods across the life-span. Vol. 1: Handbook of life-span development* (pp. 306–343). Hoboken, NJ: Wiley.

Demetriou, A., Spanoudis, G., & Mouyi, A. (2011) 'Educating the developing mind: Towards an overarching paradigm', *Educational Psychology Review*, *23*(4), 601–663.

Demetriou, A., Spanoudis, G., Shayer, M., & Kazi, S. (2013a) 'Explicating developmental reconceptualization: Differentiation and integration in intellectual development', in N.I. Chuprikova & E.V. Volcova (Eds.) *Differentiation-integration theory of development: Philosophical interpretation and application to psychology, linguistics, and education*. Moscow: Institute of Psychology RAS.

Demetriou, A., Spanoudis, G., Shayer, M., Mouyi, A., Kazi, S., & Platsidou, M. (2013b) 'Cycles in speed–working memory–G relations: Towards a developmental-differential theory of the mind', *Intelligence*, *41*(1), 34–50.

Dixon, J.A., Stephen, D.G., Boncoddo, R.A., & Anastas, J. (2010) 'The self-organization of cognitive structure', in B. Ross (Ed.) *The psychology of learning and motivation*, Vol. 52 (pp. 343–384). San Diego, CA: Elsevier.

Ennis, R.H. (1996) *Critical thinking*. Upper Saddle River, NJ: Prentice-Hall.

Fisher, A.V. (2010) 'Mechanisms of induction early in development', in M. Banich & D. Caccamise (Eds.) *Generalization of knowledge: Multidisciplinary perspectives* (pp. 89–112). New York: Psychology Press.

Gardner, H. (1983) *Frames of mind. The theory of multiple intelligences*. New York: Basic Books.

Gelman, S.A., & Coley, J.D. (1990) 'The importance of knowing a dodo is a bird: Categories and inferences in 2-year-old children', *Developmental Psychology*, *26*, 796–804.

Gentner, D. (2005) 'The development of relational category knowledge', in L. Gershkoff-Stowe & D.H. Rakison (Eds.) *Building object categories in developmental time* (pp. 245–275). Hillsdale, NJ: Erlbaum.

Glassner, A., & Schwarz, B.B. (2007) 'What stands and develops between creative and critical thinking? Argumentation?', *Thinking Skills and Creativity*, *2*, 10–18.

Halford, G.S., Wilson, W.H., & Phillips, S. (1998) 'Processing capacity defined by relational complexity: Implications for comparative, developmental, and cognitive psychology', *Behavioral and Brain Sciences*, *21*, 803–864.

Holland, J., Holyoak, K., Nisbett, R., & Thagard, P. (1986) *Induction: Processes of inference, learning, and discovery*. Cambridge, MA: MIT Press/Bradford Books.

Hupp, J.M., & Sloutsky, V.M. (2011) 'Learning to learn: From within-modality to cross-modality transfer during infancy', *Journal of Experimental Child Psychology*, *110*, 408–421.

Jensen, A.R. (1998) *The g factor: The science of mental ability*. Westport, CT: Praeger.

Kazi, S., Demetriou, A., Spanoudis, G., Zhang, X.K., & Wang, Y. (2012) 'Mind–culture interactions: How writing molds mental fluidity in early development', *Intelligence*, *40*, 622–637.

Kopp, C.B. (2011) 'Development in the early years: Socialization, motor development, and consciousness', *Annual Review of Psychology*, *62*, 165–187.

Moshman, D. (1990) 'The development of metalogical understanding', in W.F. Overton (Ed.) *Reasoning, necessity, and logic: Developmental perspectives* (pp. 205–225). Hillsdale, NJ: Erlbaum.

Moshman, D. (1994) 'Reasoning, metareasoning and the promotion of rationality', in A. Demetriou & A. Efklides (Eds.) *Mind, intelligence, and reasoning: Structure and development* (pp. 135–150), Amsterdam: Elsevier.

Moshman, D. (2011) *Adolescent rationality and development: Cognition, morality, and identity* (3rd edn.). New York: Psychology Press.

Mouyi, A. (2008) 'Developmental dynamics binding processing efficiency, working memory, and reasoning: A longitudinal study', Unpublished doctoral dissertation, University of Cyprus, Nicosia, Cyprus.

Pascual-Leone, J. (1970) 'A mathematical model for the transition rule in Piaget's developmental stages', *Acta Psychologica*, *63*, 301–345.

Presley, M., & Harris, K.R. (2006) 'Cognitive strategies instruction: From basic research to classroom instruction', in P.A. Alexander & P.H. Winne (Eds.) *Handbook of educational psychology* (pp. 265–286), Mahwah, NJ: Erlbaum.

Ricco, R.B. (2010) 'The development of deductive reasoning across the lifespan', in W.F. Overton (Ed.) *Biology, cognition, and methods across the life-span. Vol. 1: Handbook of life-span development* (pp. 391–430). Hoboken, NJ: Wiley.

Ricco, R.B., & Overton, W.F. (2011) 'Dual systems competence ↔ Procedural processing: A relational developmental systems approach to reasoning', *Developmental Review*, *31*, 119–150.

Rips, L.J. (1994) *The psychology of proof: Deductive reasoning in human thinking.* Cambridge, MA: MIT Press.

Rosch, E. (1975) 'Cognitive representations of semantic categories', *Journal of Experimental Psychology: General*, *104*, 192–233.

Shipstead, Z., Redick, T.S., & Engle, R.W. (2012) 'Is working memory training effective?', *Psychological Bulletin*, *138*, 628–654.

Siegel, H. (1989) 'The rationality of science, critical thinking, and science education', *Synthese*, *80*(1), 9–41.

Siegler, R.S. (1996) *Emerging minds: The process of change in children's thinking.* Oxford: Oxford University Press.

Simonton, D.K. (2000) 'Creative development as acquired expertise: Theoretical issues and an empirical test', *Developmental Review*, *20*, 283–318.

Sloutsky, V.M., & Fisher, A.V. (2011) 'The development of categorization', *Psychology of Learning and Motivation*, *54*, 141–166.

Téglás, E., Vul, E., Girotto, V., Gonzalez, M., Tenenbaum, J.B., & Bonatti, L. (2011) 'Pure reasoning in 12-month-old infants as probabilistic inference', *Science*, *332*, 1054–1059.

Watson, G.B., & Glaser, E.M. (1980) *WGCTA Watson-Glaser Critical Thinking Appraisal Manual: Forms A and B.* San Antonio, TX: The Psychological Corporation.

Zelazo, P.D. (2004) 'The development of conscious control in childhood', *Trends in Cognitive Sciences*, *8*, 12–17.

Zelazo, P.D., & Frye, D. (1998) 'Cognitive complexity and control: The development of executive function', *Current Directions in Psychological Science*, *7*, 121–126.

Zelazo, P.D., Qu, L., & Müller, U. (2005) 'Hot and cool aspects of executive function: Relations with early development', in W. Schneider, R. Schumann, R. Hengsteler, & B. Sodian (Eds.) *Young children's cognitive development: Interrelationships among executive functioning, working memory, verbal ability, and theory of mind* (pp. 71–93) Mahwah, NJ: Erlbaum.

Chapter 3

Learning to learn

A complex systems perspective

Ruth Deakin Crick

Abstract

This chapter explores how a complex systems thinking approach might contribute to a holistic understanding of learning to learn and the conditions necessary to support it. Learning to learn is a crucial competence for living in a context of radical change and uncertainty. By approaching learning to learn through the lens of systems thinking, it is possible to develop a design architecture for learning how to learn in a formal educational setting, which models the relationships and dependencies that contribute to what is a complex and delicate ecology. The chapter identifies six processes that contribute to learning to learn and identifies examples from theory, practice, and research, seeking to map out the terrain of relevant variables, including the classroom and system-wide practices that influence it. Finally, the chapter explores the implications of this for policy and practice, suggesting that a worldview shift of significant proportions about what matters in education is required if our schools are to prepare young people for life through the development of competence in learning to learn.

Key words: learning to learn, ecology, theory, practice, research.

Introduction

The purpose of this chapter is to explore how complex systems thinking contributes to our understanding of learning to learn and the conditions necessary to support this crucial competence for living in a context of radical change and uncertainty. First, the chapter introduces systems thinking and develops a design architecture for learning how to learn in a formal educational setting, which models the relationships and dependencies that contribute to what is a complex and delicate ecology. Next, it explores six high-level processes of a systems architecture for learning to learn and identifies examples from theory, practice, and research, seeking to map out the terrain of relevant variables, including the classroom and system-wide practices that influence the process. Finally, the chapter explores the implications of this for policy and practice, suggesting that a worldview shift of significant proportions about what matters in education is required if our schools are to prepare young people for life through the development of competence in learning to learn. It draws substantially on empirical evidence from the evaluation of the Learning Futures programme, which operated in the UK from 2009 to 2011 with 30 schools, selected for their innovation in approaches to learning and teaching (Deakin Crick et al., 2010, 2011). The purpose of the evaluation was to investigate factors that contribute to quality in Learning Futures pedagogies – designed to promote the deep engagement of students in their own learning.

Learning to learn as a complex dynamic system

Framing learning to learn as a core process in a complex, dynamic system allows us to explore patterns and relationships in the contextual factors that we know influence the capability of the individual to become an effective learner and respond profitably to change and challenge. These factors are both internal to the learner and external in the social context of the learning community. Increasingly that social context is both virtual and embodied. Complexity, rather than a reductionist focus on one aspect of learning to learn, more readily reflects the reality of learners, classrooms, schools, and communities, even though by definition it is harder to measure, describe, and predict. From a systems perspective, learning to learn can be understood as an emergent property of a social journey from purpose to performance, while knowledge and know-how can be understood as emergent properties of learning. Emergence is a term that describes something new that results from the interaction of more simple variables within a complex system. Goldstein (1999: 49) describes it as 'the arising of novel and coherent structures, patterns and properties during the process of self-organization in complex systems'. From this perspective, the key pedagogical challenge is how to create these emergent properties dependably, rather than how to measure and control a single variable such as a particular outcome, or a single indicator of learning to learn.

A complex systems lens is particularly valuable for understanding the ways in which learning to learn is dependent on history and community. It allows us to position the learner as a purposeful agent in their own process or journey, utilizing their learning dispositions, values and attitudes (learning power), and their knowledge-structuring capabilities to shape complex data into a personally negotiated product or outcome. The process of learning to learn is about learning-as-design rather than learning-as-script (Goldspink, 2010; Deakin Crick & Goldspink, 2014). In learning-as-script, knowledge and outcomes are prescribed, often enshrined in national curricula and transmitted from an expert to the learner. In learning-as-design, the learner is a purposeful agent, working in a complex context, generating and co-constructing knowledge for a particular outcome or a product which is not predefined, but which may nevertheless meet curricula targets, or specific organizational needs.

Applying systems thinking to learning to learn

Systems thinking is used to address complex and uncertain real-world problems. Learning to learn, over a lifetime, is a messy, interconnected, foggy, and contradictory process that requires principles of complex thinking in order to 'civilise our knowledge' (Morin, 2008:6). In contrast to the principles of 'disjunction, reduction and abstraction', which Morin argues are characteristic of Western civilisation introduced by Descartes, the principles of complex thinking are

> distinction/conjunction that will allow us to distinguish without disjoining, to associate without identifying or reducing . . . [it] would include a dialogical and translogical principle which would integrate classical logic whilst taking into account its defacto limitations (problems of contradiction) and its de jure limitations (problems of formalism). It would incorporate the principle of Unitas Multiplex, which escapes abstract unity whether high (holism) or low (reductionism).
>
> (Morin, 2008: 6)

Systems thinking starts with the assumption that the world is a set of highly interconnected social and technical entities that are hierarchically organized, and produce emergent behaviour. A system is essentially two or more entities that are interconnected for a purpose. The purpose of the system is what defines its boundaries and its context and the output of the system is the result of a change process. A system produces 'synergy' when the whole is more than the sum of the parts; this is also sometimes referred to as 'emergence'. Systems thinking provides a way of developing a 'design' or 'architecture' for a complex process as a foundation for understanding, analysis, intervention, and positive change. Developing an architecture for learning to learn offers a way of understanding that is useful in practice and may help to integrate the differing perspectives on what is a multi-dimensional and complex process. The outcome of such an architecture is a model – a visual representation of what we know about the system being explored. Of course any model is limited -– it is good only in so far as it is useful, either for understanding or for guiding change. However, in conditions of increasing complexity and rapid change, visualisation is an increasingly important literacy for leaders, simply because of the sheer volume and pace of input of relevant data.

Blockley (2010) argues that the starting point for developing a systems design is identifying the system's purpose. From here the task is to identify the high-level processes that provide the means of achieving that purpose. These high-level processes interact with the substance of the domain – the who, what, where, and when; in this case, the substance of what is being learned, grounded in the context in which it is being learned. These processes may be subdivided, or decomposed to generate hierarchical layers. The interactions between the processes and layers operate through feedback loops through which one entity influences another. There are multiple, many-to-many connections between entities or processes that influence or send messages to each other, thus creating uncertainty and unpredictability. A system may be relatively stable or highly unstable.

Blockley (2010) suggests that the entities in any system should be described as a process, rather than as a structure, even though as is often the case in his discipline (engineering), that structure may be apparently solid and static (e.g. a bridge). This is because everything has a life cycle – and the concept of life cycle and change is inherent in systems thinking. In the case of learning to learn, there are relatively static entities which influence the process, such as the examination system; however, to understand these as a process is helpful in practice because it implies the possibility of change and it is, in fact, a better match with how such systems operate.

Developing a systems architecture for learning to learn

The challenge of developing a systems architecture for learning to learn is one which Bauman identifies as crucial for educators in the information age – how to 'theorise a formative process which is not guided from the start by the target form designed in advance' (Bauman, 2001: 139). If the target of learning to learn is simply the acquisition of knowledge and associated summative test results that are already predefined, then we may simply continue as we are. However, if the challenge is to enable individuals to engage mindfully, wisely, and profitably with uncertainty and risk over a lifetime, then we need to re-examine our practices and it is here that complex systems design may have something to offer.

The purpose of learning to learn

The starting point therefore in developing a learning to learn systems architecture is to define its purpose. Referring to the Assessment for Learning movement in the UK, Black et al. (2006) argued that the purpose of assessment for learning is the development of learning autonomy, or intentional learning on the part of the student. The student puts discretionary effort into the learning process. This is important but not sufficient to develop a systems architecture because it still leaves the question of purpose unanswered. The question remains as to why intentional learning is important. As Marshall and Drummond (2006) pointed out, some teachers used assessment for learning in the spirit that it was developed by the Assessment Reform Group (i.e. to develop learning to learn), whereas others followed the 'letter' rather than the 'spirit' in order to help students pass tests and thus improve standards. The overall purpose in each case was different according to the goal orientation of the student (Dweck, 2000).

The idea of the development of competence in learning to learn, on the other hand, provides a more precise purpose around which to create a systems architecture. Competence is defined as the ability to utilize inter- and intra-personal resources to engage in authentic, real-world tasks or challenges (Rychen & Salagnik, 2003) and this more accurately defines its purpose. So the purpose of learning how to learn is to become a competent lifelong learner:

> Competence in learning to learn is defined as the ability to engage consciously, intentionally, and profitably with new learning opportunities, throughout the life span and to purposefully negotiate a pathway through a range of options, managing, interpreting, and re-constructing complex data

and relationships, in order to achieve personally appropriated and publicly recognized goals.

Processes that achieve this purpose

In the next section, I discuss five distinct processes that have been identified in research and practice as enabling the development of competence in learning how to learn. These form the high-level processes in the systems design that can be decomposed into sub-components. Three are related to the individual learner, and two to the context of learning, in this case the classroom and the school. These are derived from research into the application of learning power assessments in schools (e.g. Deakin Crick et al., 2004; Deakin Crick & Yu, 2008; Deakin Crick, 2012), from research into identity formation and life narrative (Sfard & Prusak, 2005; Biesta & Tedder, 2007; Biesta et al., 2008), socio-cultural theories of learning (Lave & Wenger, 1991; Wertsch, 1991; Wenger, 1998), authentic pedagogy and quality teaching (Newmann, 1996; Newmann et al., 1996; Foster, 2001; Amosa et al., 2007; Ladwig et al., 2007; Goldspink, 2008; Ladwig, 2009):

1. Forming a learning identity and purpose
2. Developing learning power
3. Generating knowledge and know-how
4. Applying learning in authentic contexts
5. Sustaining learning relationships.

These five processes are all pedagogically relevant. They are aspects of learning that teachers need to understand and negotiate in the core pedagogical tasks of (i) designing contexts for learning and (ii) facilitating learning for individuals and groups. Unlike an academic, teachers in classrooms don't have the luxury of reducing their focus to only one aspect at the expense of the other. Furthermore, to develop learning to learn as a competence for students, teachers need to progressively hand over responsibility for learning, knowledge construction, and performance to learners themselves – and this is something that requires sustained attention over time. Being able, therefore, to understand learning to learn as a complex system and to model, represent, and evaluate that system in professional dialogue is a core competence for teachers.

Forming a learning identity and purpose

The first core process that is crucial for developing competence in learning to learn is the formation of identity and agency in learning. Wenger's (1998) social theory of learning explores the processes of learning from an intensely practical or engaged perspective, rather than taking a single slice of this multidimensional construct. His assumptions are that: (i) humans are essentially social beings and this is a central aspect of learning; (ii) knowledge is a matter of competence with respect to valued enterprises; (iii) knowing is a matter of participating in such enterprises; and (iv) meaning-making – making sense of our experience in the world and our engagement with it – is ultimately what learning is about. His initial inventory of the components of such learning includes:

- identity – or learning as becoming;
- community – or learning as belonging;
- meaning – or learning as experience; and
- practice - or learning as doing.

These interconnected and mutually defining elements of his systemic model constitute the concept of 'communities of practice'. Without using the term learning to learn, he describes these elements as a way of talking about learning. It is this 'talking about' one's identity, experience, activities, and relationships constituting social participation as a process of learning which gives a profound insight into the heart of the concept of learning to learn.

What Wenger's model brings into sharp relief is the importance of the 'person' who is learning: their emerging identity, belonging, meaning-making, and purpose in the world. This core idea is about agency – the intentional engagement of the individual in the learning process – something that is achieved, rather than possessed, through the active engagement of individuals with aspects of their contexts-for-action (Biesta et al., 2008). Biesta and colleagues argue that learning about the particular composition of one's agentic orientations and how they play out in one's life can play an important role in the achievement of agency. They further argue that life-narratives, stories about one's life, can be an important vehicle for such learning.

Stories about persons are at the heart of Sfard and Prusak's model of identity. They equate identities with stories about persons, defining identities as collections of stories about persons that are 'reifying, endorsable by others and significant' (Sfard & Prusak, 2005: 14), and argue that a person's stories about themselves are profoundly influenced by the stories that important others tell about that person. Identities are discursive counterparts of one's lived experiences – they are stories, which are told, witnessed and re-told, and which are open and susceptible to change.

The importance of this for understanding learning how to learn is that positive identity talk enables individuals to develop a sense of purpose and belonging. By understanding their actual (here and now) identity and their designated identity – the person they are in the process of becoming – an individual is able to engage in identity-making as a communicational practice (Hall, 1996; Gonzalez, 1999; Gee, 2001). According to Sfard and Prusak (2005), this makes a person more able to engage with new challenges or opportunities in terms of their past experiences, and provides tools to plan for the future. It is a foundation for the achievement of agency in learning how to learn. At its heart, it is about enabling *the individual to appropriate their own purpose in learning*, which draws on their unique story and passion.

Identity as a discursive activity thus becomes an important bridge between the lived experience (history and story) a person brings to the learning encounter and the movement forwards towards the construction of a new identity. Sfard and Prusak (2005) go so far as to suggest that the notion of identity is the missing link between learning and its socio-cultural context:

> We believe that the notion of identity is a perfect candidate for the role of 'the missing link' in the researchers' story of the complex dialectic between learning and its socio-cultural context.
>
> (Sfard & Prusak, 2005: 15)

The formation of identity is thus an important factor in learning to learn, and one which is perhaps least understood in the context of pedagogy in the classroom. Of course it is theory dependent. Where school systems are organized, explicitly or implicitly, around a worldview that sees knowledge as an entity, pieces of information that are stored in the brain, then there is no particular pedagogical reason to engage in identity formation – other than ensuring compliance in the process of acquiring knowledge. However, if this is only a small part of knowing, and knowledge is about active meaning-making and agentic participation in a learning community, then attending to identity formation becomes a pedagogical imperative and a core process in facilitating students in becoming competent in learning how to learn. It is through first engaging with one's identity, then discursively engaging with a sense of 'becoming' or designated identity that critical agency can be achieved.

Reason (Heron & Reason, 1997; Reason, 1998) sees 'critical subjectivity' at the heart of a participatory worldview, with its notion of reality as subjective-objective. It involves the knower participating in the world through four interdependent ways of knowing: experiential, presentational, propositional, and practical. These four forms of knowing constitute the manifold of human subjectivity and offer the challenge of critical subjectivity: how do we understand and mobilize these ways of knowing so that we achieve agency and develop an understanding of reality that is 'unclouded by a restrictive and ill-disciplined subjectivity' (Heron & Reason, 1997: 5).

Developing learning power

Moving from the deeply personal, the second core process concerns the development of the dispositions, attitudes, and values necessary for an individual to engage profitably with new learning opportunities. Identity – reifying, endorsable, and significant stories about persons – is the foundation for meaning-making and agency. What follows from this is that dispositions, values, and attitudes towards learning are crucial for the achievement of agency in learning how to learn because they empower, or dis-empower, the individual in closing the gap between actual and designated identities, or to put it another way, in fulfilling their chosen purpose.

A study conducted as part of the Teaching for Effective Learning programme in South Australia, exploring the components of engagement in learning, found that the learner's orientation towards the unknown, uncertainty and ambiguity, and their tendency to either retreat from it or move into it contributed very substantially to their model of engagement as a primary causal factor. This dispositional factor predicted interest, positive affect towards learning, and involvement in classroom learning (Goldspink & Foster, 2013). The disposition of retreating from new learning opportunities effectively precludes learning to learn because the orientation of the individual is to close down and disengage, whereas being open and moving towards the unknown is a beginning point for it. This orientation operates at a visceral level and has the hallmarks of what Damasio and his colleagues describe as affective pre-appraisal – a rapid emotional assessment of the presenting situation (Damasio, 2000; Priestley et al., 2012). What we know from the literature is that negative affect is associated with a narrowing and closing down of behaviour that presents as fight or flight mechanisms. In classrooms, these could manifest as passive dis-engagement or compliance, physical absence, or disruptive behaviour. However, positive affect is associated with openness to new ideas, to appropriate risk-taking and making-meaning – and thus to the possibility of deep learning.

The disposition variable used by Goldspink and Foster drew on Dweck's (2000, 2006) research into mindsets, which shows that people who believe success is based on hard work and learning have 'growth' mindsets or an 'incremental' theory of intelligence as opposed to an 'entity' theory of intelligence. People with a growth mindset are more likely to overcome setbacks as resilient learners than those who have a 'fixed' theory of intelligence, who believe intelligence is about innate ability. The latter see failure as a negative reflection on the self – on their sense of identity as a learner. These basic orientations (reflected in Goldspink and Foster's research) are fundamental dispositions – tendencies to behave in a certain way that are crucial to learning how to learn.

This work also informed more recent research into learning dispositions. Deakin Crick et al. (2004) identified seven learning dispositions that constitute what has come to be termed 'learning power', and these have demonstrated their reliability and validity in successive quantitative studies, as well as their trustworthiness and credibility in pedagogical and theoretical studies (Deakin Crick & Yu, 2008; Deakin Crick et al., 2013b). 'Learning power' is described as a complex mix of dispositions, lived experiences, social relations, values, and attitudes that combine to influence how an individual engages with particular learning opportunities (Deakin Crick et al., 2004). The seven empirically derived dimensions of learning power are changing and learning, critical curiosity, meaning-making, learning relationships, strategic awareness, creativity, and resilience.

In the UK's Learning Futures Project (Deakin Crick et al., 2010, 2011), there was a demonstrable relationship between students' identity and self-stories as learners and their learning dispositions as measured by these seven dimensions of learning power. A sample of students with low, medium, and high learning power were selected from the cohort, through cluster analysis, and these students were invited to contribute to narrative interviews, which were then analysed for the language they used to describe themselves as learners.

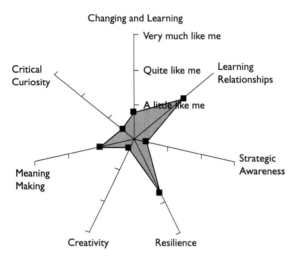

Figure 3.1 Female Year 7 student, low learning power sample.

For example, the learning power profile of a girl in one school (Fig. 3.1) was identified from raw data and categorized as 'low' and accompanied by a transcript which recorded her as saying: 'I am a little bit rubbish' and later 'sometimes I feel I hate being me and sometimes I love being me' with little focus on her own learning processes. The feedback to the user from the Learning Power self-assessment tool is represented in a spider diagram (Fig. 3.1), without numerical values, as a framework for a conversation about learning identity and purpose, which can then stimulate the achievement of agency and strategies for change.

In contrast, a student selected as 'high' on learning power (Fig. 3.2) used a rich and owned language for learning in his interview. For example, he said:

> learning is like a road . . . you can get tow trucks that can help you . . . like my friend – it doesn't have to be a friend it can be a parent – they can give

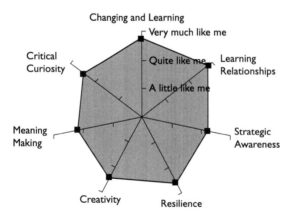

Figure 3.2 Male Year 7 student, high learning power sample.

you support and they can like say maybe you could do this. They won't actually tell you what to do but they will give you some options. You can choose them or make your own up but they will help you.

Generating knowledge and know-how

The third core process in learning to learn has to do with the individual's ability to engage with knowledge and information. In achieving competence in learning how to learn, identity, purpose, and learning power are necessary but not enough. These personal qualities interact with actual learning opportunities in formal and informal contexts. They are useful in that they enable the individual to engage profitably with the world in sense-making and achieving a purpose. Knowing how to go about structuring knowledge through collecting, selecting, collating, mapping, manipulating, analysing, and using data to achieve a purpose is a third, distinct core process in the overall design architecture of learning to learn. Using tools to do this – from pencils to mind maps to social learning apps – is an integral part of the process. As Haste (2001) argues, humans are collaborative tool users who need new competences to thrive within the changing environment of the twenty-first century.

Becoming a *generative knowledge worker* was the term used to describe those students in the Learning Futures study who demonstrated agency in their own learning. They were able to take responsibility for their own learning processes and to co-construct new and meaningful knowledge according to a personally selected purpose aligned to their own interest and passion. This was in direct contrast to students who were only able to receive and repeat 'predetermined', abstracted sets of knowledge communicated by experts in a traditional, didactic manner.

The generative knowledge worker begins from a particular, embodied place, and works from the 'bottom up' to achieve an intellectually rigorous outcome representing new knowledge (at least new to them), while learning how to learn in the process. The *knowledge receiver* begins with the knowledge itself, in packages prescribed by existing scholarship and curriculum guidelines and works from the 'top down' to integrate the knowledge and make it meaningful.

Enquiry-based learning – sometimes known as project-based learning, or problem-based learning – is a 'genus for which there are many species and sub-species' (Barrows, 1986), each of which addresses different objectives to varying degrees. What is characteristic of all of them is that the starting point for the learner is an authentic, real-world context, place or problem. The pedagogical challenge is to support the learner in making sense of the complex data they encounter and in shaping and working with this data to achieve a particular outcome or product. It is context- and purpose-driven rather than driven by a predetermined outcome, often abstracted from its authentic context.

There is substantial evidence that these context-driven approaches have a positive impact on student engagement in learning (Hmelo-Silver et al., 2006; Lynch & Prandolini 2006) and achievement (Bereiter & Scardamalia, 1989;

Marshall & Drummond, 2006; Biesta & Tedder, 2007; Biesta et al., 2008), and strengthen students' ability to contemplate, analyse, and systematically plan strategies for action (Hall, 1996). Enquiry-based learning helps students access prior knowledge leading to deep understanding, and learning that occurs in the context of real-life situations is more likely to be retained and applied (Gonzalez, 1999; Gee, 2001). Students express substantially more positive attitudes towards learning when problem-based approaches are used than when learning is irrelevant and anxiety-producing in traditional programmes (Hmelo-Silver et al., 2006; Chinn and Hung, 2007; Geier et al., 2008).

There are many common pedagogical themes in these enquiry-based approaches to learning, including the development of student agency, dialogue and debate, modelling argumentation, generating questions, mind mapping, knowledge visualization techniques, authentic contexts and assessments (cf. www.bie.org. and www.innovationunit.org). In a study emerging from the Opening Minds Curriculum programme in the UK, a set of student thinking and learning capabilities were identified which support and scaffold a personalized approach to enquiry-based learning (Deakin Crick, 2009). These were: Choosing, Describing, Questioning, Narrating, Mapping, Connecting (with existing funds of knowledge), Reconciling (with performance criteria), Presenting (assessment event), and Applying (in authentic contexts). In professional engineering contexts, complex systems designing methodologies offer generic and domain-specific methods for knowledge construction and modelling complexity. A suite of sophisticated tools, such as hierarchical process modelling, dynamic process modelling, and so on, and models such as that developed by Blockley (2010) – thinking in loops, layers, and processes – provide strategies and scaffolding for capturing and re-presenting complex data, and exploring the systems, sub-systems, their properties, and the relationships between them. From the teacher's perspective, teaching in enquiry-based learning is more like 'designing' and classroom management is more like project management, compared with traditional didactic methods in which all students do the same thing.

Knowledge structuring processes facilitate individual and collective sense-making and problem-solving. Such processes are crucial in context-driven enquiry where individual and collective cognition are stretched to the limit as people engage in sense-making (Weick, 1995), namely the construction of plausible narratives around emergent patterns. Knowledge structuring strategies replace the acquisition and repetition of abstract, predefined knowledge that is often the traditional fare of the academic curriculum, because they enable the collection, interrogation, and re-presentation of data generated in a real context and reorganized and redefined towards a novel solution.

Applying learning in authentic contexts – or becoming competent

The fourth core process in a learning to learn architecture has to do with the application of learning in an authentic context. Rychen and Salagnik (2003: 43) define the term 'competence' as: 'the ability to successfully meet complex demands in a particular context through the mobilisation of psychosocial pre-requisites (including cognitive and non-cognitive aspects)' and as the 'internal mental structures in the sense of abilities, dispositions or resources embedded in the individual' in interaction with a 'specific real world task or demand'. They go on to describe the internal structures of a competence as including dimensions of 'Knowledge, Cognitive skills, Practical skills, Attitudes, Emotions, Values and Ethics and Motivation' (Rychen & Salagnik, 2003: 44).

The site of a competence is at the interface between the person and the demands of life in the world. Competencies are broader than knowledge or skills, and are acquired in an ongoing, lifelong learning process across the whole range of personal, social, and political contexts. A competence refers to a complex combination of knowledge, skills, understanding, values, attitudes, and desires that lead to effective, embodied human action in the world, in a particular domain.

To understand competences, the spotlight is on the accomplishment of 'real-world tasks' and on a multiplicity of ways of knowing – for example, knowing how to do something, knowing oneself and one's desires, or knowing why something is important as well as knowing about something. This is similar to Delor's four pillars of learning developed for UNESCO: 'learning to live together, learning to know, learning to do and learning to be' (Delor, 1996). Importantly, competencies are expressed in action and by definition are embedded in narratives and shaped by values – this action, or way of doing something, is more important or desirable than another because it leads to a particular end. Just as a competence is recognized in the context of the real world, the development of competences is also based in real-world experiences and takes into account the full spectrum of learning opportunities (informal, non-formal, and formal learning) throughout the life span.

Competence as authentic, skilful engagement in the world is explicitly related to identity and purpose. In the qualitative findings of the Learning Futures Project, the term 'authenticity' was chosen to describe a pervasive theme in the data to do with self-authorship together with a process that is genuine and mean-ingful in the life of the learner beyond the classroom or school. It had to do with the degree to which a person was able to integrate personal motivation and inter-est with public requirements and demands and thus become the author of their own story in the world. The theme 'authenticity' had five sub-components: intrinsic interest and flow, active learning, authentic performance, connecting to the real world, and pride in achievement.

Students who were deeply engaged in an authentic learning task described an intrinsic passion about what they were learning. What they were learning actually mattered to them personally and they described the feeling of flow as 'being stuck in' and getting on with it. When intrinsic interest and flow were involved, students described how they continued learning at home, and one of the highly engaged students described the most important thing in learning as 'liking what you do'. With some students it was also evident that this flow continued into their lives beyond school and led to changed behaviour. When intrinsic interest and flow were present, learning was fun, playful, and part of a process; when it was absent, learning was 'work' and students framed learning and school in terms of different 'entities' that you get, or do, rather than as an integrated, incremental process. Authentic learning was active and described by students as motivating, meaningful, and desirable. What students meant by active learning was being actively involved in making decisions about what, where, and how to learn something, as agents in their own learning. The opposite of active learning was sitting in the classroom and the teacher telling the students what they needed to know. Active learning was still 'active' even if the activity was within the classroom simply using the Internet to find resources, but it extended to going into the town to research something, engaging with peers, and creating a product.

Authentic learning was supported by authentic performance as a formative or summative assessment event. The Learning Futures Project included video pre-sentations, Skype vivas, and presentations of student learning to the community as formal assessment events. Students described the process of 'doing something real' in a meaningful way for assessment or evaluation as a natural development of their learning. Authentic assessments were supported by owned and negotia-ted assessment criteria: students explained why they had chosen a particular outcome and how they had arrived at it. Where authentic assessments took place, they were taken seriously by both those who were assessing and by the students themselves. They involved numerous members of the non-teaching staff and older students, and many students presented their learning in creative ways. They were an opportunity for students to describe not only the new knowledge they had discovered, but to talk about what they had learnt about themselves as learn-ers, and to respond to questions posed to them by their 'assessors'. In this way, their learning could be celebrated and issues that needed remedying could be addressed. In contrast to authentic assessment were 'tests' that generated fear and a test-performance-orientation.

Students were most engaged in their learning when it was meaningful in their lives beyond the classroom. They could see its relevance and application or it was something that people in the real world do. Their learning was integrated inside and outside of the classroom and school. In contrast, when learning was apparently meaningless – apart from preparing for tests – it was not engaging. Students showed real pride in their achievements when learning was authentic. An authentic, successful product or outcome formed part of their emerging identity in a positive way – part of the story they tell about themselves and that others tell about them.

Sustaining learning relationships

The fifth process in the architecture is sustaining learning relationships. Humans are essentially social beings and social relationships are at the heart of learning to learn that operates in communities of practice. The nature of relationships between stakeholders in a learning community is a core and critical process that either facilitates or inhibits the development of learning to learn. Relationships are primarily between human beings; however, they can be asynchronous over time (as when engaging with the works of Shakespeare) or virtual (as when engaging in social networking or online forums) or both, and they can be mediated through tools of all sorts.

Furthermore, the currency of relationships is communication – primarily spoken and written language, but also the shared repertoire in a community of practice. A synergy is created in a community of practice that feeds back messages to participants about what matters, what is okay and what is not okay, and how to go about learning. It provides the 'shoulds and oughts', the 'values and permissions', and the defining stories that shape what is possible.

Wenger (1998) identifies three dimensions of practice through which meaning is negotiated and relationships are sustained in a community of practice. These are mutual engagement, joint enterprise, and shared repertoire. Classrooms and schools that are designed to promote learning to learn will be characterized by these qualities – students will enter into the experience of learning to learn by simply engaging in the community. The quality of relationships between participants, the mutuality of engagement and shared purpose, and the shared repertoire of practices, routines, words, tools, stories, gestures, concepts, etc., that the community adopts as part of its practice, all mediate the process of learning how to learn and the development of competence. All of these modes of relationships carry feedback messages for students, and impact upon developing identities, learning power, knowledge, and the development of competence.

A key question in understanding a systems architecture for learning to learn is how the key learning relationships in a community of practice can facilitate identity formation, develop learning power, sustain the generation of knowledge, and enhance competence. This extends the traditional notion of teacher as expert conveyer of knowledge to teacher as facilitator of learning in community.

Learning how to learn requires significant variety in the modes of teacher/ student relationship. In transmitting expert knowledge, a teacher takes the tradi-tional role relationship of expert/novice, and at times this may be the most effec-tive way to communicate certain types of knowledge. However, in identity formation, the most effective mode of teacher/learner relationship is that of coach/coachee, in which the purpose is to enable the coachee to identify and develop their own identity and purpose and to find their own strategies for change. At other times, the teacher/learner relationship may be that of a mentor/ mentee, in which the teacher shows the student how to do something, or that of a counsellor/counselee, in which the teacher seeks to enable the student to nego-tiate a pathway through a challenging personal or social issue. Another form of teacher/student relationship is simply that of co-learners, or learning together on a particular task. These modes of relationship form a continuum in 'learning facilitation' and a teacher needs to be able to move between different roles and make effective professional judgements about when and which role to take. It perhaps goes without saying that trust is a core resource for the sustenance of such learning relationships. Bond (2004) defines trust as the confidence that a relationship can withstand the challenges of risk, uncertainty, inequality, and dif-ference. Without trust, an individual is unlikely to expose their authentic identity, desire, and purpose to another, or operate collaboratively. Fear in a relationship is the opposite of trust, and this closes learning down because the learner is unlikely to be willing to explore the unknown, or expose their 'ignorance' to another.

These findings indicate the complexity and contextual nature of teaching as learning facilitation, which is a way of describing the differing forms of learning relationships that teachers may adopt with students and students with each other. When the desired outcome is the development of 'generative knowledge workers', the relationships between student and teacher vary dynamically and teachers need to use professional discretion about which mode of relationship is appropriate for a particular purpose in a particular context. Thus teaching is about learning design, rather than following a predetermined script.

Systems designing and learning to learn

The formula developed by Blockley (2010) to represent the process of systems designing is: Why = How (Who, What, Where, When). This, they argued, was not meant to be interpreted as an algebraic formula, but an attempt to represent the idea that purpose (why) is the difference of potential that drives the transformation processes (how) in the flow of change in a particular domain, which is defined by the attributes who, what, where, and when. They say:

> The purpose, functionality, success and failure criteria, concerning a given process at a given level of definition, derive from all the relevant why questions that can be identified. Answers to all how questions define the transformations or methods that will change the starting or input state to a finishing or end state in a defined time period. Answers to all who questions define players or actors, clients and stakeholders. Answers to what questions define all state variable and performance indicators. Answers to all where questions define place and context. Answers to all when questions define parameters of time.
>
> (Blockley, 2010: 191)

If we understand learning to learn as a complex process, then the question of purpose is paramount. It is the purpose or intention to learn something that drives the process of learning and the meta-process of learning to learn. In a context of innovation and risk, particularly in the Bauman (2001) context where the 'target form is not designed in advance', the quality of the learner's intention will sustain the process. To put it another way, the more a learner owns their own purpose in learning, the more energy will drive the processes of change. The more they will be likely to explore their learning identity, develop their learning power, construct new knowledge, apply it in authentic contexts, and sustain learning relationships. The 'domain' has to do with the actual focus of learning, the content, the knowledge, skills and understanding, and the stories that constitute the 'curriculum'.

Learning to learn cannot be divorced from its context because the process of learning to learn is always about something. Bateson (1972) identified three levels of learning which explain this. The first level is proto learning – learning

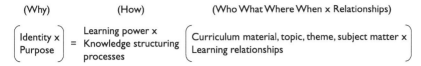

(Why)   (How)   (Who What Where When x Relationships)

$$\begin{pmatrix} \text{Identity x} \\ \text{Purpose} \end{pmatrix} = \begin{matrix} \text{Learning power x} \\ \text{Knowledge structuring} \\ \text{processes} \end{matrix} \begin{pmatrix} \text{Curriculum material, topic, theme, subject matter x} \\ \text{Learning relationships} \end{pmatrix}$$

Figure 3.3 A systems architecture for learning to learn.

about something unreflectively. The second level, deutero learning, is a process where the learner identifies meta-patterns and relationships in the process and context of learning and thus learns how to go about learning. The third level he describes as tertiary learning – a higher level of consciousness again which involves some form of personal transformation. Where there is no personal choice and something is being learned for external reasons, rather than from an internal, self-organizing purpose, there may be a recognition of patterns, but it is unlikely that transformative learning will take place. The individual is unlikely to be changed as a person because of what they have learned.

In seeking to represent learning to learn as a complex, dynamic process, the 'why' is defined by the learner's intention, which depends significantly on their sense of identity and purpose. The 'how' of learning to learn can be defined by the personal dispositions, values, and attitudes the learner brings to the task and the knowledge structuring processes that they utilize for their purpose. The 'what', 'where', 'when', and 'who' can be defined as the immediate subject matter of what is being learned – the topic, project or theme in curriculum terms. In communities of practice, learning relationships influence all aspects of learning. Those relationships are complex and multi-layered – proximal and distal. While they may take different forms at different stages of the process, relationships are the medium through which the individual negotiates the journey from purpose to performance and the context in which learning takes place. Relationships provide the vehicle for feedback, both formal and informal, self-generated and other-generated.

Applying this architecture to learning to learn, we arrive at the following: Understanding learning to learn through a systems thinking lens invites a focus on purpose, and it is the purpose of something which provides the energy for sense-making and ownership of the process – and Bateson's deutero and tertiary learning which is important for the development of competence in learning to learn. We can describe this type of learning as 'endogenous learning'.

It is very easy to ignore purpose – but to take it into account in learning design makes a significant difference to how we organize learning and schooling. As an analogy, for example, if we see a bridge only as an engineering structure, it is very different from seeing its purpose, which is to transport people from one side to another.

Discussion

If competence in learning to learn is a desired outcome of schooling, then learning to learn cannot be treated in isolation. It is not simply another slot to be added to the timetable. It is an emergent property of a social journey from purpose to performance. The quality of pedagogy depends on learning design that facilitates relationships and connections (feedback and feed-forward loops) between purpose, learning power, knowledge construction, and performance.

Linking learning to identity and purpose is a pedagogical necessity. The task of enabling the individual learner to make authentic connections with what they are learning is important precisely because it is literally the means for the individual to make sense of their experiences in the world. It allows reflection on 'me and my purpose' and contributes to the formation of learning identity – who I am and who I am becoming. Authentic learning is self-directed learning which is real and meaningful in the lifeworld of the learner. It is endogenous because it originates from within the learner as a self-organizing system.

Starting with an authentic purpose, the individual is able to move beyond compliance to identify a personally chosen goal, to appropriate and achieve agency in learning, and thus to sustain their engagement with new learning opportunities fuelled by the transformative energy of human intention. The development of learning power facilitates critical reflection on identity and purpose and serves the journey towards the achievement of that purpose.

A second key connection is between purpose and performance – in this case, competence in learning to learn about something that matters in the world. An individual's authentic learning purpose will always have an application in the world, even if the purpose is limited to the acquisition of an academic qualification, and is therefore somewhat abstracted from context. Purpose drives behaviour and shapes what is possible for that individual. Where a learning purpose is personally chosen, because it is meaningful and authentic in the life of the learner, not only is the energy for pursuing learning more readily available but, by definition, the outcomes will have an application in the life of the learner beyond the classroom and the school.

This model of the learner is an 'inside-out' model (Fig. 3.4). Learning about something (generating knowledge) is integral to learning how to learn, and the process is fuelled by the intention and purpose of the learner, which results in authentic application in the life of the learner beyond the classroom.

Learning to learn as a journey

Understanding learning to learn through a systems lens means that it cannot be reduced to one isolated process. Rather, it is a relational journey of authentic enquiry from purpose to performance. The interrelationships and feedback loops between the core processes mean that it is difficult – maybe impossible – to control from the outside, particularly in the 'messy' contexts of classrooms, so often constrained by instrumental values imposed from the outside. Individual learners receive feedback data constantly from a range of people and processes and their impact may not always be predictable. The implications for pedagogy are that teachers need a rich understanding of the processes and relationships that are significant in learning to learn as a complex process, and the professional skill to design contexts for learning that best enable these processes to work together

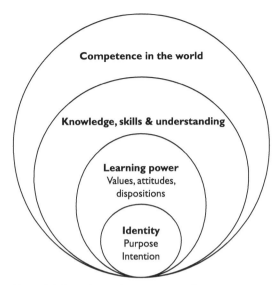

Figure 3.4 Learning to learn as a complex process.

to create the synergy that is learning to learn – young people able and willing to become self-directed learners.

A key part of the teacher's lexicon of pedagogical skills is in providing feedback loops for learners – assessment strategies, which, at the personal end of the spectrum, facilitate the formation of identity and purpose and at the public end of the spectrum, provide summative feedback on performance. Within that spectrum, a facilitator of learning may need to move between coaching for the development of learning power, providing formative feedback on knowledge construction in a specialized domain, and mentoring in a particular skill or counselling in the formation of healthy learning relationships.

Conclusions

Learning how to learn is a complex human, social process that cannot be reduced to a single entity or process. This perspective is important particularly for teachers and leaders of learning where the task is to facilitate the whole process as well as the parts. It is also important for understanding the relationship between learning in formal educational settings and learning that takes place beyond the classroom and school, and in the application of learning theory to authentic contexts such as the community or the workplace. Learning how to learn is a crucial twenty-first-century competence that will enable individuals to respond productively to uncertainty and risk and to develop the resilience to withstand radical personal, professional, and social challenges. The systems design for the process explored in this chapter uses the idea of authentic purpose to define the system boundaries, and identifies learning power and knowledge structuring processes as key means of achieving an authentic learning purpose, which always relates to learning about something meaningful in the world of the person concerned and results in an authentic performance. The implications of this for policy and practice are significant because if learning to learn is understood as a curriculum entitlement for all, then teaching needs to move beyond the transmission of knowledge towards teaching as learning design: creating a context in which learning to learn competence emerges from the interaction between the core processes of learning as a journey from purpose to performance.

References

Amosa, W., Ladwig, J., Griffiths, T., & Gore, J. (2007) 'Equity effects of quality teaching: Closing the gap', Paper presented to the Australian Association for Research in Education Conference, Fremantle, WA, 25–29 November.

Barrows, H.S. (1986) 'A taxonomy of problem-based learning methods', *Medical Education, 20,* 481–486.

Bateson, G. (1972) *Steps to an ecology of Mind.* San Francisco, CA: Chandler.

Bauman, Z. (2001) *The individualized society.* Cambridge: Polity Press.

Bereiter, C., & Scardamalia, M. (1989) 'Intentional learning as a goal of instruction', in L. Resnick (Ed.) *Knowing, learning and instruction: Essays in honour of Robert Glaser* (pp. 361–392). Hillsdale, NJ: Erlbaum.

Biesta, G., Field, J., Goodson, I., Hodkinson, P., & Mcleod, F. (2008) 'Learning lives: Learning, identity and agency in the life course', *TLRP Research Briefing, 51.*

Biesta, G., & Tedder, M. (2007) 'Agency and learning in the lifecourse: Towards an ecological perspective', *Studies in the Education of Adults, 39,* 132–149.

Black, P., McCormick, R., James, M., & Pedder, D. (2006) 'Assessment for learning and learning how to learn: A theoretical enquiry', *Research Papers in Education, 21,* 119–132.

Blockley, D. (2010) 'The importance of being process', *Civil Engineering and Environmental Systems, 27,* 189–199.

Bond, T. (2004) *Ethical guidelines for researching counselling and psychotherapy.* Rugby: British Association for Counselling and Psychotherapy.

Chinn, C., & Hung, C. (2007) *Learning to reason about the methodology of scientific studies: A classroom experiment in the middle school.* Chicago, IL: American Educational Research Association.

Damasio, A. (2000) *The feeling of what happens: Body, emotion and the making of consciousness.* London: Vintage Books.

Deakin Crick, R. (2009) 'Inquiry-based learning: Reconciling the personal with the public in a democratic and archaeological pedagogy', *Curriculum Journal, 20*(1), 73–92.

Deakin Crick, R. (2012) 'Student engagement: Identity, learning power and enquiry – a complex systems approach', in S. Christenson, A. Reschly, & C. Wylie (Eds.) *The handbook of research on student engagement.* New York: Springer.

Deakin Crick, R., Broadfoot, P., & Claxton, G. (2004) 'Developing an effective lifelong learning inventory: The ELLI Project', *Assessment in Education: Principles Policy and Practice, 11,* 247–272.

Deakin Crick, R., & Goldspink, C. (2014) 'Telling identities: Learning as script or design?', *British Journal of Educational Studies,* (forthcoming).

Deakin Crick, R., Haigney, D., Huang, S., Coburn, T., & Goldspink, C. (2013) 'Learning power in the workplace: The effective lifelong learning inventory and its reliability and validity and implications for learning and development', *International Journal of Human Resource Management, 24*(11), 2255–2272.

Deakin Crick, R., Jelfs, H., Huang, S., & Wang, Q. (2011) *Learning Futures: Final report*. London: Paul Hamlyn Foundation.

Deakin Crick, R., Jelfs, H., Ren, K., & Symonds, J. (2010) *Learning Futures*. London: Paul Hamlyn Foundation.

Deakin Crick, R., & Yu, G. (2008) 'The Effective Lifelong Learning Inventory (ELLI): Is it valid and reliable as a measurement tool?', *Education Research, 50*(4), 387–402.

Delor, J. (1996) *Learning: The treasure within*. Paris: UNESCO.

Dweck, C.S. (2000) *Self-theories: Their role in motivation, personality, and development*. New York: Psychology Press.

Dweck, C.S. (2006) *Mindset: The new psychology of success*. New York: Random House.

Foster, M. (2001) *Learning our way forward*. Adelaide, SA: Department of Education, Training and Employment.

Gee, J. (2001) 'Identity as an analytic lens for research in education', *Review of Research in Education, 25*, 99–125.

Geier, R., Blumenfeld, P.C., Marx, R.W., Krajcik, J.S., Fishman, B., Soloway, E. et al. (2008) 'Standardized test outcomes for students engaged in inquiry-based science curricula in the context of urban reform', *Journal of Research in Science Teaching, 45*, 922–939.

Goldspink, C. (2008) *Learning to Learn: Phase three evaluation report*. Adelaide, SA: Department of Education and Children's Services.

Goldspink, C. (2010) *Learning to Learn and teaching for effective learning: A summary of research findings and recommendations for the future*. Adelaide, SA: Department of Education and Children's Services.

Goldspink, C., & Foster, M. (2013) 'A conceptual model and set of instruments for measuring student engagement in learning', *Cambridge Journal of Education, 43*, 291–311.

Goldstein, J. (1999) 'Emergence as a construct: History and issues', *Emergence, 1*(1), 49–72.

Gonzalez, N. (1999) 'What will we do when culture doesn't exist any more?', *Anthropology and Education Quarterly, 30*, 431–435.

Hall, S. (1996) 'Introduction: Who needs "identity"?', in S. Hall & P. Du Guy (Eds.) *Questions of cultural identity*. London: Sage.

Haste, H. (2001) 'Ambiguity, autonomy and agency', in D. Rychen & L. Salganik (Eds.) *Definition and selection of competencies: Theoretical and conceptual foundations*. Seattle, WA: OECD/Hogreffe & Huber.

Heron, J., & Reason, P. (1997) 'A participatory inquiry paradigm', *Qualitative Inquiry, 3*, 274–294.

Hmelo-Silver, C., Golan, D., & Chinn, C. (2006) 'Scaffolding and achievement in problem-based and inquiry learning: A response to Kirschner, Sweller, and Clark', *Educational Psychologist, 42*, 99–107.

Ladwig, J.G. (2009) 'Working backwards towards curriculum: on the curricular implications of *Quality Teaching*', *Curriculum Journal, 20*(3), 271–286.

Ladwig, J., Smith, M., Gore, J.M., Amosa, W., & Griffiths, T. (2007) 'Quality of pedagogy and student achievement: Multi-level replication of authentic pedagogy', Paper presented to the Australian Association for Research in Education Conference, Fremantle, WA, 25–29 November.

Lave, J., & Wenger, E. (1991) *Situated learning: Legitimate peripheral participation.* Cambridge: Cambridge University Press.

Lynch, C., & Prandolini, A. (2006) 'Thinking it through: Articulating thinking through inquiry-based learning', *Learning Matters, 11*(1): 56–58.

Marshall, B., & Drummond, M.J. (2006) 'How teachers engage with Assessment for Learning: Lessons from the classroom', *Research Papers in Education, 21,* 133–149.

Morin, E. (2008) *On complexity.* Cresskill, NJ, Hampton Press Inc.

Newmann, F.M. (1996) *Authentic achievement: Restructuring schools for intellectual quality.* San Francisco, CA: Jossey-Bass.

Newmann, F.M., Marks, H.M., & Gamoran, A. (1996) 'Authentic pedagogy and student performance', *American Journal of Education, 104*(4), 280–312.

Priestley, M., Biesta, G., & Robinson, S. (2012) 'Teachers as agents of change: An exploration of the concept of teacher agency', Teacher Agency and Curriculum Change Working Paper (ESRC reference RES-000-22-4208).

Reason, P. (1998) 'A participatory worldview', *Resurgence, 168,* 42–44.

Rychen, S., & Salagnik, L. (2003) 'A holistic model of competence', in S. Rychen & L. Salagnik (Eds.) *Key competencies for a successful life and a well-functioning society.* Gottingen: Hogrefe & Huber.

Sfard, A., & Prusak, A. (2005) 'Telling identities: In search of an analytic tool for investigating learning as a culturally shaped activity', *Educaitonal Researcher, 34,* 14–22.

Weick, K. (1995) *Sensemaking in organizations.* Thousand Oaks, CA: Sage.

Wenger, E. (1998) *Communities of practice: Learning, meaning and identity.* Cambridge: Cambridge University Press.

Wertsch, J. (1991) *Voices of the mind: A sociological approach to mediated action.* Hemel Hempstead: Harvester Wheatsheaf.

Chapter 4

Learning to learn for the individual and society

Aureliana Alberici and Paolo Di Rienzo

Abstract

This chapter adopts a critical approach to address the concepts of lifelong learning and learning to learn in their multifaceted dimensions – individual, social, and ecological. In the first section, we conceive development as freedom and consider individuals' capability of learning to learn as a fundamental resource for personal and social development. We emphasize the qualitative nature of such an approach and focus on learning to learn as a core strategic competence for lifelong learning, since it can mobilize reflective and proactive behaviours. Learning to learn is interpreted as a capacity *for all*, which eventually facilitates the development of democracy. The next section offers a reflection and detailed analysis on learning to learn as a resource for facilitating lifelong learning and particularly adult learning, from international models found in literature. Reference is made to the concept of learning energy or learning power as a key feature of learning to learn. The last section provides a key to interpreting learning to learn as a competence, recalling the holistic dimension of lifelong learning where multiple personal, cultural, and social elements are involved. Learning to learn is considered ecologically according to Bateson's theories, in which individuals are part of social living systems. The core of the discourse is placed on the need to move beyond a mere functionalist approach to embrace a broader transformative and constructive view of learning, in which learning to learn is a fundamental resource, due to its transformative and evolutionary nature, for individuals' fulfilment and active citizenship.

Key words: lifelong learning, competence, personal and social development.

Introduction

This chapter develops the concept of learning to learn, from a lifelong learning perspective, as a resource for the benefit of individuals and society. Our theoretical argument starts with a critical overview of a wealth of sociological, psychological, and pedagogical literature, related to lifelong learning and learning to learn, particularly in relation to learning in adulthood. We consider learning to learn a strategic competence for individuals, which mobilizes individuals' energies for lifelong learning. This in turn provides individuals with the necessary tools to adapt to the challenges of ever-changing global societies. Since societies today are part of a fluid global network, this chapter stresses the importance of learning to learn as a tool and lever for global and ecological social change. The relevance of transformative learning for deep, aware, value-driven social change is also highlighted for both individuals and societies.

Learning to learn is interpreted as a capacity *for all*, which eventually facilitates the development of democracy. It is identified as one of the European Council's key competencies, and the discussion is informed by international models found in literature. Learning to learn is then discussed from an ecological perspective, drawing on Bateson's theories, in which individuals are understood as part of social living systems.

The conclusions point to a potential solution to educational and social problems through lifelong learning, learning to learn, and related pedagogy: we maintain there is a need to move beyond a mere functionalist approach (founded on learning things and facts) and underline the importance of embracing a broader transformative and constructive view of learning, with learning to learn as a core construct. This involves having a holistic understanding and vision of learning and achievement that includes multiple personal, cultural, and social processes. This approach could be described as critical socio-cultural pedagogy.

Democracy, globality, lifelong learning, and learning to learn

Lifelong learning is central to the interpretation of the complexity of today's world. For some time, it has been part of a debate about the democratic development of societies (Ceruti, 1985). The complexity of contemporary societies is evident on the one hand in the crisis of the 'pensée unique'[1] and the failure of values founded on certainty and completeness; and on the other, by the acknowledgement of the variety of interpretive worldviews, as a widespread literature on this subject shows (Morin, 1999a).

There is a close connection between democracy in today's society and the development of lifelong learning (Jarvis, 2008). Democracy and lifelong learning share the values of diversity and freedom in a globalized world and the need for an integrative, interdisciplinary approach to learning and change. Lifelong learning goes beyond the psychological processes of learning and includes cultural, anthropological, and social processes (Jarvis, 2009) that are increasingly relevant in the political and economic analysis of today's global society (Griffin, 2009).

Touraine (2006) makes a distinction between the concepts of *globalization* and *globality*. The word 'globality' not only includes the economic features of the globalization process but also social, technological, and political transformations and the challenges coming from the unprecedented complexity of human relationships. The concept of globality enables us to go beyond the perception of planetary homologation and limited ways of thinking, values and beliefs systems, usually associated with the phenomenon of globalization. This meaning of globality offers a new resource for the improvement of human beings (Beck et al., 1999).

The concept of globality is particularly relevant to lifelong learning: it is no longer possible to understand ourselves in separate worlds; rather, we are all part of an interconnected global society. No country or community can isolate itself from another, although we cannot take for granted that human beings in different cultural settings perceive themselves as interconnected. What is required to foster democratic citizenship in this context is the development of individual and community self-awareness and reflectiveness. In other words, it is necessary to promote reflective understanding (Giddens, 1990; Beck et al., 1999) and reflective and inclusive political and cultural strategies, as basic requirements for the development of individuals and societies (Alberici, 1998).

Lifelong learning, therefore, is more and more a political decision and a necessary condition for enacting the rights and responsibilities of becoming active citizens. New cultural, political, and educational benchmarks, then, must deal with the features of today's global knowledge society, including: technological changes; new forms of employment; the ever increasing relevance assigned to knowledge and human resource management and the pervading and permanent dimensions of learning in the life of individuals (Delors, 1996). The studies, guidelines, and resolutions released by the European Union (EC, 2000, 2001, 2010) and by international organizations (OECD, 2010; World Bank, 2011) underline the key relevance of lifelong learning for the acquisition of knowledge and the capacity to live effectively, to work, to face change, to plan the future, and to actively engage with the society in which individuals live. These are guiding principles of lifelong learning policies (OECD, 2011).

Nevertheless, the functional-economic model of human capital development, based on the leading role of the market and on the idea of human capital conceived as an economic resource, still poses a threat to our understanding of lifelong learning and democratic development (Rubenson, 2009). When educational strategies are framed by a functionalist worldview, they become subordinated to economic principles (Jarvis, 2009). From this perspective, the learning process becomes a tool for exacerbating inequalities and social, cultural, and professional gaps in different contexts; thus the deprivation of capabilities. We refer instead to Amartya Sen's theories that conceive of human *development as freedom*, in general terms, and consider the individual's capability as a fundamental resource for social development. Here, the word 'capability' refers to an ability that can be possibly achieved and acquired by individuals in their social contexts, going beyond those abilities connected only to economic and productive tasks (Sen, 1999).

The development of such capability is a challenge in contemporary contexts where the educational process is aimed almost exclusively at the acquisition of skills and adaptive behaviours in individuals considered by élites as potential manageable consumers. In such a scenario, we observe that adaptive educational policies and strategies often turn out to be just a means to an end, missing their specific *use-value*, and thus are imbued with a mere *exchange value* (Bailey, 1988). This is likely to affect their effectiveness in personal and social development.

The establishment and consolidation of a learning society is one of the most effective and desirable political solutions to address and overcome the economic-functionalist approach, particularly in the light of the present economic crisis and of the failure of the neo-liberal development model (Wain, 2009). The global dimension of the learning society is the new framework, in which the new cultural and operational benchmarks underlying educational strategies are: technological changes, new forms of employment, the ever increasing relevance of knowledge and human resources, the pervading and permanent features of lifelong learning (Delors, 1996; EC, 2000). This implies moving beyond a functionalist standpoint (Usher & Edwards, 2007) to consider lifelong learning as a resource for personal and social growth, embedded with intrinsic value. The concept of lifelong learning has been examined from different perspectives, as it deserves a prominent positioning. Usher and Edwards (2007: 2–3) argue that

> . . . learning is neither invariant nor unchanging because 'learning' is a socio-culturally embedded set of practices. Given this, lifelong learning therefore is a way, and a significant way, in which learning is fashioned . . . in which learning is signified in a variety of contemporary discourses.
>
> (Usher & Edwards, 2007: pp. 2–3)

In this chapter, we base lifelong learning on two concepts: first, on holistic human development incorporating the development of knowledge and learning to learn, involving psychological, spiritual, ethical, and socio-cultural dimensions; and second, on the concept of capability, as it has been previously described. The key idea behind these concepts is that individuals have the freedom to realize themselves and to widen the range of opportunities open to them (Sen, 1999). We are referring here to what Sen describes as a *capability-raising* process, to be achieved through a new strategic role for education, aimed at providing individuals with the capabilities needed in everyday life and in promoting social development. The conception of lifelong learning suggested here and its implication for educational paths, places the focus not only on the formal dimension of educational systems but also on the lifelong and lifewide[2] learning potential of individuals and on educational policies that will support this. The focus is thus on the human capability to generate and use knowledge effectively, intelligently, creatively, and proactively. In today's knowledge society, individuals, with their set of knowledge and competencies, are the actual 'treasure for themselves' and for the community (Delors, 1996).

This notion of lifelong learning requires the development of the competence of learning to learn as a core focus of educational systems. Through assisting individuals in developing competence in learning to learn, education systems can facilitate the establishment of a democratic society that features inclusive cultural models and policies (Alberici, 2008).

Morin's theories (1999a) regarding the reform of thinking provide a useful indication for the development of competence in learning to learn. Such theories recall the need to develop a new mental model as a crucial resource for gaining the knowledge required to live in complex global societies. Such a goal can be achieved through a deep reform of education in which learning to learn becomes a necessary tool for all. Learning to learn is a competence that is based on the empowerment and enhancement of personal experiences and of prior learning. It is necessary for becoming a lifelong learner, for pursuing individual fulfilment, and for the democratic development of societies. Learning to learn focuses on the learner – owing to the importance of motivation, volition, and critical reflection on one's own learning experience (Carr & Claxton, 2002). It includes being critically reflective of one's own learning – meant as an open process in which anyone can find one's own internal resources – exploiting one's own potential, developing the ability to actively engage in one's own life.

From these assumptions, we argue that learning to learn can be a key resource for personal development and active citizenship. The European Framework for Key Competencies for Lifelong Learning, released at the end of 2006, includes learning to learn among the eight key abilities and knowledge that everyone needs in order to achieve employment, personal fulfilment, social inclusion, and active citizenship in today's rapidly changing world. According to this framework:

> Learning to learn is the ability to pursue and persist in learning, to organise one's own learning, including through effective management of time and information, both individually and in groups. This competence includes awareness of one's learning process and needs, identifying available opportunities, and the ability to overcome obstacles in order to learn successfully. This competence means gaining, processing and assimilating new knowledge and skills as well as seeking and making use of guidance. Learning to learn engages learners to build on prior learning and life experiences in order to use and apply knowledge and skills in a variety of contexts: at home, at work, in education and training. Motivation and confidence are crucial to an individual's competence.
>
> (EC, 2006: 7)

The development of learning to learn requires individuals to know their preferred learning strategies, and includes the motivation and confidence to pursue and succeed in learning throughout one's life. A positive attitude incorporated in learning to learn is the desire to apply prior learning, life experiences, and curiosity to look for opportunities to learn and apply learning in a variety of life contexts (EC, 2006: 7). Basic competencies such as literacy, numeracy, and ICT are an essential foundation for learning (EC, 2006; OECD, 2010). Thus, learning *how* to learn (Gibbons, 1990) is a *strategic* competence, as it supports all learning activities throughout life, enabling individuals to display their social and civic competencies (Hoskins & Deakin Crick, 2008).[3] According to the European Recommendation, such social and civic competences include:

> personal, interpersonal and intercultural competence and cover all forms of behavior that equip individuals to participate in an effective and constructive way in social and working life, and particularly in increasingly diverse societies, and to resolve conflict where necessary. Civic competence equips

individuals to fully participate in civic life, based on knowledge of social and political concepts and structures and a commitment to active and democratic participation.

(EC, 2006: 7–8)

This implies an original vision of the value of the learning process in the life of individuals and communities. Educational systems across the European Union are required to support the development of such a competence. As a consequence, educational systems and policies should then be re-oriented to promote and support the learning process. This implies assisting individuals in the development of those competencies required for effective functioning in life and work (e.g. literacy and professional, emotional, and social competences), with the aim of self-realization as free and responsible active citizens (Burbules & Torres, 2000).

To achieve such goals, a key pedagogic response is to focus on the reflective dimension of education, which is based on the continuum of change/transformation (Demetrio, 1991; Bee, 1996; Saraceno, 2001),[4] on the concept of life-long learning potential, and on the role of experience in learning. This new educational dimension is embedded with complexity and dynamism; in other words, it expresses a dialectic synergy between knowledge and experience in educational processes and practice (Jarvis, 2004), particularly in adult learning. Actually, this perspective on education takes into account how learning can be fostered through the transfer of knowledge. Above all, this educational dimension considers how learning can turn personal experiences into knowledge and competencies. This should enable individuals to achieve conscious, reflective, proactive, and meaningful thinking and behaviour to be used through their entire life cycle and in different contexts (Brookfield, 1987).

A large literature in the fields of politics, sociology, and economics calls on the need for reflectiveness and meaning-making as strategies to deal with complexity and more generally to face present and future social challenges (Giddens, 1990; Beck et al., 1999; Sen, 1999). Hence, we can consider a new theoretical perspective on education, following a humanistic and holistic approach to learning: a reflective, transformative, and empowering approach, focused on the development of individuals and assisting them in actively engaging as social players; more generally, an approach focused on human development (Rubenson, 2004). This requires a new educational strategy conceived of as reflective and critical thinking, often divergent thinking in opposition to homologation. This new strategy originates from and takes into account the critique to the role of human capital in the functionalist theory. This educational strategy therefore considers learning to learn and lifelong learning, with their intrinsic value, as two interrelated aspects of a new paradigm in education and as key processes to achieve human development. This new paradigm focuses on the ability to actively and strategically engage in the society in which we live and deal with the complexity of everyday life. This means individuals should be equipped with proactive, reflective, and meaning-making abilities.

Accomplishing one's own life, responding dynamically to the many challenges of being members of a social and work context requires the individual to achieve and update a set of capabilities and competencies all life long. This in turn requires appropriate policy measures to foster such competencies. Learning to learn plays a key role as a tool for supporting individuals in tackling their social, civic, and professional tasks. To achieve learning to learn, individuals should develop strategic dimensions such as the ability to discover, assign, and modify meanings for oneself and for others within given contexts, to act as active social players in a democratic society (Bruner, 1986). The learning to learn model suggested here is a meta-competence, or deuteron-competence (Bateson, 1972), seen as the ability needed by everyone to be a lifelong learner. Such a strategic competence is conceived here as a turning point for mobilizing individual resources and strategic reflective behaviour in complex modern societies.

Following Le Boterf (2000), we claim that a competence cannot be considered as a status; a competence does not consist of knowledge acquired once and for all. A competence does not lie in the resources of individuals, but rather in the actual *process of mobilization of such resources* (knowing-how, knowing-that, knowing how to learn, knowing how to do, knowing what to do, etc.). All this applies to learning to learn, since its essence lies in its reflective dimension and in its ability to mobilize resources in order to enhance the quality of learning processes in diversified life contexts.

In today's society, learning to learn should be considered as a useful resource *for all* adults and a tool for human development policies and social and economic development (OECD, 1996). In this respect lifelong learning, when focused on the competence of learning to learn, can be a lever for facilitating social and cultural transformations to promote active citizenship in the contemporary world. We thus define learning to learn as a *strategic competence* for lifelong learning and, in a broader sense, for social and cultural empowerment, in today's knowledge society. In the next section, we investigate this concept further.

Learning to learn as a strategic competence for lifelong learning

Lifelong learning implies both the development of basic functional competences, such as literacy and numeracy, and the strategic competence of learning to learn, which is the necessary prerequisite to be able to learn all life long. Learning to learn consists in the *ability to mobilize* a cluster of activities and processes providing individuals with cultural, professional, and social tools (competencies) needed for their personal, professional, and social accomplishment (EC, 2006). These competencies, just like the learning to learn competence, are characterized by their evolving nature and can be described as forming the cultural profile of each individual.

Research offers further evidence that learning to learn is central in encouraging active citizenship and, more generally, social development and meaning-making processes (Gibbons, 1990; Deakin Crick et al., 2004; Hoskins & Deakin Crick, 2008). In learning practices, the meaning-making process requires a focus both on disciplinary knowledge (cognitions) and on the development of a proactive attitude, which is at the heart of learning to learn: the so-called *learning power*

(Deakin Crick et al., 2004). Learning to learn is thus a polysemic concept, including several dimensions of cognitive and holistic human activity (Gardner, 1983). It includes the ability to be critically reflective of one's own assumptions and to engage effectively in discourses to validate one's beliefs (Mezirow, 1991), the ability of self-orientation in different cultural environments, the ability to make decisions (responsibility), to communicate (participation), to make plans (problem-solving and innovation) (Alberici, 2004). The notion of learning power as learning energy is associated with the notion of learning potential, from a neuroscience perspective (Levi Montalcini, 1998), yet it differs from it. The latter concept draws the attention to the word 'potential' and thus basically refers to the natural and biological dimension of learning (Gibbons, 1990), achieved by human beings in the continuum of a life cycle. Learning power, considered as an energy infused into learning, should rather include socio-cultural and psychological dimensions too, in order to be successfully performed in the *hic et nunc* of the individual. In this view, we can assume that the final purpose of all activities aimed at the promotion and acquisition of learning to learn is the development of such learning energy. This can be achieved through prior learning and experiences, knowledge and behaviours that individuals bring about in their learning paths. Deakin Crick et al. (2004) offer an interpretation of learning to learn as learning power and describe it as a complex combination of learners' identities, dispositions, values, attitudes, beliefs, and skills that coalesce to shape an individual's engagement with learning opportunities. Learning to learn is thus generated by the capability to mobilize a compound of integrated dimensions of knowledge and action, connoting the adult cultural profile, and assisting individuals in the development of the reflectiveness that modern societies require. Modern complex societies, especially knowledge societies, offer evidence of the key importance of lifelong learning, and the learning to learn process plays a relevant part in it (Van Damme, 2000).

Learning to learn is thus a *dynamic competence and an empowering tool* that cannot be defined once and for all or accomplished permanently, or be achieved merely through an appropriate learning process. The notion of learning to learn we refer to rather implies an ever-changing human condition, rolling through the different stages in the lives of individuals and connoted by their different private, professional, organizational, and social experiences; in a wider sense, by the cultural dimension of individuals, placed in their historical context.

From this point of view, we can consider a new vision of competence in learning to learn as the ability of individuals to learn their own learning process (EC, 2006). This is a fully individual resource that nevertheless can be accomplished only within experiential contexts, particularly when personal experiences do not fall into the category of individuals' habitual frames of reference (Jarvis, 2004). This learning to learn framework implies a wider conception and a critical practice of experience, involving the idea of reflectiveness. Experience, as a learning resource, is not to be considered as a generic motivating force, or as an implicit asset of adulthood, but rather as a complex dimension of thinking. Through specific educational strategies and paths, such a dimension enables the learner to demonstrate understanding and interpretive abilities, facilitating meaning-making, continuous self-assessment, and development of a sense of responsibility (Schön, 1987).

Enabling individuals to engage in self-examination, and consequently, to control their own learning process, must involve analysis and reflection *in* and *on* the texture of emotional, biographical, cognitive, professional, and social relations and experiences, in which such learning process takes place. In this respect, following Dewey's theories, experience certainly plays a relevant role in individual and social transformations, as is the case of learning to learn activity (Dewey, 1938). Hence, becoming lifelong learners – that is, being capable of performing the strategic competence of learning to learn – implies a reflective attitude towards experience (Kolb, 1984; Jarvis, 2004). In fact, the ability to debate, analyse, and assess the deepest premises behind our actions and our diversified approach to experiences involves the biographical, cognitive, and emotional dimensions of this strategic competence, and all this is likely to facilitate a proactive, reflective, diverging education process (Dominicé, 2000). Such a reflective attitude, meant as a critical evaluation of one's own assumptions, can enable individuals to assess their learning approach, and can place them in a perspective of never-ending change and growth, thus facilitating the development of the strategic competence of learning to learn in a lifelong learning perspective.

In a democratic environment, emphasis should be placed on the ability to perform learning to learn for an ever-increasing number of individuals; in other words, learning to learn should be *for all* to promote active citizenship and employability (OECD, 1996; EC, 2013). The prerequisite for the implementation of this ability is the definition on the one hand of new cultural codes, including competencies, knowledge, skills, and abilities aimed at lifelong learning; and on the other, the shaping of activities aimed at the development of the learning to learn strategic competence.

The approach we describe involves dimensions of learning and teaching and the final objectives of learning and of lifelong learning. If the aim is to promote learning power, as previously described, then the educational approach should deal with how we create meaning; how our understanding changes in different settings; how multiple intelligences develop. In addition, a pedagogy for learning to learn should reflect on what is the most suitable environment and what type of quality is to be pursued in the educational process in order to foster learning capability.

Considering the general purpose of enabling an ever-increasing number of individuals to become lifelong learners and active citizens, we can outline two different functions of learning to learn, which are independent yet interconnected (Alberici, 2008):

- an *instrumental* function: learning to learn, as a set of working tools, emphasizing the cultural and proactive dimensions of those activities and processes providing individuals with cultural, professional, and social competencies which can assist them in tackling the challenges of complex learning societies;

- a *generative* function: learning to learn emphasizes higher-order learning (double loop or deuteron-learning, according to Bateson, 1972), which is the precondition for implementing the lifelong learning power that is a autopoietic ability – that is, an ability of individual self-construction.

In this respect, the notion of learning to learn implies a complex semantic field: *in primis*, the relevance of its generative quality; then the relevance of the cultural dimension, enabling individuals to perform effectively in their socio-historical backgrounds and as lifelong learners.

We can claim that the knowledge dimensions, abilities/skills, behaviours and volitions, which are distinctive features of competence in learning to learn, are the hallmark of the adult cultural profile and can produce the reflectiveness needed for operating in given contexts. Internationally, we can observe a variety of interpretive models of learning to learn, beginning with the Helsinki model (Hautamäki et al., 2002). For our argument, those models which are focused on the founding abilities of learning to learn in adult education and in lifelong learning are particularly relevant. We refer to the social and cultural approach of Carr and Claxton (2002) and to the assumptions of Collett (1990), which generated the Alberta project for illiterate adults at the beginning of the 1990s. Our outlook on learning to learn as a strategic competence for lifelong learning is also founded on the models of Gibbons (1990) and Deakin Crick et al. (2004). The former describes learning to learn as a higher-order function in learning, supporting individuals' ability to manage their own learning processes and focused on the need for individuals to make sense of their activity; the latter, ELLI model is based upon the relevance of the learning energy needed to learn all life long.

In accordance with studies focused on the different theoretical-operational models of learning to learn, on the multiple dimensions of intelligence, on the relevance of emotional and social competences (Gardner, 1983; Goleman, 1998), we can assume that what characterizes learning to learn lies in several cultural and functional dimensions. The learning energy – which moves in the direction of a holistic improvement of individuals – can be reached through such dimensions (Alberici, 2008). The four dimensions are:

- *biographical*: self-awareness, meaning-making, self-guidance, strategic planning, decision-making;
- *meta-cognitive*: like, for example, the strategies for reviewing existing mental schemes (awareness of one's own cognitive schemes, problem-solving abilities, etc.), self-management, and development of competencies;
- *cognitive-symbolic*: like the symbolic competence of verbal comprehension and logical reasoning (literacy, numeracy); the disposition to create new knowledge;
- *social and emotional*: use of emotional intelligence, relational competences, interpersonal communication in different environments.

In line with the model developed by Gibbons (1990), we intend to highlight the meta-dimension of learning to learn and its dynamic quality, hence its *energy*. A learning energy conceived of as a driving force, relevant not only for lifelong learning but also enabling individuals to actively engage in those tasks connected to adulthood in a complex society.

Ecology of learning to learn, social values, and perspectives on meaning

In this section, learning to learn from an ecological perspective is examined according to Bateson (1972). This is to respond to the functionalist approach to learning: there seems to be the need to embrace a broader transformative view of learning and of individuals' change processes in today's complex societies, a perspective in which learning to learn is a fundamental resource owing to its evolutionary nature.

The concept of learning to learn itself, with its double-loop character, embodies such complexity. In the history of the development of knowledge, we can distinguish two modes through which change can occur: first, when we acknowledge there are things we do not know; second (more seldom), when we do not know that there are things we do not know.[5] The latter in particular calls into question the issue of learning to learn and requires a transformation in learning dynamics (Ceruti, 1985). The concept of learning to learn we are referring to is related to awareness, described by Bateson (1972) as ecological awareness, since it is connected to changes in individuals' epistemologies involving perspectives of meaning (Mezirow, 1991).

We consider the issue of learning to learn from an ecological perspective (Bateson, 1972; Morin, 1999b). From this perspective, learning to learn can be seen as a tool for facilitating reflection upon the autopoietic nature of competences, meant as individuals' ability to self-renew their knowledge, taking into account the continuous nature of the learning process in diversified contexts (Maturana & Varela, 1980).

Learning to learn from a functionalist perspective refers to learning concepts and practices in which predefined answers are provided to a predefined set of well-known questions (Rubenson, 2009). Here, the prearranged answers have no power to modify the common frames of reference like, for example, those founded on economic considerations. The neo-liberal economic globalization project, and the policies related to it, have a built-in tendency to promote homologation in cultural and social models and to bring about short-term changes and solutions. If the process of knowledge acquisition becomes subordinated to a functionalist approach, it follows that it cannot have any influence on meaning perspectives and it cannot provide any strategic response to the human quest for a good future, as its horizons are constrained to the short term (Jarvis, 2009). This argument on functionalist and neo-liberal learning theories is important, because it shows the connection between learning dynamics and meaning-making processes and how these vary according to the epistemologies of a particular environment.

We assert that any society is founded on values and on meaning perspectives:[6] the belief systems that keep human beings connected are distinctive features also in today's global societies, as the World Value Survey demonstrates. This clarifies the meaning we assign to the notion of ecology, which should not be confused or restricted to the positions of environmentalists. We are rather referring to an ecology of mind; here the word 'mind' is not seen merely as a feature belonging to each individual and it is not fitting in the boundaries of the *envelope of the skin* of each individual (Bateson, 1972). According to Bateson (1979), the mind is a unit of interacting parts, an ecological context in which information is elaborated, distinctions are outlined, and differences are created. Thus, we are all part of a mental system. The ecology of ideas has to do with the interconnection of human beings and involves the nature of organized systems and life contexts. Therefore, the word 'ecology' refers to the study of the origin and evolution of ideas and their interconnections. The ecology of ideas uses the language of relationships to facilitate our understanding of the global knowledge that interconnects human beings.

According to a systemic and ecological vision as, for example, in Gregory Bateson's theory of living systems, learning processes do not fall into just one dimension, but operate at multiple levels (Bateson, 1979). Such a perspective acknowledges the double-loop nature of the concept of learning to learn, meant as learning of higher order, pertaining to the human disposition to operate within given contexts of relationships. Bateson's theory provides an ecological key to interpreting the complexity of learning dynamics. Bateson recommends classifying the learning process according to logical levels:

- Type Zero learning: stereotyped reaction generated mostly by genetic factors
- Type I learning: automatic change in the peculiarity of response
- Type II learning: learning to learn, relational learning, transformation of epistemologies
- Type III learning: deep reorganization of an individual's personality.

As we can see, type II learning is clearly a complex form of learning, involving complex mental processes, based on self-orientation abilities, understanding of micro-universes of relationships – the contexts – and on making sense of life experiences. The mental processes we have described are likely to generate a variety of attitudes, for example, a constructive attitude, or supremacy, or passivity, or energy, or free will, and so on. The making of sense is thus connected with the human ability of *assigning punctuations* to a sequence of experiences in order to arrange the complex dimension of human relationships and create the possible social contexts (Bateson, 1972). Learning to learn is the core of the meaning-making process, a process which places us into a more complex system which we belong to as individuals.

In accordance with this ecological perspective, we need to examine the nature of our life contexts, the overall shaping of organized systems, and critically assess our responsibility as players engaged in a system founded on interrelations (Di Rienzo, 2006). We will also need to define lifelong learning from an educational perspective. Such a perspective implies a complex notion of time that, hardly compatible with a linear scheme, places individuals and organizations into an ecological, historical, and evolutionist dimension, embodied in a cyclic conception of time. Thus, we are seeing a shift from a simplifying, discontinuous, local, rigid notion of time to a fluid one, imbued with a world of relationships; an extensive and expandable notion of time, in other words, a running flow of experiences (Fabbri, 1990: 22). In the light of this notion of time, we can say that we can learn continuously, as we are embedded in a web of diversified relations, intentional and non-intentional, visible and invisible, which bring about incessant processes of transformation and meaning-making.

The lifelong learning model, founded on the idea of individuals producing their own biographies, considers human development processes according to a transformative, diverging, and re-orientating perspective, as opposed to a linear development model (Alberici, 2008). In this respect, the concept of learning to learn represents a heuristic principle of the adopted holistic approach and generates a theoretical perspective in which lifelong learning is seen as a vital and ecological process. Learning to learn, in fact, facilitates the adoption of additional points of view, the transformation of perspectives, the critical assessment of complexity, the deconstruction and recreation of meanings, and the benefit of social transformations.

The issue that we are considering here is the creation of habits of mind in tackling a constellation of life experiences: we are referring to the variously perceived human condition of being influenced by one's own epistemology. In the light of this perspective, emphasis should be placed on personal responsibility and on reasoning abilities, meant as critical awareness of one's own assumptions, as a key to transforming those taken-for-granted frames of reference underlying human behaviours.

From this perspective, it becomes clear that the key dimension of learning to learn lies in reflectiveness. The notion of reflection is often connected to the categories of hypothetic-deductive thinking (rational dimension) or the awareness of the cognitive process. Here we suggest a partially different and broader interpretation, based on reflectiveness, or critical reflection, as conceived by Mezirow (1991). This implies going back to a broader human dimension founded on the analysis of the frames of reference underlying human actions. In this context, reflective learning, meant as the transformation of individuals' interpretive schemes and perspectives of meaning, has a role in effecting changes and in turning the transformation process into a meaningful experience. The dimension of reflectiveness, as a capability of human beings, is likely to generate profound changes in the learning dynamics: these changes are related to knowledge acquisition processes taking place in a life cycle enabling individuals to make sense from experiences, involving critical awareness. In other words, learning is here meant not just as acquisition of simple facts and procedures, instrumental to work environments, but as a way to make sense of reality and participate in it democratically.

Through the learning to learn activity, we do not merely react to what we can call, with a behaviourist language, the stimuli of the experimenter. We rather achieve a configurational and aesthetic knowledge of the complex system in which we live. Here is further evidence of the strategic dimension of learning to learn, empowering the individual in different life experiences. Through learning to learn, we can outline the features of our life contexts: such contexts can be understood and recognized through our thinking habits, which, in Bateson's words, allow the segmentation of sequences of experiences and the punctuation of sequences of events in which we are embedded. This leads to uninterrupted elaboration, and uninterrupted assessing and reassessing of one's own decisions, to finally achieve a higher level of abstraction and understanding. This can be reached since human beings, as mammals, are able to learn their context; hence, they are able to make distinctions and assign logical levels to a large number of inputs/signals (Bateson, 1972).

Nevertheless, the human ability of learning to learn might fail. In this case, the individual could run the risk of misapplying learning to learn, sticking to an unsuccessful mental scheme that could cause pain and lead to incapability. This raises a question of epistemology, involving knowledge acquisition and learning styles and a deep change in the assumptions shared by individuals (Di Rienzo, 2006). The achievement of such transformations in individuals' frames of mind calls for the need for a new educational strategy and a new approach to learning. From this perspective, the learning process should imply a deep transformation of individuals' epistemologies, of their assumptions about knowledge, expectations, values, and beliefs, to allow the acquisition of useful tools for functioning in their lives and for performing active citizenship (Bauman, 2001). We are talking about a comprehensive concept of learning, with an impact on the educational process: this means going beyond and integrating present learning theories; it means also going beyond a reductive and mechanistic vision of education, in which the knowledge acquisition process implies a passive attitude from learners. The concept of learning we are suggesting here is rather founded on the active engagement of individuals. The idea behind it is that individuals' learning activity can be accomplished not only through what and how much has been learnt, but through how the cognitive processes have been implemented; through individuals' perception of knowledge; through the participation of individuals in the meaning-making process (Candy, 1989).

In today's world, with its complexity of social contexts, we must abandon a reductionist approach and adopt a holistic one. The perspective we espouse is that of Morin (1999a), concerning planetary evolution and the development of living systems. In this frame of reference, also described as cohabitation of world and society, we have to accomplish: a better understanding of ourselves; a critical reflection about our well-established habits of mind; a sense of self-responsibility and a reflection on the hidden vital threads which interconnect human beings and the whole ecosystem of living creatures. Nowadays, we all have to deal with the ecological challenge, as we are living in a world of relationships, engaged as responsible players within it. Being members of such a world requires the practice of systemic awareness and a continuous implementation of critical thinking (Di Rienzo, 2006). As human beings placed within given historical contexts, we share the responsibility of co-determining a set of values for the future. At the same time, we are responsible of taking into account the premises coming from our past (Pasolini, 2003).

Conclusions

We researchers, like all humans, have values and worldviews too. We deem the above ecological approach to be useful for educational strategies in today's global societies and have tried to demonstrate this: an ecology of learning generates a wider perspective on learning dynamics, involving personal beliefs, values, and assumptions about knowledge, knowledge acquisition, and meaning perspectives. We are talking about deep changes in learning, affecting individuals' epistemologies for the sake of a wider and deeper democratic participation and active citizenship.

In this chapter, we have tried to delineate a theoretical argument in favour of an ecological perspective on learning and learning to learn, considered as a new educational dimension, in a lifelong learning perspective. Following critical socio-cultural pedagogies, this dimension brings to mind the concepts of reflectiveness, transformation, centrality and responsibility of the individual, meaning-making and relevance of the socio-cultural contexts. Such an educational perspective is characterized by a situated approach that considers the social dimension in the shaping of knowledge and competencies. It considers learning practices placed in social contexts; it implies that individuals themselves can make sense of their own life experiences. In other words, it makes human action meaningful, going beyond mere effectiveness and efficiency criteria, typical of the functionalist approach to learning. Finally, this educational approach gives relevance to the development of cognitive strategic competences (understanding) and critical awareness.

From this educational perspective, the implementation of educational activity thus moves beyond the functionalist dimension of learning – operating outside of the individual – and gives relevance to the development of meta-competences, such as the strategic competence of learning to learn (Alberici, 2008), making the learning process meaningful inside the individual. We consider this approach to be particularly useful when tackling the many issues of adult education, formal and non-formal, in addition to school education. The biographic methodology, with a series of activities aimed at empowering people through responsible and critical reflection on their own experience, can be fruitful, especially when addressing learning needs of adults in non-formal settings.

Notes

1 The concept of *pensée unique* (single thought) refers to a notion developed at the end of the past century in a socio-political milieu. It describes the primacy of neo-liberal economic ideology over politics. This notion has been subsequently adopted in its general meaning also in cultural settings to denote a prevailing dominant conception, pretending to provide the one and only explanation to socio-cultural and political processes.
2 Lifelong relates to a temporal dimension, whereas lifewide relates to different social contexts in which learning takes place and is displayed.
3 In the context of this book, it is not possible to analyse all the connections between learning to learn and civic competencies. However, we would like to underline the importance of promoting both in order to equip current and future citizens of democratic societies with the necessary tools to solve social problems.

4 A wide psychological, sociological, and pedagogical literature on the topic of adult age and adult learning highlights the concept of change as a continuous yet non-linear process of individual transformation all life long.

5 Laing (cited in Mezirow, 1991: 25) acutely notices that it is difficult to change until we are not aware that our unawareness of the needed change models our thoughts and our actions in different ways.

6 For an extensive outlook on world values, see for instance the works of Ronald Inglehart, President of the World Value Survey at http://www.worldvaluessurvey. org/ The shift from survival to self-expression values is highlighted in World Value Survey's *Values Change the World*: 6–9 (available at: http://www.worldvaluessurvey. org/wvs/articles/folder_published/article_base_110/files/ WVSbrochure6-2008_11.pdf). See also the human developmental sequence according to Welzel and Inglehart (2008), based on economic prosperity, self-expression, and democratic values. Within this value framework, independent thinking and ability, motivation, and entitlement to govern our own lives are key to human development.

References

Alberici, A. (1998) 'Toward the learning society', in J. Holford, P. Jarvis, & C. Griffin (Eds.) *International perspectives on lifelong learning*. London: Kogan Page.

Alberici, A. (2004) 'Prospettive epistemologiche. Soggetti, apprendimento, competenze', in D. Demetrio & A. Alberici, *Istituzioni di Educazione degli adulti. Saperi, competenze e apprendimento permanente*. Milano: Guerini.

Alberici, A. (2008) *La possibilità di cambiare. Apprendere ad apprendere come risorsa strategica per la vita*. Milano: Franco Angeli.

Bailey, C. (1988) 'Lifelong education and liberal education', *Journal of Philosophy of Education*, 22(1), 121–126.

Bateson, G. (1972) *Steps to an ecology of mind*. New York: Ballantine.

Bateson, G. (1979) *Mind and nature: A necessary unity*. New York: Dutton.

Bauman, Z. (2001) *The individualized society*. Cambridge: Polity Press.

Beck, U., Giddens, A., & Lash, S. (1999) *Modernizzazione riflessiva*. Trieste: Asterios.

Bee, H. (1996) *The journey of adulthood*. Englewood Cliffs, NJ: Prentice-Hall.

Brookfield, S.D. (1987) *Developing critical thinkers: Challenging adults to explore alternative ways of thinking and acting*. San Francisco, CA: Jossey-Bass.

Bruner, J. (1986) *Actual minds, possible worlds*. Cambridge, MA: Harvard University Press.

Burbules, N.C., & Torres, C.A. (2000) *Globalization and education: Critical perspectives*. New York: Routledge.

Candy, P.C. (1989) 'Constructivism and the study of self-direction in adult learning', *Studies in the Education of Adults*, 21, 95–116.

Carr, M., & Claxton, G. (2002) 'Tracking the development of learning dispositions', *Assessment in Education: Principles, Policy and Practice*, 9, 9–37.

Ceruti, M. (1985) 'La hybris dell'onniscienza e la sfida della complessità', in G. Bocchi & M. Ceruti (Eds.) *La sfida della complessità*. Milano: Feltrinelli.

Collett, D. (1990) 'Learning to learn needs for adult basic education', in R.M. Smith and Associates (Eds.) *Learning to learn across the lifespan*, San Francisco, CA: Jossey-Bass.

Deakin Crick, R., Broadfoot, P., & Claxton, G. (2004) 'Developing an effective lifelong learning inventory: The ELLI Project', *Assessment in Education: Principles, Policy and Practice*, 11(3), 247–272.

Delors, J. (1996) *Learning: The treasure within*. Report to UNESCO of the International Commission on Education for the Twenty-first Century. Paris: UNESCO.

Demetrio, D. (1991) *Tornare a crescere. L'età adulta tra persistenze e cambiamenti*. Milano: Guerini.

Dewey, J. (1938) *Experience and education*. New York: Collier Books.

Di Rienzo, P. (2006) *Apprendere ad apprendere. Una lettura per l'educazione degli adulti. Note su una cibernetica dei sistemi viventi*. Roma: Anicia.

Dominicé, P. (2000) *Learning from our lives*. San Francisco, CA: Jossey-Bass.

European Commission (EC) (2000) *A memorandum on lifelong learning*, SEC (2000) 1832. Brussels: European Commission.

European Commission (EC) (2001) *Making a European area of lifelong learning a reality*, COM (2001) 678 final. Brussels: European Commission.

European Commission (EC) (2006) *Recommendation of the European Parliament and of the Council of 18 December 2006 on key competences for LLL* (2006/962/EC). Brussels: European Commission.

European Commission (EC) (2010) *EUROPE 2020: A strategy for smart, sustainable and inclusive growth*, COM (2010). Brussels: European Commission.

European Commission (EC) (2013) *Learning for all*. Brussels: European Commission.

Fabbri, D. (1990) *La memoria della regina*. Milano: Guerini e Associati.

Gardner, H. (1983) *Frames of mind: The theory of multiple intelligences*. New York: Basic Books.

Gibbons, M. (1990) 'A working model of the learning-how-to-learn process,' in R.M. Smith and Associates (Eds.) *Learning to learn across the lifespan*, San Francisco, CA: Jossey-Bass.

Giddens, A. (1990) *The consequences of modernity*. Stanford, CA: Stanford University Press.

Goleman, D. (1998) *Working with emotional intelligence*. New York: Bantam Books.

Griffin, C. (2009) 'Policy and lifelong learning', in P. Jarvis (Ed.) *The Routledge international handbook of lifelong learning*. London: Routledge.

Hautamäki, J., Arinen, P., Eronen, S., Hautamäki, A., Kupiainen, S., Lindblom, B. et al. (2002) *Assessing Learning to Learn: A framework*. Helsinki: National Board of Education.

Hoskins, B., & Deakin Crick, R. (2008) *Learning to learn and civic competences: Different currencies of two sides of the same coin?* Luxembourg: The European Communities. Retrieved from: http://publications.jrc.ec.europa.eu/repository/bitstream/111111111/4954/1/reqno_jrc45123_learning%20to%20learn%20and%20civic%20competence%5B2%5D.pdf.

Jarvis, P. (2004) *Adult education and lifelong learning: Theory and practice*. London: Routledge.

Jarvis, P. (2008) *Democracy, lifelong learning and the learning society*. London: Routledge.

Jarvis, P. (2009) 'Lifelong learning: a social ambiguity', in P. Jarvis (Ed.) *The Routledge international handbook of lifelong learning*. London: Routledge.

Kolb, D.A. (1984) *Experiential learning*. Englewood Cliffs, NJ: Prentice-Hall.

Le Boterf, G. (2000) *Construire les competénces individuelles et collectives*. Paris: Les Éditions d'Oganisation.

Levi Montalcini, R. (1998) *L'asso nella manica a brandelli*. Milano: Baldini & Castoldi.

Maturana, H., & Varela, F. (1980) *Autopoiesis and cognition: The realization of the living*. Dordrecht: Reidel.

Mezirow, J. (1991) *Transformative dimensions of adult learning*. San Francisco, CA: Jossey-Bass.

Morin, E. (1999a) *La Tête bien faite*. Paris: Seuil.

Morin, E. (1999b) *Les sept savoirs nécessaires à l'éducation du futur*. Paris: UNESCO.

Organization for Economic Cooperation and Development (OECD) (1996) *Lifelong learning for all*. Paris: OECD Publishing.

Organization for Economic Cooperation and Development (OECD) (2010) *PISA 2009 results: Learning to learn: Student engagement, strategies and practices (Vol. III)*. Pisa/Paris: OECD Publishing.

Organization for Economic Cooperation and Development (OECD) (2011) *Education at a glance 2011: OECD indicators*. Paris: OECD Publishing.

Pasolini, P.P. (2003) *Lettere luterane*. Torino: Einaudi.

Rubenson, K. (2004) 'Lifelong learning: A critical assessment of the political project', in P. Alheit, R. Becker-Schmidt, T. Gitz Johansen, L. Ploug, H. Salling Olesen, & K. Rubenson (Eds.) *Shaping an emerging reality: Researching lifelong learning*. Roskilde: Roskilde University Press.

Rubenson, K. (2009) 'Lifelong learning: Between humanism and global capitalism', in P. Jarvis (Ed.) *The Routledge international handbook of lifelong learning*. London: Routledge.

Saraceno, C. (2001) 'Dalla sociologia dell'età alla sociologia del corso della vita', in C. Saraceno (Ed.) *Età e corso della vita*. Bologna: Il Mulino.

Schön, D.A. (1987) *Educating the reflective practitioner: Toward a new design for teaching and learning in the professions*. San Francisco, CA: Jossey-Bass.

Sen, A. (1999) *Development as freedom*. New York: A. Knopf.

Touraine, A. (2006) *Un nouveau paradigme. Pour comprendre le monde au jourd'hui*. Paris: Fayard.

Usher, R., & Edwards, R. (2007) *Lifelong learning: Signs, discourses, practices*. Dordrecht: Springer.

Van Damme, D. (2000) 'Adult learning as strategic behaviour and strategic learning as competence', in P. Alheit, J. Beck, E. Kammler, R. Taylor, & H. S. Olesen (Eds.) *Lifelong learning inside and outside schools: Collected papers of the European Conference on Lifelong Learning*. Roskilde: Roskilde University.

Wain, K. (2009) 'Lifelong learning and philosophy', in P. Jarvis (Ed.) *The Routledge international handbook of lifelong learning*. London: Routledge.

Welzel, C. and Ingleart, R. (2008) 'The role of ordinary people in democratization', *Journal of Democracy*, 19(1), 126–140.

World Bank (2011) *Learning for all: Investing in people's knowledge and skills to promote development*. Washington, DC: World Bank.

Chapter 5

Learning to learn from a Confucian perspective
Insight from China

Kai Ren

Abstract

Confucian ideas on learning have impacted generations of learners in China and the Far East for over 2000 years. However, there is scant literature both internationally and domestically that investigates the connections between Confucian learning theory and learning to learn and how these connections can enlighten policy and practice. This chapter presents a critical review of Confucian thinking about learning to learn and how it has influenced the way the Chinese learn from past to present, as well as of its implications for educational policy and practice. It draws on a literature review and qualitative data from interviews with learners. The main aims of the chapter are to explain how the Confucian conceptualization of learning to learn as 'learning to conduct oneself, to think and do, and to enjoy learning for life' has contributed to the lifelong learning culture in China, and to discuss its implications for promoting learning to learn worldwide.

Key words: Confucian conceptualization of learning, policy and practice.

Introduction

> *Learning without thought is labour lost; thought without learning is perilous.*
>
> *When walking in a company of three, one is certainly my teacher.*

These two quotes from the Analects of Confucius (551–479 BCE) are sayings about learning that have been learned by heart and followed by generations of Chinese learners since ancient times. 'Confucius' is a Romanization of Kong Fu Zi, i.e. Master Kong (the family name of Confucius). He was a thinker, political figure, and above all, an educator, honoured by the Chinese as 'a teacher for ten thousand generations'. Although he did not leave any writings of his own, the teachings of Confucius were preserved in the Analects (Confucius, 479 BCE/2008, hereafter cited by book and chapter number only) by his followers, which is a collection of dialogues between Confucius and his students. Viewed as one of the greatest learning innovators in history (Tweed & Lehman, 2002), Confucius was probably the first to have developed a theory about learning to learn, even though he did not use the term himself. Learning to learn can be seen as a meta/higher-order learning that not only includes learning approaches, but also the attitudes and values a learner holds towards learning. As Confucius taught, learning is an essential part of human life and not only is it a cognitive activity but also a social activity. Therefore, to study learning to learn, one needs to examine both cognitive and social aspects. Cognitive factors include learning styles and patterns, and being able to adjust these to a particular learning task; social factors include how one engages in a learning opportunity, makes the best of the resources available, and deals with relationships in learning. There is also an ideological factor that guides one's values and aspirations as well as emotions for learning and affects one's self-regulation of learning. Many of these factors were reflected in Confucian pedagogy, which was centred on learning rather than teaching. The ultimate goal of a teacher, from the Confucian perspective, was to identify effective ways to help students learn. This is manifest in that the Analects start with a quote about learning from Confucius: 'To learn and then practise it time and again is a pleasure, is it not?'

Confucian thoughts on learning have impacted generations of learners in China and the Far East for over 2000 years. His learning theories have contributed to a strong tradition and culture of learning in Chinese society (Li, 2003b). Furthermore, some of his teachings share a universal appeal with contemporary educational issues (Lee, 2005) and, in particular, have much to contribute to learning to learn and lifelong learning both in the East and West. However, there is scant literature both in China and abroad that investigates the connections between Confucian learning theory and learning to learn and how these connections can enlighten policy and practice of learning to learn in the twenty-first century. This is the rationale for writing this chapter.

Methodology

This chapter reports on a study that aimed to investigate how a Confucian conceptualization of learning to learn has contributed to a lifelong learning culture in China, and its implications for promoting learning to learn worldwide. It examines and draws insights from the Analects, which is a record of the classical teachings of Confucius. It also reviews the literature on 20 studies conducted in China and overseas. In addition, a qualitative comparative analysis is made in terms of the differences between learning to learn in China and in the West and of the changing definitions of learning to learn in China. Given that there is little empirical research in this area, qualitative interviews were conducted with four participants, which aim to provide original in-depth data about the interviewees' thoughts and experiences with Confucian learning beliefs in their particular settings and life history.

Confucian learning to learn perspective: A critique

Confucian learning beliefs

The word *xue* (learning) appears 64 times across the 55 pages of the Analects, while the word *jiao* (teaching) only appears seven times. This to some extent

Table 5.1 The Confucian view of learning

What is learning?	Learning is a self-aware and self-initiated activity that combines the learner's cognitive and non-cognitive attributes and promotes their rounded development
Why learn?	To become more virtuous and more skilled
What to learn?	Life-wide learning, including morality, ethics, proper speech, government, and the 'Six Arts' (ritual, music, archery, chariot-riding, calligraphy, and computation)
Learning principles	Be aspired and persistent to learn, keep learning for life, and seek joy from learning

demonstrates the greater importance Confucius attached to learning. In a broad sense, he regarded learning as a process of observation of some subject matter followed by reflection, judgement, and actions (Li, 2002a). Confucius believed that the essence of any good teaching is guiding and encouraging students to learn by themselves. He saw learners as agents of learning, as he once commented: 'It is Man who is capable of broadening the Way. It is not the Way that is capable of broadening Man' (4: 9). Therefore, learning was a starting point for Confucius to address pedagogical problems and carry out teaching activities. The Confucian philosophy of teaching was not lengthy lecturing and spoon-feeding, but instructing, guiding, and inspiring students to learn. His learning theory consists of the purpose of learning, the contents of learning, and the principles for learning (see Table 5.1). Next, we will examine his teachings about learning from a learning to learn perspective.

Acquiring the moral-virtuous values and attitudes for learning

> The way of great learning consists in illuminating innate virtues.
> (Opening Statement of Great Learning, one of the 'Four Books' in
> Confucianism, as quoted by Song and Yang, 2009)

Confucius emphasized the significance of a learner's self-awareness and stressed that the purpose of learning plays a crucial part in one's learning. He believed that learning should be oriented towards higher morality and contribute to society and the state rather than merely personal utilitarian gains. Confucius' long-lasting influence resides in his fundamental teaching of the concept of *ren* (goodness, humanity), that is, a lifelong striving for any human being to become the most genuine, sincere, and humane person one can become (Tu, 1979). Those who deserve the name of *junzi* commit themselves to the process of *ren* though self-cultivation, a typical way of achieving a high moral and virtuous standard as advocated by Confucius (Tu, 1979; Li, 2003a). Confucius also emphasized intellectual honesty and held that one should be modest and honest in learning. He was quoted as telling his students, 'if you know a thing, say that you know; and if you don't, admit that you don't, that is knowledge' (2: 17). He believed that admitting one's ignorance is the right attitude for learning and can be the reason for starting to learn.

Cultivating a passion for learning throughout life

> At fifteen I set my heart on learning; at thirty I firmly took my stand; . . .
> At seventy I followed my heart's desire without overstepping the boundaries
> of right.
>
> (2: 4)

Confucius believed in lifelong learning that must become both a joy and a passion for the individual. He held that the greatest virtue of his was 'the eagerness to learn' (*haoxue*) (5: 28). In fact, having a passion for learning became one of the key criteria when he evaluated his students. Yet not only did he emphasize 'being fond of learning', but he also paid more attention to 'finding joy in learning' (6: 20). He advocated that the very idea of a love or passion for learning is an end in itself, given that learning to him was the only pathway towards lifelong moral striving. Confucius thus emphasized one's emotional experience in the learning process because only those who are genuinely keen on what they are learning and enjoy the learning process can really master the subject.

Making meaning for learning

> A man is worthy of being a teacher who gets to know what is new by keeping
> fresh in his mind what he is already familiar with.
>
> (2: 11)

To Confucius, learning is an interconnected rather than intermittent process. He suggested a learner regularly revisit what he has learned to generate new ideas. Confucius particularly highlighted the importance of making connections in learning and believed that a good learner can find links between what they learn and then make better meaning of it (7: 8). He once asked Ci, a student of his, if in Ci's opinion he was 'the kind of man who learns widely and retains what he has learned in his mind'. When Ci gave an affirmative answer, Confucius said: 'No. I have a single thread binding it all together' (15: 3). This comment explicitly disapproves of rote learning but highlights the importance of finding threads to link the vast amount of knowledge, facts, and understanding that one has learned.

Learning to think and ask questions

> Learning without thought is labour lost, thought without learning is
> perilous.
>
> (2: 15)

Confucius conceptualized thinking as self-reflection and he advocated that it is important to strike a balance between learning and thinking. Confucius regarded thinking as an indispensable part of learning because proactive thinking can help internalize knowledge and experience that has been learned (Zhang, 2001). He believed that thinking could also point out directions for future learning. Yet he also warned against excessive thinking without learning from external resources (15: 31). Meanwhile, Confucius was aware that being able to ask questions was a product of thinking in learning, and in turn it would also promote one's thinking (Yang & Lin, 2003). He elaborated on the importance of raising questions in learning and strongly suggested that a learner remain curious about things around him. In particular, he stressed that a learner should be quick and eager to learn and be 'not ashamed to seek the advice of those who were beneath him in station' (5: 15). To Confucius, one does not lose 'face' to learn from someone who might not be as learned as oneself.

Learning by doing

To learn and then practise it time and again is a pleasure, is it not?'

(1: 1)

Confucius was among the first educators in history to have advocated the complementary relationships between learning and doing (Zhang, 2001). He believed that an effective way to learn is to put what one learns into practice and he regarded this as an enjoyable experience. He often encouraged his students to use what they had learned to deal with problems in reality such as social, political, and ethical issues. Otherwise, what one has learned, no matter how much it is, may be of no real value. On the other hand, he warned against the tendency to neglect learning from textbooks and only concentrate on practice. He was aware that in an educational context, the main task of a student is to learn from a curriculum and acquire knowledge, and that studying theoretical knowledge must by no means be replaced by practical work.

Creating harmonious learning relationships

When walking in company of three, one is certainly my teacher. If someone is wise, learn from him; if not, reflect on his behaviour for your own sake.

(7: 22)

Confucius viewed learning not only as an individual process but also an interpersonal one. He held that harmonious learning relationships based on mutual respect are conducive to learning. From his perspective, every person is always in need of improving themselves and, ideally, always open and ready to learn from anyone, whether a sage or a person on the street (Li, 2003a). This humble attitude towards learning stems from the concept of humility associated with Confucian *ren* and *junzi* (Tu, 1979). As for the relationship between teachers and students, he believed both parties are learning but in different ways. Students should have respect for teachers, while it is essential for teachers to discipline themselves, and earn the respect of the students by inspiring them rather than by imposing their ideas on the students. He suggested to his students that 'when faced with the opportunity to practise "ren", do not yield precedence even to your teacher' (15: 36). Confucius also offered advice to learners on how to get on with someone who is above or below them in learning. Whereas he suggested that those better learners be modest, he advised those who are behind to learn from their peers and strive to catch up.

Being resilient in learning

Learn without flagging and teach without growing weary.

(7: 2)

Confucius encouraged learners to make dedicated efforts in learning throughout life. This is because learning to become a *junzi* is bound to be fraught with all kinds of obstacles, and being able to overcome the obstacles is intimately related to one's commitment to the process of self-perfection (Li, 2002b). From the Confucian perspective, learning is an enduring and hard journey and one needs to be hardworking and persevere. Yet this also is a process full of joy that makes one forget one's worries when immersed in it (7: 20). In addition, Confucius suggested a learner be unperturbed when others do not appreciate his achievement. As far as making mistakes is concerned, he held that it is human to err but one must learn from the mistakes so as to avoid them in the future.

A Confucian learning to learn framework

To this attainment there are requisite the extensive study of what is good, accurate inquiry about it, careful reflection on it, the clear discrimination of it, and the earnest practice of it.

(20: 19, Doctrine of the Mean, one of the 'Four Books'
in Confucianism, as quoted by Song and Yang, 2009)

This is believed to be a quote from Confucius about how to be an effective learner. In a sense, Confucius established a learning to learn framework that combines learning with inquiring, learning with thinking, and learning with doing. In particular, he emphasized the importance of *xi*, which means both 'practice' and 'revision' in Chinese. He suggested that *xi* should be done constantly and is an enjoyable thing to do. Confucius also highlighted the steps one takes in the learning process and stressed that learning should follow a certain order and be well organized. It goes from shallow to deep, from simple to difficult, and from concrete to abstract and cannot be achieved all in one move (13: 17). He also valued experiential learning, although he was aware it is hard and one of the learning approaches he often used himself was taking field trips. In addition, as repeatedly evidenced in the Analects, Confucius advocated learning with stories, by metaphors and analogies, which he held is more effective than learning merely theories and facts. Confucius believed that through learning one should acquire six qualities: richness in knowledge, proficiency in practical skills, nobleness in spirit, braveness and perseverance, good behaviour, and graceful composure (Chang, 2009). This depicts a more concrete goal for lifelong and lifewide learning that a learner can aim for in the process of self-perfection.

Limitations of the Confucian learning to learn perspective

As Biesta and his colleagues (2005: 3) point out:

> Human learning is always located in a certain social and cultural context with a particular history, including both the individual's life history and the history of the practices and institutions in and through which learning takes place.

Confucian learning to learn theory was established in an age when values were distorted and actions and behaviour no longer corresponded to the labels originally attached to them. Moral education was overwhelmingly important to Confucius because it was the very means by which this situation could be rectified and meaning restored to language and values to society (Tu, 1979). To him, the acquisition of knowledge and skills was merely a preparation and means for moral education. This aspiration for learning therefore may be over-oriented towards ethics and morality, yet it suited the historical context and the personal story of Confucius. Due to the overwhelming emphasis he placed on ethics and politics, Confucius encouraged the learner to focus on learning arts and politics rather than science and technology. He also thought less of farming and other manual skills. *Junzi* in his eyes should contribute to the state/government and peace by becoming an official and engaging in public duties rather than taking up 'minor arts'. Meanwhile, Confucius strongly detested the sycophantic 'petty men', who win themselves an audience by clever talk and a pretentious manner. He therefore strongly advocated being quick in action but cautious in speech (1: 14, 4: 24). This extreme caution in speaking may discourage people from speaking up and engaging in learning debates, especially with authoritative figures. Although he advocated mutual respect between teacher and student, Confucius noted the respect that students paid to teachers as authorities in the first place and students were not supposed to be disobedient except in extreme circumstances, such as a violation of *ren*.

Despite the importance that Confucius attached to imitation, reflection, and experience, he did not encourage creativity in learning or being critical as well as appreciative of the classics (7: 1). He suggested that learners follow certain rules and orders, but neglected the importance of unorthodox means of learning or making an unconventional leap in learning. While Confucius was fully aware of the 'order' of learning, he seemed to neglect the 'alternative sequence' and 'miracles' in it.

Effects of Confucian teachings on the learning to learn of the Chinese people

As the most important traditional Chinese learning theory, Confucian learning beliefs have had the most extensive and long-lasting influence on the way the Chinese learn (Li, 2003a). Even today, extracts from the Analects on learning are selected for Mandarin textbooks used in Chinese secondary schools nationwide.

Despite the struggles and challenges as witnessed during social upheaval and political setbacks in recent Chinese history, children grow up in China internalizing the age-old values that benefit their learning (Li, 2002a). The Confucian learning-centred pedagogy reveals the nature of learning and teaching, and develops a framework as well as a philosophy for learning to learn. The effects of the Confucian perspective on learning to learn in China, both positive and negative, can be examined in the following areas.

Holding a positive attitude towards learning

Confucius intimately related learning to one's commitment to the process of self-perfection and contributing to the state and society. This has inspired generations of Chinese learners, intellectuals in particular, to set high aspirations for learning, dedicate themselves to the learning process, and enjoy it throughout their lives, even in times of setbacks and hardships. Research by a number of researchers (Tu, 1979; Lee, 1996; Li, 2002a) demonstrates that Chinese children express highly positive and consistent values about learning. The overall moral orientation of Chinese learners is largely consistent with the Confucian learning tradition, which links a person's moral and virtuous purposes in life to their lifelong search for knowledge (Li, 2002b: 263).

Nurturing self-regulated learning habits

The Confucian learning to learn perspective encourages Chinese learners to self-regulate and organize their learning. This includes revising what they have learned regularly and trying to find connections between what they have learned and what they are learning. It also helps many Chinese learners to focus on their learning, which, according to Confucius, is one of the most important things in life. In particular, *haoxue* (eagerness to learn), a phrase often used in the Analects, has become an essential part of the Chinese discourse for learning. Furthermore, under the influence of a Confucian learning to learn perspective, the Chinese are more likely to make efforts for learning instead of giving up in the face of obstacles and difficulties, which they deem as an inevitable part of their learning. On the other hand, the Confucian ideology may hinder people from taking risks and discourage unsuccessful trials. This to some extent has a negative impact on the development of creativity in learning.

Being humble and respecting teachers

Based on the Confucian concepts of *ren* and *junzi*, the Chinese believe that humility ensures better learning (Tu, 1979; Li, 2003a). Therefore, in learning and other social communications, they are taught to listen attentively and to question only after they have understood others (Li, 2002a). It would be considered rude and inappropriate to make an inquiry without listening carefully to the master first. In fact, Chinese students often state 'listening to teacher' as their most frequent activity in a school context (Liu & Littlewood, 1997).

Therefore, Chinese learners are likely to be less critical of the authorities and will be highly cautious in criticizing those who are supposed to be more knowledgeable than them. Teachers' answers are usually regarded as the standard and students tend to guess what their teachers' answers will be rather than having their own thinking (Biggs & Watkins, 2001).

Introverted learning

Influenced by the Confucian perspective on thinking and learning, Chinese learners favour thinking-oriented and reflective learning styles (Littrellin, 2005). Oxford and Burry-Stock (1995) found that Chinese and Japanese are concrete-sequential learners, and use a variety of strategies such as planning, memorization, analysis, sequenced repetition, detailed outlines and lists, structured review, and a search for perfection. This quiet introverted learning style is also in line with the Confucian perspective that one should be quick in action but slow and simple in words. Hence a good learner is expected to read extensively and think about what he has learned before he can discuss it with others, as Confucius would do himself.

Confucian heritage culture learner's phenomenon

The last two decades have seen students from Asian countries with a Confucian heritage culture such as China, Korea, Singapore, and Japan outperform their counterparts in international standardized assessments such as PISA (Program for International Student Assessment). In 2010, with China's debut in PISA, students in Shanghai surprised experts by outscoring their counterparts in a total of 65 countries, in reading as well as in maths and science (Dillon, 2010). Researchers and educators attribute in part the academic success of these Confucian heritage culture countries to the diligence and dedication of students to academic learning to which they give high priority (Wong, 2008). These characteristics are influenced by the Confucian heritage. In addition, the Confucian perspective on aiming high for learning is often seen as the origin of the strong achievement-orientation of Confucian heritage culture societies (Lee, 2005). Interestingly, although Confucian learning to learn theory was originally developed for learning arts, it showed strong transferability as students in Confucian heritage culture applied it in science and maths, on which they outperformed their Western peers in international tests (Wong, 2008; Dillon, 2010).

Common misunderstandings of Confucian learning theory

As critiqued by Li (2003a), the sometimes cursory portrayal of the Confucian learning approach inevitably leads to misunderstanding and the perpetuation of stereotypes. This includes the neglect of the core of the Confucian learning theory, which, as discussed previously, is humility and moral striving associated with Confucian *ren* and *junzi* (Tu, 1979). For example, Tweed and Lehman (2002: 91) asserted that Confucius' purpose of learning was 'pragmatic', aimed at obtaining a civil service job, which took Confucius' words out of context. What the sage actually meant was to contribute to the state and society through becoming an official. Another misunderstanding of Confucian learning theory is attributing the current learning environment in China to the impact of Confucius, such as rote learning and whole-class teaching. In fact, Confucius never discoursed at length on a subject. The very content of Confucius' Analects is in the style of questioning and response. It must be noted that the passive transmission and uncritical assimilation of knowledge stems from the authoritarian values of Confucianism developed by his followers, rather than those of Confucius himself (Ng, 2000). In addition, as the Analects were written in concise ancient Mandarin, which is very different from the modern Chinese language, there sometimes are different interpretations of what Confucius actually meant (see, for example, Yang & Lin, 2003).

Learning to learn in comparison

Learning to learn in China: From past to present

About 100 years after the death of Confucius, *On Learning* (Xue Ji) was written. As the earliest work on pedagogy in Chinese history and one of the greatest classics on education in China, it theorized the learning viewpoints of Confucius and further developed them. Yet different from the Analects, *On Learning* placed much emphasis on the role of the teacher and was more about learning to teach rather than learning to learn. This may be one of the fundamental reasons why Chinese education later became predominately teacher-centred and -driven with both the teacher and text regarded as authoritative sources of knowledge (Forrester et al., 2006). The Sui Dynasty in the seventh century instituted a civil service examination system and since then a standardized examination system has been a major way of selecting students, which contributes to a strong examination-oriented culture in China. The learning principles that Confucius originally advocated gradually changed into examination-oriented learning. As the exams were largely based on memorization and diligence, rote learning gained much popularity in China. Meanwhile, the altruistic pursuits for learning in the Confucian ideology were being increasingly challenged by learning for personal gains.

In the early twentieth century, Western educational ideas were formally introduced to China as subjects like mathematics and science were made part of official curricula for the first time (Yu, 2005). Students started to try new and more creative ways of learning and rote learning was less popular than before. After the founding of the People's Republic of China, learning was given a strong political tone as the general public were effectively motivated to do their best in learning in order to catch up with the West (Tian, 2009). However, learning was largely reduced to memorizing and reciting Mao's works during the Cultural Revolution (1966–1976), when Confucian teachings were virtually banned. As soon as the political catastrophe was over, the national college entrance examination was restored, which also saw a resumption of examination-oriented learning and teaching. Although the Confucian thoughts were reintroduced as compulsory curriculum for readings in classical Mandarin and his classic learning strategies were re-adopted by Chinese learners, learning to learn has become increasingly domain-specific in China ever since the 1980s. For example, there are numerous papers and popular books on how to study a certain subject (see, for example, Wei, 2010). Apart from rote learning, the so-called 'sea of items' pedagogical techniques, which prioritize factual knowledge and memorization, also are becoming common among Chinese learners.

The Chinese Government has realized the serious damage rote learning can have on Chinese students mainly because their potential to utilize knowledge is restricted, and they are instructed to act mainly as passive recipients of knowledge and lack creativity and critical thinking (Biggs & Watkins, 2001). Another development was that the Chinese version of the UNESCO report *Learning to Be* (UNESCO, 1972), which has been republished several times in China ever since its first publication in 1984, was well received by Chinese educational authorities, educators, and academia (Gao, 2000). It has had a continuing positive impact on the making of Chinese educational policies. The book listed 'learning to learn' as one of the pillars of 'learning to be' and the term 'learning to learn' was formally introduced to China. Therefore, the last decade saw a number of educational initiatives that encouraged inquiry-based learning and learning-centred education in China. In particular, the nationwide curriculum reforms that have been carried out since 2004 made learning to learn a legitimate part of the national policy by advocating that the process of acquiring fundamental knowledge and skills should also be the one of learning to learn (Ministry of Education, 2005).

A cultural dimension on learning to learn: From East to West

Learning to learn may be seen as a higher-order entity but within a context that incorporates general principles of effective learning and should not be separated from learning itself (Black et al., 2006). Humans conceptualize and approach learning in rich but varied ways and human understanding of learning may differ substantially due to cultural values and priorities (Li, 2002a). The cultural models of learning as suggested by Li (2002b) are meaning systems that are more complex than single notions of intelligence and discrete or dichotomous concepts. Therefore, when investigating issues of learning to learn, we must take into account different cultural contexts, diversified general principles of effective learning, and various cultural models of learning.

Confucius' influence in Chinese history can be compared with that of Socrates in the West (Aoki, 2006). They both have a strong impact on the way people learn in the two cultures. Socrates, nevertheless, held a very different approach to learning from Confucius. From his perspective, learning is focused mainly on questioning, evaluating, and generating knowledge (Jacobsen, 1999). Socrates went as far as to encourage learners to challenge or even publicly humiliate authority figures. This is in sharp contrast to the Confucian ideal of modest and introverted learning mainly from respected others.

Socratic-oriented learning in a Western cultural context, as defined within the framework of Tweed and Lehman (2002), views overt and private questioning, the expression of personal hypotheses, and a desire for self-directed tasks as general principles of effective learning. Based on the data collected from college students in China and the USA, Li (2002a, 2002b, 2003b) found that the contemporary American and Chinese conceptions about learning are quite different. According to Li's work, the US learning model basically presents a 'mind orientation' towards learning, denoting the very active nature of mental processes and inquiry-oriented activities that follow the principles of Socratic-oriented learning. However, this learning model does not seem to evoke passionate affect or to be intimately connected to the emotional, spiritual or moral lives of the respondents (Li, 2002a: 56). On the other hand, Li (2002a, 2003b) found that members of Chinese culture often regard learning as a personal relationship built by the individual between themselves and the knowledge that they aim to acquire. Chinese learning beliefs therefore display a person orientation elaborating on personal causation of learning (Li, 2002a). It is demonstrated in general principles of effective learning in a Chinese culture where an exemplary learner is expected to cultivate high aspirations and the eagerness to learn. They engage in lifelong learning and remain humble, diligent, concentrated, and steadfastly perseverant, even in poverty or other adverse learning conditions. These are consistent with the Confucian values for learning.

Pratt and Wong (1999) found that culturally Chinese learners are likely to view learning as a sequential four-stage process: memorizing, understanding, applying, and questioning or modifying. The possible criticism set at the end of the learning process is in contrast with learners' questioning and evaluating throughout the process as often encouraged in the West. Chinese learners also seem to be more sensitive to power relationships in learning than their Western counterparts because they tend to believe that overt doubt may disrupt harmonious learning relationships. Therefore, Chinese students are more likely to withhold questions that threaten the power distance between themselves and respected others. Taking the Socratic approach in a Chinese context and being insensitive to the social consequences of public criticism of authorities can result in the disruption of learning (Tweed & Lehman, 2002).

Real-world Chinese learners' narratives on the Confucian learning to learn perspective

Enculturation does not produce one-to-one mirror correspondence between a given learning cultural model and members of the culture but results in individuals' varied appropriations of the cultural model (Strauss, 1992). Below are four learning narratives from Chinese university students and university graduates. They provide original in-depth data about individual Chinese learners' experiences with the Confucian theory of learning to learn in their particular setting and life history.

> The Confucian influence is in our blood, though we cannot say for sure what he said exactly. He was a great person being able to say those things about

learning 2000 years ago. 'When walking in a company of three, one is certainly my teacher' [quote from the Analects] is always a great inspiration to me. It reminds me to see the merits of others and maintain a sense of humility in learning, so that I will benefit from good learning relationships and can learn a lot from others.

(Student A, a female third-year major in Oil Painting)

I think a thorough grasp of Confucius' thoughts about learning allows you to avoid detours in your studies. It can also help improve your performance in learning. For example, '. . . to know what is new by keeping fresh in his mind what he is already familiar with'. If you keep on doing new items but don't summarize what you have learned, then the effect is likely to be unsatisfactory. Also, 'Do not be ashamed to seek the advice of those who are of lower status.' I feel that every person has something worthy for you to learn, so I will ask the people around questions and do not care who it is.

(Graduate A, 10 months after graduation, about to pursue his Master in Mechanics)

Many of us learned about the Analects when we were little. Although we may learn differently from the ancients, it is still a memory shared by generations. Confucius' learning theory offered great help to my learning. In fact what my parents taught me orally about how to learn was in essence based on his theory. This is a unique experience for many Chinese people and it's irreplaceable now or ever. If someone asks me about the Confucian learning theory, I will blurt out 'Learning without thought is labour lost, thought without learning is perilous.' Having studied in the UK for such a while, I can still think of it immediately. Confucius taught us to learn to think, which is very important. But in my own learning experience, during the last 16 years I have not really thought much in my learning. A lot of things that I did were the repeated memorizations of the necessary knowledge about geography, history, literature, or mathematical formulas, chemical experiment and physics theories, etc. I think we should be required to think more and given more space to think in our learning.

(Student B, just completed her postgraduate foundation course for Business Studies in London)

Neither of my parents is intellectual but I have longed to become one ever since I was a little girl, perhaps because my grandpa was a knowledgeable person and civil official, and my granny took much pride in it. I carried on learning even though my father did not offer me much support. But Chinese society is becoming increasingly impetuous nowadays and there is a serious decay in morality. Although the Confucian moral striving sounds like a great idea, my real-life experience is that 'kind people are more likely to be bullied'. Also academic learning is less valued than before. We girls frequently hear people say, 'it is better to marry well than learning well'. Meanwhile, how well you learn often is not so important as whom you know, or what social connections you have. It's all very frustrating sometimes.

(Graduate B, two years after getting her MA in Hong Kong, currently back in China working as a language school teacher)

Discussion

Times are certainly very different now from when Confucius lived. Nevertheless, Confucius still offered much incisive insight to the development of learning to learn in contemporary times. In particular, his perspective of learning to learn has strong implications for educational policy and practice both in China and worldwide.

First of all, Confucius' learning theory consolidates the holistic concept of learning to learn as suggested by Ó Murchú (2007). On the one hand, Confucius highlighted the significance of learning by doing and asking questions, and by constant revision and practice. On the other hand, he paid special attention to such non-cognitive psychological factors as developing 'aspirations' and 'interest' for learning, and fostering 'enjoyment', 'humility', 'diligence', and 'perseverance' in learning. These are underlying psychological conditions that initiate, maintain, and promote effective learning (Zhang, 2001). In addition, Confucius attended to learners' selfhood and advocated sustainable learning throughout one's life by self-perfection. This demonstrates his belief in humans' learning and changing abilities, that one can become a better learner and a better person. Even though his thoughts originally featured a lifelong moral striving, what he described as 'an insatiable desire to learn' (7: 2) can be extended to all learning activities. It is particularly essential for learners in the twenty-first century when they must constantly update their knowledge, understanding, and skills to keep up with the rapid development of the Information Age.

Few have stressed the significance of ethics and morality for learning like Confucius did. From his perspective, moral life aspirations helps a learner be constantly motivated for learning and remain enthusiastic and persistent in the life-long learning process, which should be a journey of moral striving as well as intellectual and skill improvement. In contrast, learning to learn theories and practice in the West seem to be more focused on learners' cognitive abilities, psychological traits, and learning styles (see, for example, Riding & Rayner, 1998; Pashler et al., 2008). A good case in point is the VARK (Visual, Aural, Read/Write, and Kinaesthetic) model of learning styles developed by Neil Fleming (Fleming & Mills, 1992) that has been used widely in teaching and learning in schools in the West over the past two decades (Hawk & Shah, 2007). Yet the success of Confucian heritage culture students in international tests suggests the strength of Confucius' work ethics. Indeed, the moral integrity of a learner, such as patriotism and ethical values, is a major contributing factor in fostering life-long diligence, persistence, and concentration for learning, and above all is one of the primary purposes of education. Policy-makers and practi-tioners need to take this into account when promoting learning to learn, which means they should become more aware of the significant part that effective citizenship education plays in helping students become better learners. This is supported by the findings of the EPPI Centre (Evidence for Policy and Practice Information and Coordinating Centre, Institute of Education, University of London) review of the impact of citizenship education on student learning and achievement. They demonstrate that citizenship education pedagogies and curricular experiences can enhance student learning and achievement, resulting in the improvement in cognitive learning as well as in personal and social learning (Deakin Crick et al., 2005).

Confucius considered the role of the teacher to be highly important in promoting student learning because a good teacher spontaneously teaches students how to learn alongside imparting them subject knowledge. The Chinese Government is currently promoting learning to learn by encouraging and helping teachers to adapt their teaching to this end (Ye, 2009), and domain-specific learning to learn workshops and seminars are being held nationwide. The challenge for teachers, nevertheless, will be to move beyond the traditional didactic pedagogy to cultivate learning to learn in the classroom. Teachers also need to be active learners themselves so that they can serve as change agents in promoting learning to learn among students (Lee, 2005).

Many of the Confucian ideas on learning later became sayings, proverbs, and idioms, which have been widespread among the Chinese people for centuries. Along with other Chinese proverbs and idioms about learning to learn (see Table 5.2), they inspired many Chinese learners on their learning journey as learning mottos. Simple as proverbs and sayings are, they may be much more effective in popularizing learning to learn among the general public than academic or political discourse.

The narrative data in the study demonstrates that individual learners may appropriate, negotiate, and even reject the Confucian learning cultural values in different personal settings. However, as D'Andrade (1995) suggests, provided that children are socialized in their own cultural contexts, the learning values of their cultures are bound to exert a directive force on their thinking, feelings, behaviour, and outcomes of learning. So the development of a strong learning to learn culture is essential to having an impact on individual learners. Tweed and Lehman (2002) point out that those students who can flex their learning approach

Table 5.2 Popular Chinese proverbs about learning

Learning to learn ideas	Proverbs
One needs to pursue lifelong and lifewide learning	'Keep on learning as long as one lives' 'There is no boundary to learning'
Learning is essential to being human	'A knife will rust without sharpening; a person will fall backwards without learning'
Diligence, steadfastness, and concentration are required to achieve any serious learning	'Long-term diligence is the road to the mount of knowledge; endurance of hardship is the boat to the boundless sea of learning' 'It takes more than one cold day for the river to freeze three feet deep'

in response to different cultural cues in the academic environment may hold an advantage in the frequent international educational exchanges at the moment. The cultural dimension of learning to learn developed in this study thus means that in this age of globalization, learners need to adapt how they learn to different learning cultures. It also suggests that learners should be encouraged and instructed to combine different learning cultural models to optimize their learning. Given both the strengths and weaknesses of the Eastern and Western learning models, the East and the West should come and discuss at the 'middle zone' how learners can benefit from the general principles of effective learning in another culture. Some scholars have made attempts at this initiative. For instance, Perkins (1992) encourages both thoughtful acquisition (Confucian) and critical inquiry (Socratic) so that students obtain knowledge and thinking skills that become fully understood and active in many domains. This leads to the development of a 'third way' for learning that integrates the best of the East and West approaches to learning to learn in response to global challenges. As Fig. 5.1 shows, it is a more holistic model that is set in a harmonious learning ecology built of respect, trust, and willingness to share. The model combines the morality and ethics of learning, the reflective acquisition of knowledge, and the readiness to seek joy from lifelong learning with critical inquiry and making the best of learning styles and strategies that suit the individual.

Conclusions

The last decade saw a renaissance of the Confucian philosophy in China including his teachings about learning to learn (Mooney, 2007). His conceptualization of learning to learn as 'learning to conduct oneself, to think and do, and to enjoy learning for life' was revisited by many Chinese educators and practitioners to reform the way Chinese learn, which has been overly examination-oriented. Confucian teachings about learning to learn also have a universal appeal, since they provide a framework that supports the holistic concept of learning to learn and leads to all-round development of the learner in the form of lifelong self-perfection. Confucius thus offered useful perspectives for discussion on the kind of forces that would shape the future of effective learning in school and beyond (Lee, 2005).

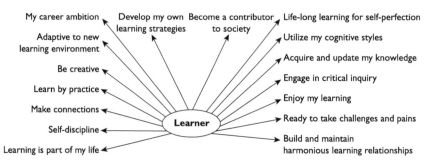

Figure 5.1 A holistic learning to learn model integrating Eastern and Western ideas.

Further research is certainly needed into this topic. There needs to be more empirical research on the effects of the Confucian learning to learn perspective on Chinese learners, especially its transmission to the young, and how it may benefit learning in other cultural contexts. Also, as suggested by Li (2002b), the complexity of the Confucian learning model merits careful examination both in theory and practice. In addition, the holistic learning to learn model proposed in this chapter needs further conceptualization and development and the benefits of integrating both East and West approaches to learning to learn in the contemporary globalized world we live in should be validated by research. Besides the word 'learn', Confucius also used 'study' in his teaching, which warrants an in-depth investigation into how 'study' and 'learn' are conceptualized in different ways. Furthermore, academic domain-specific learning to learn as well as the possible differences between learning to learn in an academic domain and a non-academic domain also merit further inquiry.

Confucian learning to learn perspectives have endured and are very likely to survive challenges such as social upheaval and political setbacks as well as materialism. This is because his thoughts concern the ethical selfhood of the learner, which is the essence of being human. Educational policy-makers, researchers, and practitioners should develop the vision to build a learning to learn culture where learning flourishes for all. That was the very ideal Confucius had for human learning.

References

Aoki, K. (2006) 'Confucius vs. Socrates: The impact of educational traditions of East and West in a global age', *International Journal of Learning*, *14*, 35–40.

Biesta, G., Hodkinson, P., & Goodson, I. (2005) 'Combining life history and life-course approaches in researching lifelong learning: Some methodological observations from the "Learning Lives" Project'. Paper presented at the TLRP Research Capacity Building Network (RCBN) Conference, Cardiff, 22 February.

Biggs, J.B., & Watkins, D. (2001) 'Insights into teaching the Chinese learner', in D. Watkins & J.B. Biggs (Eds.) *Teaching the Chinese learner: Psychological and pedagogical perspectives*. Hong Kong: Comparative Education and Research Centre.

Black, P., McCormick, R., James, M., & Pedder, D. (2006) 'Assessment for learning and learning how to learn: A theoretical enquiry', *Research Papers in Education*, *21*, 119–132.

Chang, G. (2009) 'Confucian viewpoints about learning and their implications for the construction of a learning society', *Adult Education*, *11*, 15–17.

Confucius (2008) *The Analects* (Chinese-English edition, B. Yang & D.C. Lau, trans.). Beijing: Zhonghua Book Company (Original work published ca. 479 BCE).

D'Andrade, R. (1995) *The development of cognitive anthropology*. Cambridge: Cambridge University Press.

Deakin Crick, R., Taylor, M., Tew, M., Samuel, E., Durant, K., & Ritchie, S. (2005) *A systematic review of the impact of citizenship education on student learning and achievement*. Research Evidence in Education Library. London: EPPI Centre, Social Science Research Unit, University of London Institute of Education.

Dillon, S. (2010) 'Top test scores from Shanghai stun educators', *The New York Times*, 7 December.

Fleming, N., & Mills, C. (1992) 'Not another inventory, rather a catalyst for reflection', *To Improve the Academy*, *11*, 137–155.

Forrester, G., Motteram, G., & Liu, B. (2006) 'Transforming Chinese teachers' thinking, learning and understanding via e-learning', *Journal of Education for Teaching*, *32*, 197–212.

Gao, W. (2000) 'Learning to learn and learning strategies', *Review of Foreign Education*, *21*, 48–52.

Hawk, T.F., & Shah, A.J. (2007) 'Using learning style instruments to enhance Student learning', *Decision Sciences Journal of Innovative Education*, *5*(1), 1–19.

Jacobsen, D.A. (1999) *Philosophy in classroom teaching: Bridging the gap*. Upper Saddle River, NJ: Merrill.

Lee, W.O. (1996) 'The cultural context for Chinese learners: Conceptions of learning in the Confucian tradition', in D.A. Watkins & J.B. Biggs (Eds.) *The Chinese learner*. Hong Kong: Comparative Education Research Centre.

Lee, Y.P. (2005) 'Forces shaping the future of teaching and learning of mathematics', *Educational Research for Policy and Practice*, *4*, 169–179.

Li, J. (2002a) 'Learning models in different cultures', *New Directions for Child and Adolescent Development*, *96*, 45–63.

Li, J. (2002b) 'A cultural model of learning: Chinese "heart and mind for wanting to learn"', *Journal of Cross-Cultural Psychology*, *33*, 248–269.

Li, J. (2003a) 'The core of Confucian learning', *American Psychologist*, *57*, 146–147.

Li, J. (2003b) 'U.S. and Chinese cultural beliefs about learning', *Journal of Educational Psychology*, *95*, 258–267.

Littrellin, R.F. (2005) 'Learning styles of students in and from Confucian cultures', in I. Alon & J.R. McIntyre (Eds.) *Business and management education in China: Transition, pedagogy and training*. Singapore: World Scientific.

Liu, N.F., & Littlewood, W. (1997) 'Why do many students appear reluctant to participate in classroom learning discourse?', *System*, *25*, 371–384.

Ministry of Education (2005) *Fundamental theories for the new curriculum reform*. Beijing: Ministry of Education.

Mooney, P. (2007) 'Confucius comes back: In China, once-banned works by the country's most influential philosopher are studied and celebrated', *Chronicle of Higher Education*, 20 April.

Ng, G.W. (2000) 'From Confucian master teacher to Freirian mutual learner: Challenges in pedagogical practice and religious education', *Religious Education*, *95*, 308–319.

Ó Murchú, D. (2007) 'Interactive technologies, active citizenship and learning to learn: A global challenge', in *Proceedings of Society for Information Technology and Teacher Education International Conference*. Chesapeake, VA: AACE.

Oxford, R.L., & Burry-Stock, J.A. (1995) 'Assessing the use of language learning strategies worldwide with ESL/EFL version of the Strategy Inventory for Language Learning (SILL)', *System*, *23*, 153–175.

Pashler, H., McDaniel, M., Rohrer, D., & Bjork, R. (2008) 'Learning styles: Concepts and evidence', *Psychological Science in the Public Interest*, *9*, 105–119.

Perkins, D. (1992) *Smart schools: Better thinking and learning for every child*. New York: Free Press.

Pratt, D.D., & Wong, K.M. (1999) 'Chinese conceptions of "effective teaching" in Hong Kong: Towards culturally sensitive evaluation of teaching', *International Journal of Lifelong Learning*, *18*, 241–258.

Riding, R., & Rayner, S. (1998) *Cognitive styles and learning strategies: Understanding style differences in learning and behaviour.* London: David Fulton.

Song, T., & Yang, L. (2009) *A contemporary annotation and translation of Great Learning and The Doctrine of Mean.* Chongqing: Chongqing Press.

Strauss, C. (1992) 'Models of motives', in R.G. D'Andrade & C. Strauss (Eds.) *Human motives and cultural models.* Cambridge: Cambridge University Press.

Tian, J. (2009) 'Essence of the "learning to learn" educational ideology of Qian Wei Chang', *China Adult Education, 21,* 115–116.

Tu, W.M. (1979) *Humanity and self-cultivation: Essays in Confucian thought.* Berkeley, CA: Asian Humanities Press.

Tweed, R.G., & Lehman, D.R. (2002) 'Learning considered within a cultural context: Confucian and Socratic approaches', *American Psychologist, 57,* 89–99.

UNESCO (1972) *Learning to be: The world of education today and tomorrow.* Paris: UNESCO.

Wei, G. (2010) *Learning to learn.* Nanjing: Southeast University Press.

Wong, N.Y. (2008) 'Confucian heritage culture learner's phenomenon: From "exploring the middle zone" to "constructing a bridge"', *Mathematics Education, 40,* 973–981.

Yang, W., & Lin, L. (2003) 'The contemporary significance of Confucian teachings on learning', *Journal of China Southeast Guizhou National Teachers' College, 21,* 87–92.

Ye, L. (2009) *Research of the basic education reform and reconstruction of pedagogical theory in China.* Beijing: Economic Science Press.

Yu, Q. (2005) *A brief history of Chinese education.* Beijing: Central Open University Press.

Zhang, C. (2001) 'Learning-centred pedagogy of Confucius and its implications', *Studies of Educational History, 2,* 1898–1905.

Part II

International research and practice

Chapter 6

Learning to learn in early childhood

Home and preschool influences on Chinese learners

Nirmala Rao, Jin Sun, and Li Zhang

Abstract

This chapter considers how the attitudes and skills related to learning to learn are facilitated among Chinese learners in the home and preschool during the early years. First, we review research on early cognitive socialization focusing on studies that have considered how children's learning to learn skills, including behavioural regulation and problem-solving skills, are promoted in Chinese families. Next, we consider the role of preschool curricula and teachers' practices on the development of skills related to learning to learn. We then discuss the ways in which experiences at home and in early childhood programmes work together to promote learning to learn and achievement among young Chinese children.

Key words: early cognitive socialization, Chinese learners, preschool curricula, home context.

Introduction

Researchers from different parts of the world have been interested in explaining the consistently high performance of Chinese students in cross-national tests of achievement such as the Trends in International Mathematics and Science Study (TIMSS) (Mullis et al., 2004a, 2004b) and the Programme for International Student Assessment (PISA) (OECD, 2007, 2009). Chinese children have also been found to exhibit higher levels of behavioural regulation than their counterparts from other cultural backgrounds during the early years (Rubin et al., 2006; Wanless et al., 2011). Why do these children do so well in tests of achievement and behavioural regulation? One explanation is that as 'Chinese learners' (Watkins & Biggs, 1996) they are influenced by the Confucian value system, which emphasizes academic achievement, diligence in academic pursuits, the belief that all children can do well through the exertion of effort regardless of innate ability, and the significance of education for personal improvement and moral self-cultivation (Lee, 1996; Li, 2003; Rao & Chan, 2009). These Confucian values are evident in Chinese families regardless of the political structure of the society in which they live and influence Chinese families in Mainland China, Hong Kong, Taiwan, Singapore, and those living in non-Chinese societies. We consider the influences of Confucian values and their influence on learning to learn.[1]

We consider learning to learn as both a basic competence and a process relevant to knowledge construction, application, and generalization. It includes cognitive, metacognitive, motivational, and socio-affective processes enacted in a cultural context. Given our focus on the early years, our definition of learning to learn privileges young children's learning-related skills such as persistence, attentiveness, and interest in learning, and the role of parents and teachers in the cultivation of this competence.

In the following sections, we review studies that have considered how children's learning to learn skills, including problem-solving and self-regulation, are promoted in preschools and families in rural and urban China. Specifically, we report on studies that have addressed: (i) parental involvement in early learning in Beijing, Shenzhen, Hong Kong, and Singapore (Li & Rao, 2000; Lau et al., 2011); (ii) pedagogical practices in mathematics teaching in pre-primary classes and early primary classrooms, and teacher-child interactions in kindergartens in Hong Kong (Ng & Rao, 2008; Chen & Rao, 2011); (iii) scaffolding interactions of Chinese mothers and teachers in problem-solving with preschool children in Beijing (Sun & Rao, 2012a, 2012b); and (iv) the influence of different types of preschool experience on the development of self-regulation in children in rural China (Zhang & Rao, 2012). The results from these studies help us to better understand how learning to learn is facilitated in Chinese families and preschool programmes.

Early cognitive socialization in Chinese families

The family, the first and most influential context of development for a child, is where educational competence is developed and nurtured (Cole, 1985). The family environment influences childhood cognitive abilities directly through environmental transmission and indirectly through correlations with parents' child-rearing behaviours (Coon et al., 1990). We focus on the latter in this chapter.

Child-rearing behaviours, including parenting style, parenting beliefs, socialization goals, and parenting practices, influence child development (Darling & Steinberg, 1993). Using the dimensions of warmth and control, Western theories classify parenting as reflecting authoritative, authoritarian, permissive or neglectful styles (Baumrind, 1971). Authoritarian parenting reflects low warmth and high control. Chinese parents have been considered more authoritarian than their American counterparts (Chiu, 1987; Lin & Fu, 1990), but they have also been shown to facilitate children's performance through exercising a combination of both authoritarian and authoritative parenting in a single situation (Xu et al., 2005). For example, Chinese parents foster children's ability by stressing obedience to rules and adult authority but they also express warmth in a more subtle way by being supportive and sensitive to their children's needs (Chao, 1994). Chinese parenting reflects *guan* ('to govern', 'to care for', and 'to love') and *chiao shun* (training), behaviours that cannot be adequately captured by the terms authoritarian or authoritative parenting (Chao, 1994). *Guan* (governing) is considered as parents' responsibility and *chiao shun* (training) is the continuous monitoring and correcting of children's behaviour to ensure that children are not falling short of societal standards.

The culturally relevant constructs of *guan* and *chiao shun*, which are manifestations of Chinese parenting, are important in understanding the development of learning to learn in Chinese children. Chinese parenting practices and parental expectations for children's behaviour may be the reason why Chinese children show relatively high behavioural and emotional inhibition, which is an important precursor of learning to learn. In support of this contention, research indicates that Chinese mothers report using more physical coercion and higher levels of directiveness than American mothers (Wu et al., 2002). Chinese parents socialize children to avoid expression of thoughts and feelings, to show behavioural conformity (Ho, 1996), and to regulate their behaviours at home, especially around older family members (Hsieh, 2004). For example, children are required to greet senior family members and show respect to elders in multiple daily scenarios such as eating after the elders, sitting still, and remaining silent when older family members are speaking. They are also taught to be modest, shy, sensitive, cooperative, and to take responsibility for their actions (Wu et al., 2002).

Chinese parents' emphasis on academic achievement may also influence children's learning to learn. Chinese mothers have reported a stronger emphasis on socialization for academic achievement, exertion of effort, and filial piety than mothers from English and Indian cultures (Pearson & Rao, 2003; Rao et al., 2003). Furthermore, Chinese parents, regardless of whether they are the urban privileged or urban poor, emphasize school learning as the path to upward social mobility (Chi & Rao, 2003). Parents of rural preschoolers reported that mastering some pre-academic skills and liking preschool were keys to children's school readiness (Zhang, 2008).

Research has also indicated that Chinese parents' involvement is related to their children's school readiness and literacy achievement. Lau and colleagues (2011) examined involvement in early cognitive and academic learning at home among parents of kindergarten children from Hong Kong and Shenzhen, two economically advanced cities in China. Parents reported being involved in their children's early education at home through homework supervision and the provision of language and cognitive activities, and their home-based involvement predicted children's school readiness. The extent of parental involvement in literacy activities at home also significantly contributed to their children's Chinese literacy attainment in Beijing, Hong Kong, and Singapore, even though there were differences in overall literacy attainment in the three cities (Li & Rao, 2000).

These findings suggest the socialization of young Chinese children by their parents to achieve academic learning goals, which reflect the motivational component of learning to learn from an early age. Furthermore, research also shows that Chinese children show better effortful control, which is an important component of learning to learn skills, than American children, as early as infancy (Gartstein et al., 2006). Taken together, these results suggest that Chinese children are encouraged to exert great effort in learning during the early years and this may set the stage for the development of learning to learn skills.

It is also important to consider societal changes when examining children's early socialization. Since the 1980s, Mainland China has experienced considerable economic growth and felt the impact of westernization. Social and economic changes have not only improved standards of living and education, but have also offered more opportunities for learning about other parts of the world. Mainland Chinese parents who have been exposed to western patterns of child-rearing are more likely to appreciate inductive reasoning, democratic forms of control, flexibility, and respect for individualization over power, assertive, restrictive, and directive approaches to child-rearing (Chen et al., 2000; Xu et al., 2005). In the past, Chinese parents merely wanted children to achieve high grades so they could progress to the next stage in the highly competitive pyramidal system of education. However, we believe that in addition to the focus on academic achievement, contemporary educated urban Chinese parents are now keen to cultivate in their children an interest in learning. This is partly due to the influences of western ideology.

Another important factor influencing Chinese socialization in Mainland China is the one-child policy, which was implemented in the 1980s. In urban areas, the majority of couples have only one child and this has eliminated the sibling system in the family. In line with traditional norms, most Chinese parents are immensely devoted to their children and sacrifice much to meet their children's needs (Chang et al., 2004). Thus, the only child might have a closer relationship with parents, receive more instruction and care, and be provided with more resources to facilitate his or her development.

Against this background, we believe that, on the one hand, Chinese urban parents tend to adopt more democratic and permissive approaches to parenting because of socio-contextual changes. On the other hand, deeply embedded Confucian values are still evident in Chinese parenting practices. Children are taught to be modest, obedient, self-disciplined, and diligent through *guan* or *chiao shun* in a loving family environment. The latter may help to promote the learning to learn skills of young children. However, very few studies have directly addressed how children's skills related to learning to learn are facilitated within Chinese families.

Preschool practices and the early development of learning to learn in Chinese contexts

As is the case for parenting practices, preschool education in Chinese societies is markedly influenced by Confucian values. Hence the nature of preschool experience in these societies may also promote the development of children's behavioural regulation. For example, the Confucian doctrine places a premium on respect for teachers and proper behaviour. Children are expected to obey their teachers' instructions and Chinese preschool children generally appear to be more orderly, attentive, and show more self-discipline in the kindergarten than their counterparts in western countries, such as the United States where independence is encouraged and children are given both the time and the liberty to choose to engage in a range of activities in preschool settings (Pang & Richey,

2007). Furthermore, relatively large class sizes and the prevalence of whole-class/large group teaching in the Chinese setting necessitate a considerable degree of discipline by the teacher and compliance on the part of the students for classroom learning to occur. Children have to listen carefully and follow the teacher's instructions and control their impulsiveness. Indeed these skills – attention, memory, inhibition – are three key components of behavioural regulation (McClelland et al., 2007) and children's learning to learn skills.

Although preschools in Mainland China have been characterized as being rigid and over-regimented due to the influence of Confucian values, these characteristics may have actually facilitated children's behavioural and emotional regulation (Pang & Richey, 2007). Yet, over the years, there have been progressive changes in preschool education due to the influence of globalization and research-based knowledge about how children learn best. Steps to foster child-initiated activities, independence, and creativity have been taken in preschools and the early education context now reflects the combined influences of both Chinese and western ideas (Tobin et al., 2009). It should be noted that the academic orientation in the Chinese educational system is not accompanied by a neglect of other domains of development at least during the early years. Young children's social and emotional development has gained as much attention as physical, cognitive, and language development in the preschool curriculum.

In 1989, the State Education Commission in Mainland China released *The regulations on kindergarten education practice (on a trial basis[2])*, a watershed for Chinese preschool and early education (Chan & Mellor, 2002). Western educational beliefs, such as respecting children, supporting children's interests, encouraging child-initiated learning, and cultivating children's approaches towards learning (see Table 6.1) rather than academic knowledge were gradually being accepted and promoted in Chinese preschools (Liu & Feng, 2005). In the *Kindergarten educational practice guidelines*, released by the Ministry of Education in 2001, it is clearly stated that one of the general rules for preschool

Table 6.1 Comparison of the features of traditional Chinese and Western approaches to child rearing in preschool programmes

Dimensions	Traditional Chinese culture	Western culture
Perspective on children	A dependent child	An independent child
Atmosphere in the classroom	Teacher-centred/-controlled	Child-centred/-initiated
Learning goal	High academic achievement	Creativity and interest in learning
Method of learning knowledge	Memorization and repeated practice	Learning through understanding
Learning dispositions	Impulse control, persistence, attentiveness, exertion of effort, and following teachers' instructions	Self-exploration, self-direction, individuality, and curiosity

education should be to facilitate children's active learning through the provision of learning activities related to their daily lives. The main components of learning to learn skills and attitudes, including promoting children's curiosity, problem-solving, collaborative learning, pleasure and engagement in learning, emotional regulation, and appropriate behaviour have been explicitly emphasized as the educational goals for domains of health, science, and social education.

The development of children's skills related to learning to learn has also been increasingly recognized as an important outcome of high-quality preschool education in Shanghai (Shanghai Education Commission, 2008).[3] It has been recommended that children's approaches to learning are evaluated as part of the early childhood programme evaluation strategy. These are defined as having an interest in learning, being good at asking questions, observing and listening carefully, enjoying trying new things, being serious and persistent in completing learning tasks, being satisfied with learning outcomes, and using educational materials and toys carefully.

The trend towards emphasizing holistic, child-centred preschool education is also evident in pre-primary curriculum guidelines in Hong Kong. The Hong Kong Government issued *Guides to the pre-primary curriculum* in 1996 and in 2006 (Education Department, 1996, 2006). The 1996 guide was concerned with principles of curriculum design and implementation, while the 2006 guide was more explicit in advocating a child-centred approach to education and stressed children's enjoyment of learning. The 2006 guide stated that the teacher's role was to help children construct knowledge and not merely to transmit knowledge to children. Emphasis was also placed on helping children acquire appropriate learning-related skills and attitudes.

The relevant changes in terms of the preschool curriculum guidelines and the incorporation of western ideologies in Chinese societies suggest that increased efforts have been exerted to foster the early development of learning to learn abilities. These changes have been reflected in teachers' pedagogical practices. For example, Ng and Rao (2008) examined early mathematics instruction in Hong Kong and found that a child-centred and play-based approach, which is important for promoting children's interest, motivation, and engagement in learning, was evident in classrooms (Table 6.2). However, teachers also emphasized discipline and diligence during teaching because of traditional Chinese beliefs. Chen and Rao (2011) observed teacher–child interactions and peer exchanges in four kindergartens in Hong Kong and the results indicated that teachers spent a considerable amount of time ensuring that children displayed proper behaviour (sitting and lining up appropriately) and self-control, although there were gender differences in their interactions with boys and girls. Children's active learning and engagement are also facilitated via 'Eduplay', a form of play-based education with 'Chinese characteristics' prevalent in urban preschools in Mainland China (Rao & Li, 2008). In this form of play, teachers promote the learning of basic concepts during 'free-play' time. For example, if a child is playing with blocks, the teacher asks the child to name the colours of the different blocks or to count the blocks.

Table 6.2 Mathematics teaching during the early years in Hong Kong

Characteristics of teaching	Description
Child-centred approach	Children were offered the opportunity to make their own decisions, for instance, how to use the materials
Play-based approach	In kindergartens, discovery learning was promoted through manipulatives and activities. Hands-on and minds-on activities were used to help children construct meaningful knowledge
Emphasis on discipline	Children were required to remain silent in classrooms and listen to and follow the teachers' instructions
Emphasis on effort and practice	Repeated practice was stressed in the process of teaching and diligence was emphasized as a key to success

Note: Data were collected through observation of 27 lessons and teacher interviews in three preprimary schools and three primary schools in Hong Kong.

Analyses of state curriculum documents in Hong Kong and Mainland China suggest that the importance of learning to learn in early education contexts is recognized, and observations suggest that Confucian values, which ostensibly support the development of learning to learn skills, are evident in classrooms. Under such values, children are required to show respect for their teachers, adhere to classroom discipline, and control their behaviour. But how do specific preschool experiences influence learning to learn? Do children with and without preschool experience differ in their learning to learn skills? Zhang and Rao (2012) examined the relationship between preschool experience and the development of self-regulation in rural China. A total of 190 children who had attended kindergarten, attended separate pre-primary classes, 'sat in' Grade 1 classes,[4] and had no preschool experience were administered the revised Head-Toes-Knees-Shoulders task (Ponitz et al., 2009) both at the beginning (Wave 1) and the end of Grade 1 (Wave 2), and seven executive function tests[5] at the end of Grade 2 (Wave 3) (see Fig. 6.1) (Zhang, 2013). Results indicated that preschool experience significantly influenced children's self-regulation. Children from kindergarten and the separate pre-primary classes showed better self-regulation than the other two groups through the three waves of study. Children 'sitting in' Grade 1 classes had better self-regulation skills than those without preschool experience in the latter two waves. Further classroom observations showed that the kindergarten teachers engaged in more of the behaviours that are conducive to the development of children's learning to learn skills than teachers of pre-primary or Grade 1 classes. They posed open-ended questions to engage children, and provided children with a variety of learning activities and clear instructions. The separate pre-primary class teachers prepared fewer activities for children and frequently required them to sit still and follow the class rules just like primary school children. Preschool-aged children in Grade 1 classes were neglected by their

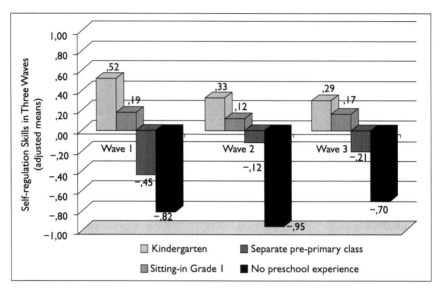

Figure 6.1 Pattern of differences in self-regulation skills for children with different preschool experience across the three waves.

Note: Children's scores in self-regulation tests across the three waves were standardized.

teachers and were only disciplined when these young children's inappropriate behaviours seriously disrupted the learning processes.

In summary, we believe that traditional Chinese (Confucian) values, which stress politeness and proper behaviours, respect for the teacher, and self-control are manifest in early Chinese classrooms. Some of these values are important components of learning to learn in Chinese contexts. At the same time, more progressive views about how to support early learning, including child-initiated activities, fostering the enjoyment of learning, and a holistic approach to the curriculum are also reflected in contemporary Chinese early childhood class-rooms. Just like 'Eduplay' mentioned earlier, both play and learning have been accorded importance in Chinese early childhood classrooms. Children are provided with different choices. In these contexts, teachers play a role of a supporter, collaborator, and guide and maintain order and discipline in the classrooms. There is a fusion of the old and the new (Rao et al., 2009) and we posit that contemporary early education in Chinese societies promotes the early development of learning-related skills and attitudes.

Home and preschool practices and learning to learn in early childhood

The family and school are two primary contexts for early child development and both are part of the microsystem in Bronfenbrenner's (1979) ecological model. Furthermore, behaviour in one setting influences behaviour in the other, and positive connections between microsystem settings support child development (Ritchie & Howes, 2003). Parent–child interaction at home is likely to affect caregiver–child interaction in the child-care setting, and vice versa. For example, if both teachers and parents read to the child, this better promotes early literacy development.

Since the publication of the Coleman Report (Coleman et al., 1966) in the USA and the Plowden Report (Plowden, 1967) in the United Kingdom, there has been a vigorous debate about the extent to which families and schools influence children's school outcomes (Hung & Marjoribanks, 2005). However, researchers acknowledge that it is very important that the family and school stress similar values and hold similar priorities for child development. According to Hess and Holloway (1984), a match between children's experiences in the family and school appears to be advantageous for children, whereas a mismatch may delay or hinder children's optimal development, because of parents' and teachers' distinct purposes in their interactions with children (Lehrer & Shumow, 1997). Therefore, a smooth and successful transition between the home and school largely depends on the adequacy of communications between the two contexts, whether activities in the two contexts reinforce each other, and whether teachers and parents are respectful of each other and work together for the benefit of children (Laosa, 1977). In addition, Pianta and Walsh (1996) proposed a 'contextual systems model' to describe an organized system in which children develop. According to this model, the family and school systems operate together to shape children's academic outcomes and school experiences. When parents and teachers give students consistent (positive) messages and guidance about academic and behavioural expectations, children are likely to attain their optimal learning outcomes.

Do home–preschool interactions in the Chinese context typically facilitate the development of learning to learn skills and attitudes in early years? Studies have shown that Chinese parents are more directive and knowledge-centred than their western counterparts. For example, researchers comparing Euro-American and Chinese parents' interactions with children in mathematics learning have found that Chinese parents instruct in a more formal, structured, and direct way and provide more encouragement for children's mathematics-related activities than do Euro-American parents (Huntsinger et al., 1997). Chinese parents also offer a more supportive family environment for children's mathematical learning than western parents (Wang, 2004). In addition, Pan and her colleagues (2006) found that both Chinese and American mothers adopted concept-focused and calculation-focused instructions in their interactions involving mathematics-related activities. Chinese mothers taught more calculation in daily life than American mothers; and unlike their American counterparts, their instructions were related to children's learning of proportional reasoning. As mentioned earlier, such interaction patterns reflect traditional Chinese beliefs about early learning and education. However, are parent–child interaction patterns similar to teacher–child interaction patterns in situations related to academic learning? Does the extent of congruence between mother–child and teacher–child interaction patterns affect children's specific learning outcomes and general learning to learn skills?

Sun and Rao (2012a, 2012b) and Sun (2009) compared both the interaction patterns and processes of adult–child interactions in different types of problem-solving tasks. The dyadic interactions in four problem-solving tasks (supermarket, jigsaw puzzle, worksheet, and map) between fifty-seven 5-year-old Chinese children and their mothers and teachers were observed, and adults' scaffolding during problem-solving was coded and analysed. The results indicated that teachers demonstrated a higher level of cognitive support and gave more feedback than did mothers. They adopted more heuristic scaffolding strategies, gave less negative feedback, and showed more appropriate shifts of scaffolding after children's failure to follow or lack of response than mothers (see Table 6.3). However, both mothers and teachers were inclined to be directive in terms of both their scaffolding content and scaffolding manners and tended to transfer the responsibility of problem-solving to the children (see Table 6.4). The findings further support the view that western values are increasingly evident in early childhood education in China – teachers have started to use strategies that are more helpful in children's independent problem-solving and promote children's active learning.

Such adult–child interactions may be important for the early development of learning to learn. One of the most commonly used scaffolding strategies was progress control (Sun & Rao, 2012b). Mothers and teachers used this strategy in about half of their interaction turns with children, a strategy characterized by the adult explicitly giving children step-by-step instructions to complete the task.

Table 6.3 Mothers' and teachers' scaffolding modifications after children's failure to follow or lack of response[a] (mean ± standard deviation)

	Mothers	*Teachers*
After children's failure to follow		
No shifts[b]	0.44 (0.15)[e]	0.57 (0.16)
Lower-level shifts[c]	0.30 (0.23)	0.27 (00.20)
Heuristic scaffolding content[d]	0.51 (0.13)	0.56 (0.13)
Heuristic scaffolding manner[e]	0.54 (0.13)	0.62 (0.13)
After children's lack of response		
No shifts	0.41 (0.17)	0.57 (0.17)
Lower-level shifts	0.25 (0.10)	0.26 (0.11)
Heuristic scaffolding content	0.46 (0.12)	0.58 (0.13)
Heuristic scaffolding manner	0.53 (0.13)	0.63 (0.15)

Note:
[a] All the contrasts between teachers and mothers were significant.
[b] *No shifts*: There were no differences of scaffolding level between two contiguous adult–child interaction turns.
[c] *Lower-level shifts*: Adults provided more specific support than that provided in the prior interaction turn.
[d] *Heuristic scaffolding content* refers to adults': (1) meta-cognitive supports; (2) provision of problem-solving clues when the child encountered difficulties; (3) review of the problem-solving progress or summarization of the results; and (4) recall of children's related experience to help them get the correct solution.
[e] *Heuristic scaffolding manner* refers to the way information was transferred to children in a manner of asking reflective questions or elaborating specific problem-solving steps to the child.

Table 6.4 Mothers' and teachers' scaffolding behaviours in four tasks (mean ± standard deviation)

Measures	Supermarket		Jigsaw puzzle		Worksheet		Map	
	Mother	Teacher	Mother	Teacher	Mother	Teacher	Mother	Teacher
Duration (min)	3.32 (2.91)	4.08 (2.85)	9.24 (4.07)	7.98 (3.17)	3.28 (1.71)	3.27 (2.16)	4.64 (2.02)	6.08 (2.59)
Heuristic scaffolding content	0.43 (0.15)	0.55 (0.13)	0.40 (0.15)	0.48 (0.13)	0.40 (0.15)	0.49 (0.16)	0.35 (0.09)	0.39 (0.08)
Heuristic scaffolding manners	0.63 (0.16)	0.72 (0.12)	0.31 (0.15)	0.45 (0.15)	0.49 (0.17)	0.56 (0.18)	0.70 (0.09)	0.74 (0.10)
Transfer of responsibility to child	0.68 (0.24)	0.87 (0.06)	0.70 (0.15)	0.81 (0.15)	0.86 (0.12)	0.87 (0.11)	0.68 (0.14)	0.79 (0.09)

Adults also typically transferred the responsibility of problem-solving to children. This enabled children to master more 'mature' or 'effective' ways to solve problems, which facilitated their engagement in the learning task and motivated them to focus their attention and even persevere in difficult tasks. At the same time, teachers started to apply more heuristic strategies[6] to promote children's higher-order thinking. They also faded their control of children's behaviours in problem-solving so that children learned from their mistakes.

Sun and Rao (2012a, 2012b) found that a family's socio-economic status (SES) was associated with adult–child interactions. For example, more educated mothers' scaffolding strategies were more similar to those of teachers than those of less educated mothers. By providing relatively more heuristic guidance and more positive feedback, mothers from the middle to high SES families shifted their scaffolding levels more appropriately than those from low SES backgrounds. These variations were assumed to be due to differences in available educational resources, exposure to western ideas, and maternal education. In addition, the scaffolding by teachers of children from the low SES group was less optimal than that by teachers of children from the high SES group; they were less capable of scaffolding children's problem-solving in the play-like activities than in the school-like activities. Apart from the fewer resources and lower support available to teachers of children from low SES families than for teachers of middle or upper SES children (Duke, 2000), the especially high expectations from low SES parents might influence teachers' instructions in kindergartens; as for children from a low SES background, education was considered the only path to upward social mobility. The teachers of children from the low SES families have to stress children's academic performance and consequently put more value on school-related tasks rather than the play-like tasks to prepare these children for primary schools as well as to satisfy parents. Therefore, family socio-economic status impacts scaffolding strategies and behaviours of mothers at home and teachers on preschool programmes, which further affect children's development of learning to learn skills. As a result, children from low SES families may actually have fewer opportunities to develop learning interests in non-academic domains compared with children from middle or upper SES families because of the input from both the family and preschool. This may hinder the long-term development of these disadvantaged children and exaggerate the achievement gap in the long run. Therefore, it is important for pre-service and in-service teacher training as well as parental programmes to consider the current scaffolding strategies teachers and mothers adopt and to facilitate children's learning to learn, which should include not only persistence and engagement, but also children's interest and motivation in learning, as well as flexibility in problem-solving in the early years.

The research reviewed suggests that the links between home and preschool practices have set the stage for learning to learn and learning for high achievement in Chinese contexts. What children are taught in preschool programmes is usually reinforced at home and vice versa. For example, children's self-control is emphasized in both families and preschools. The shared values between these two contexts help to promote the development of learning to learn skills in children. On the one hand, the traditional approach to child rearing in both preschools and families, including directive teaching, intense control during the learning process, and focusing on knowledge acquisition, effectively transmits formal knowledge to children in the early years and fosters their exertion of effort and persistence in learning. On the other hand, under the influences of western ideology, pedagogical practices that encourage active learning and problem-solving are gradually being adopted by parents and teachers. These will foster children's learning-related skills and attitudes, such as interest and pleasure in learning, intrinsic motivation, curiosity, and creativity.

Summary

In this chapter, we have considered how families and preschools help to promote children's learning to learn skills in Chinese societies. Parent–child interactions, teacher–child interactions, and positive home–preschool collaborations are crucial in assisting children to acquire learning to learn competencies. Both Chinese parenting and preschool education are markedly influenced by Confucian values. In the home context, Chinese parents are likely to engage children in academically-oriented activities. Children are also socialized to have good manners, follow rules and adults' instructions, and display a relatively high level of self-discipline. Similarly, in the preschool context, children are taught to be well-behaved and to follow teachers' instructions. In addition, the predominant large-group teaching approach places a high demand on children's behavioural regulation. These practices contribute considerably to the development of children's early learning-related skills. The components essential for early learning and success of children such as engagement in learning, following instructions, and self-control are promoted. With the gradual permeation of western ideology, Chinese parents and teachers have attached increasing importance to cultivating children's interest in learning, approaches to learning, their independence and creativity. Traditional parenting practices, which rely on parental control and directiveness, have waned and urban parents have now adopted some aspects of western parenting practices, including using more democratic forms of control, being more flexible, and showing respect for the individuality of children. The curriculum reform in preschools has brought new ideas on how to facilitate children's learning-related skills, and children are provided with a more active play-based curriculum. Preschools have focused on promoting children's interest in and positive attitudes towards learning. Hence, traditional Chinese pedagogy and western ideas about effective teaching and learning have been integrated in Chinese classrooms.

The linkage between home and preschool further enforces the development of children's skills related to learning to learn. The concordance of practice between home and preschool is particularly important to promote children's optimal early learning. Studies have shown that teachers tend to adopt more heuristic strategies to foster children's interest and independence in problem-solving than parents. With the support of teachers, parents may also learn how to use more effective strategies to promote learning.

However, it should also be acknowledged that children from economically disadvantaged families in China still have not been offered enough opportunities to fully develop their skills related to learning to learn. Owing to the emphasis on academic achievement, only examination performance is stressed at both home and school. These children are offered few learning opportunities in non-school-related tasks, and other skills related to learning to learn – such as interest in learning, motivation to learn, and creativity – are neglected by parents and teachers. Therefore, more effort should be exerted to better prepare children from less advantaged backgrounds for formal schooling so they too can enjoy learning to learn.

Notes

1 A more detailed discussion of Confucian values and their influence on learning to learn can be found in Chapter 5 of this volume.
2 *The regulations on kindergarten education practice (on a trial basis)* (State Education Commission, 1989) emphasized catering for individual differences and developmental appropriateness in early childhood education. In addition, it suggested that learning should be based on children's interest and that children's good habits in learning should be cultivated through daily routine and play.
3 In 2008, the Shanghai Education Commission launched the *Guidance on the evaluation of quality of early childhood care and education in Shanghai kindergartens (a trial version)* to facilitate the curriculum reform and promote the quality of early childhood care and education in kindergartens. According to the document, child development and curriculum were two main targets for evaluation. Children should be evaluated in terms of seven domains, including physical development, habits, self-awareness and self-help, cognitive development, language ability, social development, and aesthetic feelings and expression. 'Approaches to learning' was a very important aspect of the domain of habits.
4 In China, some rural primary schools allow children below 7 years of age to attend Grade 1 classes so that they can have some exposure to formal learning environments before they are officially enrolled in Grade 1. These children typically sit at the back of the class and receive exactly the same curriculum and schedule as children officially enrolled in Grade 1.
5 The seven tests tapped three main components of executive function: working memory, inhibitory control, and attention shifting. All the tests were adapted from the age-appropriate and easy-to-administer tests in literature and were modified to be more like school learning tasks. The counting span and listening recall tests were used to assess working memory. The directional Stroop, animal Stroop, and number Stroop tests were used to administer inhibitory control. The contingency naming and plus–minus tests were used to assess attention shifting skills.
6 Heuristic strategies refer to adults' provision of heuristic scaffolding content or delivery of scaffolding content in a heuristic manner in adult–child problem-solving interactions. Such strategies may include: (1) adults' metacognitive support, such as planning, reflection, and justification in problem-solving; (2) provision of problem-solving clues when the child encounters difficulties; (3) review of problem-solving progress or summarization of results; and (4) recall of children's related experience to help them get the correct solution. The adults may deliver the strategies in a manner of asking reflective questions or elaborating specific problem-solving steps to the child.

References

Baumrind, D. (1971) 'Current patterns of parental authority', *Developmental Psychology Monographs*, 4, 1–103.

Bronfenbrenner, U. (1979) *The ecology of human development*. Cambridge, MA: Harvard University Press.

Chan, L.K.S., and Mellor, E.J. (2002) *International developments in early childhood services*. New York: Peter Lang.

Chang, L., Lansford, J.E., Schwartz, D., & Farver, J.M. (2004) 'Marital quality, maternal depressed affect, harsh parenting, and child externalising in Hong Kong Chinese families', *International Journal of Behavioral Development, 28*, 311–318.

Chao, R.K. (1994) 'Beyond parental control and authoritarian parenting style: Understanding Chinese parenting through the cultural notion of training', *Child Development, 65*, 1111–1119.

Chen, E.S.L., & Rao, N. (2011) 'Gender socialization in Chinese kindergartens: Teachers' contributions', *Sex Roles, 64*, 103–116.

Chen, X., Liu, M., Li, B., Cen, G., Chen, H., & Wang, L. (2000) 'Maternal authoritative and authoritarian attitudes and mother–child interactions and relationships in urban China', *International Journal of Behavioral Development, 24*, 119–126.

Chi, J., & Rao, N. (2003) 'Parental beliefs about school learning and children's educational attainment: Evidence from rural China', *Ethos, 31*, 330–356.

Chiu, L.H. (1987) 'Child-rearing attitudes of Chinese, Chinese-American, and Anglo-American mothers', *International Journal of Psychology, 22*, 409–419.

Cole, M. (1985) 'The zone of proximal development: Where culture and cognition create each other', in J.V. Wertsch (Ed.) *Culture, communication and cognition: Vygotskian perspectives* (pp. 146–161). Cambridge: Cambridge University Press.

Coleman, J.S., Campbell, E., & Hobson, C. (1966) *Equality of educational opportunity*. Washington, DC: US Government Printing Office.

Coon, H., Fulker, D.W., DeFries, J.C., & Plomin, R. (1990) 'Home environment and cognitive ability of 7-year-old children in the Colorado Adoption Project: Genetic and environmental etiologies', *Developmental Psychology, 26*, 459–468.

Darling, N., & Steinberg, L. (1993) 'Parenting style as context: An integrative model', *Psychological Bulletin, 113*(3), 487–496.

Duke, N. (2000) 'Print environments and experiences offered to first-grade students in very low- and very high-SES school districts', *Reading Research Quarterly, 35*, 456–457.

Education Department (1996) *Guide to the pre-primary curriculum*. Hong Kong: Government Printer.

Education Department (2006) *Guide to the pre-primary curriculum*. Hong Kong: Government Printer.

Gartstein, M.A., Gonzalez, C., Carranza, J.A., Ahadi, S.A., Ye, R., Rothbart, M.K. et al. (2006) 'Studying cross-cultural differences in the development of infant temperament: People's Republic of China, the United States of America, and Spain', *Child Psychiatry and Human Development, 37*, 145–161.

Hess, R.D., & Holloway, S. (1984) 'Family and school as educational institutions', in R.D. Parke, R.N. Emde, H.P. McAdoo, & G.P. Sackett (Eds.) *Review of child development research: Vol. 7. The family* (pp. 179–222). Chicago, IL: University of Chicago Press.

Ho, D.Y.F. (1996) 'Filial piety and its psychological consequences', in M.H. Bond (Ed.) *The handbook of Chinese psychology* (pp. 143–154). Hong Kong: Oxford University Press.

Hsieh, M.-F. (2004) 'Teaching practices in Taiwan's education for young children: Complexity and ambiguity of developmentally appropriate practices and/or developmentally inappropriate practices', *Contemporary Issues in Early Childhood, 5*, 309–329.

Hung, C.L., & Marjoribanks, K. (2005) 'Parents, teachers and children's school outcomes: A Taiwanese study', *Educational Studies, 31*, 3–13.

Huntsinger, C.S., Jose, P.E., Liaw, F.-R., & Ching, W.D. (1997) 'Cultural differences in early mathematics learning: A comparison of Euro-American, Chinese-American, and Taiwan-Chinese families', *International Journal of Behavioral Development, 21*, 371–388.

Laosa, L.M. (1977) 'Inequality in the classroom: Observational research on teacher–student interactions', *Aztlan: International Journal of Chicano Studies Research, 8*, 2–3.

Lau, E.Y.H., Li, H., & Rao, N. (2011) 'Parental involvement and children's readiness for school in China', *Educational Research, 53*, 95–113.

Lee, W.O. (1996) 'The cultural context for Chinese learners: Conceptions of learning in the Confusion tradition', in D.A. Watkins & J.B. Biggs (Eds.) *The Chinese learner: Cultural, psychological and contextual influences* (pp. 25–41). Hong Kong/ Melbourne: Comparative Education Research Centre, The University of Hong Kong/Australia Council for Educational Research.

Lehrer, R., & Shumow, L. (1997) 'Aligning the construction zones of parents and teachers for mathematics reform', *Cognition and Instruction, 15*, 41–83.

Li, H., & Rao, N. (2000) 'Parental influences on Chinese literacy development: A comparison of preschoolers in Beijing, Hong Kong, and Singapore', *International Journal of Behavioral Development, 24*, 82–90.

Li, J. (2003) 'The core of Confucian learning', *American Psychologist, 58*, 146–147.

Lin, C.C., & Fu, V.R. (1990) 'A comparison of child-rearing practices among Chinese, immigrant Chinese, and Caucasian-American parents', *Child Development, 61*, 429–433.

Liu, Y., & Feng, X. (2005) 'Kindergarten educational reform during the past two decades in Mainland China: Achievements and problems', *International Journal of Early Years Education, 13*, 93–99.

McClelland, M.M., Ponitz, C.C., Connor, C.M., Farris, C.L., Jewkes, A.M., & Morrison, F.J. (2007) 'Links between behavioral regulation and pre-schoolers' literacy, vocabulary, and math skills', *Developmental Psychology, 43*(4), 947–959.

Ministry of Education. (2001) *Kindergarten educational practice guidelines.* Retrieved from: http://www.moe.gov.cn/publicfiles/business/htmlfiles/moe/s3327/201001/xxgk_81984.html.

Mullis, I.V.S., Martin, M.O., Gonzalez, E.J., & Chrostowski, S.J. (2004a) *TIMSS 2003 International Mathematics Report: Findings from IEA's Trends in International Mathematics and Science Study at the fourth and eighth grades.* Chestnut Hill, MA: Boston College.

Mullis, I.V.S., Martin, M.O., Gonzalez, E.J., & Chrostowski, S.J. (2004b) *TIMSS 2003 International Science Report: Findings from IEA's Trends in International Mathematics and Science Study at the fourth and eighth grades.* Chestnut Hill, MA: Boston College.

Ng, S.S.N., & Rao, N. (2008) 'Mathematics teaching during the early years in Hong Kong: A reflection of constructivism with Chinese characteristics?', *Early Years, 28*, 159–172.

Organization for Economic Cooperation and Development (OECD) (2007) *PISA 2006 Science competencies for tomorrow's world.* Paris: OECD.

Organization for Economic Cooperation and Development (OECD) (2009) *PISA 2009 results.* Retrieved from: http://www.oecd.org/document/61/0,3746,en_32252351_32235731_46567613_1_1_1_1,00.html.

Pan, Y., Gauvain, M., Liu, Z., & Cheng, L. (2006) 'American and Chinese parental involvement in young children's mathematics learning', *Cognitive Development, 21,* 17–35.

Pang, Y., & Richey, D. (2007) 'Preschool education in China and the United States: A personal perspective', *Early Child Development and Care, 177,* 1–13.

Pearson, E., & Rao, N. (2003) 'Socialisation goals, parenting practices and peer competence in Chinese and English preschoolers', *Early Child Development and Care, 173,* 131–146.

Pianta, R.C., & Walsh, D.J. (1996) *High-risk children in schools: Constructing sustaining relationships.* New York: Routledge.

Plowden, B. (1967) *Children and their primary schools* (The Plowden Report). London: HMSO.

Ponitz, C.C., McClelland, M.M., Matthews, J.S., & Morrison, F.J. (2009) 'A structured observation of behavioral self-regulation and its contribution to kindergarten outcomes', *Developmental Psychology, 45*(3), 605–619.

Rao, N., & Chan, C.K.K. (2009) 'Moving beyond paradoxes: understanding Chinese learners and their teachers', in C.K.K. Chan & N. Rao (Eds.) *Revisiting the Chinese learner: Changing contexts, changing education* (pp. 3–31). Hong Kong: The University of Hong Kong Comparative Education Research Centre/Springer.

Rao, N., & Li, H. (2008) '"Eduplay": Beliefs and practices related to play and learning in Chinese kindergartens', in I. Pramling Samuelsson & M. Fleer (Eds.) *Play and learning in early childhood settings: International Perspectives* (pp. 73–92). Berlin: Springer.

Rao, N., McHale, J.P., & Pearson, E. (2003) 'Links between socialization goals and child-rearing practices in Chinese and Indian mothers', *Infant and Child Development, 12,* 475–492.

Rao, N., Ng, S.S.N., & Pearson, E. (2009) 'Preschool pedagogy: A fusion of traditional Chinese beliefs and contemporary notions of appropriate practice', in C.K.K. Chan and N. Rao (Eds.) *Revisiting the Chinese learner: Changing contexts, changing education* (pp. 255–279). Hong Kong: The University of Hong Kong Comparative Education Research Centre/Springer.

Ritchie, S., & Howes, C. (2003) 'Program practices, caregiver stability, and child–caregiver relationships', *Applied Developmental Psychology, 24,* 497–516.

Rubin, K.H., Hemphill, S.A., Chen, X., Hastings, P., Sanson, A., Coco, A.L. et al. (2006) 'A cross-cultural study of behavioral inhibition in toddlers: East-West-North-South', *International Journal of Behavioral Development, 30*(3), 219–226.

Shanghai Education Commission (SEC) (2008) *Guidance on the evaluation of quality of early childhood care and education in Shanghai Kindergartens (a trial version).* Shanghai: SEC.

State Education Commission of the People's Republic of China (1989) 'The Regulations on Kindergarten Education Practice (on a trial basis)', in Chinese Preschool Education Research Society (Ed.) *A collection of major documents on early childhood education in the People's Republic of China* (pp. 288–298). Beijing: Beijing Normal University Publishing Group.

Sun, J. (2009) 'Scaffolding preschool children's problem solving: Commonalities and differences between Chinese mothers and teachers', Unpublished doctoral dissertation, The University of Hong Kong, Hong Kong.

Sun, J., & Rao, N. (2012a) 'Scaffolding interactions with preschool children: Comparisons between Chinese mothers and teachers across different tasks', *Merrill-Palmer Quarterly, 58,* 110–140.

Sun, J., and Rao, N. (2012b) 'Scaffolding preschool children's problem solving: A comparison between Chinese mothers and teachers across multiple tasks', *Journal of Early Childhood Research, 10*(3), 246–266.

Tobin, J.J., Hsueh, Y., & Karasawa, M. (2009) *Preschool in three cultures revisited: China, Japan, and the United States.* Chicago, IL: University of Chicago Press.

Wang, D.B. (2004) 'Family background factors and mathematics success: A comparison of Chinese and US students', *International Journal of Educational Research, 41*, 40–54.

Wanless, S.B., McClelland, M.M., Acock, A.C., Ponitz, C.C., Son, S.-H., Lan, X. et al. (2011) 'Measuring behavioral regulation in four societies', *Psychological Assessment, 23*, 364–378.

Watkins, D.A., & Biggs, J.B. (Eds.) (1996) *The Chinese learner: Cultural, psychological and contextual influences.* Hong Kong/Melbourne: Comparative Education Research Centre, The University of Hong Kong/Australian Council for Educational Research.

Wu, P., Robinson, C.C., Yang, C., Hart, C., Olsen, S., Porter, C. et al. (2002) 'Similarities and differences in mothers' parenting of preschoolers in China and the United States', *International Journal of Behavioral Development, 26*, 481–491.

Xu, Y., Farver, J.A.M., Zhang, Z., Zeng, Q., Yu, L., & Cai, B. (2005) 'Mainland Chinese parenting styles and parent–child interaction', *International Journal of Behavioral Development, 29*, 524–531.

Zhang, L. (2008) 'The cognitive school readiness development of preschool left-behind children in rural China', Unpublished Master's thesis, East China Normal University, Shanghai.

Zhang, L. (2013) 'Preschool experience, school readiness, self-regulation, and academic achievement: A longitudinal study in rural China', Unpublished doctoral dissertation, The University of Hong Kong, Hong Kong.

Zhang, L., & Rao, N. (2012) 'Preschool experience and self-regulation skills: Lessons from rural China', Poster presented at the 2012 ISSBD Biennial Meeting, Edmonton, Canada, July.

Chapter 7

Learning to learn at a whole-system level

Development of the South Australian Teaching for Effective Learning Framework

Chris Goldspink and Margot Foster

Abstract

In this chapter, we present an analysis of a learning to learn change initiative within the state education system in South Australia. The programme was first introduced in 1999 and in this boutique phase involved some 77 schools – approximately 13% of the total public schools in the State. Following its success, it has been extended and widened to provide a foundation for pedagogy development under the banner of Teaching for Effective Learning. Research has been undertaken at all stages, involving teachers, students, school leaders, and key policy officers in order to identify the effectiveness of strategies and the outcomes. Here, we highlight some of the lessons drawn about school change and compare these with the more general findings on school-based reform drawn from the literature.

Key words: school improvement, learning to learn, educational reform.

Introduction

There is broad agreement among educational policy advocates that the role of education and the way in which it is delivered needs to change (Bingler, 1998; OECD, 1999; Delors, 2000). This claim is driven in part by observation of changing economic, social, and geo-political settings (OECD, 1999; Sterling, 2001) and in part by growing concern about the efficacy of current approaches (Louis & Miles, 1990; Newmann, 1996; Caldwell & Haywood, 1998). In response, many countries have introduced a succession of change programmes. These have varied in their objectives both over time and by country but have many similarities. Through decades of attempts to improve school performance, the broad conclusion is that school reform is difficult (Louis & Miles, 1990; Sarason, 1990; Fullan & Hargreaves, 1991; Fullan, 1994; McDonald, 1996).

In recent times, particularly in the UK, USA, New Zealand, and Australia, it is possible to distinguish at least two distinct foci of reform – those directed at institutional arrangements, in particular an increased emphasis on school-based management and accountability (Cranston, 2000), and those directed at the relationship between teacher and student. The former have, along with many other public sector reforms, been influenced significantly by what has become known as 'managerialism' and/or public choice theory (Goldspink, 2007a), and the latter by a variety of learning theories. The approach to implementation has also varied markedly, with many being imposed top-down while a few have been advanced at a local level.

This chapter documents research undertaken into the effect of a programme undertaken over a ten-year period starting in 1999 (and now ongoing) in the state school sector in South Australia. The focus of this programme was initially school level – concerned to improve learning outcomes for students by deepening teachers' understanding of learning theory and their capacity and willingness to apply it in their classrooms and through this students' capacity to learn how to learn. This was then expanded to become a state-wide pedagogy improvement programme called Teaching for Effective Learning. While the research is continuing and has increasingly adopted a more system-wide policy focus, here we focus primarily on what was learned about achieving school-level change.

Context and background to the programme

Learning to Learn

The programme, initially known as the Learning to Learn Project, was originally funded for three years, ending in June 2001. Two subsequent rounds with expanded scope were subsequently funded and these segued into the current state-wide Teaching for Effective Learning programme.

The programme grew out of dissatisfaction with earlier approaches to curriculum development. As has been found elsewhere, the take-up of central improvement initiatives by teachers can be 'patchy' at best (Louis & Miles, 1990; Spillane, 1999). In the local context, the way in which curriculum development had previously been undertaken was seen to suffer the following limitations. It did not assist with: 'The generation of new thinking and understandings about the learning process – knowledge generation . . . [and] . . . The translation of this knowledge and learning outwards to the system as a whole' (Foster et al., 2000). The Learning to Learn Project, therefore, was focused on the redesign of learning experiences for the entire school community. The stated aim was to support the development of a leading-edge, futures-oriented pedagogy.

The following key precepts were identified as informing the design (inferred from Foster, 2001):

- Meta-learning skills are increasingly important to society and business as a basis for knowledge.
- Education is increasingly expected to be future oriented.
- There was a need for a catalyst or leader to trigger partnership to bring this change in orientation about.
- Complex problems need complex solutions, and these can come from those who are confronting them at a local level.

- Vocation matters and constitutes a motivational resource in the context of education.
- Learning comes through trust and acceptance of risk.
- Reflection on deeply held worldviews and a questioning of identity was needed, not just administrative change, for sustainable benefit.
- Transformation was needed, not incremental improvement.
- Change and uncertainty are ubiquitous and form the backdrop for transformation.
- Sustainable change would only come through responsibility taken at a local level, not through imposition.

This project drew on and promoted 'constructivism' as a theory base appropriate to rethinking learning processes and towards achieving improved meta-learning and life-long learning skills. It was also influenced by systems thinking and concepts (Stein et al., 1994; Baxter Magolda, 2004; Le Cornu & Peters, 2005b).

A summary of the strategies

A number of specific strategies were adopted as a part of the programme. First, schools were selected for their commitment, ideas for focus of curriculum inquiry and cultural factors. *Service agreements* specified a minimum set of conditions and established the respective commitments and obligations of the parties. This included the provision of funding to allow for teacher release for professional development, participation in meetings and cross-school forums, and payment for professional development organised at school level. Importantly, the approach to accountability was designed to be congruent with the values informing the programme. The emphasis was on evaluating what was important and valued rather than evaluating what was easily measured. This can be considered as an attempt to focus goals onto longer-term learning and system-wide outcomes rather than more short-term tangibles or outputs. This had important implications for the direction of the research, which increasingly shifted from a focus on understanding the change process to developing measures that would inform actors and policy-makers about the effectiveness of change strategies used.

South Australia has an experienced teaching force that has developed particular ways of working. While they have participated in ongoing professional development, this was highly varied. The aim was to ensure all principals/directors, school-based project leaders, and staff were exposed to leading-edge research regarding learning and complementary constructivist pedagogies and methodologies. The programme was also supported by a number of project colleagues – 'outside' professionals with a range of backgrounds, including specialists in learning and cognition, community education, learning to learn, and educational administration and research. The capacity to draw on and encourage teachers to engage with a diverse range of leading experts was seen as necessary to loosen the boundaries around established thinking and practice. Harnessing the potential innovation from learning across sectors and through the establishment of non-traditional networks was seen as important to establish new knowledge and practice.

Significant emphasis was placed on having teachers learn from one another. This was intended to open up and deepen teachers' professional networks and facilitate the transfer of learning from one site to another. The primary formal mechanism for doing this was the 'practicum'. Practicums were three-day professional development programmes hosted by Project sites that provided teachers and leaders with opportunities to share and learn from one another about their particular approach to reform.

Site-level leadership was seen as essential to the effective generation of change. To support learning among leaders themselves about what worked and how to better support and encourage change, leaders were invited to share experiences regularly in learning circles. These provided site leaders with a basis for support and learning from a small group of trusted colleagues. They also provided a forum for the project manager to canvas leaders' views regarding project directions and management.

Methodology

The aim of the research undertaken in relation to the programme has changed over time. In the early stages, it was primarily directed towards investigating the impact of the Learning to Learn Project on professional practice and theorizing about that impact. More recently, it has focused on measuring the relationship between school climate, quality of practice, learner engagement, and quality of learning outcomes. This later work has had a focus more on wider policy influence.

Changes such as those pursued by this programme are subject to a wide range of influences. Some of these are apparent while others may be indirect and difficult to identify. In addition, alternative stakeholders can be expected to apply alternative interpretations and values to the evidence collected. There was a need therefore for robust methods. Qualitative data played a key role in the early stages but as a better understanding of the issues was gained, this led to the development and/or incorporation of a range of quantitative instruments. These have focused in particular on measuring the quality of professional practice, student engagement, and the resulting learning to learn skills of students.

The research was designed both to inform policy and programme design but also to provide rapid feedback to practitioners and leaders. Over the history of the programme, a broad mixture of methods has been adopted, including the use of:

- case studies
- narrative analysis
- semi-structured interviews
- measurement of quality of pedagogy, engagement and outcomes, including problem-solving skills and skills associated with lifelong learning
- data analysis of extant qualitative and quantitative materials.

The findings reported here draw primarily on the first three of these. Towards the end of the chapter, some comment will be provided on the move to greater quantification – albeit with the overriding goal of measuring what matters.

Building a capacity to learn how to learn: Early findings

The following account describes the emergent model distilled from the early evidence on school change. Three distinct phases were identified in the change trajectory of schools. Schools passed through these in the same order but at different times.

Phase One: The keys to establishment

The evidence suggests that Learning to Learn became established in schools as a result of the convergence of five critical factors: funding, attracting 'committed' schools, appealing to teachers' intrinsic motivation, pursuing change with high levels of flexibility and devolved responsibility, and timely and flexible exposure of teachers to diverse new ideas on learning.

Funding provided a means for schools to access critical input including, for rural schools, overcoming geographical distance. More generally, it provided the means for supporting and covering the absence of teachers as they participated in the programme, releasing them from day-to-day demands, to engage more deeply and fully in rethinking their own and others' practice. The need for time to research, learn, reflect, plan, and experiment may seem self-evident, but as Adelman and colleagues (1997) found, is all too often lacking. In this sense, the effect of funding was practical: reflecting a realistic appreciation of the minimum conditions needed for teachers to participate effectively.

Equally important to the practical importance of funding was the symbolic importance. The provision of financial support sent a signal about the Department's seriousness and was widely interpreted as recognition of and valuing of teachers. However important funding was, and several school leaders stated that in the early days they had little expectation or confidence in the programme and were motivated due mainly to the funding, it was not in the end regarded as sufficient. In retrospect, school leaders reflected that had they been given the resource but no further guidance they would not have been able to put it to such effective use. The overall framework of the programme was a necessary adjunct.

The importance of funding raises a number of issues for the future. Louis and Miles (1990) have observed that the provision of excessive funding can lead to failure of reform efforts as it lets schools off the hook: 'when the soft money goes away so will the program'. They argue that schools should be asked to show commitment by using local resources. Louis and Miles also believe that inadequate resources and/or excessive reliance on 'volunteers' signals a lack of institutional commitment. It is apparent from the Learning to Learn experience that a refusal to fund would have been widely interpreted as yet another demand by 'the system' for more from teachers and yet further evidence of a lack of appreciation of existing demands. Conversely, the more recent experience of providing schools with a dedicated resource to support the Teaching for Effective Learning programme as it is now called, has provided some leaders with a means to delegate responsibility, potentially limiting effective change. These observations, taken together, suggest that un-tied resource that can be deployed in accordance with local needs and priorities may be the most effective approach.

The readiness of schools and attention to necessary preconditions has been found to be important. The project managers state that initially schools with a predisposition for change and some of the preconditions (such as leadership support, learning culture) were sought to increase the likelihood of success. There were concerns, however, about how such capabilities may be meaningfully assessed. Upon reflection, the project management report remained unconvinced that this made much of a difference in the outcomes, with some schools that scored highly against such criteria failing to deliver as expected and others that were initially considered questionable making above average progress. That said, the schools included in the first round of the Project, by and large, had a history of involvement in developmental programmes and many regarded themselves as 'innovators' – albeit in diverse directions, not all of which were consistent with the values and philosophy informing the Learning to Learn Project. Within these schools there did appear to be a pool of interested and willing leaders who were prepared to work to involve their staff and have them commit (at least in part) to involvement with the programme.

Factors influencing change

A great number of past attempts to improve school education have foundered due to the failure to effectively engage teachers and produce changes within the classroom (Spillane, 1999; Evans, 2001). There is very strong evidence that there is a culture among teachers that values a notional 'social good' as part of teaching. Based on extensive research in several Western countries (Australia included), Dinham and Scott (2000) note that satisfaction among teachers was due to factors:

> . . . intrinsic to the role of teaching. Student achievement, helping students to modify their attitudes and behaviour, positive relationships with students and others, self-growth, mastery of professional skill, and feeling part of a collegial, supportive environment are powerful satisfiers.

The underlying value of 'concern for student learning' seems widely present and has had a significant effect on past attempts at reform. Such research demonstrates that teachers respond badly when they feel that programme or change priorities detract from or are in conflict with this overall objective of teaching. As far back as 1990 Louis and Miles stated that:

> . . . starting an innovation program with an effort that centres on curriculum and instruction is the most effective strategy for getting teachers interested and involved . . . Even where organizational variables, such as morale or climate, need to be worked on, these should usually come after teachers have been excited about an innovation that reaches into the pedagogic core.
>
> (Louis & Miles, 1990: 201)

The focus of the Learning to Learn Project on classroom and school-level improvements for students resonated well with this underlying value. It therefore met little resistance even from the more cynical teachers and inspired and excited the more committed ones.

Critics may well ask, however, if teachers are so concerned with the quality of learning and outcomes for students and communities, why is there such concern at deficiencies in our schools? What is striking in this regard, is that teaching practice varies relatively little internationally. Furthermore, it has remained much the same despite substantial environmental change and in the face of community criticism and evidence that current practices are not the best that can be achieved. It has to be concluded that some intrinsic motivation to do better for students, in and of itself, is not sufficient to generate real improvement. Rather, it appears to act as an abstract value, important as a foundation to teachers' sense of who they are and of their self-worth but motivating them to 'do the best within the existing system' rather than to support its transformation or to lead them to reflect deeply on their own practice.

Tyack and Cuban's (2000) work provides some insights into why this may be the case. They argue that attempts to change schools run across deeply held views as to how a school 'should' look and operate. Unlike many fields, teaching is one experience that everyone has some knowledge of – even if only from having been on the receiving end. Members of the community, teachers as well as politicians and educational administrators all have a view of what education is and how it does or 'should' work. As the primary reference for what a school 'is' and 'should be' is based on most (non-student) stakeholders' personal experience, this can act as a significant conservative force to the extent that these stakeholders find it difficult to imagine alternatives to those that they experienced. Change will tend to focus on 'tinkering' with what is known and taken for granted as necessary, rather than any deeper questioning. In addition, under pressure, there will be a tendency for teachers to retreat to what they know rather than to innovate and try radical new approaches. Reform attempts that fail to address and challenge these intrinsic sources of conservatism are unlikely to make much headway. Indeed, this has become a significant issue as the programme has moved from working with the initial 'coalition of the willing' to attempts to scale across a wider range of schools.

Research and local experience show that teachers have, as a mature workforce, tended to become cynical and somewhat suspicious of agendas for change. Sarason (1990: 64) noted the depth of mistrust in genuine power sharing in the schools he studied and concluded, 'everything in [teachers'] experience taught them two things: don't believe the sincerity of what you are told, and don't allow yourself to hope that real change is possible because you will be disappointed'.

It is to be expected that teachers will be suspicious of programmes for change, even those that ostensibly stand for values that they embrace. There is some evidence from the data collected that this was the case in relation to Learning to Learn. Even the schools that were motivated to apply indicated some scepticism about whether the delivery would match the words. The initial incentive to become involved was the funding that many thought would allow them to do some of what they wanted to even if the other support and direction proved a disappointment. Leaders and teachers were particularly suspicious of the open-ended and exploratory focus of the programme, although they later came to value this highly. Many schools reported the congruence and integrity experienced from the project managers as an important ingredient in deepening their commitment. Project managers report repeated 'testing' by schools particularly around the autonomy and exploratory values of the programme. For many schools, the development of trust took some time to mature (commonly 12 months or more).

Engaging schools in learning and change

Perhaps in large part due to this deliberate challenging of previously taken-for-granted 'rules of engagement', in the early stages of the Project, schools reported considerable confusion and lack of direction – an uncertainty about how to use and work with the scope and flexibility open to them. The Core Learning Programme helped to assist clarity. That this was targeted at classroom practice and school organization was clearly important. The diversity of the programme offering was also regarded as important, as it provided alternative points of entry and motivation to teachers starting from different places in commencing a critical review of their past practice. This need to find a local locus for change has some support from within the literature. Louis and Miles (1990: 206) note, for example, that in their study:

> The more successful of our schools had no a-priori mission statements for the program of the school itself. Instead multiple improvement efforts coalesced around a theme or set of themes only after activity had begun.

Many teachers and leaders identify this early stage of tentative engagement as very challenging. The intrinsic flexibility of the programme was unlike what they were used to and many sought clearer direction. Project managers deliberately declined to give this to encourage schools to take responsibility for their own learning. For this responsibility to become established, there was a need for a genuine renegotiation of power between centre and sites. The need for this is again well supported in the literature. Sarason (1990: 28) concludes, for example, that '[a]ny effort to deal with or prevent a significant problem in a school system that is not based on a reallocation of power – a discernable change in power rela-tionships – is doomed'. Once trust had been established and confusion gave way to a growing sense of control and direction, commitment to the change process grew and deepened. At this point, feelings of confusion gave way to excitement.

An important aspect of the theory and professional development offered as a part of the Project was that it was inspiring. In addition, it needed to have direct application in the classroom. The aspects of the theory that proved most challenging varied significantly, individual by individual and school by school. Similarly, people differed in which approach they found inspiring and which style of presentation they preferred. The theory adopted by the Project was somewhat eclectic while being broadly consistent with the systems orientation and a commitment to constructivism. While this could be seen as a weakness, it facilitated an open and exploratory approach by teachers and avoided the risk of being seen to be prescriptive of 'the one best way'. This, too, has become more difficult to sustain, as in more recent attempts to scale the programme. It was and remains very significant that the theory advocated focuses not on structure of education or content but on pedagogy.

As trust deepened between sites and the centre and new ideas were gained, some of the more innovative teachers began to experiment with new ways of teaching. This occurred more quickly where leaders were actively involved. The extent of impact in the early stage was frequently reported to be relatively minor, while the focus remained on individual development and before a broader collegiality began to operate throughout the school. Important catalysts to moving it on included the practicum, as it was the need to prepare to communicate with others that compelled teachers to work actively with others to achieve a result.

Evans (2001) argues that changes at this level are particularly difficult in that they imply the need for teachers not only to acquire new knowledge but new ways of thinking about knowledge and knowing. The implication is that teachers must unlearn much of what they know. The importance of unlearning was highlighted in several of the school interviews and in cases. For example, in their account, the project managers state:

> Although there had been some thought about the need to investigate the mental models and assumptions which drove the industrial paradigm of schooling, it was through the learned pattern about what constituted pressure for change and how sites were experiencing this that the critical nature of this idea was revealed. Unlearning became our conscious work.

The project managers note that for schools it was the unlearning of their passive dependence on the centre that most needed to change (Foster et al., 2000). For teachers, the most commonly mentioned unlearning was to do with their relationship with students, in particular the power relationships. As the research has progressed, however, we have identified a significant gap in teachers' ability to surface and articulate what they do and why they do it. This suggests that much of their practice is tacit – operating at the level of habit – rather than conscious choice. We have also established that many of these habits may be inconsistent with a teacher's stated intent and beliefs. This makes the process of unlearning far more of a challenge.

Phase Two: Deepening engagement

Emergent collegiality

The process of deepening engagement as change moved beyond initiation and individual interest was markedly different from that of the early phase. In particular, it is characterized by a significant growth of collegiality rather than localized individual action. The importance of collegiality and collaborative engagement as a part of teacher development has been well established (see, for example, Emihivitch & Battaglia, 2000). Immediate feedback, as more innovative teachers try out new ideas, was important for deepening the commitment of those initiators and served to widen involvement as others were inspired by the gains.

The programme clearly attracted most strongly those teachers who had values consistent with the student-centred nature of the change. The initial phase supported these teachers and gave them a voice in their schools. In this way, they found each other and began to make local change. Initially, this was in their own classrooms. In many cases, it led to immediate positive feedback from students and in some cases from parents also. Effective leaders encouraged these local efforts. This led to feedback that was important for building commitment and increasing the spread of engagement, particularly from teachers with a 'wait and see' approach. Spillane (1999) has observed that for change to be effective, teachers need to be able to learn the practical knowledge necessary for teaching in the ways implied by the reform. Local conversations that were grounded in the reform ideas and in teachers' efforts to work with them in practical ways in their classrooms were important. These developed where teachers were simultaneously involved in practising the new ideas and learning about how to deal with the problems that arose from putting into practice the new and possibly more challenging pedagogy. This 'action' or 'experiential' learning was an explicit aspect of the design of the Learning to Learn Project. Leaders can connect with what it might mean for teachers to become learners as they learn to challenge their own behaviours that limit change. Teachers can connect better to how their choices impact on students when they become more aware of themselves in the learning role. The effectiveness of this approach was clearly evident through the research data. The research specifically pointed to a conflict between the 'managerial' role they were being asked to perform as a result of some aspects of concurrent reform and the 'letting go of power', implicit in allowing others to become effective learners – including by making mistakes while experimenting with new approaches (Peters & Le Cornu, 2004, 2006). This opening up of the system to learning at multiple levels – the fractal nature of learning – has also proven more difficult to sustain in a policy climate that has become increasingly concerned with centralization and standardization.

Alignment of values

As the programme progressed, it became clear that an individualist approach was not fostering a deeper learning culture. Staff who attended core learning events hosted by the programme reported problems, including difficulties doing justice in presenting the material back to colleagues. In addition, the intrinsic motivation of learning from 'international experts' was lost through this process of re-transmission. McDonald (1996: 354) notes that there is a tendency for site-driven change to overemphasize individualistic approaches:

> . . . reform initiatives launched on the inside of schools, by principles or small groups of teachers with or without consultants, typically put too much trust in add-on programs and one shot professional development.

To their credit, this limitation was recognized early in many schools and increasingly group-centred approaches were adopted.

Increasingly, leaders sought opportunities to send small groups to development relevant to their areas of interest and/or to bring key colleagues to the school to involve more or all staff. Leaders often regarded this as a critical step. Importantly, rather than being localized, the possibility of all teachers in the site learning a new way of thinking and talking about learning became established. This establishment of a 'common language', provided it was broadly based, reduced the likelihood of 'in-group' and 'out-group' formation within the school. Where insufficient attempts were made by leaders to maintain the inclusivity of the work being undertaken, it had the reverse effect, creating a division within the school. The wider use of group professional development, in particular the use of 'internal' experts to share new ideas and lessons from experimenting with new approaches enabled the better-led schools to broaden the effect – engaging a wider network of teachers in the process. The eclectic nature of the developmental options was important – providing multiple possible entry points for teachers with differing experience and approaches. The approach offered a non-deficit view of change led and driven by teachers for students, their communities, and themselves.

Through this phase more innovative teachers began reporting a good response to change by their students and in some cases by parents. This encouraged leaders and other staff, providing further affirmation for those teachers who had taken the risk of trying something new. With many teachers having lengthy service and significant experience, and in a context of declining morale, the sense of capacity to 'make a difference' that arose through this process cannot be underestimated. As Evans (2001: 95) notes, 'There is much research to confirm the importance of a sense of efficacy – the sense of making a meaningful difference, of true accomplishment – in teachers' motivation and performance.' Many teachers reported feeling excitement as they realized that their experiments based on the new ideas yielded benefits for students.

Collaborative learning across sites

Gradually, in most schools, this short-term immediate feedback at the local site encouraged a broadening of the change and deepened teachers' and leaders' commitment to the process and its possibilities. For some schools, this came to a head with the first practicum. The need to prepare to share beyond the immediate site and the learning that resulted was reported to be a major factor leading to a deeper commitment to change. The practicums provided staff time to reflect on what they had collectively achieved and to gain affirmation from a wider collegiate network for what they had done. The exchanges between schools also began to link teachers and leaders to others with like mind, expanding networks beyond school boundaries. This is significant, as teaching has been identified as a potentially isolating and individual occupation (Evans, 2001). Evans notes that a sense of collegiality is relatively rare in schools yet, as Day et al. (2000) observe, it is essential for effective change. Fullan and Hargreaves also note the problem of isolation inherent in teaching as providing a powerful check on change. They state, for example, that:

> The professional isolation of teachers limits access to new ideas and better solutions, drives stress inward to fester and accumulate, fails to recognise and praise success, and permits incompetence to exist and persist to the detriment of students, colleagues and the teachers themselves.
>
> (Fullan & Hargreaves, 1991: 5)

Spillane (1999) observed that by engaging in new praxis in a collaborative environment, teachers learned from one another about what worked and this helped consolidate and diffuse the changes. Isolation, whether imposed or self-chosen, significantly reduced the chances of success. For McDonald also, where reform is effective:

> ... direct instruction in isolated, departmentalized classrooms yields to a community of learners and teachers sharing common standards, striving for connections, staying open intellectually, cultivating and respecting diverse viewpoints.
>
> (McDonald, 1996: 354)

The de-privatisation of practice and a focus on building communities of practice became the main focus of the subsequent Teaching for Effective Learning Programme, more on which shortly.

Devolving and sharing power

With the expansion to site-level engagement, there was commonly a period of confusion where a focus and common commitment emerged. For some leaders, this was a challenging time, as they felt pressure to provide direction but felt that more learning would take place if teachers found their own pathways forward. Noting the work of Lee and Smith (1994), Foster et al. (2000) state:

> It is clear that the extent to which school leaders are prepared to devolve power to others and provide the support for others to assume leadership roles is critical in transforming school culture from 'bureaucratic organisation' to 'communal organisation'.

It was not formal authority that mattered in the context of Learning to Learn but relationship management. Indeed, the most successful leaders recognized that formal authority was a potential barrier and that a genuine need to renegotiate power and to strive to establish a genuinely collegiate basis for decision-making was a key to success at school level. This need is well reflected in the literature. Newmann (1996: 194), for example, notes: 'In the more successful schools, individuals in leadership positions defined themselves at the centre of the schools staff rather than at the top. This was not to say that they moved to the background. They did give up some 'visible' leader behaviour such as chairing meetings, but maintained a strong presence – focusing on facilitative roles rather than directive ones. This may have included focusing on values and leading debate about values, helping staff negotiate difficult situations and make their way through differences. It is just this style that is evident in the most successful learning to learn schools. Newmann's results show clearly that schools that found ways to genuinely move to a shared power situation were most successful at improving their teaching performance. This is confirmed by the work of Marks and Louis (1999) and Fullan and Hargreaves (1991). Newmann did identify several instances of where highly centralized power was effective but this was only found in a context of high levels of agreement about values and objectives for student learning. Again the lessons drawn from this early stage found clear articulation in what is now referred to as Domain 1 of the Teaching for Effective Learning Framework – a domain that has as its focus leading for effective teaching.

The South Australian Learning to Learn Programme was not a top-down change but one that was facilitated and enabled by central initiative. It was driven at a local level as individuals connected and deepened their commitment due to a strong values base connection with the purpose of the reform.

Respecting group diversity

Social identity theorists note that the tendency towards group differentiation is endemic to all social systems. The evidence from the research suggested that there was some in-/out-group formation within schools as a result of the programme. Effective leaders worked to reduce this by expanding involvement of teachers as widely as possible and avoiding stigmatizing those who chose not to participate. Where such groups did form, there were a variety of positions evident with some leaders clearly viewing it as undesirable. Others, however, respected this choice and sought ways to turn it to advantage, recognizing it as a source of diversity and a check and balance on the enthusiasm of others – another source of learning. This respect for difference is consistent with the overall philosophy of the Project. The philosophy of 'moving towards the threat' and of seeking to engage and include it as a component in a learning network rather than isolating or attacking would be consistent with the past approach and consistent with expanding the influence of the ideas and practices informing Learning to Learn. This was a substantial challenge, as there is no doubt that these differences did constitute a threat to the ongoing viability of the Project. Not all players would respect the new rules of engagement, resorting instead to the more typical political play characteristic of bureaucracies.

Phase Three: School-level change

Once a site moved past the initial confusion and found direction, leaders worked to focus efforts and to deepen involvement. This was extended in some cases to widen involvement, increasingly bringing in parents and the community. This development was however patchy. The evidence suggests that local community environmental factors, while shaping the particular approach or focus, were seldom a factor in enhancing or inhibiting the success of the programme. Moreover, changing expectations of parents and students helped reinforce and stabilize the change. At the same time, inter-school collegiality and growing inter-school networks were an important ingredient in facilitating the spread and development of experimentation at a classroom level. Community attitudes have been identified as potentially important inhibitors of change. Tyack and Cuban (2000) have observed, for example, that many in the community hold multiple and sometimes contradictory views about what they want from schools. Pursuing these may lead to contradictory directions and/or cycles of change. As school decision-making is increasingly devolved, such conflict will be felt at a local level.

Accountability – a critical risk factor

Accountability was clearly a sensitive issue for teachers and schools and was most commonly interpreted as a negative – holding to account as questioning and potentially punitive – reflecting distrust of teachers' and leaders' professionalism. In addition, many schools reported that the mechanisms of accountability currently in place imposed an administrative burden ('make-work') while contributing little policy intelligence for the system. This was confirmed by an examination of a random selection of school annual reports. These reflected a standard approach, with a heavy emphasis on reporting against a selection of metrics, including such things as literacy performance benchmarks by year-group, retention rates, and so on. These may be valuable at the level of the State, but in many cases, particularly for small rural schools or junior primaries, were often perceived as meaningless. Given this, it is no surprise that the Learning to Learn Project managers were very sensitive to the symbolic power of the term 'accountability' and the associations and connotations it carried at school level. In their case account they report, for example:

> . . . we were preoccupied with the knowledge that the accountability processes for the Project had the potential to undo all the learning gains which had been made by invoking a 'compliant mindset'. 'Teaching to the test', 'just tell us what to do' were products of a particularly strong view in the department about accountability as proof. We needed accountability processes which provided stocktake points for site learning, reflection points which contributed to the overall learning process – not just 'proving' they had fulfilled their Service Agreement. If the project was to create a different atmosphere where new possibilities

could be conceived we couldn't have accountability processes which constrained this.

By all accounts they succeeded. There was seldom mention of formal reporting requirements during interviews, and the accountability points included in Learning to Learn were not commonly perceived as such. Far from being eschewed, they were commonly identified as the most powerful learning points in the Project. Accountability was transformed to mean learning and celebration – a cultural shift managed through the careful use of language and avoidance of invoking historically sensitive negative associations. Perhaps most importantly the accountability points provided an opportunity for meaningful collaborative and collective critical reflection on performance by those who were responsible, and had accepted responsibility for the achievement of the outcomes. The information, fresh insight and new ideas, the lessons learned from success and failure, were useful to teachers/practitioners in improving their practice.

Leaders letting go of control

The changes that began to take place at this level presented a significant challenge for many leaders. Many reported that they felt quite early on that they needed to let go of more and more control and allow teachers to take greater responsibility for the directions and approach to experimenting with change and developing directions of change in areas consistent with their collective motivation (Foster et al., 2000; Le Cornu et al., 2002, 2005). This included dealing with perceived conflicting demands, such as:

*   leading learning and managing the site;
*   acknowledging the past and initiating new directions;
*   building relationships and challenging professional identity;
*   routine ('surface') decision-making and reflective ('deep') decision-making;
*   responding emotionally and analytically (Peters & Le Cornu, 2004).

Those schools that responded to this and actively renegotiated power were able to advance quickly. This meant challenging their own and teachers' assumptions about roles and responsibilities. It also meant the need to adopt new practices and to maintain congruence with a new set of behaviours. This is not easy to initiate and it can be even harder to maintain.

Rethinking power relations in the classroom

If renegotiation of power was a challenge for leaders, it was no less so for teachers. In addition to having to deal with changed expectations from the centre and the local leadership, their engagement with the Project compelled them also to rethink their traditional role in the classroom (Le Cornu & Peters, 2005a, 2005b). Many teachers were now actively working to be more responsive and more flexible in order to accommodate and work with students' diverse and individual needs. Hence power in the classroom loomed as a significant issue. Many recognized a broader implication of this power change – a shift to empowering students and the equity issues associated with a more individually responsive approach to learning, while recognizing a need to consider the learning impacts of the wider social context of students. For some, this reorientation was made explicit, through establishment of a set of core values, negotiated at school level. For others, it was embraced through a school-level vision.

Creating learning networks with policy-makers and academics

Activities such as the practicums helped teachers explore beyond their immediate site. The core learning programme also had allowed teachers to begin to form wider networks of relationships. For leaders, strategies such as the Learning Circles (Peters & Le Cornu, 2005) broadened their networks with other leaders and also served to connect them to academics within the teaching universities. This was experienced as a challenge. Many schools reported looking at their own work and feeling inadequate compared with others. There was common reporting also of a stock take and reflection with schools feeling that, as they were doing things differently, they must be doing something wrong. These feelings gradually dissipated and confidence grew through key events such as the practicums. Thus from being essentially isolated practitioners with a lack of self-confidence in dealing with and engaging with peers, participating teachers report much increased confidence and a delight in working with others, both within and beyond the school. The Core Learning Programme and project partners served to connect teachers in participating schools to a national and international network of leading practitioners and academics. This served to raise self-esteem, confidence, and willingness to rethink and learn from others.

Relational and cultural changes in schools

Research into school change concludes that one of the most important determinants of a capacity to sustain change is local school culture. For Evans (2001: 229), for example, 'School improvement is embedded in an ethos of empowerment and collegiality.' For Newmann and Wehlage (1996: 288), schools that were successful in making change to improve student achievement were built on an ethos of 'trust, respect, and sharing of expertise and power'. For Marks and Louis (1999) also:

> A key finding is the significance of the relationship between 'empowerment at the middle range' and the capacity for organizational learning. The finding suggests two conclusions: first, that schools can't 'take off' in terms of getting teachers fully involved in taking collective responsibility for making the school a good working environment for both themselves and students until they have the capacity for organizational learning that permit them to

be professional. Second, both the capacity for organizational learning and empowerment are, once the school is provided with autonomy, largely a matter of internal relationships among people, in which school staff provide each other with support, exchange ideas and reach consensus, and treat each other in professional and egalitarian ways. These are not aspects of reform that cost a great deal of money: they are reforms of culture and not of external resources, buildings, assessment programs, or student schedules.

The building of collegiality, the development of expanded networks, staff empowerment, and growing staff confidence and skill in the facilitation of their own and each other's learning led to an embedding of an ethos for change and improvement within many of the schools' cultures.

As noted above, many past reforms have emphasized the importance of structural change. With Learning to Learn, the emphasis was on relational and cultural change. Structure and culture are, however, related and this was confronted by a number of schools as they advanced the change process at whole-school level. The evidence suggests that as the development of a shared commitment to change deepened, there arose a need to confront structural impediments. Many schools made significant changes to the way in which they organized staff and scheduled programmes and delivery in order to become more flexible and to use more effectively the diverse talents of teachers. Significantly, though, these changes to structure came after cultural acceptance had been gained and were commonly designed and implemented by teachers themselves.

Going mainstream: The Teacher for Effective Learning Programme

The Learning to Learn Project demonstrated some substantial achievements. These were, however, mixed in that some schools achieved considerably more than others. It must be remembered also that this was initially a boutique programme involving schools that actively sought to be involved. A key challenge was, therefore, how to take the lessons from the early stages and apply them to a wider range of schools – how to scale up.

There were some significant new challenges to face in expanding the scope and depth of the Project. The lessons drawn from the experience of the Learning to Learn phase were helpful, especially the need to:

- consolidate and maintain change at existing sites in the face of changing staff and new staff;
- support staff who had been a part of the change as they moved to new schools that had not been involved;
- find new ways to stimulate and excite those who had engaged with the first round to maintain a momentum for change;
- broaden the involvement of community and parents in local change;
- link change at site level to higher level organizational learning and ensure it impacted on policy;

- expand the involvement of schools, increasingly having to confront less supportive school cultures and conceive of new strategies for involving more reluctant stakeholders;
- manage the anticipated backlash as increasing numbers of people at all levels of the system felt that their established ways of working were threatened by the inexorable 'influence' of Learning to Learn.

Scaling up the lesson from Learning to Learn

Beginning in 2010, the Project entered a fundamentally new stage directed at addressing these issues. At this time, it was renamed the Teaching for Effective Learning Programme. The brief of this programme was to scale many of the lessons. The goal was to provide a developmental framework for the support of teacher learning and pedagogical improvement that was rigorous and grounded in theory. This was greatly supported by additional federal funding to support research into disadvantaged schools. This led to the development of a set of structured interventions that also addressed two research goals:

1. To evaluate the effectiveness of Teaching for Effective Learning (TfEL) as an intervention to improve quality of pedagogy and learning outcomes in schools with pupils of low socio-economic status.
2. To continue research aimed at establishing a comprehensive framework for measurement of variables impacting on student learning outcomes in primary and secondary schooling.

In both of these research goals, the concern was to understand how school climate and quality of practice were linked to higher-order thinking and learning skill development as well as academic attainment.

In contrast to the earlier work, which had avoided the production and distribution of frameworks and programme artefacts – with the view that these would suggest that directions for change were fixed and answers about how to change already known – one early product was the Teaching for Effective Learning Framework (DECS, 2010). This framework both brought together research-derived ideas and resources to support practitioner reflection and illustrate alternative practice. Importantly, it also was designed to provide a measurement framework for evaluating quality of practice linked to higher-order thinking and learning skills development. The trial and refinement of this measurement framework was a core component of the research.

Involving, engaging, and supporting schools as stakeholders

Strategies to involve, engage, and support schools drew on some of the prior learning from the Learning to Learn phase. These included the importance of five critical factors: funding, attracting 'committed' schools, appealing to teachers' intrinsic motivation, pursuing change with high levels of flexibility and devolved responsibility, and timely and flexible exposure of teachers to diverse new ideas on learning. These were incorporated into the design of the Teaching for Effective Learning Programme in that:

1.   Sites volunteered – they were not co-opted.
2.   Dedicated resources were provided in the form of specialist teachers. The role of the specialist teachers was to support local learning and meaning-making as well as to facilitate the development of local learning communities around the dimensions of quality and principles of practice established within the TfEL framework. It was also envisaged that the specialist teachers would work closely with leaders in developing change strategies at the site and between site levels (specialist teachers were shared between up to three geographically proximal sites, working with the school community in each).
3.   Accountability continued to be about staff and site learning. The research strand was designed to collect rigorous data about the relationship between what was done and a range of outcomes. The aim also was to feed as much of the evidence collected as possible within confidentiality constraints to those directly involved, particularly teachers and leaders. Accordingly, the service agreement that schools entered into with the project team requires participation and cultural change towards staff engagement with the programme and meaning-making about the elements of the TfEL framework, not the implementation of others' thinking. There was recognition that teachers and leaders first needed to construct their own meaning of what the framework was about and how it connected to their context.
4.   Choice was afforded sites regarding their focus for working with TfEL – for example, which learning area they wished to peruse and which level of schooling.
5.   Professional learning communities were a required aspect of the service agreement. This linked to the key principle of de-privatizing practice and building a community of practice focused on improving pedagogy. This was also based on the assumption that teachers can learn best from their peers but was also directed at injecting inspiration into the work with a core learning programme and feeding back results from the research to deepen engagement and focus local action.
6.   In recognition of the pivotal role of leaders in creating the conditions for rich learning at the site level, a leader and specialist teachers learning programme was also established.

Key differences between the TfEL approach and that of learning to Learn included:

•   In the case of Teaching for Effective Learning, a pre-established framework and set of resources was 'provided' rather than asking sites to create their own stance about learning at their site and to decide what quality meant in their context. This both disempowered some and empowered others.
•   Local support was provided in the form of specialist teachers who were given extensive support in understanding the TfEL framework and were expected

to work with local leaders and staff to build a local community of practice around these ideas. This may have reduced the need for direct involvement of leaders, reducing their taking responsibility for the process and outcomes.

- A distinct research strand was established alongside the professional learning programme. This became a professional development strand in itself as the rigorous analysis teachers were involved in to score practice and justify their evidence – particularly around the use of the TfEL framework for observing and assessing quality of practice – was an intensive learning experience.

- During Learning to Learn, the introduction of rigorous yet diverse and thought-provoking professional development was new and exciting. Prior to this, professional development had been more programmatic training linked to top-down programme implementation. However, there were signs that this was losing its impact and by the time of TfEL, and in the context of a wider return to impositional and standardized programmes, teachers were becoming reform-weary and had little time to work in more reflective and exploratory ways.

At the same time, there was a change in the wider policy context at both a State and Federal level. This was – largely in keeping with international trends – a growth in concern for centralized standards and an accountability regime that was increasingly focused on the results measured by standardized academic testing. There was also a rapid expansion of targeted intervention programmes – directed in particular at disadvantaged and 'underperforming' schools. This may have significantly reduced the space for teachers to think together and construct their own professional knowledge to inform their actions. The proliferation of interventions also meant that TfEL was competing for limited time and conceptual space at a time that leaders were also finding that there was growing expectation that they operate more as managers rather than educational leaders.

The research component

Throughout the research into school transformation discussed above, work had also been undertaken into the development of quantitative instrumentation to support measurement of the effect of school change on learner engagement and outcomes. This had included various trials to instruments taken from the literature or invented anew. The aim was to assemble an integrated set of tools to measure the effect of school climate, leadership behaviour, quality of practice, student engagement, and learning outcomes. The rich qualitative data collected as part of the research, along with a wide literature review and involvement of several project colleagues, contributed to the design of these methods and tools. To narrow the scope, the initial focus was on better understanding the relationship between pedagogy and engagement. In 2005, a small case study had been conducted to establish the feasibility of measuring such a relationship. This study involved two Learning to Learn schools – one that had undertaken extensive change over the period of the programme and another that was just beginning change (Goldspink, 2008). The school that had undertaken considerable cultural transformation and pedagogical change showed clear evidence of learners having:

- greater choice in what to learn;
- greater choice in how to learn;
- learning that was more social;
- learning that was less class-centred;
- teachers who were more professionally engaged.

These differences, as well as some unmeasured differences in site (possibly a culture of regard and trust) and context, contributed to statistically significant:

- higher scores for both numeracy and literacy;
- higher meta-cognitive/thinking skills;
- higher 'on-task' behaviour associated with greater interest and less boredom;
- higher happiness and satisfaction;
- higher social functioning;
- higher disposition to learning;
- higher observed thinking skills;
- overall higher well-being.

These students also performed more strongly on a test of problem-solving/thinking trialled from the Finnish Learning to Learn work (Hautamäki et al., 2002; Hautamäki & Kupiainen, 2002).

This convinced us that it was feasible to measure these relationships and further investment was made in both:

- developing practitioner-based resources to support change – drawing on the key lessons of Learning to Learn (DECS, 2010); and
- a framework of multi-item measures for quality of pedagogy and learner engagement (Goldspink & Winter, 2008; Goldspink & Foster, 2013).

A framework for teacher self-evaluation

It was at this time that it was also decided that the developing Teaching for Effective Learning Framework should also be designed to work as a measurement tool (Atkin & Foster, 2011).

Learning for effective teaching

The resulting framework grouped dimensions of professional practice identified in wider research to be important in supporting engagement and learner achievement in both academic and social and emotional outcomes. One of these domains related primarily to teachers' own learning and leadership aspects which support learning – learning for effective teaching. This domain encapsulated the lessons drawn from the Learning to Learn Project, including that to markedly improve their practice leaders needed to open up the possibility for deeper professional learning at a whole-site level, effectively adopting the principles that had guided the Learning to Learn Project, including the use of an invitational rather than directive stance, supporting wide experimentation with accountability operating through a process of shared learning. In addition, this element emphasized the need for ongoing professional development to deepen pedagogical and content knowledge and learning design orientated school systems, structures, and practices.

Teaching for effective learning

The remaining three domains focused on teacher practices – teaching for effective learning. In addition to drawing on research into effective practice, development of these domains also gave cognisance to pre-existing frameworks in other Australian States. This work indicated that there was an opportunity for South Australia to make a distinctive contribution in areas addressed by the Australian National Goals for Schooling (MCEETYA, 2008), particularly goal 2, which was concerned with meta-cognitive, problem-solving, and social skills outcomes, and positive self-concept as a learner (Sellar & Cormack, 2007). These three domains each comprised four elements of practice, which were framed in terms of observable behaviours. These formed the basis of the measurement instrument. The instrument and therefore this aspect of the framework went through several trial data collection and refinement iterations.

At the same time, it was decided to expand the range of outcome measures used, particularly those that related to the development of higher-order thinking and learning skills. From 2011 on, the Effective Lifelong Learning Inventory (Deakin Crick et al., 2004; Deakin Crick, 2007) was introduced as a means for measuring students' learning dispositions. Measures drawn from Carol Dweck's (2000) research into the effect of children's assumptions about themselves as learners was also adopted.

We are currently at the stage of reporting findings to government and the funders and the results will be published over the next few months and years.

Conclusions

The Learning to Learn and now Teaching for Effective Learning Project shows that school reform that is driven by an emphasis on learning and the attendant attention to relationships and cultural change can effect school-level change. It reinforces many of the conclusions of the literature, in particular that:

- reform should be curriculum/learning focused;
- successful change involves teachers directly;
- teachers respond well to being treated as professionals;
- innovation is possible with attention to school environment and with the injection of new ideas.

It also offers significant new insights into factors important to the achievement of successful outcomes from change (Goldspink, 2007b). These include:

- appealing to teachers' intrinsic motivation is key to prevent resistance and that this can ameliorate other de-motivating factors present in the general environment;
- pursuing change with high levels of flexibility and a learning and risk tolerant approach to accountability can lead to rigorous approaches to change and a focus on results, contrary to 'managerialist' assumptions;
- maintaining a high level of congruence to core values informing the change is vital;
- a non-deficit approach to reform opens up possibilities for institution-wide learning.

At this stage, it is not clear that the strategies employed can be effectively scaled. Furthermore, it has often proven difficult to sustain change. Early suggestions are that the largely site-based and developmental approach of TfEL is not sufficient to achieve change in the absence of a high level of pre-existing local commitment or in the face of unhelpful wider policy settings. Some strategies detracted from the level of leader commitment and engagement meaning that in many schools progress was slow. Issues impacting significantly on the sustainability of change included the effect of leader and staff turnover and these need a policy response. More will be understood of these effects and the major factors influencing the capacity to scale the lessons when the results of the research are known in mid 2013.

References

Adelman, N.E., Walking Eagle, K.P., & Hargreaves, A. (Eds.) (1997) *Racing with the clock: Making time for teaching and learning in school reform.* New York: Teachers College Press.

Atkin, J., & Foster, M. (2011) *South Australian Teaching for Effective Learning Review tools handbook: A resource for reflecting on teaching and learning in South Australia.* Adelaide, SA: Department of Education and Children's Services, Government of South Australia.

Baxter Magolda, M.B. (2004) 'Evolution of a constructivist conceptualization of epistemological reflection', *Educational Psychologist, 39*(1), 31–42.

Bingler, S. (1998) *Less is more: Learning environments for the next century.* Retrieved from: www.newhorizons.org [accessed 22 May 2002].

Caldwell, B.J.H., & Haywood, D.K. (1998) *The future of schools: Lessons from the reform of public education.* London: Falmer Press.

Cranston, N. (2000) 'The impact of school-based management on primary school principles: An Australian perspective', *Journal of School Leadership, 10*(3), 214–232.

Day, C., Harris, A., Hadfield, M., Tolley, H., & Beresford, J. (2000) *Leading schools in times of change.* Buckingham: Open University Press.

Deakin Crick, R. (2007) 'Learning how to learn: The dynamic assessment of learning power', *The Curriculum Journal, 18*(2), 135–153.

Deakin Crick, R., Broadfoot, P., & Claxton, G. (2004) 'Developing an effective lifelong learning inventory: The ELLI Project', *Assessment in Education*, *11*(3), 248–272.

Delors, J. (2000) *Learning: The treasure within*. Paris: UNESCO.

Department of Education and Children's Services (DECS) (2010) *South Australian Teaching for Effective Learning Framework: Framework guide*. Adelaide, SA: DECS, Government of South Australia.

Dinham, S., & Scott, C. (2000) 'Enhancing teacher professionalism: The need to engage with the "Third Domain"', Paper presented to the ACEA International Conference, Hobart, Tasmania, 9–12 September.

Dweck, C.S. (2000) *Self-theories: Their role in motivation, personality, and development*. New York: Psychology Press.

Emihivitch, C., & Battaglia, C. (2000) 'Creating culture for collaborative inquiry: New challenges for school leaders', *International Journal of Leadership in Education*, *3*(3), 225–238.

Evans, R. (2001) *The human side of school change*. New York: Jossey-Bass.

Foster, M. (2001) *Learning our way forward*. Adelaide, SA: Department of Education Training and Employment.

Foster, M., Le Cornu, R., & Peters, J. (2000) 'Leadership for learning', Paper presented to the Australian Association for Research in Education Conference, Sydney, NSW, 4–7 December.

Fullan, M.G., & Hargreaves, A. (1991) *Working together for your school*. Hawthorn, VIC: ACEA.

Fullan, M.J. (1994) 'Coordinating top-down and bottom-up strategies for educational reform', in R.F. Elmore & S.H. Fuhrman (Eds.) *The governance of curriculum* (pp. 186–202). Alexandria, VA: Association for Supervision and Curriculum Development.

Goldspink, C. (2007a) 'Rethinking educational reform – A loosely coupled and complex systems perspective', *International Journal of Educational Management, Administration and Leadership*, *35*(1): 27–50.

Goldspink, C. (2007b) 'Transforming education: Evidential support for a complex systems approach', *Emergence: Complexity and Organization*, *9*(1/2): 77–92.

Goldspink, C. (2008) *Constructivist classroom case studies: Final report*. Adelaide, SA: Department of Education and Children's Services.

Goldspink, C., & Foster, M. (2013) 'A conceptual model and set of instruments for measuring student engagement in learning', *Cambridge Journal of Education*, *43*(3), 291–311.

Goldspink, C., & Winter, P. (2008) 'Student engagement and quality pedagogy', Paper presented to the European Education Research Conference, Göteborg, Sweden, 10–12 September.

Hautamäki, J., Arinen, P., Eronen, S., Hautamäki, A., Kupiainen, S., Lindblom, B. et al. (2002) *Assessing Learning to Learn: A framework*. Helsinki: National Board of Education.

Hautamäki, J., & Kupiainen, S. (2002) *The Finnish Learning-to-Learn Assessment Project: A concise report with key results*. Brussels: Centre for Educational Assessment.

Le Cornu, R., & Peters, J. (2005a) 'Reculturing primary classrooms: Renegotiating the four R's (rules, roles, responsibilities and relationships)', *Change: Transformations in Education*, *8*(2), 16–30.

Le Cornu, R., & Peters, J. (2005b) 'Towards constructivist classrooms: The role of the reflective teacher', *Journal of Educational Enquiry*, *6*(1), 50–64.

Le Cornu, R., Peters, J., Foster, M., Barrett, R., & Stratfold, J. (2005) 'What constitutes significant change in reforming schools?', Paper presented to the British Educational Research Association Conference, University of Glamorgan, Pontypridd, 14–17 September.

Le Cornu, R., Peters, J., Foster, M., & Shin, A. (2002) 'Leadership for school improvement', Paper presented to the British Educational Research Association Conference, Exeter, 12–14 September.

Lee, V., & Smith, B. (1994) 'High school restructuring and student achievement: A new study finds strong links', *Issues in Restructuring Schools*, 7, 1–16.

Louis, K.S., & Miles, M.B. (1990) *Improving the urban high school*. New York: Teachers College Press.

Marks, H.M., & Louis, K.S. (1999) 'Teacher empowerment and the capacity for organizational learning', *Educational Administration Quarterly*, 35(4), 707–751.

McDonald, J.P. (1996) 'Below the surface of school reform: Vision and its foes', in L. Schauble & R. Glaser (Eds.) *Innovations in learning: New environments for education*. Mahwah, NJ: Erlbaum.

Ministerial Council on Education, Employment, Training and Youth Affairs (MCEETYA) (2008) *Melbourne Declaration on Educational Goals for Young Australians*. Melbourne, VIC: MCEETYA.

Newmann, F.M. (1996) *Authentic achievement*. San Francisco, CA: Jossey-Bass.

Newmann, F.M., & Wehlage, G.G. (1996) 'Conclusion: Restructuring for authentic student achievement', in F.M. Newmann (Ed.) *Authentic achievement: Restructuring schools for intellectual quality*. San Francisco, CA: Jossey-Bass.

OECD (1999) *Innovating schools*. Centre for Educational Research and Innovation, OECD Publications.

Peters, J., & Le Cornu, R. (2004) 'Leaders in transition: Living with paradoxes', Paper presented to the British Educational Research Association Annual Conference, University of Manchester, Manchester, 16–18 September. Retrieved from: http://www.leeds.ac.uk/educol/documents/00003783.htm.

Peters, J., & Le Cornu, R. (2005) 'Beyond communities of practice: Learning circles for transformational school leadership', in P. Carden & T. Stehlik (Eds.) *Beyond communities of practice*. Teneriffe, QLD: Post Pressed.

Peters, J., & Le Cornu, R. (2006). 'Co-constructing transformational leadership in new settings', *Leadership in Focus*, Spring (3), 26–29.

Sarason, S.B. (1990) *The predictable failure of educational reform*. San Francisco, CA: Jossey-Bass.

Sellar, S., & Cormack, P. (2007) *Framing pedagogies: A review of frameworks and research designed to promote effective approaches to teaching and learning*. Adelaide, SA: Centre for Studies in Literacy Policy and Learning Cultures, Hawke Institute, University of South Australia.

Spillane, J.P. (1999) 'External reform initiatives and teachers' efforts to reconstruct their practice: The mediating role of teachers' zones of enactment', *Curriculum Studies*, 31(2), 143–175.

Stein, M., Edwards, T., Norman, J., Roberts, S., Sales, J., & Alec, R. (1994) *A constructivist vision for teaching, learning, and staff development*. ERIC Document Reproduction Services No. 383 557.

Sterling, S. (2001) *Sustainable education: Re-visioning learning and change*. Foxhole, Devon: Green Books.

Tyack, D., & Cuban, L. (2000) *Tinkering towards Utopia*. Cambridge, MA: Harvard University Press.

Chapter 8

Learning to learn in Finland

Theory and policy, research and practice

Jarkko Hautamäki and Sirkku Kupiainen

Abstract

The Finnish National Board of Education published the framework for evaluating educational outcomes in 1995, of which learning to learn competences and motivation for lifelong learning were key objectives. These were viewed as outcomes that *do not fall into the domain of any particular school subject*; rather, they were to be seen as *common pedagogical goals* for all school subjects. The definition of learning to learn was *the ability and willingness to adapt to novel tasks*, or the adaptive and voluntary mastery of learning action. This means that learning to learn is seen to comprise a cognitive component – basic knowledge and (thinking) skills – and an affective component that steers the use of these competences. In the Finnish framework, ability or competence refers to thinking or reasoning, and to the knowledge of relevant facts; to the ease with which the student can access that previously learned and can apply general, earlier acquired procedures to adapt to new tasks. The scales cover reading comprehension, basic mathematical operations, deductive and analytical reasoning, and formal operational thinking. The affective dimension encompasses both self-related and context-related beliefs and attitudes, and is assessed using self-report questionnaires. In addition, the assessment includes questions regarding background data (gender, parents' education, language spoken at home, school achievement). The objectives of the Finnish Learning to Learn Project are twofold: first, to provide 'epidemiological' data of the measured learning-related factors for system-level evaluation, and second, to serve individual schools and municipalities as a tool for school development.

Key words: learning to learn framework, cognitive component, affective component, mastery of learning action, assessment.

> *No one can become really educated without having pursued some study in which he took no interest – for it is a part of education to learn to interest ourselves in subjects for which we have no aptitude.*
>
> (T.S. Eliot, 1932/1969)

Theory and practice

The start

The comprehensive school, comprising the first nine years of education (7–16 years), was adopted in Finland in 1968, and implemented across the country during the 1970s. In the 1980s, the Finnish education system was largely decentralized, giving the municipalities a stronger role in education (Aho et al., 2006). This decentralization led, among other things, to the abolition of school inspections and of the mandatory approval of textbooks by the education authorities. Moreover, the first very detailed national curriculum was replaced in 1985 by a core curriculum that outlined fairly general goals and norms on which every school was to build their own curriculum.

However, by the 1990s, a concern had arisen over educational equality between different parts of the country, and the National Board of Education (NBE) launched a project to develop a strategy for the evaluation of the effectiveness of education (NBE, 1995). It is worth noting that except for the matriculation or exit exam at the end of the academic track of upper secondary education, the Finnish equivalent of high school, sixth-form or gymnasium, there is and never has been any national exams or testing in Finnish schools. Following this tradition, the NBE implemented the evaluation strategy by introducing sample-based assessments in core subjects in the form of bi-annual assessments at Grade 9 in Finnish and in mathematics, with assessments in other subjects and at other grades on a less regular basis. The NBE also began to look for ways to assess the more equivocal outcomes of education, often referred to as cross-curricular competences (cf. NBE, 1998). During concurrent discussions within the European Union (EU) and in the Organization for Economic Cooperation and Development (OECD), learning to learn was seen to have a central position among the cross-curricular competences as a precursor for lifelong learning. In the Recommendation of the European Parliament of 2006 (2006/962/EC), learning to learn was included in the eight key competences and aptitudes deemed necessary for personal fulfilment and development, social inclusion, active citizenship, and employment in the present and future knowledge society.

The Finnish National Board of Education published the first framework for evaluating educational outcomes in 1995, and a slightly revised framework in 1998 (NBE, 1995, 1998; Yrjönsuuri, 1995). Learning to learn competences and motivation for lifelong learning were key objectives of the framework. These intertwined constructs were viewed as outcomes that *do not fall into the domain of any particular school subject*; rather, they were to be seen as *common pedagogical goals* for all school subjects. As a public administrative document, the evaluation strategy created an opening and an incentive for developing a more detailed framework for learning to learn.

In 1996, the National Board of Education gave a group of researchers at the University of Helsinki the task of developing a framework for learning to learn and a tool for its assessment. This led to the founding of the Centre for Educational Assessment. In the Finnish Learning to Learn Framework, published in English in 2002 (Hautamäki et al., 2002), learning to learn is seen to encompass general cognitive and affective goals that are not the sole domain or responsibility of any one subject, but formed through the contents of, and good educational practices in, different subjects. Accordingly, the assessment of learning to learn is seen to provide the schools participating in the assessment, as well as state, municipal, and school-level education authorities, information on how well schools are succeeding in fostering in students the capacities necessary for the application of the knowledge and skills acquired across the curriculum in later life, in work as well as in leisure-time and civic activities.

The core definition for learning to learn in the Finnish framework can be stated as *the ability and willingness to adapt to novel tasks*, or the adaptive and voluntary mastery of learning action (Hautamäki et al., 2002; Hautamäki et al., 2010). This means that learning to learn is seen to comprise a cognitive component – basic knowledge and (thinking) skills – and an affective component that steers the use of these competences. Yet, while learning to learn in its 'fulfilled form' might be considered close to self-regulated or voluntary learning, the tool built for its assessment also covers factors that impede successful learning (to learn). This is based on the understanding – supported by later empirical evidence in the Finnish assessments – that to foster students' future readiness and willingness to learn, preventing the formation of dysfunctional beliefs and attitudes can be at least as important as supporting the formation of beliefs and attitudes that promote (further) learning.

In the Finnish Learning to Learn Framework, ability or competence refers to thinking or reasoning, and to the knowledge of relevant facts; to the ease with which the student can access that previously learned and can apply general, earlier acquired procedures to adapt to a new task at hand. The cognitive tasks cover reading comprehension (text macro-processing), basic mathematical operations, deductive and analytical reasoning, and formal operational thinking. These are all understood to be malleable skills that can be developed and fostered by good teaching (e.g. Adey et al., 2007). Accordingly, shortcomings revealed in the assessment can be utilized to direct later teaching and can thus improve the effectiveness of education.

The affective dimension of learning to learn encompasses both self-related and context-related beliefs and attitudes, and is assessed using self-report questionnaires. The self-related beliefs comprise motivation (e.g. Dweck, 1990; Deci & Ryan, 2000; Gottfried et al., 2001), goal orientation (e.g. Elliot & Dweck, 1988; Elliot & Church, 1997; Niemivirta et al., 2001; Harackiewicz et al., 2002), control and agency beliefs (e.g. Chapman et al., 1990; Zimmermann, 2000; Little et al., 2001), learning strategies (e.g. Ames & Archer, 1988; Clayton et al., 2010), means–ends beliefs (e.g. Dweck et al., 1995a, 1995b), academic self-concept in thinking, maths, reading, and writing (e.g. Marsh & Shavelson, 1985; Markus & Wurf 1987; Marsh, 1990a, 1990b; Harter, 1999; Marsh et al., 2006), general self-esteem (e.g. Buhrmester et al., 2011; Zeigler-Hill, 2013), self-handicapping (e.g. Eronen et al., 1998; Midgley & Urdan, 2001; Urdan & Midgley, 2001), fear of failure (e.g. Bartels & Magun-Jackson, 2009; De Castella et al., 2013), students' perceptions of their school and classroom, socio-moral view of oneself as a student (e.g. Brugman et al., 2003), and group work behaviour. The context-related beliefs include the perceived support of significant others (parents, teachers, peers; Grolnick et al., 1991) in school and in learning-related activities. Scales to measure students' motivation for, or orientation towards, later learning are also included in the assessment of older students.

In addition to the cognitive tasks and the affective questionnaires, the assessment includes questions regarding background data (gender, parents' education, language spoken at home, school achievement). Furthermore, data regarding class, school, type of municipality (urban vs. rural), and province are collected to allow for multi-level analyses. More recently, the assessment studies have also included teacher questionnaires. The focus has not only been on teaching methods and on teachers' appraisal of their students or the classes they teach, but also of the school where they work.

The objectives of the Finnish Learning to Learn Project are twofold: first, to provide 'epidemiological' data of the measured learning-related factors for system-level evaluation, and second, to serve individual schools and municipalities as a tool for school development. The first objective, achieved originally in collaboration with the National Board of Education, included the creation of national norms for the measured characteristics at different grades (end of primary, end of lower secondary, and second year of upper secondary schools, i.e., 12-, 15-, and 17-year-olds). The normative data for the turn of the millennium covered some 15,000 students with two data collections at Grade 6 and Grade 9 (1996/2002 and 1997/2001, respectively), and one for the two-track Finnish upper secondary schools (general and vocational track) in 2000. A new nationally representative assessment at Grade 9, replicating the 2001 sample, was implemented in 2012, to facilitate appraisal of possible changes in the Finnish comprehensive school students' competences (presently under preparation).

All studies have been conducted in the spirit of Finnish educational legislation, which stipulates that national and local assessments should support advancement of local education. This has meant that all necessary measures have been used to prevent publication of 'league tables'. Also, efforts have been made to develop means to communicate results to local municipalities and even to single schools (see below).

In total, some 120,000 students have participated in the different national, municipal, and school-level assessments between 1996 and 2013, providing one of the largest data sets worldwide of the competences and learning-related attitudes of students of different ages, gathered with statistically comparable instruments.

Modelling learning to learn

The concept of *learning to learn competences*, or 'cross-curricular knowledge, skills, and attitudes', refers to the cognitive and affective factors central to the application of existing skills to novel tasks and to new learning. Instead of cross-curricular knowledge, a new concept of transversal skills is emerging, even if still without a commonly agreed definition (cf. Zuliani, 2008; Sicilia, 2009; Brunello & Schlotter, 2010). It should be noted that in this chapter we use concepts such as ability and aptitudes as being synonymous with 'competence' or 'competencies' (for the term competence, see also Hoskins & Deakin Crick, 2010), and are aware of the many meanings ascribed to them in the literature. No commitment to any specific theory is thus to be read into their use (however, see Adey et al., 2007), in the manner of Richard Snow's way to approach learning to learn (Snow & Swanson, 1992; Snow, 1996).

On a general curricular-philosophical level, the Finnish quest for learning to learn can be classified under E.D. Hirsch's theme, 'Tool Conception of Education' (Hirsch 1996). Hirsch includes in this theme such notions as accessing skills, critical thinking skills, higher-order skills, lifelong learning, metacognitive skills, and problem-solving skills. The Finnish framework embraces this idea of general tools formed through good teaching but acknowledges the many structural constraints embedded in learning and development.

On a measurement level, the Finnish Framework and Indicator for learning to learn are based on a modified version of Snow's models for educational assessment (Snow, 1990, 1995). In these models, the components assessed are Conceptual Structures, Procedural Skills, Learning Strategies, Self-Regulatory Functions, and Motivational Orientations. Snow then examines each component from three different perspectives: 'Aptitude Constructs and Initial States', 'Learning–Development Transitions', and 'Achievement Constructs and Desired End States'. A certain aptitude is assumed to provide the starting point for a new learning activity, and to (re)appear as a new achievement. If learning to learn assessment is based on tasks that require adaptation in the learning–development transition stage by the student, the tasks can be seen as both aptitude and achievement assessment while also tapping the student's attitudes or beliefs.

Snow also shows in his model that, before being accepted, a task activates orientation to task type, to subject-matter characteristics (relevance to learner, novelty to learner, dominant symbol system), to treatment dimensions (ambiguity, risk and evaluation, stress and importance of outcome, novelty, meaningfulness, complexity of information processing required, structured-ness and completeness, adaptive-ness to learner), and to instructional-social contexts.

In the Finnish framework, the concept of *learning function* (cf. Häyrynen & Hautamäki, 1976) is used to make a distinction between knowledge (*to know*), skill (*to be able*), exploration (*to study*), and wish (*to hope*). Knowledge refers to the knowing of facts, i.e. to declarative knowing or conceptual structures (Snow, 1990, 1995). Skill refers to knowing how, i.e. to the ability to apply knowledge or to procedural knowledge (Snow, 1990, 1995). Yet, the mere knowing of facts and knowing how to proceed do not by themselves lead one to undertake a task. What is needed is the act of exploration, i.e. the readiness to assess the situation, to set a goal, and to act on it through perseverance (covering, but not limited to, the concepts of learning strategies and self-regulation in Snow's model). In addition, the component of hope, in the form of a perspective of personal goal attainment, is an integral but conceptually distinct part of exploration. With it we want to emphasize the courage needed to face the challenge of a task – and possible defeat.

In the framework, learning to learn is seen to comprise and adhere to several theoretical traditions within the educational sciences. The indicator is built to operationalize this diverse theoretical background to a practical solution for a valid and reliable assessment of this multi-dimensional phenomenon in the school setting with the guidance of the teacher.

The cognitive psychological tradition sees thinking and higher cognitive functions as malleable (Resnick, 1987; Klauer, 1988, 2000; Gardner, 1991; Nuthall, 1999; Shayer & Adey, 2002; Adey et al., 2007; Demetriou et al., 2011). From this tradition derive the different modes of the tasks, the idea of assessing automated skills in new contexts, the idea of identifying and using propositions, and the idea of mental tools. Due to the requirements of limited testing time, the scales have been reduced to cover only the most critical areas and modes within the field (reading comprehension, mathematical thinking, and reasoning skills).

The socio-cultural tradition (Lompscher, 1972; Häyrynen & Hautamäki, 1976; Lurija, 1976; Leontjev, 1978; Vygotsky, 1978; Moll, 1990; Cole, 1996; Claxton, 2007) has provided ideas relating to learning activity, to relations between motives, goals, and actions, to the roles of context factors and significant others, and to the general idea of a new 'epistemic mentality'.

The motivational and volitional traditions (Marsh & Shavelson, 1985; Marsh, 1990a, 1990b; Bandura, 1997; Harter, 1999; Pintrich, 2000) attest to both the positive and the negative effects of attitudes or beliefs in goal-oriented action. In the Finnish framework and in the indicator, these have been tuned to school-subject-specific topics and to schooling as the developmentally important setting for the formation of learning to learn.

Students' goals at school are linked to learning tasks that the teacher provides and the students are expected to accept as their own. In this process, the outer social context is complemented by the inner context of the self. The solution – be it positive or negative – is to be evaluated by the student socially and internally. Social comparison and achievement assessment tie it to the social system – to teachers, classmates, and parents – whereas inner evaluation ties it back to the goals set by the student. These two comparisons lead to a confirmation of present self-understanding or provide an incentive for change. This double process then continues throughout the years of schooling, and, gradually, results in more stable self-understanding, and the acceptance or rejection of the roles of student.

In the case of learning to learn assessment, students are given novel tasks that they are invited to accept as their own with all the motivational, goal- and aptitude-related conditions attached, and the processes of learning to learn are set in motion in this acceptance. Regardless of the knowledge or skill level of the student, the acceptance of the assessment task (or the refusal of it) activates processes that either enhance or hinder flexible intellectual work. Yet, with the non-curricular nature of the learning to learn tasks, it is easier to see the task itself as summoning up in the student the skills and abilities needed to begin to solve the tasks. Therefore, the assessment tasks can be seen to better anticipate the students' behaviour in further learning contexts as a part of lifelong learning.

The non-curricular nature of the Finnish learning to learn assessment means the cognitive items are not directly derived from the curriculum of the respective grade(s). Instead, the tasks are modified to include an element of surprise, to offer an impression of being related to but different from typical school tasks, hence requiring a wider use of skills and abilities acquired during the school years and also in learning outside of school. There is an axiomatic claim here – good tasks call for the use of plastic general abilities accumulated throughout the years while also arousing interest. In this, the cognitive tasks do not represent a return or relapse into the notion of fixed intelligence. Instead, the claim that both cognitive skills and learning-related attitudes are outcomes and effects of (good) schooling is central to the endeavour of the Finnish learning to learn assessment. Hence, the formation of learning to learn can be called epigenetic by nature, using concepts of modern developmental psychology. Moreover, the claim is that in assessing the future-oriented concept of learning to learn, students should be presented with – and given the incentive to solve – tasks that are not overtly familiar, as this is the kinds of tasks they will meet as adults in working careers or in further studies.

To summarize, the Finnish Learning to Learn Framework (Hautamäki et al., 2002, 2006), commissioned by the Finnish National Board of Education together with the City of Helsinki Education Department, was developed by the Centre for Educational Assessment (CEA) at the University of Helsinki. The framework posts learning to learn as two-dimensional: 'Mastery of Thinking' and 'Perspective of Hope', and encompasses several theoretical traditions within educational and developmental psychology. The conceptual core can be summarized as understanding learning to learn as the 'ability to adapt to novel tasks'.

Hence, learning to learn is seen to encompass general educational goals that are not the sole domain or responsibility of any one subject but

- are formed in good pedagogical practice in different subjects;
- guide students' learning at school and are present in school achievement;
- can be understood as a precursor to lifelong learning in indicating students' (cognitive) propensity and (affective and volitional) willingness for learning and self-development.

In assessment, learning to learn is divided into competences (knowledge and thinking skills) and into school and learning-related beliefs, attitudes, and motivation.

In the Finnish framework, learning to learn is defined as the ability and willingness to adapt to novel tasks, activating one's *mastery of thinking* and the *perspective of hope* by means of maintaining one's cognitive and affective self-regulation in and of learning action (Hautamäki et al., 2002; Hautamäki et al., 2010, Hautamäki, 2010). The definition includes three central concepts, which will be specified in more detail:

- *Adaptation*: the student's active action (reflective abstraction and reflective intentionality or mentality) for attaining a balance between the current and the anticipated (goal) state.

- *Mastery of thinking*: the active use of intellectual competences relevant for task performance and for accommodation.
- *Perspective of hope or personal goal attainment*: the balance between facilitating and inhibiting affective and motivational forces that influence the activation of relevant skills and abilities as well as their effectiveness in relation to the given task.

The core supposition

As mentioned above, the central claim of the Finnish model is that any task (e.g. learning and assessment situation) activates students' prior knowledge and skills (the learning domain), the cognitive tools for acquiring new contents and intellectual schemes at their disposal (the reasoning domain), and the beliefs, attitudes, and mental frames [the 'value and sense orientation' of Galperin (see Arievitch and Stetsenko, 2000; Podolskij 2010), or 'intellectual transcendent mode' of Donaldson (1993)]. Tasks are accepted as personal motives and goals within a particular social situation through the process of orientation. This, in turn, activates processes of adaptation where emotions and cognition are coordinated to enable the appropriate cognitive acts, such as learning new competencies, and the monitoring of progress (goal state and actual state comparisons).

The stages of accepting the task and activating the general cognitive abilities can be understood as cognitive activities taking place in a particular context. The context frames the learning activity (cf. Zuckerman, 2004) during which diverse dimensions relevant for task acceptance and learning are initially monitored (oriented to) and taken into account or are taken for granted. Generally, these aspects can be understood as constraints that are universal, objective, and socio-historical. Learning to learn takes place within these conditions (Figs. 8.1 and 8.2).

Universal conditions refer to the general physical and biological conditions of human beings and to the actual situation and estimated risks for well-being of the learning situation. When learning or assessment takes place in school, the universal conditions can be assumed to be standard for the respective community (no real danger even if children are tired, hot or cold, or hungry).

Figure 8.1 Three major contextual conditions for learning activity.

The dynamic field of learning to learn activity

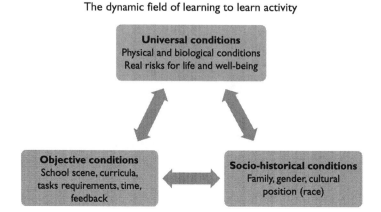

Figure 8.2 Learning to learn as an activity takes place in a constrained space, where several explicit and implicit conditions are taken into account as frame-factors.

Objective conditions include the schooling scene, the curriculum in force and textbooks in use, the actual task requirements given in test instructions, time given for the testing (say 2 hours in PISA, or 90 minutes in the Finnish test), and the role of feedback (often not instant; might even be given after each item when the testing is computerized). Often, objective conditions are left unanalysed or are not understood as such; but they do have their effects on the scores, which should be understood.

Socio-historical conditions include general societal factors and individual student-related characteristics such as gender and socio-economic or immigration status. These are the key variables used in breaking down the variance in learning outcome and change due to their role in influencing students' learning and school-related attitudes. They also constitute the major educational equity variables critical for interpreting differences in scholastic achievement both nationally and internationally (cf. Hautamäki et al., 2008, 2009; Carnoy & Rothstein, 2013).

A learning or assessment task appears to the student in a particular context defined by the three constraints of the universal, objective, and socio-historical conditions, activating students' orientation to the subjective meaning of the situation to them and to the objective requirements of the task. The objective structure of a task may be described using the terms of Sternberg's triarchic theory: analytical, practical or creative, and verbal, numeric or pictorial (Sternberg et al., 2001), or by using Piagetian or neo-Piagetian theories (Adey et al., 2007) to claim that the task demands certain formal operational schemata like control-of-variables. There are also other parallel ways to describe the objective structure of tasks.

Students' adaptation to the task situation and to the task is processed through two analytically separate processes of affective and cognitive modulation (Fig. 8.3). The former can be called reflective intentionality or mentalizing

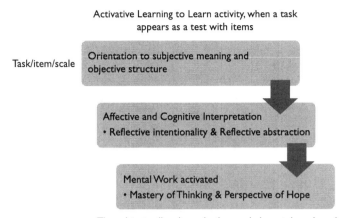

Figure 8.3 Learning to learn activity as a process in which cognitive and affective elements are interpreted and united in an attempt to solve tasks and respond to attitude questions.

(Hautamäki, 2010) and the latter reflective abstraction (Piaget, 1985, 2001). These lead to processes that we have called the mastery of thinking and the perspective of hope or personal goal attainment. If either of these two vectors is not activated, the student does not provide a valid response to the task, leading to underachievement and, in assessment, to an underestimate of competence.

The task can be rejected and not attempted; it can be accepted and attempted by solving or not solving. The task can be a real life task or, in a testing situation, a test item. The idea is, of course, in all testing, that the scores have a predictive validity and predict success later in working life.

Measuring learning to learn

Whereas PISA can be seen to take a step *forward* regarding some school subjects by looking at students' proficiency in applying their skills and knowledge in everyday-like tasks even if presented as narratives of the real situation, read about and answered in the classroom, the Finnish learning to learn assessment takes a step *backwards* to the factors that *lead to* the learning of those subjects. Accordingly, it seeks to disentangle the diverse cognitive and affective factors that lead to learning at school and beyond school – though, like PISA, measuring it in the classroom with paper-and-pencil or computerized tasks and questionnaires.

Regarding the three constraints of learning activity described above, the measurement situation can be described as follows: The universal conditions are controlled through the assessment taking place in safe circumstances in students' own classrooms. The objective conditions differ from (high-stakes) subject-specific achievement testing through the non-curricular nature of the tasks, the addition of personal questions, and the low-stakes nature of the assessment even if the assessment situation is based on students' familiarity with teaching and learning situations where formal thinking and doing one's best are required. The socio-historical conditions are present and will be used in the analysis of the results in the form of educational equity indicators regarding the relative role of students' gender, family background (socio-economic status), possible immigration status, and language spoken at home as the key explanatory variables.

The measurement model

As stated above, the Finnish Learning to Learn Framework differs from some related constructs in its emphasis on the general cognitive competence of students *before* they enter formal education but constantly developed through good curricular teaching and learning. This difference is seen clearly in the comment of Black and colleagues regarding the Finnish model: 'This exploration [the Black et al. paper] examines the [Finnish] construct of L2L and argues against its implication that there is a distinct capacity with generality of application across all forms of learning' (Black et al., 2006). We indeed imply that there is and should be something general for the learning to learn notion to be useful in educational discourse, and we start from the premise that learning a task-specific strategy leads to transfer effects that build on and are dependent on general strategies. The reverse, however, is not true.

The learning of a general strategy does not lead to transfer effects in learning situations, which are always dependent upon specific strategies. *A general strategy is used, a specific strategy is learned* (Klauer, 2000). Klauer calls these higher-order skills or general strategies *analytical thinking*, and the related specific strategies *inductive thinking*. He sees the formation of inductive thinking as a means of promoting learning and the formation of higher-order general strategies. Following Klauer, we claim that learning to learn competency is therefore a general-ability concept. It is, however, brought about through the learning and application of specific strategies that can be specified in a curriculum-relevant manner and which are connected to their respective curricular or achievement domains.

This raises the following essential questions: How do we measure a general-ability concept? What kinds of tools or tasks and tests are needed for the estimation of this generalized learning activity, which in our framework is called learning to learn activity? Gustafsson (2002) presents his idea of referent generality and three axioms to be used in assessing such constructs. The axioms are:

1. To measure constructs with high referent generality, it is necessary to use heterogeneous measurement devices.
2. A homogeneous test always measures several dimensions.
3. To measure constructs with low referent generality, it is also necessary to measure constructs with high generality.

The danger in basing the measurements on too limited a pool of items is construct under-representation. A way to avoid the problem of construct under-representation in the measurement of high referent generality constructs is the construction of heterogeneous measures. If the measurement is interpreted in terms of the low referent generality construct, the variance due to the more general constructs takes the form of construct-irrelevant variance. Understanding learning to learn as a low referent construct would be to claim that there are several distinct learning to learn capacities, and thus different forms of learning in different academic subjects. Using such modelling, the measurement of learning to learn will involve the affective domain only – maybe including metacognition without its cognitive component – with the cognitive component of learning left out. In addition to presenting a reduced version of learning (to learn), we would face other problems, one of which is the poor comparability of results based on Likert and other measurement scales due to cultural differences in response style (cf. Kupiainen et al., 2008; Buckley, 2009). Without the possibility to anchor students' attitudinal responses to their cognitive competence, attempts to understand the role of the affective domain in learning and in scholastic achievement – and as an independent outcome of schooling – is hard to interpret (for PISA, see Olson, 2003; Buckley, 2009).

If learning to learn competence is understood as comprising the mastery of thinking and the perspective-of-hope – or cognition and emotion/attitudes – it is necessary to measure it with diverse cognitive and affective scales (cf. Gustafsson, 2002). Yet, as learning to learn is understood to develop through education in the different subjects, there is no need for too strict a definition of the set of scales or cognitive tasks which satisfy the conditions but that these should be heterogeneous enough to call for or to afford different (earlier) learning experiences. This will also allow for a wider scope of student interest in the assessment situation, supporting the notion of learning to learn as 'a learning set of the prepared mind' (Hautamäki et al., 2010).

The Finnish learning to learn endeavour is by no means the only one, not least since learning to learn is one of the eight key competences in the European Reference Framework of Key Competences (EU 2006) (e.g. Csapò, 2007; Deakin Crick, 2007; Fredriksson & Hoskins, 2007; Hoskins & Fredriksson, 2008). Yet it seems that many of these position their approaches to the Finnish framework, either neutrally or more critically. Therefore, it is important to try to analyse learning to learn using also PISA and other general solutions to worldwide assessments of students' competence. In the Appendix, we present the relations of some of the Finnish cognitive scales to PISA tasks. We have used released PISA items for maths and science. Using IRT-scaling, the scales can be placed in the same metric suitable for comparisons.

Research and practice

Learning to learn assessment in Finnish comprehensive schools

In the 1970s, Finland adopted a nine-year comprehensive basic schooling, pedagogically divided into primary Grades 1–6 with classroom teachers and lower secondary Grades 7–9 with subject teachers. After compulsory basic schooling, more than 90% of students continue their schooling in the tracked upper secondary education, either in general academic or in vocational schools, both lasting 3–4 years and providing a gateway to tertiary education (cf. Kupiainen et al., 2009).

The Finnish learning to learn studies have been implemented at all major transitions of the school continuum with nationally representative samples Fig. 8.4), enriched with repetitive cross-sectional and longitudinal studies at the municipal level. For Grade 1 students, the data are from the Helsinki metropolitan area. All studies have been comprehensive in the sense that all students of the respective grades participated in the studies.

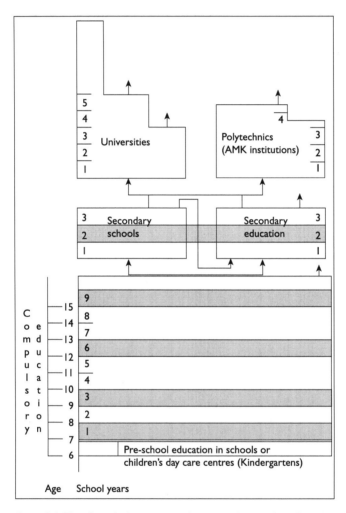

Figure 8.4 The Finnish learning to learn studies within Finnish education. (1st, 3rd, 6th, and 9th grades. Grade 10 is optional for students wishing to raise their Grade 9 GPA.)

The Finnish Learning to Learn Assessment Battery

Since 1996, several sets of scales for the cognitive component (mastery of thinking) and the affective component (the perspective of hope) have been tested, used, and refined. One of the early versions is presented in Hautamäki et al. (2002), another in the report of the European Union learning to learn pilot project of 2008 (Kupiainen et al., 2008).

Some of the cognitive scales are modifications (with permission) of instruments developed by others; some have been constructed specifically for the Finnish learning to learn endeavour. All have been modified and extended to allow for the assessment of students at different grades based on empirical evidence, with the national studies providing normative standards for assessments at the municipal and school level. All modifications have been done using classical test theory and IRT-scaling (see the Appendix, where the scales used in the EU pilot are presented). The affective scales were constructed at the Centre for Educational Assessment, most notably by Airi Hautamäki, Markku Niemivirta, and Patrik Scheinin.

We present here some of the scales that have been used in the recent studies (Kupiainen, Marjanen, Vainikainen, and Hautamäki, 2011) in the Helsinki metropolitan area.

Cognitive tasks

The cognitive tasks in the instrument have been chosen to provide a well-rounded picture of students' cognitive competence. The scales are analysed and reported both individually and as the weighted first principal component. In the later examples, this dimension is called simply learning to learn competence. Most of the cognitive tasks have eight items with three to five multiple-choice answers each, coded 0 or 1 first for each variable (when necessary 2011) and then for the whole item.

Control of variables

The task is a modified version (Hautamäki, 1989; Hautamäki et al., 2002) of the Science Reasoning Task the 'Pendulum' (Shayer, 1979), regarding the control of variables and is based on one of the formal schemata identified by Inhelder and Piaget (1958). The students are presented with comparisons set in the world of Formula 1 races with four variables: driver, car, tyres, and track. A variation of the task, called CHOCO, a chocolate comparison task, was used in the EU pilot project of 2008 (Kupiainen et al., 2009; see Appendix).

Hidden arithmetic operators

The task is based on the quantitative-relational arithmetic operators task of Demetriou and colleagues (e.g. Demetriou et al., 1991, 1996). The task comprises problems with one to four operators (e.g. '6 = (5 a 3) b 4. In this task, letter a / b stands for: addition (+) / subtraction (–) / multiplication (×) / division (÷)').

Invented arithmetic operators

The task is a modified group-version of Sternberg's Triarchic Test (H-version) Creative Number Scale (Sternberg et al., 2001), where arithmetic operators are conditionally defined depending on the value of the digits they connect. The task uses two operators with differing definitions and can comprise several operations in the same equation (e.g. 'a *lag* b; If a > b, then *lag* stands for subtraction, else for multiplication'; 'What is 4 *lag* 7 *sev* 10 *lag* 3?').

Missing premises

The task is adapted from the Ross Test of Higher Cognitive Processes, Section III (Ross & Ross, 1979). In each of the eight problems, students are presented with a fact (premise) and a conclusion, and their task is to choose the second fact (premise) from among five alternatives to make the conclusion valid.

Reading comprehension

The task is based on Kintch and van Dijk's (1978) model of text comprehension, using a Finnish translation of a text by Winograd regarding the development of US cities in the late nineteenth century (cf. Lyytinen & Lehto, 1998; Lehto et al., 2001). After reading the text, the student is presented with 16 statements and asked to evaluate their relevance with reference to the text using a 3-point scale with labels 'a good description of the text as a whole', 'gives vital information regarding the text', and 'information that is trivial regarding the topic of the text'.

Affective scales

The self-report questionnaires for the affective domain comprise scales for a range of factors relevant for new learning and for school achievement (e.g. academic self-concept, academic withdrawal, achievement goal orientation, agency beliefs, fear of failure, learning strategies, means–ends beliefs, self-efficacy, and self-esteem) with additional scales regarding homework, listening in class, relationships with parents, and leisure-time activities.

Five scales are described here. All affective items are answered using a 7-point Likert scale ranging from 1 ('Not true at all') to 7 ('Very true'). The results are presented using the Likert scale, but also applying standardized national norms for each grade. The scales are analysed and presented in the reports both individually, as clustered according to their relation to achievement, and as the weighted first principal component. In the later examples, this dimension is called simply learning to learn attitudes. Also, profile-oriented analyses have been implemented in specific studies.

Achievement goal orientation

Achievement goal theory has been one of the major sub-fields of motivation theory since the 1980s (e.g. Nicholls, 1984; Elliot & Dweck, 1988; Pintrich, 2000). Of the extended five-dimension model applied in the Finnish learning to learn studies, two scales are given as examples: mastery-intrinsic (e.g. 'To acquire new knowledge is an important goal for me in school') and mastery-extrinsic (e.g. 'My goal is to succeed in school') (Niemivirta et al., 2001; Niemivirta, 2002; Tuominen-Soini et al., 2008).

Agency beliefs

Agency beliefs are generally understood to form one component of the trio of means–ends or causality beliefs, agency beliefs, and control expectancies (e.g. Little et al., 1995, 2001). In the Finnish instrument, only the two key dimensions of ability and effort have been used, to complement the more specific scales for academic self-concepts (maths, reading, writing, and thinking), control expectancy, and means–ends beliefs (ability, effort, and chance).

Control motivation

Based on Strube and colleagues' work, the Finnish instrument comprises a scale for *control motivation* (e.g. 'If I get a problem wrong, I want to know where I made the mistake') to tap students' quest to understand the reasons for failure in order to learn from the mistakes they make (Shalon & Strube, 1988; Strube & Yost, 1993; Niemivirta, 2004).

Self-efficacy

The Finnish learning to learn instrument comprises two separate scales for general self-efficacy, one referring to school achievement and the other to learning.

Communicating assessment results to stakeholders

From the beginning, the Finnish Learning to Learn Project has been both a scientific and policy endeavour. Hence, communication of the goals and the outcomes of the assessments to the schools assessed and to the municipal/national school administration has been of paramount importance from the beginning. But, as Olson (2003: 276–277) states, it is a difficult task:

> Educational discourse and educational theory are polemical rather than constructive to the extent that they fail to distinguish these two quite different agendas, the causal analysis of the factors relevant to the functioning of schools as an institution and the intentional analysis of the processes relevant to teaching and learning . . . [and] . . . different methods of analysis are required. Analysis of the school as an institution focuses on the causal factors relevant to the optimal

functioning of the institution as a whole, whereas analysis of pedagogy focuses on the intersubjectivity and intentionality of the teachers and students involved.

It would appear that – in an ideal model – communication takes place in one of three ways. Learning to learn assessment outcomes inform:

- teachers of their success in communicating during and through lessons how failures and errors are treated reflectively, i.e. it is how pupils learn that errors and failures can be useful in the process of learning;
- how well teachers have relayed the criteria for records and marks delivered to pupils at the end of term, i.e. how well the seriousness of schooling has been understood; and
- how well and accurately the school as a whole has understood the tasks and goals of education, as a mediator of precious knowledge of past generations to the next generation, as we have described elsewhere (Hautamäki et al., 2010).

The report developed for communicating the results to the assessed schools offers the key results of the assessment tied to either national or municipal-level standards or means. The main results are presented to the schools in an eight- or twelve-page booklet, where the evaluation project is described, all the scales are briefly presented, and the results are given as box-plots or other figures automatically generated from the data. These are accompanied by an interpretation of the results to assist the independent reading of the report at schools. Each school receives the results of its students and classes referenced to the results of the other schools participating in the assessment but the schools can only be identified by the municipal administration commissioning the assessment. Additional teacher in-service training is offered to schools and municipalities to allow for a deeper insight into the pedagogical implications of the results.

In the report, the overall results are first presented as a two-dimensional model with students' cognitive competence and their learning-enhancing attitudes as the two dimensions, both standardized for the assessed cohort. The results are given for school, class, and student level to demonstrate the role of between-student, between-class, and between-school differences (Fig. 8.5). For each school, its position in the different charts (school, classes, and students) is highlighted.

To further help the interpretation of the later more detailed results, separate charts are provided for the relationship of students' home background (mother's education) and gender with regard to their cognitive competence and learning-related attitudes. After that, more detailed results are given for each cognitive and affective dimension using class-level box-plots with a separate insertion for gender (Fig. 8.6). Both present norm-lines for the cohort median (bold line), the upper / lower limit of the 25th and 75th percentile (dashed line), and their means (thin line). Detailed instructions for reading the charts are always provided in the report.

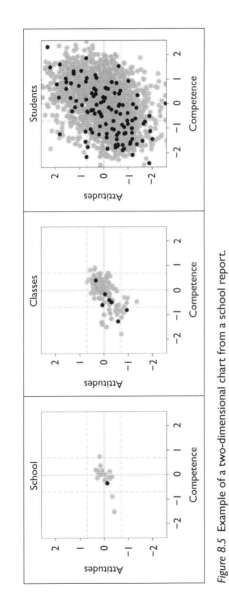

Figure 8.5 Example of a two-dimensional chart from a school report.

Note: Panels from the left: schools, classes, and students. x-axis = cognitive component; y-axis = affective component. All values are normed for the assessed student cohort with mean = 0 and standard deviation = 1.

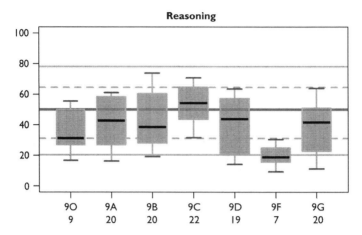

Figure 8.6 Example of a box-plot for a cognitive task from a school.

Note: y-axis = percentage of correctly solved items; x-axis = classes identified by their codes with the number of participating students. Bold line = cohort median; dashed lines = upper/lower limit of the 25th and 75th percentile; thin line = cohort mean of 25th and 75th percentile.

On the side of the school reports, a full report of each study is published for disseminating the outcomes of the assessment to the wider education community (for an example in Finnish, see Kupiainen et al., 2011a).

Summary

The Finnish learning to learn assessment presents a 16-year-old tradition of work between education policy and educational practice. The original quest for a prototype for a common European indicator for the key competence of learning to learn has not been reached but the work has generated a versatile tool for educational evaluation at the national level. Furthermore, the use of the Finnish learning to learn test in successive cross-sectional and longitudinal assessments has provided valuable information on the development of students' general cognitive competence and of their learning and school-related attitudes during the past 15 years. The inclusion of both the cognitive and the affective components of learning – in their role of fostering new learning and as outcomes of education – has given new insight into the development of the relationship between students' cognitive competence, learning-related attitudes, and scholastic achievement through the school years (Kupiainen et al., 2011b).

At the level of school development and praxis, the Finnish learning to learn endeavour has played a seminal role in developing means to disseminate not only assessment results but also more general education policy views and pedagogical topics to schools through the assessment reports and in-service training seminars. While referencing the competences and attitudes of students in individual classes to national or municipal norms (means), their simultaneous referencing to factors such as gender and home background has helped to direct the discussion not to ranking of schools or teachers but to ways to try to overcome the obstacles to the realization of educational equity.

References

Adey, P., Csapó, B., Demetriou, A., Hautamäki, J., & Shayer. M. (2007) 'Can we be intelligent about intelligence? Why education needs the concept of plastic general ability', *Educational Research Review*, 2, 75–97.

Aho, E., Pitkänen, K., & Sahlberg, P. (2006) *Policy development and reform principles of basic and secondary education in Finland since 1968*, Education Working Paper Series 2. Washington, DC: The World Bank.

Ames, C., & Archer, J. (1988) 'Achievement goals in the classroom: Students' learning strategies and motivation processes', *Journal of Educational Psychology*, 80(3), 260–267.

Arievitch, I.M., & Stetsenko, A. (2000) 'The quality of cultural tools and cognitive development: Galperin's perspective and its implication', *Human Development*, 43, 69–92.

Bandura, A. (1997) *Self-efficacy: The exercise of control*. New York: W.H. Freeman.

Bartels, J.M., & Magun-Jackson, S. (2009) 'Approach-avoidance motivation and metacognitive self-regulation: The role of need for achievement and fear of failure', *Learning and Individual Differences*, 19, 459–463.

Black, P., McCormick, R., James, M., & Pedder, D. (2006) 'Learning how to learn and assessment for learning – a theoretical inquiry', *Research Papers in Education*, 21, 119–132.

Brugman, D., Heymans, P.G., Boom, J., Podolskij, A.I., Karabanova, O., & Idobaeva, O. (2003) 'Perception of moral atmosphere in school and norm transgressive behaviour in adolescents: an intervention study', *International Journal of Behavioural Development*, 27, 289–300.

Brunello, G., & Schlotter, M. (2010) *The effect of non cognitive skills and personality traits in labour market outcomes*, Analytical Report for the European Commission prepared by the European Expert Network on Economics of Education (EENEE). Retrieved from: http://www.epis.pt/downloads/dest_15_10_2010.pdf.

Buckley, J. (2009) 'Cross-national response styles in international educational assessments: Evidence from PISA 2006', Paper presented to the NCES Conference on the Program for International Student Assessment (PISA), 'What We Can Learn From PISA', Washington, DC, 2 June. Retrieved from: https://edsurveys.rti.org/PISA/.

Buhrmester, M.D., Blanton, H., & Swann, W.B., Jr. (2011) 'Implicit self-esteem: Nature, measurement, and a new way forward', *Journal of Personality and Social Psychology*, 100(2), 365–385.

Carnoy, M., & Rothstein, R. (2013) *What do international tests really show about U.S. student performance?*, Economic Policy Institute Report. Washington, DC: Economic Policy Institute. Retrieved from: http://www.epi.org/publication/us-student-performance-testing/.

Chapman, M., Skinner, E.A., & Baltes, P.B. (1990) 'Interpreting correlations between children's perceived control and cognitive performance: Control, agency or means–ends beliefs', *Developmental Psychology*, 26(2), 246–253.

Claxton, G. (2007) 'Expanding young people's capacity to learn', *British Journal of Educational Studies, 55*, 115–134.

Clayton, K., Blumberg, F., & Auld, D.P. (2010) 'The relationship between motivation, learning strategies and choice of environment whether traditional or including an online component', *British Journal of Educational Technology, 41*(3), 349–364.

Cole, M. (1996) *Cultural psychology: A once and future discipline.* Cambridge, MA: Harvard University Press.

Csapò, B. (2007) 'Research into learning to learn through the assessment of quality and organization of learning outcomes', *Curriculum Journal, 18*, 195–210.

De Castella, K., Byrne, D., & Covington, M. (2013) 'Unmotivated or motivated to fail? A cross-cultural study of achievement motivation, fear of failure, and student disengagement', *Journal of Educational Psychology, 105*(3), 861–880.

Deakin Crick, R. (2007) 'Learning how to learn: The dynamic assessment of learning power', *Curriculum Journal, 18*, 135–153.

Deci, E.L., & Ryan, R.M. (2000) 'The "what" and "why" of goal pursuits: Human needs and the self-determination of behaviour', *Psychological Inquiry, 11*(4), 227–268.

Demetriou, A., Pachaury, A., Metallidou, Y., & Kazi, S. (1996) 'Universals and specificities in the structure and development of quantitative-relational thought: A cross-cultural study in Greece and India', *International Journal of Behavioural Development, 19*(2), 255–290.

Demetriou, A., Platsidou, M., Efklides, A., Metallidou, Y., & Shayer, M. (1991) 'The development of quantitative-relational abilities from childhood to adolescence: Structure, scaling, and individual differences', *Learning and Instruction, 1*, 19–43.

Demetriou, A., Spanoudis, G., & Mouyi, A. (2011) 'Educating the developing mind: Towards an overarching paradigm', *Educational Psychology Review, 23*, 601–663.

Donaldson, M. (1993) *Human minds: An exploration.* London: Penguin.

Dweck, C.S. (1990) 'Motivational processes affecting learning', *American Psychologist, 41*(10), 1040–1048.

Dweck, C.S., Chiu, C.Y., & Hong, Y.Y. (1995a) 'Implicit theories and their role in judgments and reactions: A word from two perspectives', *Psychological inquiry, 6*(4), 267–285.

Dweck, C.S., Chiu, C.Y., & Hong, Y.Y. (1995b) 'Implicit theories: Elaboration and extension of the model', *Psychological Inquiry, 6*(4), 322–333.

Elliot, A.J., & Church, M.A. (1997) 'A hierarchical model of approach and avoidance achievement motivation', *Journal of Personality and Social Psychology, 72*, 218–232.

Elliot, A.J., & Dweck, C.S. (1988) 'Goals: An approach to motivation and achievement', *Journal of Personality and Social Psychology, 54*, 5–12.

Eliot, T.S. (1932/1969) 'Modern education and the classics', in *Selected essays* (3rd enlarged edn.). London: Faber & Faber.

Eronen, S., Nurmi, J.-E., & Salmela-Aro, K. (1998) 'Optimistic, defensive-pessimistic, impulsive and self-handicapping strategies in university students', *Learning and Instruction, 8*, 159–177.

Fredriksson, U., & Hoskins, B. (2007) 'The development of learning to learn in a European context', *Curriculum Journal, 18*, 127–134.

Gardner, H. (1991) *The unschooled mind: How children think and how schools should teach*, New York: Basic Books.

Gottfried, A.E., Fleming, J.S., & Gottfried, A.W. (2001) 'Continuity of academic intrinsic motivation from childhood through late adolescence: A longitudinal study', *Journal of Educational Psychology*, 93(1), 3–13.

Grolnick, W.S., Ryan, R.M., & Ceci, E.L. (1991) 'Inner resources for school achievement – motivational mediators of children's perceptions of their parents', *Journal of Educational Psychology*, 83(4), 508–517.

Gustafsson, J.-E. (2002) 'Measurement from a hierarchical point of view', in H.I. Braun, D.N. Jackson, & D.E. Wiley (Eds.) *The role of constructs in psychological and educational measurement*. Mahwah, NJ: Erlbaum.

Harackiewicz, J.M., Barron, K.E., Pintrich, P.R., Elliot, A.J., & Thrash, T.M. (2002) 'Revision of achievement goal theory: Necessary and illuminating', *Journal of Educational Psychology*, 94, 638–645.

Harter, S. (1999) *The construction of the self: A developmental perspective*. New York: Guilford Press.

Hautamäki, A. (2010) 'Attachment and parental sensitivity in a low-risk Finnish sample', in P. Aunio, M. Jahnukainen, M. Kalland, & J. Silvonen (Eds.) *Piaget is dead, Vygotsky is still alive, or?* Research in Educational Sciences No. 51. Jyväskylä: Jyväskylä University Press.

Hautamäki, A., Hautamäki, J., & Kupiainen, S. (2010) 'Assessment in schools – Learning to learn', in P. Peterson, E. Baker, & B. McGaw (Eds.) *International encyclopedia of education*, Vol. 3 (3rd edn., pp. 268–272). Oxford: Elsevier.

Hautamäki, J. (1989) 'The application of a Rasch model on Piagetian measures of stages of thinking', in P. Adey & M. Shayer (Eds.) *Adolescent development and school science*. London: Falmer Press.

Hautamäki, J. (2010) 'Task-commitment and developmental tasks – a theoretical scenario with a case study', in P. Aunio, M. Jahnukainen, M. Kalland, & J. Silvonen (Eds.) *Piaget is dead, Vygotsky is still alive, or?* Research in Educational Sciences No. 51. Jyväskylä: Jyväskylä University Press.

Hautamäki, J., Arinen, P., Eronen, S., Hautamäki, A., Kupiainen, S., Lindblom, B. et al. (2002) *Assessing Learning to Learn: A framework*. National Board of Education Evaluation 4/2002. Helsinki: National Board of Education.

Hautamäki, J., Harjunen, E., Hautamäki, A., Karjalainen, T., Kupiainen, S., Laaksonen, S. et al. (2008) *PISA06 Finland: Analyses, reflections and explanations*, Publication 2008:46. Helsinki: Ministry of Education.

Hautamäki, J., Hautamäki, A., & Kupiainen, S. (2009) 'Educational equity account in Nordic countries', in T. Matti (Ed.) *Northern light on PISA 2006: Differences and similarities in the Nordic countries*, TemaNord 2009:547. Copenhagen: Nordic Council of Ministers.

Hautamäki, J., Kupiainen, S., Arinen, P., Hautamäki, A., Niemivirta, M., Rantanen, P. et al. (2006) 'Learning-to-learn asassessment in Finland – versatile tools to monitor and improve effectiveness and equity of the education system', in R. Jakku-Sihvonen & H. Niemi (Eds.) *Research-based teacher education in Finland – reflections by Finnish teacher educators*, Research in Education 25/2006. Jyväskylä: Jyväskylä University Press.

Häyrynen, Y.-P., & Hautamäki, J. (1976) *Människans bildbarhet och utbildningspolitiken [Educability and educational policy]*. Stockholm: Wahlström & Widstrand.

Hirsch, E.D. (1996) *The schools we need and why we don't have them*. New York: Doubleday.

Hoskins, B., & Deakin Crick, R. (2010) 'Competences for learning to learn and active citizenship: Different currencies or two sides of the same coin?', *European Journal of Education: Research, Development and Policy*, 45(1), 121–137.

Hoskins, B., & Fredriksson, U. (2008) *Learning to learn: What is it and can it be measured?*, JRC Scientific and Technical Report, EUR 23432 EN, ISPRA. European Commission/Joint Research Centre/CRELL.

Inhelder, B., & Piaget, J. (1958) *The early growth of logic in the child*. London: Routledge & Kegan Paul.

Kintsch, W., & van Dijk, T.A. (1978) 'Toward a model of text comprehension and production', *Psychological Review*, 85(5), 363–394.

Klauer, K.J. (1988) 'Teaching for learning-to-learn: A critical appraisal with some proposals', *Instructional Science*, 17, 351–367.

Klauer, K.J. (2000) 'Das Huckepack-Theorem Asymmetrischen Strategietransfers. Ein Beitrag zur Trainings- and Transfertheorie', *Zeitschrift fur Entwicklungspsychologie und Pädagogische Psychologie*, 32, 153–165.

Kupiainen, S., Hautamäki, J., & Karjalainen, T. (2009). *The Finnish education system and PISA*, Publication 2009:47. Helsinki: Ministry of Education.

Kupiainen, S., Hautamäki, J., & Rantanen, P. (2008) *EU pre-pilot on learning to learn: Report on the compiled data*, 2008-1190/001-001 TRA-TRINDC. Brussels: EU Commission.

Kupiainen, S., Marjanen, J., Vainikainen, M.-P., & Hautamäki, J. (2011a) 'Oppimaan oppiminen Vantaan peruskouluissa. Kolmas-, kuudes- ja yhdeksäsluokkalaiset oppijoina keväällä 2010'. Vantaan kaupungin sivistysvirasto ja Helsingin yliopiston Koulutuksen arviointikeskus. Retrieved from: http://www.vantaa.fi/instancedata/prime_product_julkaisu/vantaa/embeds/vantaawwwstructure/74425_web_kolmas_kuudes_yhdeksas.pdf.

Kupiainen, S., Marjanen, J., Vainikainen, M.-P., & Hautamäki, J. (2011b) 'Relations between Finnish students' cognitive abilities, learning-related attitudes and GPA at grades 3, 6 and 9', Paper presented at the EARLI 2011 Conference, Exeter, UK.

Lehto, J., Scheinin, P., Kupiainen, S., & Hautamäki, J. (2001) 'National survey of reading comprehension in Finland', *Journal of Research in Reading*, 24, 99–110.

Leontjew, A.N. (1978) *Activity, consciousness, and personality*. Englewood Cliffs, NJ: Prentice-Hall.

Little, T.D., Lopez, D.F., Oettingen, G., & Baltes, P.B. (2001) 'A comparative-longitudinal study of action-control beliefs and school performance', *International Journal of Behavioural Development*, 25, 237–245.

Little, T.D., Oettingen, G., Stetsenko, A., & Baltes, P.B. (1995) 'Children's action-control beliefs about school performance: How do American children compare with German and Russian children?', *Journal of Personality and Social Psychology*, 69, 686–700.

Lompscher, J. (1972) *Theoretische und experimentelle Untersuchungen zur Entwicklung geistiger Fähigkeiten*. Berlin: Volk & Wissen.

Lurija, A.R. (1976) *Cognitive development: Its cultural and social foundations*. Cambridge, MA: Harvard University Press.

Lyytinen, S., & Lehto, J. (1998) 'Hierarchy rating as a measure of text macro-processing: Relationship with working memory and school achievement', *Educational Psychology*, 18, 157–169.

Markus, H., & Wurf, E. (1987) 'The dynamic self-concept: A social psychological perspective', *Annual Review of Psychology*, 38(1), 299–337.

Marsh, H.W. (1990a) 'Causal ordering of academic self-concept and academic achievement: A multiwave longitudinal panel analysis', *Journal of Educational Psychology*, 82(4), 646–656.

Marsh, H.W. (1990b) 'The structure of academic self-concept: The Marsh-Shavelson model', *Journal of Educational Psychology*, 82(4), 623–636.

Marsh, H.W., & Shavelson, R. (1985) 'Self-concept: Its multifaceted, hierarchical structure', *Educational Psychologist*, 20, 107–123.

Marsh, H.W., Trautwein, U., Lüdke, O., Köller, O., & Baumert, J. (2006) 'Integration of multidimensional self-concept and core personality constructs: Construct validation and relations to well-being and achievement', *Journal of Personality*, 74(2), 403–456.

Midgley, M., & Urdan, T. (2001) 'Academic self-handicapping and achievement goals: A further examination', *Contemporary Educational Psychology*, 26, 61–75.

Moll, C.L. (1990) *Vygotsky and education: Instructional implications and applications of socio-historical psychology*. Cambridge: Cambridge University Press.

National Board of Education (NBE) (1995) *Koulutuksen tuloksellisuuden arviointimalli* [*Model for evaluating educational outcomes*], Evaluation 1995:9. Helsinki: NBE.

National Board of Education (NBE) (1998) *Koulutuksen tuloksellisuuden arviointimalli* [*Model for evaluating educational outcomes*], Evaluation 1998:7. Helsinki: NBE.

Nicholls, J.G. (1984) 'Achievement motivation: Conceptions of ability, subjective experience, task choice, and performance', *Psychological Review*, 91, 328–346.

Niemivirta, M. (2002) 'Individual differences and developmental trends in motivation: Integrating person-centred and variable-centred methods', in P.R. Pintrich & M.L. Maehr (Eds.) *Advances in motivation and achievement, Vol. 12: New directions in measures and methods* (pp. 241–275). Amsterdam: JAI Press.

Niemivirta, M. (2004) *Habits of mind and academic endeavours: The correlates and consequences of achievement goal orientations*, University of Helsinki, Department of Education, Research Report 196. Helsinki: Helsinki University Press.

Niemivirta, M., Rijavec, M., & Yamauchi, H. (2001) 'Goal orientations and action-control beliefs: A cross-cultural comparison among Croatian, Finnish and Japanese students', in A. Efklides, J. Kuhl, & R. Sorrentino (Eds.) *Trends and prospects in motivation research* (pp. 163–183). Dordrecht: Kluwer Academic.

Nuthall, G. (1999) 'Learning how to learn: The evolution of students' minds through the social processes and culture of classrooms', *International Journal of Educational Research*, 31, 139–257.

Olson, D. (2003) *Psychological theory and educational reform*. Cambridge: Cambridge University Press.

Piaget, J. (1985) *The equilibration of cognitive structures: The central problem of intellectual development*. Chicago, IL: University of Chicago Press.

Piaget, J. (2001) *Studies in reflecting abstraction*. Hove: Psychology Press.

Pintrich, P.R. (2000) 'An achievement goal theory perspective on issues in motivation terminology, theory, and research', *Contemporary Educational Psychology*, 25, 92–104.

Podolskij, A. (2010) 'The P. Galperin's theory of planned stage-by-stage formation of mental action as a tool to improve teaching/learning activity', in P. Aunio, M. Jahnukainen, M. Kalland, & J. Silvonen (Eds.) *Piaget is dead, Vygotsky is still alive, or?* Research in Educational Sciences No. 51. Jyväskylä: Jyväskylä University Press.

Resnick, L. (1987) *Learning to think*. Washington, DC: National Academy Press.

Ross, J.D., & Ross, C.M. (1979) *Ross test of higher cognitive processes*. Novato, CA: Academic Therapy Publications.

Shalon, M., & Strube, M.J. (1988) 'Type a behaviour and emotional responses to uncertainty: A test of the self-appraisal model', *Motivation and Emotion*, *12*(4), 385–398.

Shayer, M. (1979) 'Has Piaget's construct of formal operational thinking any utility?', *British Journal of Educational Psychology*, *49*, 265–276.

Shayer, M., & Adey, P. (Eds.) (2002) *Learning intelligence: Cognitive acceleration across the curriculum from 5 to 15 years*. Buckingham: Open University Press.

Sicilia, M.-A. (2009) 'How should transversal competences be introduced in computer education?', *SIGCSE Bulletin*, *41*(4), 95–98.

Snow, R. (1990) 'New approaches to cognitive and conative assessment in education', *International Journal of Educational Research*, *25*, 455–473.

Snow, R. (1995) 'Abilities in academic tasks', in R. Sternberg & R.K. Wagner (Eds.) *Mind in context: Interactionist perspective on human intelligence*. Cambridge: Cambridge University Press.

Snow, R. (1996) 'Aptitude development and education', *Psychology, Public Policy, and Law*, *2*, 536–560.

Snow, R., & Swanson, J. (1992) 'Instructional psychology: aptitude, adaptation, and assessment', *Annual Review of Psychology*, *43*, 583–626.

Sternberg, R.J., Castejon, J.L., Prieto, M.D., Hautamäki, J., & Grigorenko, E.L. (2001) 'Confirmatory factor analysis of the Sternberg Triarchic Abilities Test in three international samples: An empirical test of the triarchic theory of intelligence', *European Journal of Psychological Assessment*, *17*, 1–16.

Strube, M.J., & Yost, J.H. (1993) 'Control motivation and self-appraisal', in G. Weary, F. Gleicher, & K.L. Marsh (Eds.) *Control motivation and social cognition* (pp. 220–254). New York: Springer-Verlag.

Tuominen-Soini, H., Salmela-Aro, K., & Niemivirta, M. (2008) 'Achievement goal orientation and subjective well-being: A person-centred analysis', *Learning and Instruction*, *18*, 251–266.

Urdan, T., & Midgley, M. (2001) 'Academic self-handicapping: What we know and what more there is to learn', *Educational Psychology Review*, *13*(2), 115–138.

Vygotsky, L.S. (1978) *Mind in society: The development of higher psychological processes*. Cambridge, MA: Harvard University Press.

Yrjönsuuri, Y. (Ed.) (1995) *Evaluating education in Finland*. Helsinki: National Board of Education.

Zeigler-Hill, V. (Ed.) (2013) *Self-esteem*. Current Issues in Social Psychology Series. Hove: Psychology Press.

Zimmerman, B.J. (2000) 'Self-efficacy: An essential motive to learn', *Contemporary Educational Psychology*, *25*, 82–91.

Zuckerman. G. (2004) 'Development of reflection through learning activity', *European Journal of Psychology of Education*, *19*, 9–18.

Zuliani, J.-M. (2008) 'The Toulouse cluster of on-board systems: A process of collective innovation and learning', *European Planning Studies*, *16*(5), 711–726.

Finnish learning to learn tasks and open PISA mathematics and science items

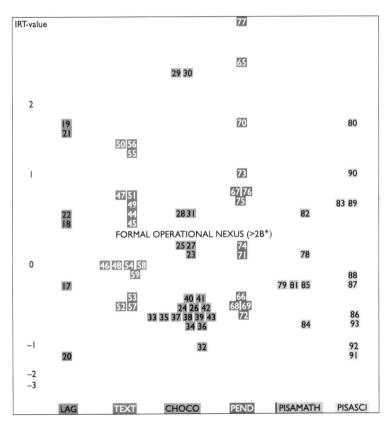

Figure 8.7 IRT-scaling within the Finnish data (N ≈ 800) of three cognitive tasks from the Finnish learning to learn instrument in the EU 2008 learning to learn pilot and two set of PISA items.

Source: Kupiainen et al. (2008).

Note: * Includes the Piagetian Pendulum task and a collection of open-source PISA items for maths and science. FORMAL OPERATIONAL NEXUS (>2B*) indicates the competence corresponding to the early formal operational stage (Piaget, 2001). Tasks: LAG = invented arithmetic operators, TEXT = reading comprehension, CHOCO = control of variables. Small numbers in the boxes refer to the number of items in the EU/Finnish test booklets. The y-axis is the IRT-scale values from −3 to +3. The distribution of students is not shown.

Chapter 9

The Spanish approach to learning to learn

Amparo Moreno and Elena Martín[1]

Abstract

In this chapter, we first analyse the concept of 'learning to learn'. We pay particular attention to how it has been developed in Spanish educational policy. In our national curriculum, learning to learn is seen as one of the most relevant competences and is incorporated in all areas of knowledge and at all levels of schooling. Next, we discuss the issue of learning to learn assessment. We review our own research on a metacognitive abilities scale related to cognitive components of learning to learn. We present the theoretical background and empirical results related to this scale. The scale was developed from a broader longitudinal research project carried out in 31 secondary schools with students of secondary school Grades 1–4, over four years. The scale was later adapted and integrated into the European test on learning to learn. Finally, we offer some guidelines to continue improving learning to learn in Spanish schools.

Key words: cognitive component, metacognitive abilities, longitudinal project, assessment.

Introduction

Society is experiencing drastic social and economic changes. Sociologists and philosophers have introduced concepts such as the society of risk (Beck, 1992) and the fluid society (Bauman, 2000), which point to the fact that, increasingly, people must act in new, changing, and very competitive circumstances. Furthermore, the phenomenon of globalization adds a complexity that demands a new paradigm for learning and teaching.

> The mastery and mechanical regurgitation of rules and facts should give way to a paradigm in which cognitive flexibility and agility win the day. The skills needed for analyzing and mobilizing to solve problems from multiple perspectives will require individuals who are cognitively flexible, culturally sophisticated, and able to work collaboratively in groups made up of diverse individuals.
>
> (Suárez-Orozco & Qin-Hilliard, 2004: 5–6)

Therefore, educational institutions must assume a duty to prepare individuals to continue learning throughout life in a complex and new world. As Claxton (1990: 66) stated: 'The prime function of education in an uncertain world should be to provide young people with the competence and self-confidence to tackle uncertainty well; in other words, to be good learners.' The issue now is what good learning is about, how it is assessed, and how it is promoted. Learning to learn is a central component of good learning that can be fundamentally understood as a process of reflection, control, and regulation that students implement within their own learning processes. In this sense, we have referred to learning to learn as meta-learning (Moreno, 2005). On the other hand, we believe that the educational problem is not so much based on the fact that our students know nothing about learning to learn, but on the way that knowledge is acquired and on what specifically is acquired.

At school, students not only build notions related to mathematics, language or the arts; in that same learning process, they develop theories related to their own school learning and the way it is undertaken to be successful in this specific context. By this we mean that their theories, practices, and values regarding learning are implicitly built through the real learning practices they experience in the classroom. These learning practices include the tasks suggested and the resources provided by the teachers, the time allocated to each task, the assessments carried out, the role given to students in the different learning stages, the spatial organization of the classroom, their success and failure in each subject. In addition, they are influenced by their overall personal, social, and cultural contexts, which include peers, school, family, and the mass media.

What is the effect of this implicit learning related to learning to learn that begins at an early age? It is the development of a habit of how to deal with knowledge and learning that is adaptable to the school context. In terms of Piagetian theory (Piaget, 1974a, 1974b), most students have learnt how to act to achieve the aim (to pass subjects and school years); to solve, from a practical point of view, the task of learning without understanding the processes involved in that task. They know if they have succeeded or not, but ignore the means used to be successful and, therefore, the reasons for their success or failure.

This automatic way of acting does not pose a problem in the case of simple learning but is a great disadvantage in the case of complex learning, which requires the control of learning itself. It is also a disadvantage when the context varies and the individual has to use a different way of learning – because, for example, the teacher's demands vary or the students must learn by themselves in their personal and professional life. The problem is a serious one, since the latter would be typical signs of good school learning: control on the part of learner. In short, our concern would not only be that students do not know how to learn to learn, but that what they have learnt on this particular matter is not what we think is the ideal way of learning to learn.

What is learning to learn

As with other psychological and educational constructs, there are multiple definitions of learning to learn (Hautamäki et al., 2002; Adey, 2006; Black et al., 2006; Stringher, 2006). These conceptions come from various fields of research, differing theoretical orientations, and even from different scales of values and contexts of application. In short, we propose three central ingredients to the notion of learning to learn related to the cognitive, affective, and social domains. Figure 9.1 shows the key elements of the learning to learn process (Martín & Moreno, 2007).

We propose a definition of learning to learn as a strategic activity whose development would require the students to be aware of (a) their reasons and intentions, (b) their own cognitive capabilities, and (c) the demands of the academic tasks. Besides this, they should be able to (d) control their resources and (e) regulate their subsequent performance (Biggs, 1988). This learning to learn approach draws on a more comprehensive notion of metacognition. This term has usually been defined as any knowledge or cognitive activity that takes as its object, or regulates, any aspect of any cognitive enterprise (Flavell et al., 2002). In the same way that metacognition refers to cognition about cognition, we could talk about meta-learning in the sense of learning about learning. Paraphrasing Flavell (1976: 232), meta-learning could refer to the active

Figure 9.1 Key elements of the learning to learn process.

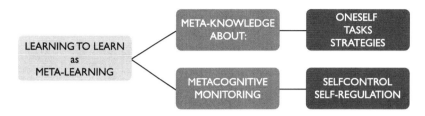

Figure 9.2 Learning to learn as meta-learning.

monitoring and consequent regulation and orchestration of these (learning) processes in relation to the objects or data on which they bear, usually in the service of some concrete goal or objective.

Based on the work of several authors (Flavell & Wellman, 1977; Brown, 1978; Paris & Paris, 2001; Zimmerman & Schunk, 2001), we have performed a theoretical analysis of the basic components that should be present in a metacognitively or self-regulated learning to learn process, including both meta-knowledge and metacognitive monitoring and self-regulation (Moreno, 2002) (Fig. 9.2).

In relation to the knowledge of *oneself* as student, learners should first assimilate that learning in the classroom requires an active mental attitude, an effort, and that this effort can be controlled by the learner. It is a type of learning in which the desire and decision to learn takes priority over spontaneous natural learning. We should also help the students become aware of their beliefs about learning and knowledge and about the specific discipline.

The student should also develop the ability to represent the state of their own mind when learning: to judge what they know, do not know, understand or do not understand in a specific learning situation. This implies the active assessment of the student's mental resources, which enable them to choose to undertake actions (to help themselves to materials, to ask teachers or classmates for help, to ask questions in other contexts) when faced with problems of understanding, gaps or generalization difficulties:

> To be a good student is, to a certain extent, to learn to become aware of one's own mind and of the level of one's own understanding. A good student may often say that he does not understand, but simply because he keeps a constant control of his own understanding. The bad student, so to speak, does not monitor himself when trying to understand, and most of the time does not know if he understands or not.
>
> (Holt, 1964, quoted in Nisbet & Shucksmith,
> 1986: 60; Spanish edition)

As a result of continuous experience with this problem of learning to learn, students will develop a general notion of themselves as a learner, a self-concept, and academic self-esteem. When students fail a task repeatedly, two problems arise: first, they do not learn the knowledge, and second, they build a representation of themselves as incompetent learners.

In relation to the *tasks* that they have to learn, students should first ask themselves about the meaning and aims of the learning tasks. They then need to assess how difficult the tasks are, and what resources should be devoted to them in terms of materials, time, and effort. The students should also know the range of *strategies* they have and how these strategies should be adapted to their own characteristics as learners, to the tasks, to the individual or team work, and so on.

The aspects related to *control and regulation* mainly include: planning (to become aware of the need to organize activities beforehand and to make decisions on how to approach the task); deciding on the specific strategies for analysis, understanding or memorization these aspects will trigger; and the personal assessment of whether the student's learning is being effective in relation to their established aim, so that he or she may continue in that direction or may change their approach to that learning.

What this suggests is an important point: learning to learn reflects intellectual and individual features, but also motivational, affective, and social aspects. In fact, students, unlike theorists and teachers, attach more importance to these affective aspects of learning to learn than to the intellectual ones.

With regard to *motivation,* autonomous and reflective learning requires an effort and perseverance that no person will devote to a task for which he or she is not motivated. If students do not receive a reward of any kind, there is very little likelihood that they will carry out a learning process in the best way possible. They will look for shortcuts in the face of any difficulty. It is fundamental that learning promotes a feeling of self-efficacy (Bandura, 1997). When we refer to meta-learning we mean that the student controls the learning process. This is only possible if students consider themselves able to make changes based on their own ability and effort. The stronger their feeling of self-efficacy and the greater their confidence in their ability to influence the future, the aims they set will be higher and they will demonstrate much greater commitment to those aims.

From the *psycho-affective* point of view, reflection should not be exclusively on the intellectual components, but on the emotions and feelings generated in the course of specific learning and in the general school context. Monitoring refers not only to the observation of external consequences, but also to one's internal responses of feeling (Claxton, 1990). What image, what self-concept does each student have about herself/himself? Do the students think of themselves as a good student? Do the students think that they are good at maths? Do they like maths? Are they afraid/not afraid of failing in this subject? Do they think maths is easy, easier or not as easy as other classmates think? How do they experience their relationship with other classmates, their teachers' attitudes to them, the support of their family, the stereotypes regarding the value of knowledge? What role do school activities play on their self-esteem?

From the *social* point of view, we know that learning is a collective task. Socio-cultural models (Vygotsky, 1978; Wertsch, 1985; Bruner, 1996) inform us about development and education as an active learning process involving adult guidance and support. Attention should be paid not only to the individual student or teacher, since the classroom constitutes a learning community. In the learning process, it is important to be a confident, self-assured, and autonomous person, but equally a person able to ask for help, to provide support, and to be part of a group that assigns an identity that that person also tries to keep. Learning to learn means that students should learn to become acquainted, to talk to each other, to listen to each other, to exchange different points of view, with the benefits that this would imply, not only within the educational context, but in all contexts where later on these young people will have to play the role of adult citizens. Several authors have discussed this relation between metacognition and cooperative learning (Palincsar & Brown, 1984; Goos & Galbraith, 1996; King, 1998; Rogoff, 1998). The role of a reflective teacher (Schön, 1987) is also at the heart of this process. The teacher, who provides the scaffolding, should be aware of these relational steps involved in the teaching–learning process.

In summary, we have highlighted some crucial ideas. First, approaching learning to learn from an analysis of metacognitive skills would appear a useful and appropriate way forward to us, but it is not the only one. Second, learning to learn cannot be isolated from the general teaching–learning process as a whole. Third, it is not a question of automatically following a series of directions as if we were cooking a dish strictly according to a recipe book. This is the problem of some handbooks on study techniques or learning strategies. What constitutes the core of reflective learning is just the opposite. It is about selecting options and not about mechanically assuming that one of them is the best. The best way of learning will be the one adapted to our aim. In this sense, the elements mentioned above constitute a basic set of skills, habits, and attitudes that each educational situation (with its particular teachers, students and their peculiarities, subject matter, and cultural values) will idiosyncratically handle, add, subtract, highlight or shade, in the same way as a good cook adjusts the recipes to her current budget, creativity or mood.

On the other hand, reflective learning does not necessarily include the awareness of the process by the learner. We refer to a level of awareness that allows for reflective abstraction (the act of thinking about the structure of actions and one's own knowledge) and not for meta-reflection (reflection about reflection) (Piaget, 1974a); and also to regulations that may be explicit but are not (Allal & Saada-Robert, 1992) or to a Level-E2 (Explicit-2) of knowledge representation available to consciousness but not verbalized (Karmiloff-Smith, 1992). The continuous explicitness of the process would imply an effort and probably a tedium that would be at odds with good results: too many questions, too frequently and obsessively posed will finally paralyse us. From our point of view, what has to be achieved is that the process triggered should operate like a habit, rather like it occurs when, with the aim of communicating with each other, we use the grammar of our mother tongue without being conscious of its rules. Good learning is the purpose here and in order to achieve it we put into practice this strategic way of learning. We argue that teachers should have it in mind as a global goal across the curriculum and they should focus on teaching this reflexive perspective.

Learning to learn in the Spanish curriculum[2]

As long ago as 1970, the importance of teaching and learning study techniques was emphasized in the General Law of Education (1970), but that emphasis was not reflected in changes to the national curriculum. Later, in 1990, the Spanish curriculum included many of the characteristics of the concept of learning to learn in the Law of General Organization of the Educational System (LOGSE). Thus, the essential educational goal is expressed in terms of competencies and, within them, those that refer to the knowledge of the cognitive processes themselves and their conscious control (Martín & Coll, 2003).

The LOGSE curriculum establishes for the first time a difference between types of content (concepts, procedures, and attitudes) that allows emphasis to be placed on learning strategies, the difference between technical and strategic use of procedures, and the importance of active reflection. The LOGSE curriculum also incorporates learning strategies in all areas of knowledge, rather than creating a curricular space of their own, separate from other subjects. This theoretical option recognizes the importance of learning to learn in specific domains to the detriment of models that understand that these abilities are content-free competencies, as in some programmes. Examples of such programmes are Feuerstein and colleagues' Instrumental Enrichment (1980), Harvard University's Intelligence Project (1983), and Lipman's Philosophy for Children (1976).

The approach of the LOGSE curriculum has these strengths but there are two important weaknesses. The first is that the evaluation criteria for LOGSE barely include learning to learn competences. The discourse is thus incomplete and contradictory. It is true that it is very difficult to define levels of learning for this type of capacity for the different educational subjects. However, by not including them in that part of the curriculum that more directly guides teachers' practice (i.e. assessment), there is the risk that teachers assign them less value and pay less attention to them. In addition, LOGSE barely incorporates the emotional dimension of the basic skill of learning to learn. It focuses above all on the cognitive strategies related to different knowledge acquisition processes. The importance of self-esteem, the perception of one's self-efficacy, and of overcoming the uncertainty generated by abandoning deep-seated study habits, these are aspects missing from the LOGSE curriculum.

Some of these limitations are better addressed in the curriculum that the Ministry of Education introduced with the new Ley Orgánica de Educación (Organic Law of Education) of 2006 (LOE). This curriculum is innovative in that it organizes learning around a series of basic competencies that are proposed as the essential goals that every student must achieve to be able to function in the future as a citizen with full rights and obligations. The basic competences established in the LOE curriculum have been selected from the proposals of the OECD Disco Project (2005) and from those set out by the European Union in the framework of the objectives for 2010 (European Commission, 2004).

Among the list of the eight competences selected – competence in linguistic communication, mathematical competence, competence in knowledge and interaction with the physical world, competence in the processing of information and digital competence, social and citizenship competence, cultural and artistic competence, and autonomy and personal initiative – the *competence of learning to learn* is inherent.

Unlike LOGSE, in this case the learning to learn competence is explicitly referred to within the basic objectives of compulsory education, which bestow upon these skills their true importance. An extensive description of what this skill means is included in the text that establishes the prescriptive curriculum. The final paragraph, reproduced here, summarizes what is set forth:

> In summary, learning to learn implies the awareness, management and control of one's own capabilities and knowledge from a feeling of competence or personal efficacy. It includes strategic thinking as well as the ability to cooperate, the ability to self-evaluate, and the efficient management of a group of intellectual work resources and techniques. All of these are developed through conscious and gratifying learning experiences, both collective and individual.
>
> (Appendix I of the Draft of Royal Decree that establishes the core curriculum for secondary education, LOE: 9)

It is obvious from this summary that the emotional dimension of the skills necessary to learn to learn is clearly captured. In addition, the new curriculum has incorporated some of these skills in the evaluation criteria for the subject matter, which, as mentioned above, could contribute to cultural change in teaching practices and in the way students learn.

The explicit introduction in the curriculum of competencies associated with learning to learn implies an important advance in the incorporation of the teaching of these skills in the Spanish educational system. Nevertheless, other necessary measures have not been implemented that would drive the educational objectives included in the curriculum to actually permeate teaching practice (Martín, 1998). Neither the initial training received by teachers, nor their ongoing training, has been adapted enough to accommodate this priority. This approach has only just recently been incorporated in the majority of educational materials, but in many cases the changes involve isolated activities, placed at the end of each lesson, and the global approach of the subject itself has not changed. Finally, these skills have yet to be considered priorities in performance evaluations. It is likely that this weak emphasis on the steps of curriculum development is one of the reasons why Spanish students do not use autonomous learning strategies to a very great extent.

A Spanish proposal for the assessment of learning to learn

Assessing learning to learn entails certain problems that are difficult to solve. First, the lack of consensus when defining the process itself leads different people to test different abilities. As a result, questionnaires can consist, for example, of standard questions about study techniques, tests that are more focused on the different stages of the scientific method, others that are centred around general reasoning, and others that are more related to metacognitive skills. Second, due to their very nature, tests do not assess the learning process directly, but rather generalization of the learning skills already acquired. Third, tests on learning strategies or metacognitive skills related to learning focus on abilities with different levels of generality, some of which are more related to a specific domain and others which are really present at higher levels. Fourth, the relationships that exist between the different abilities included in a test are usually not as strong as originally expected. Although we may assume that learning how to learn implies a general approach towards a specific domain, the results in the subscales highlight two important facts: (a) learning to learn may include a wide range of high-level skills and (b) may constitute a more specific task than was expected. Finally, most of the tests developed depend on self-reporting, along with all the problems that this technique entails.

To overcome some of the limitations of conventional learning to learn scales, we have developed a metacognitive abilities test (Moreno, 2002) based on the definition of learning to learn as *meta-learning*. We took account of three issues in particular:

1. That the scale should be focused on reflection processes so the content should be easy. The students' task should involve thinking about the process of understanding or solving a problem, not about remembering data related to a school domain.
2. That the metacognitive abilities selected should be key elements in the learning to learn process at school. Therefore, the subscales included in this Spanish metacognitive abilities test were related to essential aspects of learning to learn competence: (a) to be aware of their intentions and goals as learners, of their own affective and cognitive capabilities and difficulties, of the demands of the academic tasks; (b) to plan the learning process; (c) to use effective strategies to attain their goal; (d) to actively monitor the learning process and adjust strategy effectiveness; (e) to check the results of the learning process. Moreover, the items' content should not emerge from laboratory-based research problems – and the subjects were to be chosen mainly from school books.
3. That students should actually solve problems, practically and not hypothetically, using reflection processes.

Bearing in mind these core points, we designed a test consisting of 25 items that asked students to address problems similar to those that they might face in class. Items were divided into four subscales related to the main elements of metacognition: meta-comprehension, self-knowledge assessment, problem-solving monitoring, and learning strategies awareness.

Meta-comprehension was defined by Markman (1979, 1985) as the processes of inference that are put in place to detect whether a phrase, a verbal instruction or a story are confused or not, and whether they contain gaps, inconsistencies or contradictions. Thus, when students read a text, it is crucial that we are aware of what they understand and what they do not understand. The ability to read a text and address any difficulties that may arise in their understanding is basic at all levels of schooling and even more so in secondary education, where much of the learning can be based on the assimilation of knowledge through written texts. Baker and Brown (1980) pointed out that if students are not aware of their own limitations as learners, they cannot be expected to take preventative action to anticipate or recover from problems.

In the meta-comprehension subscale, we used five texts, each comprising four short paragraphs. The students' task was to find the inaccuracies present in each text. These mistakes stem from the inclusion of contradictory or false information in one of the paragraphs or between paragraphs. In this way, we try to determine whether students reflect on the information provided and are therefore able to detect any inconsistencies or false data. As can be seen in Fig. 9.3, the second paragraph clearly makes no sense: Levels of population cannot decrease while standards of health and nutrition rise.

Self-knowledge assessment refers to the ability to represent one's own mind in the process of learning and assess what you know or do not know. In the first version of the test, students were asked to indicate their degree of confidence about the accuracy of their answers to questions about a particular subject (language, mathematics, social sciences, natural sciences). Then, from their scores in an achievement test of that knowledge, it was determined whether or not they actually demonstrated understanding or learning. Their scores on the consciousness of their self-knowledge referred to the extent to which their level of confidence corresponded to their actual competence. The final version assessed this process by asking students about their answers to the 10 items of meta-comprehension and problem-solving monitoring.

Problem-solving monitoring. When we refer to monitoring, we mean the ability to check the plausibility of the solution. Any teacher can provide examples of students whose answers are clearly illogical if only common sense is taken into account. We chose a mathematical problem whose correct solution did not depend on mathematical knowledge but on reflecting on the problem. With this aim in mind, we designed the test so that only one of the response options was logical based on the formulation of the question.

As can be seen in Fig. 9.4, the solution to this problem does not presuppose an advanced knowledge in mathematics. We wished to check whether the chosen

---

1. The world's population has never stopped growing. By 1995 it was already approximately 5,700 million people
2. During the 19th century in Europe and America the population declined. Although the birth rate remained high, poor health and nutrition contributed to high mortality rates.
3. Despite medical advances gradually reaching them many poor countries still have large health problems.
4. The world's population is currently increasing at around 100 million per year.

Figure 9.3 Meta-comprehension item.

If I drive at 40 km per hour it takes me 20 minutes to arrive at my destination. How long will I take to make the return journey driving at 50 km per hour?

1. 16 minutes
2. 25 minutes
3. 30 minutes

Figure 9.4 Problem-solving monitoring item.

answer made sense of the context of the problem. Only one answer was logical from the formulation's point of view. If we drive faster, we will spend less than 20 minutes. Therefore, the answer is 16 minutes.

Learning strategies awareness was the last central aspect assessed on the learning to learn scale. Control of the learning processes involves judging whether the objectives have been attained and by what means they have been deployed. To assess this we added, in the monitoring problem-solving scale, a question about how they arrived at their solution. As every possibility cannot be included in the test, the student was asked about the closest choice to his or her way of reasoning (Fig. 9.5).

This metacognitive abilities scale is not only a theoretical proposal. It was developed and tested as part of a research project on the evaluation of schools (Marchesi et al., 2003).[3] This external assessment was carried out in 31 secondary schools (13,500 students in Grades 1–4 of secondary school, 13,500 parents, and 1080 teachers) within the framework of a four-year longitudinal study. In each school, four blocks of factors were assessed: socio-cultural context, initial student knowledge level in curricular subjects, learning strategies, and metacognition – with school and classroom processes and students' outcomes in the same curricular subjects assessed at the beginning. We therefore deemed it appropriate to present a summary of the results of the main test.

In general, we can identify two types of results related to the scale: first, results related to the scale itself – their level of difficulty, variations according to the socio-cultural context and the developmental aspect (i.e. the performance at

Below you will find five different ways of reasoning. In your response sheet tick the option that is closer to your own way of reasoning.

1. If you spend 20 minutes at 40 km per hour, to know how long you will take at 50 km/h you have to do the following equation 40:20=50:x
2. If you spend 20 minutes at 40 km per hour, it will take half the time at 80/h, I have thought that at 50 km/h it would take less than at 40 km/h and more than at 80km/h.
3. If we drive at 40 km/h and we spend 20 minutes to arrive, we will have done around 13 km. Then I calculated how long it takes to do around 13 km at 50 km/h.
4. I have taken away 20 minutes from 40 km and I got 10. Then I have added 10 to 20 minutes.
5. As you spend 20 minutes at 40 km/h, I have divided 50 by 2.

Figure 9.5 Learning strategies awareness item.

different levels of schooling); second, results with a predictive value with respect to performance in different subjects of knowledge.

A total score was calculated from the participants' scores on the four scales. Regarding level of difficulty, the average score achieved in this test varied according to the other two indicated factors: socio-cultural context and the age of the students. However, we prefer to provide an overview first and focus on the analysis of these two other variables later.

In general, the test proved to be slightly more difficult than expected according to the research on metacognition. The minimum average score out of 20 was 9.08 and the maximum average score 12.93. Performance can also be described in relation to the different processes evaluated. Thus, the block of questions that were most difficult were those grouped under meta-comprehension [minimum score 6.55 (Grade 1) and maximum score 8.76 (Grade 4)]. In contrast, the easiest block was, with a few exceptions, awareness of strategies [minimum score 8.55 (Grade 2) and maximum score 15.68 (Grade 4)]. Self-knowledge assessment [minimum score 9.04 (Grade 2) and maximum score 12.72 (Grade 4)] and problem-solving monitoring [minimum score 8.70 (Grade 1) and maximum score 14.87 (Grade 4)] were of an intermediate level of difficulty.

The influence of the socio-cultural context was clear both in mean scores achieved in the test as a whole and in scores by blocks. In fact, there is a nearly perfect correlation between mean scores and contexts in that a higher level of socio-cultural context leads to a higher score. Thus, the context that achieved the highest scores was, without exception, context 1. Lower scores were attained in contexts 3 and 4. Table 9.1 shows the mean score in each context for each subscale and level of secondary education.

Finally, the research design provided an excellent opportunity to analyse the developmental changes associated with levels of schooling. We could thus make various cross-comparisons (students evaluated in the same year but different courses) as well as longitudinal comparisons (the same students were evaluated in different secondary school courses). For cross-sectional comparisons, we can refer back to Table 9.1, bearing in mind that it was a longitudinal project that ran four years. Different years are removed to offer a first general overview of the

Table 9.1 Maximum and minimum scores on subscales based on contexts and secondary school grades

Subscales	Context 1	Context 2	Context 3	Context 4
Meta-comprehension	max: 10.92 (Grade 2)			min: 5.70 (Grade 1)
Problem-solving monitoring	max: 16.17 (Grade 4)		min: 7.38 (Grade 1)	
Learning strategies awareness	max: 16.80 (Grade 4)		min: 8.52 (Grade 1)	
Self-knowledge awareness	max: 13.40 (Grade 4)			min 9.23 (Grade 2)

Table 9.2 Mean scores achieved by students of different grades in different years of the research

Grade	Year			
	1998	1999	2000	2001
1	9.1	10.4	9.2	
2	11.5	11	11.6	10.2
4		12.9	13	11.5

results. Grade 1 and Grade 2 students recorded the lowest scores, while Grade 4 students, with one exception, recorded the highest scores. Table 9.2 shows the results achieved throughout the project by students from different grades in different school years.

Table 9.2 shows that mean scores achieved in the test increased with age, although the improvement was gradual. Between Grades 1 and 2 of secondary education, mean scores increased by 1 or 2 points, whereas between Grades 1 and 4, scores increased by between 2.5 and 3.5 points. Longitudinal comparisons confirmed this developmental progression. Table 9.3 shows the results achieved by the four cohorts. The average test score data corroborate what we noted above: students improved their results on the test progressively as they moved from Grade 1 to Grade 2 (improving by 1–2 points) and from Grade 2 to Grade 4 (improving by 0.5–1.5 points).

With regard to reliability, Cronbach's alpha was 0.76 for 13–14 year olds (Grade 2 of secondary school) and 0.78 for 15–16 year olds (Grade 4 of secondary school). If we look at validity, the predictive value of the test, the global research showed that the three main factors influencing the students' academic performance were previous performance in specific subjects, metacognitive skills, and the socio-cultural context (Marchesi et al., 2003). The best way to predict the students' academic performance in mathematics, language, and social sciences was to take into account their previous performance in these same subjects. The data obtained indicated that metacognitive skills made up the second factor to take into consideration (Table 9.4). All of the blocks in the test (meta-comprehension, problem-solving monitoring, awareness of strategies, and

Table 9.3 Longitudinal comparison of mean scores achieved by students from each cohort

Cohort	Year			
	1998	1999	2000	2001
1	9.1 (Grade 1)	11.4 (Grade 2)	11.5 (Grade 4)	
2	11.5 (Grade 2)		12.9 (Grade 4	
3		10.5 (Grade 1)	11.6 (Grade 2)	
4			9.2 (Grade 1)	10.2 (Grade 2)

Table 9.4 Results of multiple linear regression analysis (stepwise) for Grade 2 secondary students (mathematics, language, and social sciences)

Predictive variables	Standardized weights		
	Mathematics (n = 1184)	Language (n = 1205)	Social sciences (n = 1094)
Mathematics, language or social sciences 1st	0.491 ***	0.469***	0.391 ***
Problem-solving monitoring	0.221 ***	0.140***	0.157 ***
Meta-comprehension	0.083 ***	0.082***	0.145 ***
Self-knowledge assessment	0.081 ***	0.065***	0.098 ***
Learning strategies awareness	0.073 ***	0.078***	0.112 ***

Note: $*P < .05; **P < .01; ***P < .001$.

awareness of one's own knowledge) have functioned as predictor variables in one particular subject or another (mathematics, language, and social sciences). Of these, problem-solving monitoring has greater predictive ability in all subjects, followed by meta-comprehension (also in all subjects). These data appear to underline the importance of these skills in learning. In light of these results, metacognitive development as an element of leaning to learn should not be considered a marginal activity in the learning process but a priority. The explicit incorporation of this aim in the teaching and learning of different curricular subjects will contribute to an improvement in learning.

Metacognitive abilities are undoubtedly a key element but other important ingredients need to be added. We are currently involved in an implementation project that takes several objectives into account. As a general approach, our objectives are focused on preserving methods or techniques that help us learn better but direct us towards how we can be better learners. While we are interested in learning results, our main objective is to draw attention towards the process of learning itself, with an essential distinctive feature: the focus is on the students' own reflection on their efforts, their knowledge and its shortcomings, their own strategies for learning, and their frustrations and interests.

Implications for practice

The following are some guidelines to promote the learning to learn process more efficiently:

1. The learning process should be introduced in dialogues as an integral part of classroom routines.
2. Conceptions about the learning of students and teachers should be explored.
3. Collaborative learning should become an essential component of learning to learn.

4. A thoughtful and strategic approach towards learning tasks needs to be promoted.
5. Affective components of learning to learn should be included.
6. Assessment is an important pathway towards learning to learn.
7. The training of teachers, both initial and ongoing, should be a top priority for the future. It is also imperative that textbooks and curricular materials in general incorporate this approach. At the core of the materials there must be activities directed towards ensuring that students:

    - use reading and writing in their epistemic dimension;
    - process information in such a way that it allows them to convert it into knowledge;
    - reflect on their learning, identifying what allows them to learn more and building a representation of themselves as apprentices that makes them feel competent and wish to continue learning.

Conclusions

This chapter has given us a basic picture of the current situation of learning to learn in Spain. Our research and educational experience highlight some weaknesses in relation to the definition of learning to learn. First, learning to learn competence shows characteristics that are both innovative and difficult to define compared with other elements of the teaching and learning process. There is also some confusion between this competence and the use of procedures such as study skills and learning strategies. We therefore need to address the theoretical debate on such competences in depth and its relationship with other abilities. Our theoretical framework (Moreno, 1995) underlines the need to remember the conscious, constructive, and developmental aspects of self-regulation. Models included in the information-processing framework have not paid enough attention to these features, unlike Piagetian and Vygotskian theories. Most recent formulations can be found in the work of Karmiloff-Smith or in studies linked to theories of dynamic systems (Smith & Thelen, 2003). The constructive nature of self-regulation means that control over our actions and our mental processes is not exercised automatically (triggered by the elements of the task that we intend to fix) but that it assumes a reprocessing, a reinterpretation, a new understanding of the task, a new schema construction. Here, Piagetian and Vygotskian theories coincide with each other. Furthermore, there is a need to study these learning to learn processes from a genetic point of view, from a macro- or micro-genetic perspective. If we assume that the self-regulation of learning changes qualitatively and that these changes imply reconceptualizations, we should expect the pathway for the subject in question to take more or less time to follow, but not be an easy one.

Second, learning to learn is generally defined as a competence of a cognitive nature with little consideration for social elements and none whatsoever for emotional factors. Third, this competence is usually linked to secondary school. Our recommendation would be to devote our best efforts to build it into preschool and elementary school levels of education.

The fourth issue is connected with assessment. Our proposal constitutes a modest starting point. If educational assessments are to provide real outcomes of transformation, the more they relate to educational practices the better. This would mean assessing school contexts in which all players are included, or at least, the teachers and the students in the classroom. This implies that the assessment would be carried out through the observation of teaching practices, the students' work, specific tasks, time and space, materials and spatial organization. The most important aim of this assessment would be to improve these practices rather than to formulate a ranking.

Finally, we believe that choosing to address learning to learn means opting for a specific understanding and practice of teaching, learning, and education and, ultimately, this is a value choice about what matters. Learning to learn is learning a new way of thinking about learning that involves more than simply accumulating information. It involves asking why, questioning consequences, taking responsibility for the processes of learning, and engaging in learning as a collective enterprise.

Notes

1 We would like to acknowledge Lis Cercadillo, our colleague in the European Network on Learning to Learn, for her support.
2 This section of the chapter is based in part on Moreno and Martín (2007).
3 Problem-solving monitoring' and self-knowledge assessment' items were also included in the pre-pilot European Test on Learning to Learn. http://ec.europa.eu/education/lifelong-learning-policy/doc/pilot_survey/executive_summary_en.pdf.

References

Adey, P. (2006) 'Learning to learn – the intelligence route', in *Learning to learn network meeting report*. Ispra: CRELL/JRC.

Allal, L., & Saada-Robert, M. (1992) 'La métacognition: cadre conceptuel pour l'etude des régulations en situation scolaire', *Archives de Psychologie*, 60, 265–296.

Baker, L., & Brown, A. (1980) *Metacognitive skills and reading*. Urbana, IL: University of Illinois at Urbana-Champaign.

Bandura, A. (1997) *Self-efficacy: The exercise of control*. New York: Freeman.

Bauman, Z. (2000) *Liquid modernity*. Cambridge: Polity.

Beck, U. (1992) *Risk society: Towards a new modernity*. London: Sage.

Biggs, J. (1988) 'Approaches to learning and to essay writing', in R. Schmeck (ed.) *Learning strategies and learning styles*. New York: Plenum Press.

Black, P., McCormick, R., James, M., & Pedder, D. (2006) 'Learning how to learn and assessment for learning: A theoretical inquiry', *Research Papers in Education*, 21(2), 119–132.

Brown, A. (1978) 'Knowing when, where, and how to remember: A problem of metacognition, in R. Glaser (Ed.) *Advances in instructional psychology*. Hillsdale, NJ: Erlbaum.

Bruner, J. (1996) *The culture of education*. Cambridge, MA: Harvard University Press.

Claxton, G. (1990) *Teaching to learn*. London: Cassell.

European Commission (2004) *Key competencies for lifelong learning: A European reference framework*. Brussels: European Commission, Directorate General for Education and Culture.

Feuerstein, R., Rand, Y., Hoffman, M.B., & Miller, R. (1980) *Instrumental enrichment*. Baltimore, MD: University Park Press.

Flavell, J. (1976) 'Metacognitive aspects of problem solving', in L.B. Resnick (Ed.) *The nature of intelligence*. Hillsdale, NJ: Erlbaum.

Flavell, J., Miller, P., & Miller, S. (2002) *Cognitive development* (4th edn.). Englewood Cliffs, NJ: Prentice-Hall.

Flavell, J., & Wellman, H. (1977) 'Metamemory', in R. Kail & J. Hagen (Eds.) *Perspectives on the development of memory and cognition*. Hillsdale, NJ: Erlbaum.

Goos, M., & Galbraith, P. (1996) 'Do it this way! Metacognitive strategies in collaborative mathematical problem solving', *Educational Studies in Mathematics*, *30*, 229–260.

Harvard University (1983) *Project Intelligence overview: The development of procedures to enhance thinking skills*. Final report submitted to the Minister for the Development of Human Intelligence, Republic of Venezuela.

Hautamäki, J., Arinen, P., Eronen, S., Hautamäki, A., Kupianien, S., Lindblom, B. et al. (2002) *Assessing learning to learn: A framework*. Helsinki: Centre for Educational Assessment, Helsinki University/National Board of Education.

Karmiloff-Smith, A. (1992) *Beyond modularity: A developmental perspective on cognitive science*. Cambridge, MA: MIT Press.

King, A. (1998) 'Transactive peer tutoring: Distributing cognition and metacognition', *Educational Psychology Review*, *10*, 57–74.

Ley Orgánica de Educación (Organic Law of Education) del 2/2006 de 3 de mayo. En Boletín Oficial del Estado, num. 106, de 4 de mayo de 2006.

Lipman, M. (1976) 'Philosophy for children', *Metaphilosophy*, *7*, 17–33.

Marchesi, A., Martín, E., Martinez Arias, R., Tiana, A., & Moreno, A. (2003) 'An evaluation network for educational change', *Studies on Education and Evaluation*, *29*, 43–56.

Markman, E. (1979) 'Realizing that you don't understand: Elementary school children awareness of inconsistencies', *Child Development*, *50*, 643–655.

Markman, E. (1985) 'Comprehension monitoring: Developmental and educational issues', in S. Chipman, J. Segal, & R. Glaser (Eds.) *Thinking and learning skills*, Vol. II. Hillsdale, NJ: Erlbaum.

Martín, E. (1998) 'El papel del curriculum en la reforma educativa española', *Investigación en la Escuela*, *36*, 31–47.

Martín, E., & Coll, C. (Eds.) (2003) *Adquirir contenidos, desarrollar capacidades*. Barcelona: Edebé.

Martín, E., & Moreno, A. (2007) *Competencia para aprender a aprender*. Madrid: Alianza.

Moreno, A. (1995) 'Autorregulación y solución de problemas', *Infancia y Aprendizaje*, *72*, 51–70.

Moreno, A. (2002) 'La evaluación de las habilidades metacognitivas', in A. Marchesi & E. Martín (Eds.) *Evaluación de la educación secundaria*. Madrid: S.M.

Moreno, A. (2005) *Report: Learning to learn European Project* (Spanish Institute of Evaluation). Madrid: Ministry of Education and Science.

Moreno, A., & Martín, E. (2007) 'Learning to learn in Spain', *Curriculum Journal*, *18*, 175–193.

Nisbet, J., & Shucksmith, J. (1986) *Learning strategies*. Florence: Taylor & Francis.

Organisation for Economic Cooperation and Development (OECD) (2005) *The definition and selection of key competencies: Executive summary*. Paris: OECD.

Palincsar, A.S., & Brown, A.L. (1984) 'Reciprocal teaching of comprehension-fostering and comprehension-monitoring activities', *Cognition and Instruction*, *1*, 117–175.

Paris, S., & Paris, A. (2001) 'Classroom applications of research on self-regulated learning', *Educational Psychology*, *36*(2), 89–101.

Piaget, J. (1974a) *La prise de conscience*. Paris: Presses Universitaires de France.

Piaget, J. (1974b) *Réussir et comprendre*. Paris: Presses Universitaires de France.

Rogoff, B. (1998) 'Cognition as a collaborative process', in D. Kuhn & R.S. Siegler (Eds.) *Handbook of child psychology, Vol. 2: Cognition, perception and language* (5th edn., pp. 679–744). New York: Wiley.

Schön, D.A. (1987) *Educating the reflective practitioner*. San Francisco, CA: Jossey-Bass.

Smith, L., & Thelen, E. (2003) 'Development as a dynamic system', *Trends in Cognitive Sciences*, *7*, 343–348.

Stringher, C. (2006) 'Learning competence: An Italian exploratory research in elementary schools', in *Learning to Learn Network Meeting: Report from the Second Meeting of the Network* (pp. 32–37). Ispra: CRELL/JRC.

Suárez-Orozco, M.M., & Qin-Hilliard, D.B. (2004) *Globalization: Culture and education in the new millennium*. Berkeley, CA: University of California Press.

Vygotsky, L.S. (1978) *Mind in society*. Cambridge, MA: Harvard University Press.

Wertsch, J.V. (Ed.) (1985) *Culture, communication and cognition*. Cambridge: Cambridge University Press.

Zimmerman, B., & Schunk, D. (2001) *Self-regulated learning and academic achievement*. New York: Springer.

Chapter 10

School improvement for learning
Principles for a theoretically oriented practice

Cristina Stringher

Abstract

The purpose of this chapter is to analyse the theoretical implications for a school improvement programme conceived within the ESF (European Social Funds) evaluation in southern Italian middle schools. The first of its kind in Italy, this programme arose from the need to audit the use of ESF grants to each of the schools involved, while helping them to introduce coherent and sustainable school improvement practices. After a diachronic literature review of school effectiveness and improvement models, and a brief analysis of school self-evaluation in Italy, the chapter seeks to answer a very simple but crucial question: What should we focus on in order to improve students' learning outcomes? Here I propose a theoretical approach to school improvement that aims for coherence of practices and is grounded in learning to learn and reflection as the focus for students, teachers, and organizations. I develop a series of principles that can guide school improvements. I argue that improvement actions should stem from clearly stated objectives for students, classrooms, and schools, rather than from school effectiveness abstract reasoning or from mere statistical exercises.

Key words: learning to learn assessment, school improvement practices, socio-cultural-constructivist epistemology.

Introduction

Historically, a geographical and social divide between schools in the north and south of Italy has contributed to a dual educational system. According to PISA 2006 and 2009 data (INVALSI, 2008a, 2011), students in some northern Italian regions achieve a level of competence in language, maths, and science similar to that in the OECD most advanced countries, whereas in southern Italian schools this is not the case. A similar pattern is encountered when analysing primary school data, with the difference between northern and southern Italian regions appearing to grow in line with progression from one school level to the next, according to IEA PIRLS 2006, 2011 (INVALSI, 2008b, 2012) and TIMSS 2007, 2011 data (INVALSI, 2008c, 2012). Indeed, national and international studies show that students' basic competences in Italian Convergence regions[1] are lagging behind those of international and Italian average students, as shown in Tables 10.1 and 10.2.

There is not room here to discuss the structural and historical nature of the north–south divide in detail. However, school improvement in the southern regions is high up the Italian educational agenda and the European Social Fund (ESF), since its introduction their 1994, has been used by the Italian Government to help narrow the gap. Now in their third cycle, the 2007–13 ESF education programmes are focused on two major aims: a reduction of student drop-out rates and a concomitant increase in their key competences (MIUR – Italian Ministry of Education, 2009).

INVALSI, the Italian National Institute for the Educational Evaluation of Instruction and Training, participates in ESF programming as internal evaluator

Table 10.1 Italian north–south divide in mathematics

Average scores	Mathematics comparison		Italy*	International
	North	South		
IEA TIMSS 2007 4th grade (a)	517	496	507	515
IEA TIMSS 2011 4th grade (b)	516	496	508	524
IEA TIMSS 2007 8th grade (a)	499	457	480	509
IEA TIMSS 2011 8th grade (b)	519	474	498	512
PISA 2003 15-year-olds (c)	511	426	469	500
PISA 2006 15-year-olds (c)	496	429	464	497
PISA 2009 15-year-olds (c)	507	458	483	499
PISA 2012 15-year-olds (c)	512	455	485	494

* Italy's mean with Central regions.
(a) Invalsi processing of TIMSS 2007 data.
(b) Invalsi processing of TIMSS 2011 data.
(c) Invalsi processing of PISA 2003, 2006, 2009 and 2012 data. The modal grade level with 15-year-olds in Italy is 10th grade.

Table 10.2 Italian north–south divide in national language

Average scores	National language comparison		Italy*	International
	North	South		
IEA PIRLS 2006 IV grade (a)	555	546	553	533
IEA PIRLS 2011 IV grade (a)	551	528	541	535
PISA 2003 15-year-olds (b)	515	440	477	497
PISA 2006 15-year-olds (b)	500	434	472	495
PISA 2009 15-year-olds (b)	508	462	486	499
PISA 2012 15-year-olds (b)	513	464	490	496

* Italy's mean with Central regions.
(a) Invalsi processing of IEA PIRLS 2006 and 2011 data.
(b) Invalsi processing of PISA 2003, 2006 2009 and 2012 data. The modal grade level with 15-year-olds in Italy is 10th grade. The results for 2012 are those reported in the paper and pencil assessment.

and contributes to an evaluation strategy of the overall ESF intervention plans. Within this role, INVALSI has proposed an 'audit and mentoring' action. As the first of its kind in Italy, the project stems from the need to audit the use of ESF grants to schools for their own interventions. At the same time, INVALSI supports the schools in identifying and implementing coherent and sustainable improvements.

In this chapter, I discuss theoretical antecedents for the proposed improvement model and related data collection strategies for model validation. To achieve this aim, the chapter provides possible answers to a set of very simple yet crucial questions: Why is school improvement so difficult to achieve? Why do improvement programmes achieve such contrasting and in some cases such apparently feeble results? What is the key to helping students raise their learning outcomes?

After a methodological overview, the first section of the chapter summarizes international models on school effectiveness and improvement to identify their strengths and weaknesses and avoid similar pitfalls in the Italian context. The following two sections offer an account of previous research in school improvement in Italy and a synthesis of key findings, respectively. The next section draws on the results of the synthesis to introduce the concept of learning to learn for school improvement, a framework of improvement principles and an improvement path for implementation in southern Italy. Parameters for the improvement model are those identified within the literature review. After a discussion of these aspects, conclusions and directions for future research complete the chapter.

Methodology

The literature review was conducted between January and December 2010 (with updates to the end of 2012) using a meta-review on school improvement for learning. Key words guiding the literature search were as follows: review, improve student learning, improving one's own learning, school effectiveness models comparison, school improvement models comparison. The inclusion criteria for study selection were: intervention models to improve student learning; list of variables to take into consideration in the Italian context whenever possible. Major sources have been located through Ebsco data banks: ERIC Education Resource Information Center, ERIC Education Research Complete, PsycINFO, PsycARTICLES, Psychology & Behavioral Sciences Collection, EJS Electronic Journals Service, and Source OECD. For Italian studies, several sources were searched, including the world wide web, INVALSI's own library, and the repository of the University of Milan. The use of cross-references among articles was very useful in locating Italian resources.

A total of 657 studies were initially identified. A first screening, to remove duplications, was conducted by reading of titles and abstracts, producing a list of 123 studies potentially interesting for the purpose of this review. After this first stage, 20 studies were selected with the use of cross-references and reading of full texts. These studies were further analysed. The proposed new school improvement model is based on a critical review of the examined literature, selecting in particular those findings of most interest for southern Italian schools.

International models of school effectiveness and school improvement

Since it is a daunting task to summarize the breadth and depth of over 40 years of educational effectiveness research and school improvement studies, this section will outline their epistemological origins and identify potential strengths and weaknesses in relation to the southern Italian context. Two preliminary definitions of school effectiveness and school improvement are useful to establish the core features of the topics under discussion. Scheerens (2000), citing Van Kesteren, characterizes effective school organization as:

> the degree to which an organization, on the basis of competent manage-ment, while avoiding unnecessary exertion, in the more or less complex environment in which it operates, manages to control internal organizational and environmental conditions, in order to provide, by means of its own characteristic transformation process, the output expected by external constituencies.
>
> (Scheerens, 2000: 33–34)

The control element of the managerial organization to deliver externally defined outputs and expectations appears central in this definition. Another element is that effectiveness happens at the school level, and that above-school-level decisions should take this into careful consideration. A third aspect is an underlying assumption that improvement focuses on the added value that an individual school should be able to offer to its students and external stakeholders. Basically, the effectiveness paradigm addresses the quantitative analysis of large data sets in order to determine 'what works' in 'best practices' of the best performing schools that can be more or less easily transferred to similar institutions.

On the other hand, Elmore (2008: 45) defines improvement as 'increases in quality and performance over time' and focuses on the processes that are responsible for progress in individual schools. Typically, school improvement is mainly oriented to understand the internal qualitative processes in a school resulting in better student outcomes. In such a conception of improvement, the need to specify what is to be considered 'quality' and 'performance' is what matters, and this I will address later in the chapter. According to the Effective School Improvement (ESI) movement, the main difference between school effectiveness and improvement is the focus of the former on outputs and outcome measures of student achievement and school added value, while the latter generally addresses the internal processes necessary for a school to produce higher quality (Melchiori, 2001: 19). Creemers (2001) explains this difference, maintaining that *school effectiveness* is strongly focused on student outcomes and on the characteristics of schools and classrooms that are associated with certain outcomes. In general, school effectiveness is not especially concerned with the processes that are needed to bring about change. *School improvement* works in the opposite direction and is mainly concerned with changing the quality of teachers and schools without necessarily addressing the consequences for student outcomes. In short, school effectiveness is about finding out *what* is to be changed in schools in order to become more effective, while school improvement is about finding out *how* schools can change in order to improve. The need to integrate answers to the *what* and the *how* questions characterizes the ESI model developed in Europe (Creemers, 2001). According to this project, two factors are key at the classroom level: didactic objectives (*what* to teach, i.e. the actual curriculum taught) and didactic means (*how* to teach, i.e. disciplinary and cross-disciplinary methodologies; Melchiori, 2001).

Furthermore, the improvement process itself is characterized by some kind of change. Change management, as a field of study, has also been influential in shaping school effectiveness and improvement models (for an example applied to schooling, see Senge et al., 2000). In the USA, in the context of the Comprehensive School Reform Program (CSRP, CSR) reviewed by Borman et al. (2002: 2–3), the US Department of Education defined a school reform[2] approach on the basis of eleven stringent characteristics, the central ones being:

- employs proven methods for student learning, teaching, and school management that are based on scientific research and effective practices, and have been replicated successfully in schools;
- includes measurable goals for student academic achievement and establishes benchmarks for meeting those goals;
- meets one of the following requirements: the programme has been found, through scientifically based research, to significantly improve the academic achievement of participating students; or the programme has been found to have strong evidence that it will significantly improve the academic achievement of participating students.

Having established these basic definitions, the next step is to understand how other countries address the specific problem of improving the teaching–learning process, since this was one of the most important objectives of the Italian ESF Project.[3] In the following section, I thus summarize the international literature that I considered especially relevant in relation to the needs of Italian schools.[4]

What works to improve student learning? Evidence from international studies on school effectiveness and improvement

The first major finding derived from the examined literature is the difficulty schools have in establishing clear goals based upon scientific knowledge of what impacts student learning – causal relationships between school contextual and input factors on student learning outcomes are not easily established. Most studies on educational effectiveness are more concerned with the discovery of statistical relationships between variables rather than with the generation and testing of theories, with a consequent loss in explanatory power of such statistical exercises (Scheerens, 2000; Creemers & Kyriakides, 2006). It is evident from these studies that even elaborate analyses of large data sets, however useful, are not key to improved student outcomes, since a causal effect on learning is extremely difficult to identify (Gustafsson, 2008). The hypothesis here is that the lack of causal nexus has to do with the theoretical approach of these studies. Creemers and Kyriakides (2006) maintain that three basic approaches to educational effectiveness research have been developed to date: (a) an economic approach, focusing on malleable input variables such as student/teacher ratio to influence learning outputs (an example being Hanushek's production function); (b) frameworks addressing students' cognitive development and social antecedents, such as Carroll's and Bloom's models; (c) a generalist educational approach, attempting to integrate school effectiveness research, teacher effectiveness research, and input–output studies, in a blend of learning and organizational theories.

The CIPP (Context-Input-Process-Product) model shown in Fig. 10.1 is the established approach within the OECD for the study of factors affecting student academic performance. However, no definitive list of factor components of this model has been agreed upon, and many regard the classroom level as a 'black box' where something unintelligible happens to students (Scheerens, 2000). In the USA in particular, there has been a flourishing market in school improvement models said to be replicable in a variety of contexts;[5] however, there is also wide variation in the model components that need to be implemented and no clear priority among components has yet been identified, an exception being the number of years needed for an intervention to impact on student outputs (Borman et al., 2002).[6] In addition, these models typically yield long lists of contextual and input variables, while the output variables are not always homogeneous in terms of student learning outcomes, upon which the supposed effectiveness of a school is measured: student learning is not the only outcome, as progression to further educational levels and entry into the labour market may also be considered measures of school effectiveness from a social standpoint. This results in further complexity which cannot be handled by schools all at once: the objectives schools could set for their improvement are thus not entirely clear, and even when one could list all those factors and variables impacting student learning,

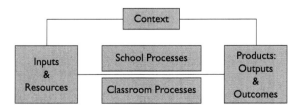

Figure 10.1 The CIPP model.

schools would need to monitor hundreds of them and possibly would be discouraged to do so.

Assuming student learning to be the most relevant school outcome, this analysis therefore focuses on factors that are at least partially under the control of the school for intervention. The next question could thus be, 'what factors impact what type of student learning?' School effectiveness studies typically analyse data sets of student learning outcomes in basic skills, primarily literacy and numeracy, thus seriously restricting the concept of 'learning' that students should acquire in school. In addition, these studies are mainly correlational in nature and the answer to our question is complicated by their eclectic nature. In his influential meta-analysis of reviews and studies carried out internationally, Scheerens (2000) offers several conclusions on improving school effectiveness that are relevant to our quest to identify the factors that impact student learning:

1. In the industrialized world, resource-input factors (such as student/teacher ratio, teacher training and experience) show negligible effects on students (correlation with achievement < 0.04), while in developing countries the significance of such factors has been established in a large proportion of studies.
2. In developed countries, some school factors were found to have a relatively limited impact on school improvement. These factors included pressure to achieve, educational leadership, staff cooperation, staff professional develop-ment, and parental involvement (correlation < 0.20); the same factors were not found to be significant in developing countries.
3. In contrast, structured teaching was found to have greater impact (with reinforcement and feedback displaying correlations ~ 0.50).[7]
4. The percent variance in student achievement explained by these malleable independent variables[8] at the school level is rather low, ranging from as little as 10% in developed to 40–50% in developing countries,[9] while the between-school variance explained by the same variables is consistent (~ 60%). Another important contextual factor in explaining students' variance is their initial aptitude.[10]
5. Scheerens underlines the greater impact of factors close to the teaching–learning process versus school or environmental conditions,[11] but then warns that training school principals on changing school factors could be more cost-effective than training many more teachers on classroom factors.[12]
6. Scheerens cites learning to learn as one of the emerging themes especially from the constructivist approach, though he warns that the effectiveness of teaching and learning according to this principle is still to be established.

From Scheerens's analysis, it seems clear that a closer look is needed at variables at the level of the teaching–learning process impacting student learning, and this could be considered a second finding from the examined literature.

The eclectic theoretical approach behind school effectiveness studies is what seems most striking and somehow it prevents the exploration of the teaching–learning process: in the search for correlational factors affecting student performance, researchers seem to lose focus on learning and their investigations are not always informed by a clear educational theory. In exploring the 'why' of 'what works' in education from a school effectiveness perspective, Scheerens states that his analysis 'brings us to the realm of theories on planning, management and organisational functioning' (Scheerens, 2000: 74) and the rationality paradigm. No specific attention, however, seems to be dedicated to broad theories explaining relationships among different factors affecting learning. Creemers and Kyriakides (2006: 3) go a step further, when they maintain that educational effectiveness research studies are atheoretical in nature. This seems rather strange: if learning is the focus, at least it would be logical to embed effectiveness and improvement studies in learning theories.

Scheerens (2000), like Creemers and Kyriakides (2006), acknowledges these pitfalls and proposes theoretical standpoints, primarily from management studies or generalist educational approaches. The international literature on organization and management identifies four primary models dealing with school effectiveness: the rational goal model (embracing also the school effectiveness models commonly referred to in educational literature), the open systems model, the human relations model, and the internal process model (Quinn & Rohrbaugh, 1983; Scheerens, 2000; Griffith, 2003). When analysed in their component parts, however, these models either do not refer directly to the teaching–learning process, or they do so partially (Griffith, 2003). In other words, the hypothesis is that in these models the low to medium explanatory power in variance explained (with an R^2 ranging from as low as 2.7% in the rational goal model to 18.9% in the open systems model) in school achievement progress can be attributable to the very items used to test such models: many variables are meant to operationalize organizational factors not directly connected with student learning.

The third piece of evidence from this exploration has to do precisely with the complexity of the teaching–learning process. In the examined literature, influences on student achievement include several factors that are multi-level in nature: there is a need to consider what happens at the student/teacher level in the classroom, as well as at the school level and possibly at the wider systemic levels in order to explain variance in students' learning results. In addition, it is not easy to clearly establish relationships among different factors at the different levels, and relationships even seem curvilinear in nature – this means, for instance, that only an 'adequate' amount of teacher content knowledge is translated into better student learning, the level of adequacy being the difficult question to answer. Moreover, factors are not one-dimensional, and this adds to the complexity of the measurement side of educational effectiveness research (Senge et al., 2000; Creemers & Kyriakides, 2006). According to Senge et al. (2000: 17), influences on learners from the learning environment should be seen primarily in the student–teacher–parents triangle at the classroom level. External environmental factors and relationships among factors representing the influences of individuals and groups of individuals upon this triangle are countless and include institutional roles inside the school (e.g. the school leader and other teachers or the school administration) and entities outside the school (e.g. mass

media, local media, extended family networks, entertainment, community institutions, government bodies, and other opinion leaders in society at large). From
Senge's perspective, it is worth noting that the human factor is key in schools and
the student level is central, as the student is the only actor within the model to
experience all school levels. However, as Senge notes, student bodies typically
exert little influence on concrete actions for improvement of their learning. This
matrix of factors, accounting for the diversity of each individual school, prevents
generalizing best practices from one school to another and shows the highly
contextual nature of improvement practices. In addition, this complexity is not
entirely manageable for concrete large-scale interventions such as the one
conceived under the European Social Fund: priorities should be identified
based upon the needs of southern Italian schools and the complexity they could
actually manage.

The fourth finding is the lack of coherence between the theory behind
improvement schemes and the actions implemented. There is a growing recognition by the OECD of the clash between social-constructivist objectives and their
relevant research approaches, still too heavily reliant on 'effect sizes', 'best practice', 'what works', and 'evidence-based' research concepts (OECD, 2008a).
Current reforms worldwide tend to be rooted in either managerialist or market
approaches, which sometimes are at odds with desired learning outcomes
(Goldspink, 2007, Bentley, in OECD, 2008a). Furthermore, there is the question of school leadership: for Elmore (2008), economic accountability
approaches[13] to school performance will not lead to increased learning outcomes,
unless they are coupled with human capital development for school improvement. In accountability systems, typically based on combinations of standards,
evaluations, classifications, supervision, and sanctions, emphasis is placed on tests
and normative control, while the competence needed from the actors in the educational system is ignored or underestimated. In such systems, it is assumed that
schools will do better simply because they are compelled to engage in the competition with their neighbouring institutions and are held accountable for the use
of public funds.[14] Experience in Great Britain and elsewhere shows that this is not
automatic: even when schools are provided with information about their students' assessments, competence in translating such information into improvement is needed (Elmore, 2008) and the threat of sanctions does not seem
satisfactory either. In addition, again according to Elmore, the variability of
effects among schools undergoing the same treatment is higher than that of
schools undergoing different interventions: the context prevails over the treatment
and this would apparently discourage any attempt to devise an improvement
model for large-scale interventions. Compliance of schools to an externally prescribed improvement programme is a necessary prerequisite for the success of
these programmes and it is often a weakness: many CSR model providers even
require up to 80% of teachers to be in favour before binding individual schools
(Borman et al., 2002; Buechler, 2002). This gives rise to the general problem of
top-down approaches, rarely effective also for their lack of adequate implementation at the classroom level. Within ESF planning, a participative intervention is
advocated rather than a top-down initiative. In their Fourth Way paths to

educational change, Hargreaves and Shirley (2009: 48) state that certain features of educational change models ought to be abandoned if progress is to be made: 'teachers' inconsistency and professional license; weak development of teachers, leaders and communities; cut-throat competition and excessive standardization; persistent autocracy, imposed targets, obsession with data, effervescent interactions'.

Thus a wider approach to student learning as the focus for school improvement models seems to be required (OECD, 2008a, 2008b), one that does not rely solely upon basic skills (Creemers & Kyriakides, 2006), but fosters what the OECD (2008a: 3) terms the central capacities of learning to learn, creativity and innovation. The most promising paths to school improvement seem to show consistently common features: (a) student-centred, customized, deep learning, connected to previous knowledge, motivating diverse student populations yet not yielding to individualistic approaches; (b) collaborative and group learning through inquiry-based activities; (c) new learning environments for the exploitation of a wide array of learning resources (including international experts reachable through ICTs); (d) assessment for learning and deeper understanding rather than rote and superficial fragmented knowledge acquisition; and (e) the emerging role of teachers as learning facilitators, experts in fostering learning and learning how to learn, and able to use assessment information for enhancement of student learning outcomes; there is also evidence that student(s)–teacher interactions have a significant impact on learning, both positive and negative: it is the quality of motivation that matters for both students and teachers (Scheerens, 2000; Harlen & Deakin Crick, 2003; Creemers & Kyriakides, 2006; Goldspink, 2007; James et al., 2007; OECD, 2008b; Vansteenkiste et al., 2009; Mouratidis et al., 2011). All these elements suggest a sociocultural-historical-constructivist epistemology for effective school improvement.[15]

Italian research on self-evaluation and quality improvement

The relatively large Italian knowledge base in school self-evaluation for quality improvement is synthesized in this section.[16] Studies using the educational effectiveness research approach are being conducted in Italy, though none of these tests established models of school effectiveness with large data sets.[17] Given the lack of such quantitative studies, it seems useful to give priority to those research and development efforts that appear to have an impact at the school level.

The experiences reported here are generally concerned with developing quality in schools through several different approaches (Castoldi, 2013). Quality certification is one of these approaches, which aims to determine the coherence between process variables in a specific school and a set of quality criteria defined by third parties (usually certification agencies). An example is the school network for quality named SIRQ (Scuole in Rete per la Qualità), started in the Piedmont region in 2000 by nine institutions that gathered together their experiences of ISO 9001 certification (http://www.sirq.it/rete/). The network now serves more than 100 schools nationwide.

External or internal accreditation is another approach, similar to the previous one. The main difference is the party defining quality criteria, which is generally some school authority such as the Ministry or the Region for external accreditation; a professional body or school network defines the quality criteria in the case of internal accreditation. An example is reported by Nicoli and Vergani (2000) of the external accreditation for quality in the VET system developed in several Italian regions, including Piedmont, Lombardy, and Emilia Romagna; an example of internal accreditation is the quality criteria set by Montessori or Steiner schools for application within Montessori or Steiner individual schools.

More quantitative are approaches based upon the systemic and periodic collection of data comparing outcomes of different schools. The REQUS Project is an example of benchmarking of school outcomes versus pre-defined organizational quality criteria (based upon TQM – total quality management – models), which has been extensively applied in schools throughout several Italian regions (http://www.requs.it/default.asp). This widespread model has had a profound influence on the conception of quality in Italian schools and has also been endorsed by the Ministry of Education. However, the model is an example of hundreds of variables, barely connected with student learning outcomes, which a school is asked to monitor.

A similar approach, yet more focused on learning outcomes, is the one adopted by the AIR network of schools for self-evaluation (http://www.progettoair.it/index.htm). This network, active since 1998, has been involved in finding a manageable solution to school self-evaluation. By applying the CIPP model, schools are encouraged to pay attention to processes that occur at the classroom level, although the chosen indicators still do not seem to touch the core of the learning processes. Examples of teaching–learning process indicators in this model are the number of problems deferred to the school leader in student–teacher relations, and the average number of hours for remedial activities per student.

An approach closer to the teaching–learning relationship in school self-evaluation is the one adopted for the improvement of professional teaching practices. There are at least four sub-types of this approach described in the Italian literature: client satisfaction orientation, organizational diagnosis, school self-analysis, and control of learning outcomes (Castoldi, 2013). Again, the projects based on these approaches, albeit centred on the teaching–learning process, often lack a clear pedagogical stance and are often informed by marketing views of students considered as customers of the school service. Alternatively, school self-evaluation is based upon a more organizational view of the teaching–learning process, with a focus on teachers' capacity to organize their own teaching within the wider context of a given school. Two examples of this approach to school self-evaluation that are more focused on student learning outcomes are the Stresa Project and the AVIMES network (http://www.avimes.it). Data collection strategies are the basis for the AVIMES Project, which makes full use of INVALSI student assessments in maths and Italian to address improvements at the teacher and school level (Scheerens et al., 2011).

Castoldi (2010) explored the concept of quality through research and development projects with schools. His most recent work identifies the classroom as the hologram of the school, and takes a quality assurance approach to school self-evaluation and improvement.[18] His proposed improvement path is divided into four phases: the first and last phases deal with quality mapping at the school level at the beginning and at the end of the process; the second and third phases concentrate on the classroom level and are aimed at self-evaluation and improvement, through an approach that underlines differences between ideal and real, internal and external quality. The internal quality is assessed by teachers, while the external quality is judged by parents and students defined as 'clients'. This improvement path is particularly useful when negotiation of different points of view is essential. It can be rather eclectic, as when researchers attempt to take different views of quality into consideration, as quality means quite different things to different stakeholders (essentially parents, students, and teachers). The approach may fall short of engaging the classroom level, as this does not appear to be the focus of the proposed interventions, though local adjustments might be possible.

Castoldi was the leading expert in another self-evaluation initiative, carried out by the SALICE Group within the Valcamonica School Network in northern Italy (Martini, 2006). The focus of this research was the teaching–learning process from a teachers' self-assessment perspective, although students and parents have also been involved in teachers' assessment. The tools used by the research team were aimed at identifying specific methodological and didactic choices and behaviours, although one of the pitfalls was the lack of instruments whose data enabled an analysis of and reflection on metacognitive aspects of learning.

Another project, carried out in southern Italy (Sicily) with a school network named Pegasus (Sammali, 2006), was based upon the CIPP model. This research intervention project involved a school self-evaluation scheme and empowering the involved parties rather than external evaluations, which are often seen as threatening. Worthy of note is the need expressed by the network leader for a tighter focus on the teaching–learning processes: when confronted with improvement demands, individual schools know that they need to focus on students' learning and are willing to tackle these weaknesses, as opposed to embracing more generic conceptions of schools' quality. Another key finding was the need for schools to 'own' the process of self-evaluation and improvement, rather than relying upon models proposed by consultants.

In all cases, these studies have mostly been developed locally and have not developed into a large-scale systemic approach.[19] School networks have been established, also in southern Italy, but have not been implemented on a large scale because of the complexity of the projects. In some cases, it seems as if school self-evaluation was the aim *per se*, which often did not reach the subsequent improvement phase.

Synthesis of findings on school effectiveness and school improvement

The above analysis of school effectiveness and improvement literature leads to the following conclusions. First, the international educational effectiveness research tradition seems to address primarily either 'what works' and the de facto situation found in schools, or hypothesis testing of improvement models. Such models are based not on the teaching–learning process, but on a variety of epistemological traditions (such as management studies), sometimes even clashing with improvement of students' learning outcomes. Accountability studies are often focused on the search for variables impacting learning, sometimes producing a 'statistical Sabbath' (e.g. overload of assessment *of* not *for* learning). Results point to so many priorities (contextual variables, parental background variables, input and resources of the school, etc.) that it is difficult for schools to focus on and to select concrete improvement activities: in tackling the complexity outside the classroom, the risk is a loss of focus on student learning. Actual learning happens during the teaching–learning cycle and this should be a priority for improvement rather than all that happens outside the classroom. In addition, even the most elaborate analyses of large data sets are not the key to improved learning outcomes, since a causal effect on student learning is extremely difficult to identify. This is particularly true in Italy where such a statistical knowledge base is yet to be fully implemented. A strong focus on the theory behind learning improvement is thus needed to advance student learning and also to advance data collection strategies connected to school improvement. As a consequence, it seems reasonable to conceive of a new school improvement model that is primarily rooted in learning and is epistemologically consistent with catering for students' learning needs.

Second, not only accountability but learning-oriented school improvement programmes also rely on intervention practices that use rewards, punishments, and controls as the main solutions for students, teachers, and schools. Such practices are not conducive to improved learning, as the literature on motivation clearly shows (Deci & Ryan, 2000; Harlen & Deakin Crick, 2003; Vansteenkiste et al., 2005, 2009; Mouratidis et al., 2011). The need for a coherent improvement approach to student learning is stringent and critical. Such an approach should take student, classroom, and teacher variables into account. Student–teacher interactions have a significant impact on learning (Harlen & Deakin Crick, 2003; Vansteenkiste et al., 2009; Mouratidis et al., 2011). What type of interaction best suits the needs of students to develop learning and learning to learn seems to be the core point, not just generic friendly relationships between teacher and students.

Third, a very different research tradition exists in Italy, with no strong focus on educational effectiveness research, but rather on schools finding their own individual path to what are sometimes generic quality improvements at different levels and in different domains of school action (administrative, managerial, and only marginally in the educational domain). There is a risk of losing focus in Italy: the emphasis placed on administrative and managerial quality control mechanisms (such as ISO) is reducing the time and effort that schools devote to teaching and learning objectives. If the focus is not correctly identified, schools run the additional risk of allocating funds and human resources to activities that are not efficient in terms of student learning and achievement. Rather than a heal-all remedy, school improvement in Italy should be grounded in national objectives, such as those stated in the national strategy for ESF. In addition, improvement should be geared towards quality teaching–learning processes in the classroom, with particular attention given to what helps students become lifelong and strategic learners. The treatment of students as clients by educational marketers within generic quality processes is not a sustainable position, if learning (and not, for instance, captivating students' benevolence) is the focus.

Key for school improvement and better student learning outcomes are the teaching and learning processes in the classroom and the drivers of students' performance, which schools can manipulate. The question is thus how to address these aspects in a way that is meaningful for students and teachers. Competence in translating student assessment information into improvement plans at the classroom level is a necessary prerequisite for improvement and something to be fully explored in Italy.

Especially within this national context, it is necessary to look carefully at what happens at the student–teacher interface to improve learning in the longer term. In other words, educational effectiveness research has introduced some core themes for the attention of Italian researchers, policy-makers, and practitioners, but it is important to prioritize such themes accurately in order to guide an improvement project.[20]

The first question posed in this chapter about obtaining improvements in student learning is an easy question that is difficult to answer: it is such a complex task, involving so many factors and relationships among factors, that it can be viewed more as an art than an established science with its own methods and recognized epistemology. In addition, the high variability in improvement results among schools undergoing the same intervention confirms the highly contextual nature of improvement. Therefore, there is a need to consider each school as a single case study, where reciprocal causation is investigated through qualitative and quantitative in-depth analyses. This complexity is not manageable for large-scale interventions such as the one conceived under the ESF, and priorities should be identified with a clear focus on what southern Italian schools could actually manage. Learning to learn has been identified as a priority (Scheerens, 2000) and should be further investigated. Professional teachers place individual students at the centre of the system, believe they can all learn, and build upon students' attitudes, beliefs, motivations, and prior knowledge (James et al., 2007; Hopkins, 2008). This approach is thus demanding in terms of the teachers' personal resources and it introduces a possible answer to the second guiding question of this exploration: school improvement obtains uncertain results not only due to the complexity examined above, but also because it actually needs a strong focus on the individual learner. Such a focus can only be achieved by teachers if they are able to critically examine and improve their usual 'common practices', in other words, if teachers themselves are able to learn how to learn. There is also a systemic answer to note here: reforms not grounded in learning will be less likely to have sustainable and long-lasting effects on students' competencies.

Learning to learn as a unifying concept for school improvement in Italy

Almost a century ago, Montessori, reflecting on the core meaning of education, came to the conclusion that education is the 'active aid to the normal expansion of life' (Montessori, 1999: 67). She observed that psychological development is self-organized around external stimuli, which must be experimentally determined (Montesssori, 2000: 63). She added that an innovative pedagogy must transform schools and act directly upon children and their teachers (Montessori, 1999: 66–67). For Montessori, not taking this approach means ultimately studying children submitted to a traditional school that does not change (Montessori, 1999: 33). Similarly, there is a risk with improvement studies carried out mainly with the idea of exploring large data sets: what really works in improving learning outcomes is not necessarily reflected in the data, unless variables relevant to learning are surveyed and analysed.

In this section, I will develop the argument of learning to learn as a unifying concept for a school improvement model to be shared by Italian schools. Learning to learn is understood here as a continuous cycle of action, assessment, and new action, through which individuals proceed in learning at progressively higher degrees of self-determination; this cycle is displayed in a time trajectory that varies at the individual level and follows the life stages of development (Bateson, 1986; Deci & Ryan, 2002; Harlen & Deakin Crick, 2003; Deakin Crick et al., 2004). Learning to learn from this perspective can be defined as the malleable side of intelligence, thus subject to change over time with optimal pedagogical interventions. As individuals do not function in a vacuum, this recursive process is both nurtured with environmental resources (from home, leisure, work, and education) and participated in by individuals contributing to their environment. The strength of learning to learn as a powerful tool for the individual in context can be extended to groups of individuals and whole settings, such as a school. In this latter case, social learning to learn and awareness of a group's drives, motives, and direction through social reflection may be developed. These learning to learn features apply equally to student learning and to teachers' professional development and more generally to schools as learning organizations at different stages of development. The emphasis here is not on a generic cybernetic process of 'evaluation → feedback → action', but rather on the deep meaning structures of the students, teachers, and leaders within a given school for their own transformation and empowerment (Mezirow, 1996; Taylor, 2008). Given these characteristics of learning to learn, a sociohistorical-constructivist paradigm and mixed methodology seems appropriate to study this domain of knowledge and practice and to frame it as a core concept for school improvement.

For the ESF initiative, which aims to help schools improve student learning and reduce the number of drop-outs, two criteria are identified to guide actions: (a) to concentrate on malleable variables and factors at each classroom and school level; (b) to precisely identify and prioritize such variables and factors. To this end, an inverted educational effectiveness research logic is applied here: the starting point is not a data set of student assessments to be explored, or a generic quality improvement organization based upon management theories, but rather a theoretical standpoint where priority is given to elements that foster cross-disciplinary methodologies to enhance student motivation and engagement. Based on the previously discussed analysis, the identified priority is to place learning[21] and learning to learn at the core of classroom practices and of each school curriculum. This logic is proposed based upon two specific contextual factors: (a) in Italy, within ESF activities, several projects already include interventions aimed at enhancing teacher effectiveness through continued professional development within their own academic discipline; therefore, the choice of learning to learn as a unifying theoretical stance seems to bring unity to otherwise monadic actions; (b) European funds are directed at the empowerment of all Italian students, and learning to learn is coherent with European policy on key competencies needed for the knowledge society.

Learning to learn is thus assumed as the nucleus of this action for three main reasons:

1. Factors close to the teaching–learning process rather than school or environmental conditions are key to student learning and should be further investigated (Scheerens, 2000).
2. Although some aspects of structured teaching have an impact on student achievement, the educational effectiveness research literature advocates learning to learn as a cutting-edge educational goal (Scheerens, 2000).
3. According to the Effective School Improvement Project, two factors are key at the classroom level: didactic objectives (what to teach, i.e. the actual curriculum taught) and didactic means (how to teach, i.e. disciplinary and cross-disciplinary methodologies; Melchiori, 2001). Learning to learn pertains to both these categories, i.e. it is an aim as well as a methodology to achieve those aims: it is not only a product of schooling but also a key process in enhancing student learning, hence its crucial importance for individuals and groups.

A route to improvement for schools: Principles of the Italian ESF improvement initiative

In this section, evidence-based principles for improvement are provided, rather than a prescribed model to be strictly followed. The intention is to offer schools a pathway to improvement in response to their differing contexts. The principles aim at theoretical coherence between the learning to learn model of Chapter 1 (with its basis in Deci and Ryan's self-determination theory) and the improvement logic outlined here. The intended route is inspired by Fourth Way paths to educational change (Hargreaves & Shirley, 2009), in an attempt to avoid some of the pitfalls identified by those authors.

In line with Creemers' attention to deductive yet evidence-based models (Creemers & Scheerens, 1994; Creemers & Kyriakides, 2006, 2010), the attempt is to delineate an approach based on each student's learning potential and on a whole-school perspective that fosters learning to learn practices. The resulting approach is an adaptation of Hopkins' (2008: 28) logic of improvement.

1. Innovation aims at the global improvement of an individual school and operates at every level (students, teaching staff, administrative staff, school leader).
2. Such improvement is finalized and focused, not scattered or dispersed: it is intended as a series of actions and processes planned by and with individual

school constituencies, directed to improving quality defined in terms of higher student competencies and reduced drop-out rates.

3. Quality certifications as well as market approaches are excluded, since they would frame a different concept of quality: an administrative quality of procedures at the expense of student learning outcomes. Also, quality perception of some non-expert stakeholders, such as parents and families, does not necessarily mean quality of teaching–learning processes and outcomes.[22] The role of schools as communities of expert learning practitioners is thus strongly advocated.

4. At the centre of such an improvement programme is the individual learner. High expectations should be placed on each learner within a school. These expectations are accurately communicated and shared among all school staff.

5. To increase student learning outcomes significantly, especially in highly disadvantaged populations, the relevant pedagogical crossroads seems to be student learning to learn, of which motivation is a primary driver, impacting on regular school attendance. The principles of self-determination theory can be taken into consideration to develop improvement routes that are coherent with the basic psychological needs of individuals, i.e. autonomy, relatedness, and competence.

6. It is important to devise ways to observe, appraise, and have a dialogue with individual students about their current status of learning and learning to learn, as a foundation for improvement.[23] The core of the intervention is thus a blend of performance data on each student learning (at least key competences) and on learning to learn. The approach is one of assessment *for* and not only *of* learning.

7. The entire process is initiated from the dialogic and participative interpretation of INVALSI data on student learning in the Italian language and maths: INVALSI experts/inspectors and the teachers/school committee meet to discuss data and to identify critical areas in need of improvement. Student assessment data are not the sole diagnostic tool, but they could be seen as a starting point for an evidence-based co-construction of the improvement project enabling benchmarking to *indicazioni nazionali* (national indications, i.e., national curriculum guidelines) on student outcomes.

8. Parallel to student performance data, students' background variables, attendance data, and a learning to learn test could inform teachers and school leaders of potential determinants of the critical areas identified through student assessments. In particular, the learning to learn test could enable a quick feedback to students about their learning profile, thus triggering learning conversations with their teachers and with learning experts or coaches. A learning dialogue between individual teachers and students on student current learning and motivation will open up creative solutions for learning enhancement. Teacher information and training is therefore needed on student learning motivation and learning to learn.

9. A series of instruments developed to sustain the practice of improvement could be made available to participating schools. Among such tools: a learning to learn test and procedures to benefit from test profiles in actual classroom environments; a teachers' guide to learning dialogues based on

INVALSI data on student learning and learning to learn; a procedure to initiate dialogue between experts and hosting schools on student learning outcomes; a planning guide for schools to deliver their own improvement project based on these principles.

10. It is important that the majority of the school community manifests its support for improvement: a top-down approach is notoriously inefficient, thus collegiality and trust in the possibility of change are fundamental. For broad effective interventions, it is not sufficient or possible to act only at the student level: the culture of the school as a learning community, forged by teachers and school leaders, but also influenced by administrative staff, contributes to the environment where students develop their capacity to learn. The improvement referred to here is a product of an effective distributed leadership and of learning motivation of an entire school community: students, teachers, school leader, other staff. The school leader's role is one of guidance and organizer of a professional learning community.

11. Each institution could create a small internal committee to develop capacity for sustainable change and improvement. Such capacity entails professional strategies openly aimed at developing and utilizing knowledge, competence, and commitment to improve student learning; however, the structural aspect of such community should not forget the core task, i.e. the development of human capital for school improvement. Sustainability of change is achievable only through a diffused improvement culture within an institution, enabling continuity also in times of personnel relocation to other schools or leadership shifts, very common in southern Italy.

12. Pre- and post-intervention assessment measures are to be taken on an annual basis. The entire improvement process should be accurately documented and monitored with simple yet frequent tools (i.e. monthly semi-structured teacher logs). The focus of the data collection strategy is not on *all* the possible variables to be controlled at the school level, but primarily on those at the micro level, directly connected to the teaching–learning process. The choice of variables to be monitored is first of all based on the following broad distinction: teachers' variables, students' variables (including socio-economic status and family background), and variables describing classroom interactions.

The core concepts of this proposal are assessment and reflection: assessment is the starting point for reflection of both students and scholastic institutions; students improve their motivation and their effort in learning based on their reflection on learning to learn competences; reflective teacher practice empowers practitioners; school self-evaluation and external evaluation trigger reflection and organizational learning.

Intervention design and data collection for learning to learn improvement purposes

A data collection strategy, consistent with both learning to learn theory and the proposed improvement path, is at the core of this model's empirical validation. Based on our current understanding of learning to learn, self-determination theory[24] would be a promising starting point to ensure consistency in the motivational approach at all levels – student and teacher as well as the whole school. In fact, if improvement is the aim, it is relevant to create environmental and social conditions at the micro classroom level that are supportive of learning to learn, both for students and for teachers.[25] In addition, self-determination theory has an already established set of empirical scales that measure different aspects of the theory and which could be used also in this endeavour.[26] However, learning to learn assessment and development implies that several other factors be considered in data collection to enable analyses of relationships among factors, the ultimate goal being to explore if and how learning to learn components are connected to learning improvement. To date, the main problem in the assessment of learning to learn has not only been to establish a list of agreed components, but also how they interact in order to produce a learning to learn output – that is, the efficient learning and application of learning to everyday life situations. The answer to this problem still evades us, yet this book points to some potential solutions.[27]

Another aim of data collection is to avoid an unnecessary statistical frenzy, but ensuring at the same time collection of what is needed to validate the model in a parsimonious way. Thirdly, data collection should enable close monitoring of the entire improvement action. Therefore, a focused data collection strategy is pursued and includes the areas identified in Table 10.3.

A quasi-experimental design in the application of the improvement path may yield data analyses that are sufficiently robust to detect effect sizes of the intervention and to allow generalizations to be made. To this end, schools could be recruited in two successive school years to allow the effects of the intervention to be shown for the group of 'first treated', while enabling a comparison against non-participating schools, which could become part of the treatment group in the following years. It is deemed that the intervention should last for three consecutive years, the time variable being one of the strongest to impact on the effectiveness of any improvement intervention.

Conclusions and future research directions

To guide action in a coherent way, school improvement needs a coherent pedagogical stance, which is more important even than funding. There is a great need for school reforms that are grounded in learning and relevant pedagogy. In fact, two specific pitfalls of existing school effectiveness and improvement models have been identified through this analysis: the risk of losing theoretical focus during the operationalization process, and a simultaneous reliance on behaviourist practices such as rewards, punishments, and controls to boost students' learning or teacher engagement.

Radical societal changes have been taking place since the inception of the school effectiveness movement in the 1980s. A useful analytic approach to change in education is that of Hargreaves and Shirley, outlined in their Fourth Way (Hargreaves & Shirley, 2008, 2009; Hargreaves, 2009). This chapter takes into account the critiques posed by Hargreaves and Shirley when they warn against a

Table 10.3 Data collection strategy

Type of information	Method	Timing of data collection
√ National assessments of student learning outcomes	Standardized assessment	Pre- and post-intervention on L2L
√ L2L competence of students	Standardized tool[a]	Pre- and post-intervention on L2L
√ Student and school background variables (including student attendance/absenteeism measures)	Student and school questionnaires	Pre- and post-intervention on L2L
√ SDT Student perceived support from teachers	SDT scale	Pre- and post-intervention on L2L
√ SDT Teacher motivation	SDT scale	Pre-intervention on L2L
√ Teachers' annotations on L2L intervention	L2L improvement logs/diaries	During intervention on L2L
√ Student and teacher participation indicators to the L2L intervention	Periodic student and teacher questionnaires	During intervention on L2L
√ School leader's perception of intervention	School leader interview	Pre- and post-intervention on L2L
√ Participants' comments on intervention and SWOT analysis	Participant focus groups and interviews	End of intervention on L2L

Note:
[a] To include the motivation scales derived from self-determination theory (SDT).

statistical frenzy and advocate the need to guide educational practice from consistent theoretical grounds. The theoretical approach of this proposal is thus rooted in learning to learn as both the focal process and the intended output for students, teachers, and schools (Deakin Crick et al., 2004; Goldspink, 2007; Stringher, 2010).

Based on the literature search, a series of principles have been extrapolated in order to plan school improvement actions. Learning to learn, self-determination theory, and a socio-constructivist approach could be the unifying theoretical basis for harmonizing routes to improvement. The proposal is informed by a sociocultural-constructivist epistemology that emphasizes situational, transformative, and organizational learning (Kolb, 1984; Resnick, 1987; Mezirow, 1996; Senge et al., 2000; Schön, 2006; Taylor, 2008). The tendency is to move away from school effectiveness literature focusing simply on statistical models, and it departs also from the educational effectiveness research tradition in that it inverts the logical approach; whereas educational effectiveness research usually analyses and compares large data sets to identify factors affecting educational outcomes, this proposal starts from what actually happens at the student level in the classroom to detect what seems to be of paramount importance in single students' performance. This socio-constructivist approach does not mean prioritizing abstract and highly contextualized processes at the expense of student learning and competences, since assessment functions as a compass for teachers and school leaders towards learning objectives that can be compared against national results.

The novelty of this approach lies in the overarching sociocultural-constructivist epistemology that attempts to inform all subsequent principles and actions, in the search for priorities and consistency. In addition, the resulting model is not one based solely on deductive reasoning, given that it makes full use of assessment for learning and outcome assessment as a basis for a reflective learning cycle. Implications for an empirical quali-quantitative model validation have been also examined.

Future developments include: (a) a detailed programme action guide for schools wanting to follow this improvement path; (b) the refinement of its operationalization in terms of actual factors and variables to be incorporated in the model for the development of a learning to learn assessment tool and for empirical validation of the model.

Acknowledgements

I wish to thank my co-editors Ruth Deakin Crick and Kai Ren, and Professor Aureliana Alberici, for their invaluable support. A special thank you also to Victor McNair and Geraldine Sutton for their help with English and reviewing. Mario Castoldi also reviewed parts of the chapter. This work is dedicated to Ciro Claudio Aversano, for his ceaseless effort to bring a ray of sunlight into my troubled days.

Notes

1 The ' Convergence Objective concerns regions characterised by low levels of GDP and employment, where GDP per head is less than 75% of the EU average as it stood between 2000 and 2002. It applies to 99 regions representing 35% of the EU-27 population and aims to promote conditions conducive to growth and ones which lead to real-time convergence in the least-developed Member States and regions.' In Italy, such regions are currently Puglia, Campania, Calabria, and Sicily, all located in the south of the country (http://ec.europa.eu/regional_policy/sources/docgener/informat/country2009/it_en.pdf. See also http://ec.europa.eu/regional_policy/atlas2007/fiche/it_en.pdf, and for education: http://ec.europa.eu/regional_policy/country/prordn/details_new.cfm?gv_PAY=IT&gv_reg=ALL&gv_PGM=1156&LAN=7&gv_per=2&gv_defL=7).

2 Within this context, the authors refer to 'reforms' as models of intervention in individual schools aimed at improving student learning and achievement, usually in basic competencies.

3 Major reviews and contributions on this topic were considered, although the aim was not a comprehensive representation of studies in the field. The studies considered include: Borman et al. (2002), Buechler (2002), Creemers and Kyriakides (2006), CSRQ (2006a, 2006b), Goldspink (2007), Hopkins (2008), OECD (2008a, 2008b), Reezigt et al. (1999), and Scheerens (2000).

4 It should be noted that school effectiveness and its public choice theoretical antecedent are not the only research fields that contributed to our understanding of how schools and classroom work to build student knowledge and competencies. They will be discussed here in more detail considering the wealth of research evidence produced.

5 Buechler's (2002) catalogue of school improvement models reviewed 27 school-wide reforms, and subsequent issues of a similar catalogue by CSRQ reviewed even more.

6 Borman et al. (2002) maintain that the number of years a reform has been implemented is a statistically significant predictor of effect size, with substantial increases in achievement from year 5 on. Their finding supports the claim that any school improvement intervention should run for a sufficient number of years to display and build on its progress. Another finding of their meta-analysis is that school reforms aimed at implementing activities for parental involvement in school governance achieve less good results than those that do not include such a feature. The authors explain this as a loss of focus, if the immediate goal is student achievement. This loss of focus is one of the biggest risks in effectiveness and improvement studies and will be discussed later in this chapter with reference to the Italian situation.

7 It should be noted that terms such as 'reinforcement' and 'feedback' do not pertain to the same epistemological tradition, the former suggesting a behaviourist approach and the latter a cognitive one. School effectiveness studies, in fact, are more interested in determining what works in improving student performance, rather than in proposing a theoretically coherent set of constructs and variables to be assessed for their impact on student learning. This eclectic approach of school effectiveness could be the major bias of these studies, not interested in a coherent set of principles guiding teaching and learning.

8 By contrast, unchanging or relatively stable determinants in student learning are for instance ascribed socio-economic status and culture. If teachers and school leaders believe learning is learnable and improvable, then the importance to find and work on malleable variables lies in the fact that schools and teachers could work on them to help their students learn better.

9 Although this could be interpreted as meaning that in general schools have not been successful in contrasting socio-economic and other variables affecting student learning, it does not automatically indicate that schools cannot make an impact: it could well be that they did not find the right way to do it, not that it is not possible to do it, or it should not be done.

10 This also should be regarded as a malleable aspect and not as an unchangeable precondition, at least with reference to student motivation affecting learning attitudes, which in turn may influence aptitudes.

11 Considering that in Italy school leaders do not have the power to hire or fire teachers (teachers are employed by the State), it is even more important in this context to take a closer look at the teaching–learning processes at the classroom level with the aim of improving student learning.

12 This point is relevant not only for policy-making, but also for research on school improvement and effectiveness. It seems this judgement has been influential in devising top-down reforms affecting school principals. However, no specific analyses were detected in the literature on the costs incurred by such reforms to understand the competitive advantage of reforms working the other way around, i.e. training many teachers on classroom factors. From an economic standpoint, it should be noted that all major western countries appear to use in-service teacher training extensively anyway. Perhaps such resources could be monitored carefully to understand their usefulness and be utilized to inform teachers about the importance of teacher-dependant variables in learning.

13 Elmore (2008: 39) defines accountability systems as those which hold schools accountable for results: 'schools, and the people in them, are expected to come to understand what policy makers (and presumably the broader society) expects of them through the application of some combination of performance standards, assessments, classification schemes, oversight and sanctions'.

14 The eventual closing of repeatedly failing schools is an extreme example of school-level sanctions in the USA. The merit pay of 'good' teachers is a counter-example of frequently used rewards to impact student learning. According to self-determination theory (Deci & Ryan, 2002), the link between rewards or sanctions and improved motivation to behave in a certain way is not automatic (see Chapter 1 for a brief explanation of the role of rewards and sanctions in human motivation).

15 Discussion of this theoretical standpoint is beyond the scope of this chapter. Reference is made here to post-Piagetian and Vygotskian approaches calling into question individuals as principal actors of their own life trajectories. I share the view that education is a process of simultaneous enculturation and transformation, where societies and their individual members are mutually constitutive. More specifically, in this perspective learning and development take place through active participation in purposeful and collaborative activity (Wells & Claxton, 2002: 2–4, 7).

16 It is not possible to provide a detail of all these projects, and a selection is made according to the criteria specified in this paragraph. One important study in northern Italy is being carried out under the supervision of Jaap Scheerens, but no empirical results have been published at the time of writing.

17 When a search was conducted with Google or Bing Web, no studies testing specific educational models within the Italian system could be found. Only statistical analyses of factors contributing to student oucomes in different subjects were identified. For an introductory volume dealing also with school effectiveness in Italy, see Paletta and Vidoni (2006).

18 The title of his project, which can roughly be translated as 'A whole school in just one classroom', synthesizes this hologram concept, meaning that a classroom can be seen as a paradigm of the teaching–learning relationship, at the heart of the school organization. This conception, totally sharable, may however run the risk of focusing too tightly on the relationships, while student learning may become a secondary objective.

19 Recently, the Ministry of Education has launched teacher training programmes with a wider national scope. They are primarily aimed at strengthening teachers' disciplinary and methodological competencies in Italian, maths, and science. The impact of such training is yet to be studied. Regarding the maths programme, INVALSI is carrying out a counterfactual analysis in southern Italian schools.

20 The proposed strategy for school improvement does not necessarily reduce the number of variables to be taken into account, but rather restricts the focus to those that are deemed to be more closely associated with student learning outcomes.

21 Reference is made here to learning the goals of the national curriculum. Recently, National Indications on what learning goals pupils should reach at the end of primary and middle secondary education have been introduced and modified in the Italian system. See MIUR (2007; 2012). See also Presidential Decree no. 89 of 20 March 2009 and Minister's Atto d'indirizzo of 8 September 2009. Retrieved from: http://www.edscuola.it/archivio/norme/programmi/ai_8909.pdf.

22 In Italy, parents are quite happy with school quality (see, for example, Maruca in Scheerens et al., 2011), while in comparative studies the country is not performing as well as other western democracies in both maths and mother tongue competencies as shown in Tables 10.1 and 10.2, respectively.

23 It is beyond the scope of this chapter to describe how this can be achieved. Other chapters in this volume address these topics in more detail.

24 See Chapter 1 for full details of how this theory is embedded in the proposed learning to learn model.

25 Teachers' incentive practices that rely on monetary rewards to perform in a certain way are quite the opposite to the principles of self-determination theory, and in

the long term produce the reverse result: through these incentives, teachers are externally determined, thus their needs for autonomy and competence are thwarted. For this reason, teachers will tend to disengage when incentives stop.

26 Relevant to this context are, for example, the Self-Regulation Questionnaire (SRQ), the Learning Climate Questionnaire (LCQ), and the Problems in Schools Questionnaire (PSQ).

27 For an analysis of the learning to learn components to be assessed, see Chapter 1 and other chapters in this volume by Goldspink, Hautamaki and Kupiainen, McCombs, and Moreno and Martín.

References

N.B. Entries marked with an asterisk (*) are those collected for the literature review.

Barber M., & Mourshed, M. (2007) *How the world's best-performing school systems come out to the top.* New York: McKinsey & Co.

Bateson, G. (1986) *Verso un'ecologia della mente [Steps to an ecology of mind].* Milano: Adelphi.

* Borman, G.D., Hewes, G.M., Overman, L.T., & Brown, S. (2002) *Comprehensive school reform and student achievement: A meta-analysis.* Report by the Center for Research on the Education of Students Placed At Risk. Baltimore, MD: CRESPAR/ Johns Hopkins University.

* Bratti, M., Checchi, D., & Filippin, A. (2007) 'Territorial differences in Italian students' mathematical competencies: Evidence from PISA (2003), *Giornale degli Economisti e Annali di Economia, 66*(3), 299–335.

* Buechler, M. (2002) *Catalog of school reform models: Program report.* Portland, OR: Northwest Regional Educational Laboratory.

* Castoldi, M. (2005a) 'Percorsi di indagine: una questione di qualità', *Dirigenti Scuola, Anno XXV* (2).

* Castoldi, M. (2005b) 'Esplorare l'idea di scuola/I: un modello di analisi', *Dirigenti Scuola, Anno XXV* (7).

* Castoldi, M. (2005c) 'Esplorare l'idea di scuola/II: da modello all'impiego diagnostico', *Dirigenti Scuola, Anno XXV* (8).

Castoldi, M. (2010) *Nell'aula la scuola – Valutare e migliorare l'insegnamento – Un progetto di ricerca.* Napoli: Tecnodid.

Castoldi, M. (2013) 'Richiesta di un parere', e-mail correspondence, 31 May.

* Comprehensive School Reform Quality Center (CSRQ) (2006a) *Report on elementary school CSR models.* Washington, DC: CSRQ.

* Comprehensive School Reform Quality Center (CSRQ) (2006b) *Report on middle and high school CSR models.* Washington, DC: CSRQ.

* Creemers, B. (2001) *A comprehensive framework for effective school improvement.* New Perspectives for Learning – Briefing Paper 27, European Commission. Retrieved from: http://www.pjb.co.uk/npl/bp27.pdf.

Creemers, B.P.M., & Kyriakides, L. (2006) 'A critical analysis of the current approaches to modelling educational effectiveness: The importance of establishing a dynamic model', *School Effectiveness and School Improvement, 17*(83), 347–366.

Creemers, B.P.M., & Kyriakides, L. (2010) 'Using the dynamic model to develop an evidence-based and theory-driven approach to school improvement', *Irish Educational Studies, 29*(1), 5–23.

Creemers, B.P.M., & Scheerens, J. (1994) 'Developments in the educational effectiveness research programme', *International Journal of Educational Research*, *21*(2), 125–140.

Deci, E., & Ryan, R. (2000) 'The "what" and "why" of goal pursuits: Human needs and the self-determination of behavior', *Psychological Inquiry*, *11*(4), 227–268.

Deci, E., & Ryan, R. (2002) *Handbook of self-determination research*. Rochester, NY: University of Rochester Press.

Deakin Crick, R., Broadfoot, P., & Claxton, G. (2004) 'Developing an effective lifelong learning inventory: The ELLI Project', *Assessment in Education*, *11*(3), 247–272.

* Elmore, R. (2008) 'Leadership as the practice of improvement', in B. Pont, D. Nusche, & D. Hopkins (Eds.) *Improving school leadership, Vol. 2: Case studies on system leadership* (pp. 37–65). Paris: OECD.

* Goldspink, C. (2007) 'Rethinking educational reform: A loosely coupled and complex systems perspective', *Educational Management Administration and Leadership*, *35*(1), 27–50.

* Griffith, J. (2003) 'Schools as organizational models: Implications for examining school effectiveness', *Elementary School Journal*, *104*(1), 29–47.

* Gustafsson, J.E. (2008) 'Effects of international comparative studies on educational quality on the quality of educational research', *European Educational Research Journal*, *7*(1), 1–17.

Hargreaves, A. (2009) 'A decade of educational change and a defining moment of opportunity – an introduction', *Journal of Educational Change*, *10*(2/3), 89–100.

Hargreaves, A., & Shirley, D. (2008) 'Beyond standardization: Powerful new principles for improvement', *Phi Delta Kappan*, *90*(2), 135–143.

Hargreaves, A., & Shirley, D. (2009) *The Fourth Way: The inspiring future for educational change*. Thousand Oaks, CA: Sage.

Harlen, W., & Deakin Crick, R. (2003) 'Testing and motivation for learning', *Assessment in Education: Principles, Policy and Practice*, *10*(2), 169–207.

* Hopkins, D. (2008) 'Realising the potential of system leadership', in B. Pont, D. Nusche, & D. Hopkins (Eds.) *Improving school leadership, Vol. 2: Case studies on system leadership* (pp. 21–36). Paris: OECD.

INVALSI (2008a) *Le Competenze in Scienze, Lettura e Matematica degli Studenti Quindicenni – Rapporto nazionale PISA 2006*. Frascati: INVALSI.

INVALSI (2008b) *Ricerca Internazionale IEA PIRLS 2006 – La Lettura nella Scuola Primaria – Rapporto Nazionale*. Frascati: INVALSI.

INVALSI (2008c) *TIMSS 2007 – Prime Valutazioni sugli Apprendimenti degli Studenti Italiani*. Frascati: INVALSI.

INVALSI (2011) *Le competenze in lettura, matematica e scienze degli studenti quindicenni italiani. Rapporto Nazionale PISA 2009*. Frascati: INVALSI.

INVALSI (2012) *Indagini IEA 2011 PIRLS e TIMSS: i risultati degli studenti italiani in lettura, matematica e scienze*. Frascati: INVALSI.

James, M., McCormick, R., Black, P., Carmichael, P., Drummond, M.J., Fox, A. et al. (2007) *Improving learning how to learn: Classrooms, schools and networks*. London: Routledge.

Kolb, D. (1984) *Experiential learning: Experience as the source of learning and development*. Englewood Cliffs, NJ: Prentice-Hall.

* Martini, M. (2006) 'Valutare l'insegnamento: un progetto di rete', *Dirigenti Scuola*, *Anno XXVI* (4/5).

* Melchiori, R. (Ed.) (2001) *Per accrescere l'efficacia dell'istruzione – Il progetto di ricerca Effective school improvement*. Milano: Franco Angeli.

Mezirow, J. (1996) 'Contemporary paradigms of learning', *Adult Education Quarterly*, 46(3), 158–172.

MIUR (Italian Ministry of Education University and Research) (2007) *Indicazioni per il curricolo per la scuola dell'infanzia e per primo ciclo d'istruzione [Indications for the curriculum of pre-school and first cycle of instruction]*. Rome: MIUR. Retrieved from: http://www.indire.it/indicazioni/templates/monitoraggio/dir_310707.pdf.

MIUR (Italian Ministry of Education University and Research) (2009) *Piano d'Azione per il Raggiungimento degli Obiettivi di Servizio del Settore Istruzione*. Retrieved from: http://archivio.pubblica.istruzione.it/fondistrutturali/allegati/piano_azione_def_4.doc#_Toc242252068.

MIUR (Italian Ministry of Education University and Research) (2012). *Indicazioni Nazionali per il Curricolo della scuola dell'infanzia e del primo ciclo di istruzione [National Indications for the curriculum of pre-school and first cycle of instruction]*. Roma: MIUR. Retrieved from: http://www.indicazioninazionali.it/J/

Montessori, M. (1999) *La scoperta del bambino [The discovery of the child]*. Milano: Garzanti.

Montessori, M. (2000) *L'Autoeducazione [The advanced Montessori method, Vols. I & II]*. Milano: Garzanti

Mouratidis, A., Vansteenkiste, M., Sideridis, G., & Lens, W. (2011) 'Vitality and interest–enjoyment as a function of class-to-class variation in need-supportive teaching and pupils' autonomous motivation', *Journal of Educational Psychology*, 103(2), 353–366.

Nicoli, D., & Vergani, A. (2000) 'La strategia dell'accreditamento nella formazione professionale', in M. Castoldi (Ed.) *Scuola sotto esame*. Brescia: La Scuola.

* OECD (2008a) *Innovating to learn, learning to innovate*. Paris: OECD.

* OECD (2008b) *Improving school leadership*, Vols. 1 & 2. Paris: OECD.

* Paletta, A., & Vidoni, D. (Eds.) (2006) *Scuola e creazione di valore pubblico. Problemi di governance, accountability e management*. Roma: Armando.

* Quinn, R.E., & Rohrbaugh, J. (1983) 'A spatial model of effectiveness criteria: Towards a competing values approach to organizational analysis', *Management Science*, 29(3), 363–377.

* Reezigt, G.J., Guldemond, H., & Creemers, B.P.M. (1999) 'Empirical validity for a comprehensive model on educational effectiveness', *School Effectiveness and School Improvement*, 10(2), 193–216.

Resnick, L.B. (1987) 'The 1987 Presidential Address: Learning in school and out', *Educational Researcher*, 16(9), 13–20.

* Sammali, A. (2006) 'Qualità nella scuola – Progettazione partecipata e autoanalisi di istituto', *Rivista dell'Istruzione, 1*.

* Scheerens, J. (2000) *Improving school effectiveness: Fundamentals of educational planning*. Fundamentals of Educational Planning No. 68. Paris: UNESCO.

Scheerens, J., Mosca, S., & Bolletta, R. (Eds.) (2011) *Valutare per gestire la scuola. Governance, leardership e qualità educativa*. Milano: Bruno Mondadori.

Schön, D.A. (2006) *Formare il professionista riflessivo : per una nuova prospettiva della formazione e dell'apprendimento nelle professioni [Educating the reflective practitioner: Toward a new design for teaching and learning in the professions]*. Milano: Franco Angeli.

Senge, P., Cambron-McCabe, N., Lucas, T., Smith, B., Dutton, J., & Kleiner, A. (2000) *Schools that learn: A fifth discipline fieldbook for educators, parents, and everyone who cares about education.* New York, Doubleday.

Stringher, C. (2010) 'What is learning to learn? An updated theoretical exploration', *Invalsi Working Paper 10.* Retrieved from: http://www.invalsi.it/invalsi/istituto.php?page=working_papers.

Taylor, E.W. (2008) 'Transformative learning theory', *New Directions for Adult and Continuing Education, 119*, 5–15.

Vansteenkiste, M., Mingming, Z., Willy, L., & Soenens, B. (2005) 'Experiences of autonomy and control among Chinese learners: Vitalizing or immobilizing?', *Journal of Educational Psychology, 97*(3), 468–483.

Vansteenkiste, M., Sierens, E., Soenens, B., Luyckx, K., & Lens, W. (2009) 'Motivational profiles from a self-determination perspective: The quality of motivation matters', *Journal of Educational Psychology, 101*, 674–688.

Wells, G., & Claxton, G. (2002) 'Introduction: Sociocultural perspectives on the future of education', in G. Wells & G. Claxton (Eds.) *Learning for life in the 21st century* (pp. 1–18). Oxford: Blackwell.

Chapter 11

Using a 360 degree assessment model to support learning to learn

Barbara L. McCombs

Abstract

A critical question for researchers and educators is how to assess the quality of learning practices and the outcomes they produce for individual learners. This chapter summarizes a learner-centred view of how to arrive at the best methods of assessment in our educational systems. Data are presented to demonstrate that the best methods are those that use a collaborative 360 degree assessment approach, contextualized within local contexts and cultures. With a 360 degree assessment approach, all stakeholders in the learning process are given the opportunity to provide their perspectives on the extent to which the student is experiencing a positive learning environment and instructional practices that meet their learning needs. This chapter also presents quantitative results to show that focusing on what the students perceive as learning supports at school and classroom levels explains the most variance in a range of learning outcomes that focus on the whole learner. The findings suggest a simpler and more valid approach to assessment that takes into account students' and teachers' perceptions of the teachers' learner-centred practices.

Key words: assessment, learning to learn, education system, school trans-formation and assessment reform.

Historical background

The foundation of the research approach to define the *Learner-Centred Psychological Principles* (LCPs) began with a special task force organized by the Education Directorate of the American Psychological Association (APA, 1993). The original principles were defined after a thorough analysis and review of persistent findings in over a century of research on individual differences in learning and what has been learned about how to best meet diverse learner needs over the life span (McCombs, 1994). All members of the task force and other experts within the educational and school psychology communities contributed to the final version of the original principles and these were distributed widely to all APA divisions and over 150,000 members for comments and suggested revisions. The resulting document contained 12 principles and a section showing how these principles could play out in school redesign efforts (APA, 1993). A subsequent revision led to the definition of two additional principles (APA, 1997) and ongoing collaborative research allowed us to further define lifelong learning and learning to learn skills in collaborations with a range of researchers in the USA and internationally (cf. McCombs & Miller, 2007, 2009).

Our collaborative research with the Learner-Centred Psychological Principles provided the rationale for the development of an approach to assessment that generates data about individual learners' perceptions of how learning practices, relationships, and contexts are supporting them. A short description of the 14 Learner-Centred Psychological Principles is provided in Table 11.1. These are summarized from the APA Work Group of the Board of Educational Affairs (APA, 1997). They have recently been used to develop evidence-based online modules for teachers' ongoing professional development and certification

Table 11.1 The Learner-Centred Psychological Principles

Cognitive and metacognitive factors

Principle 1: Nature of the learning process. The learning of complex subject matter is most effective when it is an intentional process of constructing meaning from information and experience.

Principle 2: Goals of the learning process. The successful learner, over time and with support and instructional guidance, can create meaningful, coherent representations of knowledge.

Principle 3: Construction of knowledge. The successful learner can link new information with existing knowledge in meaningful ways.

Principle 4: Strategic thinking. The successful learner can create and use a repertoire of thinking and reasoning strategies to achieve complex learning goals.

Principle 5: Thinking about thinking. Higher-order strategies for selecting and monitoring mental operations facilitate creative and critical thinking.

Principle 6: Context of learning. Learning is influenced by environmental factors, including culture, technology, and instructional practices.

MOTIVATIONAL AND AFFECTIVE FACTORS

Principle 7: Motivational and emotional influences on learning. What and how much is learned is influenced by the learner's motivation. Motivation to learn, in turn, is influenced by the individual's emotional states, beliefs, interests and goals, and habits of thinking.

Principle 8: Intrinsic motivation to learn. The learner's creativity, higher-order thinking, and natural curiosity all contribute to motivation to learn. Intrinsic motivation is stimulated by tasks of optimal novelty and difficulty, relevant to personal interests, and providing for personal choice and control.

Principle 9 Effects of motivation on effort. Acquisition of complex knowledge and skills requires extended learner effort and guided practice. Without learners' motivation to learn, the willingness to exert this effort is unlikely without coercion.

DEVELOPMENTAL AND SOCIAL FACTORS

Principle 10: Developmental influence on learning. As individuals develop, they encounter different opportunities and experience different constraints for learning. Learning is most effective when differential development within and across physical, intellectual, emotional, and social domains is taken into account.

Principle 11: Social influences on learning. Learning is influenced by social interactions, interpersonal relations, and communication with others.

INDIVIDUAL DIFFERENCES FACTORS
Principle 12: Individual differences in learning. Learners have different strategies, approaches, and capabilities for learning that are a function of prior experience and heredity.
Principle 13: Learning and diversity. Learning is most effective when differences in learners' linguistic, cultural, and social backgrounds are taken into account.
Principle 14: Standards and assessment. Setting appropriately high and challenging standards and assessing the learner and learning progress – including diagnostic, process, and outcome assessment – are integral parts of the learning process.

Source: APA (1997).

(McCombs, 2010). The Learner-Centred Psychological Principles framework provided a foundation for experts in various psychological fields to offer developmentally appropriate practice recommendations to teachers on topics they most wanted help with, such as motivating students, forming positive relationships, and providing appropriate performance feedback (McCombs, 2008, 2010).

Development of the Assessment of Learner-Centred Practices surveys

What was clear from the Learner-Centred Psychological Principles was that learning to learn is a complex process. There is no single measure that can be used to identify learning to learn, and some of the critical variables relate to students' internal perceptions and motivations and the climate and culture of the classroom, including teachers' pedagogical practices. Therefore, a single measurement of learning to learn would not be sufficient and the most robust data would represent the views of all stakeholders in a particular learning context; in other words, the measurement model would need to be 360 degrees.

The questions guiding subsequent research studies included: (a) What defines a lifelong learner at critical developmental stages from early school years through adulthood? (b) What best supports the development of lifelong learning dispositions and learning to learn skills in the home, community, and school contexts? (c) What is the role of student perceptions of teaching and learning practices at multiple system levels compared with teacher or other adult learner perspectives? (d) What is a learner-centred system and what would it look like from all stakeholders' perspectives? And (e) what assessment practices can simplify accountability concerns while supporting student engagement in learning?

These central questions defined a research agenda directed at validating 360 degree self-assessment and evaluation tools to measure the variables associated with student engagement in learning. The research programme collected data from 200 schools, 3000 teachers, 25,000 students, 200 administrators, 2500 parents, and 150 community members in the USA and beyond (McCombs & Miller, 2007, 2009). This research into validated learner-centred principles and practices led to the collection of data about students' perceptions of their teachers' and schools' teaching and learning practices and the links between these perceptions and student variables which influence learning to learn (McCombs, 2012). The multi-method research approaches meet quality standards advocated by other researchers to be the most robust and valid approach (cf. Wheatley & Frieze, 2007, 2011; Hargreaves, 2011; Scharmer, 2012).

Caine and Caine (2011) and others (e.g. Darling-Hammond, 2006; Clay, 2010; Scharmer, 2011, 2012) have argued that learning to learn dispositions are part of each learner's natural learning capacities and natural curiosity but require learner-centred teachers and learning experiences to master, sustain, and actualize them over a lifetime. Meanwhile for each learner's successful development and ability to continue a lifelong learning journey, there is agreement that context matters. There are certain key factors that must be present in the classroom and school environment (e.g. Law, 2005; Frick & Frick, 2010; Greene & Azevedo, 2010; Lee & Shute, 2010; Duffy, 2011; ETS, 2011a, 2011b). Most important from our own research are: (a) a caring and expert facilitator who allows students to have a voice in creating their unique learning goals and self-regulation skills; (b) rigour and challenge to pursue individualized and personalized learning goals in the face of learning difficulties as well as successes; (c) cooperative and collaborative learning experiences that provide reciprocal opportunities for each learner to be both a teacher in areas of expertise and to achieve high levels of performance on required skills, competencies, and subject matter knowledge; and (d) individualized attention to developmental and other unique differences that support their personal developmental trajectory in inclusive educational environments that allow for a climate and culture of trust, respect, and peer as well as adult support (Whisler & McCombs, 1989; McCombs, 1991, 2012; McCombs & Whisler, 1997; Lambert & McCombs, 1998; McCombs & Miller, 2007, 2009).

Assessment of Learner-Centred Practices surveys

Learning to learn is complex, a dynamic process, and not a single entity or single variable. As a complex human process, research and evaluation strategies for learning to learn need to reflect this complexity in promoting learning and change practices in a caring and collaborative environment (McCombs & Miller, 2007, 2009; McCombs et al., 2008; McCombs, 2013a, 2013b). Combining student or learner views in 360 degree assessment and evaluation helps educators, researchers, and policy-makers better understand what assessment and accountability approaches lead to the best pedagogical models and outcomes (e.g. Greene & Azevedo, 2010; Lee & Shute, 2010; Patall et al., 2010).

Our quantitative and qualitative data at multiple system levels (cf. McCombs & Miller, 2007, 2009; McCombs, 2012) led to the development and validation of the Assessment of Learner-Centred Practices (ALCP) self-assessment measures. These survey tools were systematically designed and validated with learners at different developmental levels to provide data on learner perceptions of what learner-centred practices were in place in their learning contexts. The ALCP surveys focus on student perceptions and ask students, their teachers, school administrators, parents, involved community members, and their peers to self-assess their beliefs and perceptions about instructional practices at the classroom, school, district, home, and community levels. Tables 11.2 to 11.7 provide descriptions of these classroom and school level ALCP surveys and their validated subscales.

We also re-validated the motivational and self-regulated learning measures that indicate a student's openness to learning, knowledge-seeking curiosity, self-efficacy, knowledge-avoidance strategies, active learning strategies, task mastery goals, and performance-oriented goals. Because the assessment tools also collect these individual measures, we were able to conduct a cross-sectional case study designed to explore the relationships between: (a) students' self-reports of their learning power measured on seven dimensions of 'changing and learning', 'meaning-making', 'critical curiosity', 'creativity', 'learning relationships', 'strategic awareness', and 'resilience'; (b) students' perceptions of their teachers' learner-centred practices, based on teachers' ability to 'create positive interpersonal relationships', to 'honour student voice', to 'stimulate higher-order thinking', and to 'cater for individual differences'; and (c) students' perception of their schools as emotionally literate places, which enable students to interact in a way that builds understanding of their own and others' emotions, and then to use this understanding to shape their actions. These three sets of variables were compared with student attainment based on teachers' assessment of national curriculum levels in English, maths, and science. These data suggested that there is a complex ecology of learning in schools and classrooms that works to promote or inhibit learning to learn skills and capabilities (Deakin-Crick et al., 2007).

In our validation process with the ALCP surveys, we study what learners self-assess as their learning and motivational orientations as well as their beliefs about their self-efficacy or ability to be a successful learner in required curriculum areas as a result of the practices they experienced in a particular classroom or school (see McCombs & Miller, 2007, 2009; McCombs, 2012). These are accompanied by consultation and professional development workshops for building communities of learner-centred practice. The learning communities include adults in the system and student leaders and were guided by transparency and collaborative involvement in all implementation and evaluation and research activities.

To demonstrate the main findings over the past 5–10 years of our collaborative national and international efforts, Tables 11.4 to 11.6 summarize our results from major multi-method studies at the middle and high school levels. Further results at the college level are shown in Table 11.7 to demonstrate the use of a 360 degree evaluation and assessment system based on the learner-centred model's research-validated principles and practices.

Figures 11.1 and 11.2 show the ALCP feedback process and the overall conceptual framework guiding our work over the past 20–25 years.

Teachers get feedback at multiple system levels (classroom, school, parent, and community) but the most meaningful for making a difference in individual student learning is the classroom level feedback they receive (see Figs. 11.3 and 11.4). As shown, the typical teacher (prior to our intervention) reaches about a third of the students (unnamed but identified in the order in which they believe their teacher is meeting their needs for positive relationships). During the individual feedback process, teachers consistently tell us they know who the students are at each end of

Table 11.2 Statistical studies with ALCP student perceptions of classroom practices

Study	Student population	Analysis	Conclusion	Notes
McCombs (2004a)	Grades 9–12; subset of ALCP surveys	Calculation of correlation between perceived LCPP performance of teachers and classroom achievement, including achievement gap issues	Students' perceptions that their teachers frequently perform the four learner-centred domains of classroom practice are significantly correlated with all motivation variables, and are particularly highly related to student self-efficacy, epistemic (knowledge-seeking) curiosity, active learning strategies, and task mastery goals. Students' perceptions that their teachers significantly perform these four domains of practice are positively correlated with classroom achievement and negatively correlated with classroom absences. Perceived teacher performance of the four domains was correlated to increasing level of academic achievement	Data derived from ALCP surveys
McCombs et al. (2008)	Grades K–3	The K–3 Assessment of Learner-Centred Practices surveys were used to examine children's and teachers' perceptions of classroom practices. A factor analysis (principal components) was conducted on the student survey data	Children's perceptions of their teacher's adherence to LCPPs significantly predicted their perceptions of competence and interest in school learning at all grade levels. Indeed, LCPPs accounted for 38.9% of variance seen in outcomes. Teachers' perceptions of their own classroom practices were less strongly related to student motivational outcomes than were students' own perceptions	Data in part derived from ALCP surveys
Vanchu-Orosco et al. (2010)	Grades 4 and 5	Profile analysis using multidimensional scaling	Two latency profiles, the mastery goal orientation (associated with LCPPs in the classroom) and performance goal orientation (associated with an absence of LCPPs in the classroom), accounted for approximately 11–13% of variance in achievement	Portions of this same dataset used in McCombs (2001) and Vanchu-Orosco and McCombs (2007)

Table 11.3 Descriptive statistics for ALCP student measures

Measure	n	mean	sd
Student attributes			
Student self-efficacy	1413	3.18	0.57
State epistemic curiosity	1413	2.91	0.51
Classroom perceptions			
Teacher fosters positive relationships	1413	3.05	0.74
Teacher honours student voice	1413	2.89	0.63
Higher-order thinking	1413	3.11	0.60
Teacher adapts to individual differences	1413	2.79	0.60
Goal measure			
Performance-oriented goals	1413	2.82	0.71
Work-avoidance goals	1413	2.27	0.68
Task mastery goals	1413	3.27	0.60
Student learning strategies			
Active learning strategies	1413	2.98	0.57
Effort-avoidance strategies	1413	2.05	0.62
Achievement			
Most recent report card grade	1413	78.15	15.04

Table 11.4 Learner-centred variables and their rubrics in ALCP surveys

Learner-centred variables	Learner-centred rubric score
Teacher learner-centred beliefs	3.16
Teacher non-learner-centred beliefs about learners	2.36
Teacher non-learner-centred beliefs about teaching and learning	2.66
Teacher perceptions of creating positive relationships	3.47
Teacher perceptions of honouring student voice	3.39
Teacher perceptions of encouraging higher-order thinking	3.31
Teacher perceptions of adapting to individual differences	3.02
Teacher self-efficacy	3.00
Teacher beliefs they can influence learning in middle childhood	3.31
Teacher beliefs that middle childhood is a difficult stage	2.90
Teacher reflective self-awareness	3.00
Teacher moderately controlling beliefs	2.96
Teacher highly controlling beliefs	3.12
Teacher moderately autonomy supportive beliefs	2.60
Teacher highly autonomy supportive beliefs	2.99

(Continued)

Table 11.4 (Continued)

Learner-centred variables	Learner-centred rubric score
Student perceptions of creating positive relationships	3.07
Student perceptions of honouring student voice	2.92
Student perceptions of encouraging higher-order thinking	3.13
Student perceptions of adapting to individual differences	2.80
Student self-efficacy	3.54
Student active learning strategies	3.06
Student effort-avoidance strategies	1.88
Student epistemic (knowledge seeking) curiosity	3.05
Student task mastery goals	3.35
Student performance-oriented goals	2.68
Student work-avoidance goals	2.07
Student classroom achievement	90.34

Table 11.5 Descriptive statistics for ALCP Grades 4–8 student measures

ALCP measure	n	mean	sd
Student attributes			
Student self-efficacy	1413	3.18	0.57
State epistemic curiosity	1413	2.91	0.51
Classroom perceptions			
Teacher fosters positive relationships	1413	3.05	0.74
Teacher honours student voice	1413	2.89	0.63
Teacher promotes higher-order thinking	1413	3.11	0.60
Teacher adapts to individual differences	1413	2.79	0.60
Student goal measures			
Performance-oriented goals	1413	2.82	0.71
Work-avoidance goals	1413	2.27	0.68
Task mastery goals	1413	3.27	0.60
Student learning strategies			
Active learning strategies	1413	2.98	0.57
Effort-avoidance strategies	1413	2.05	0.62
Student achievement			
Most recent report card grade	1413	78.15	15.04

Table 11.6 ALCP school level survey (K–12): Sample items

PRACTICE GOAL		ALREADY EXISTS
1. Expectations for Students		
1. A B C D E	Students are expected to be responsible for their own learning	**2. A B C D E**
<u>SD</u>　　<u>SA</u>	_____	<u>SD</u>　　<u>SA</u>
2. Instruction and instructional Management Practices		
15. A B C D E	Students are given choices in how, when, and with whom they want to learn	**16. A B C D E**
<u>SD</u>　　<u>SA</u>	_____	<u>SD</u>　　<u>SA</u>
3. Curriculum Structures		
29. A B C D E	Curriculum is thematic and integrated across disciplines and content areas	**30. A B C D E**
<u>SD</u>　　<u>SA</u>	_____	<u>SD</u>　　<u>SA</u>
4. Assessment and Grading Practices		
43. A B C D E	Assessment practices foster student responsibility for learning (e.g. self-evaluation)	**44. A B C D E**
<u>SD</u>　　<u>SA</u>	_____	<u>SD</u>　　<u>SA</u>
Professional Development Practices		
57. A B C D E	Teachers are given training in adapting to individual differences in student learning needs	**58. A B C D E**
<u>SD</u>　　<u>SA</u>	_____	<u>SD</u>　　<u>SA</u>
5. Parent and Community Involvement Strategies		
71. A B C D E	Mentoring programmes are available for parents and community members to work with students	**72. A B C D E**
<u>SD</u>　　<u>SA</u>	_____	<u>SD</u>　　<u>SA</u>
7. Leadership Style and Practices		
85. A B C D E	Leadership provides learning environments that allow students and teachers to engage in individual or group learning	**86. A B C D E**
<u>SD</u>　　<u>SA</u>	_____	<u>SD</u>　　<u>SA</u>

(Continued)

Table 11.6 (Continued)

PRACTICE GOAL		ALREADY EXISTS

8. Policies and Regulations

99. A B C D E   Policies promote the integration of   **100. A B C D E**
technology curriculum, instruction,
and staff development

SD   SA   _____   SD   SA

Table 11.7 Descriptive statistics for ALCP Grades 4–8 survey variables

Measure	n	mean	sd
Student attributes			
Student self-efficacy	1413	3.18	0.57
State epistemic curiosity	1413	2.91	0.51
Classroom perceptions			
Teacher fosters positive relationships	1413	3.05	0.74
Teacher honours student voice	1413	2.89	0.63
Teacher promotes higher-order thinking	1413	3.11	0.60
Teacher adapts to individual differences	1413	2.79	0.60
Student goal measures			
Performance-oriented goals	1413	2.82	0.71
Work-avoidance goals	1413	2.27	0.68
Task mastery goals	1413	3.27	0.60
Student learning strategies			
Active learning strategies	1413	2.98	0.57
Effort-avoidance strategies	1413	2.05	0.62
Student achievement			
Most recent report card grade	1413	78.15	15.04

the continuum. The issue for them is that they have been unaware of how to reach them. This simple feedback motivates teachers to apply learner-centred strategies we suggest or they suggest in our guided reflection process.

Ecological and living systems perspectives

The living systems principles emerged as essential to the success of our programme along with its 360 degree assessment structure. These principles include ownership or self-organization in defining and delivering new learner-centred practices, collaboration, and active participation in the improvement of the

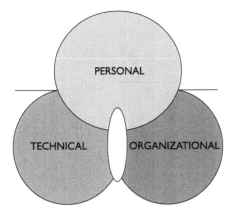

Figure 11.1 Conceptual framework: domains of living systems as levels of interventions related to systemic research on engagement.

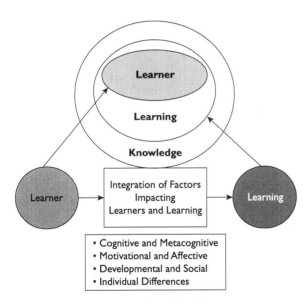

Figure 11.2 Learner-centred model: a holistic perspective.

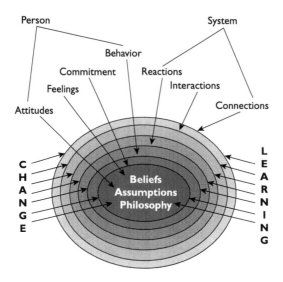

Constituencies: Students, Teachers, Administrators,
Parents, Business and Community Members

Figure 11.3 Beliefs and the change process.

system by stakeholders (Wheatley & Frieze, 2011). Success was defined in a mixed-methods, quantitative and qualitative set of studies to continually refine our knowledge and empirical validity of our assessment measures for students, teachers, and others connected to each student's learning.

As in similar 360 degree learner-centred models (cf. Duffy & Kirkley, 2004; Hargreaves, 2011), we looked for simplicity and common sense solutions that were empirically supported by sound research data. Our processes of research and evaluation attempted to reduce assessment complexity and lead to a smaller set of powerful individual person or learner variables demonstrating the success of learner-centred classroom and school practices in the eyes of all learners, from children to adults. The qualitative and quantitative data continue to define an emergent view of learning that assumes individual learners are capable of describing their learning processes and learning experiences as they change over time with different teachers, different subject matter, and different overall schooling practices (McCombs, 2013a, 2013b).

The concept and assessment of learning to learn thus emerged in our research from a theoretical and evidence-based perspective of learning as a natural process in all humans that occurs in multiple human contexts. We identified that what is learned and the dispositions developed in a variety of learning experiences – in different contexts as one moves from infancy through adulthood – are interdependently part of a larger understanding of complex living systems (cf. Deakin-Crick, 2012; McCombs, 2012).

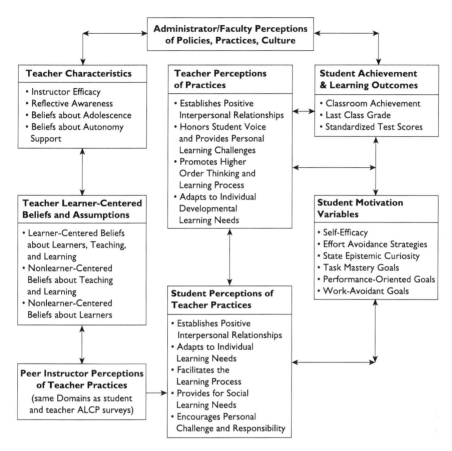

Figure 11.4 A learner-centred model of relations between K–12 level faculty beliefs, teacher practices, and student outcomes: 360 degree learner perspective.

Features of the ideal 360 degree assessment and evaluation model

A 360 degree assessment and evaluation process leads to data that provide stakeholders accountability information about the quality of the learning experiences and environment for each learner in the system (McCombs, 2008, 2009). Combining research and evaluation methodologies is one way to provide more robust and reliable accountability information (e.g. Barton & Coley, 2010). Research seeks to understand phenomena at basic or applied levels while evaluation is focused on seeing what happened as a result of an intervention, including research results that may have been overlooked or required a different methodology. For example, more qualitative data were needed in a quantitative study, and so was more participation or transparency on the part of the researcher(s) to more completely understand what is actually happening in a particular learning context or culture (Adams et al., 2009; Clay, 2010; Caine & Caine, 2011).

Beyond these practical needs, a 360 degree assessment and evaluation framework assists students and their teachers in knowing themselves, each other, and how they learn best – an important element of learning to learn (Deakin-Crick, 2012). Most teachers know experientially and intuitively that learning is a natural process driven by inherent learner interests, natural curiosity, and perceived talents and abilities. This would lead to contextually relevant and emergent assessment and accountability systems built by the people who need it most to improve their practice. Thus, we and other living system thinkers are researching and advocating a continuous improvement model built on the foundation of research-validated principles and practices derived from ongoing collaborative research ventures (Fullan, 2010a, 2010b; Senge, 2011).

Major findings from ongoing research with the learner-centred 360 degree model

What follows is a description of key findings from our ongoing research programme on the theoretically grounded learner-centred principles and practices (cf. McCombs, 2007, 2008, 2009, 2011, 2012, 2013a, 2013b). Overall, the findings suggest that the individual learner's perspective on their own learning is a crucial part of a 360 degree model to produce assessment and practices that lead to simpler (easier to understand and implement), higher quality, and more robust assessment approaches. In a 360 degree model, all learners are included and the perspective of the student learners at all ages (Kindergarten–12) are considered. When the teacher is also the learner, his or her views of the quality of instructional practices are the focus. Thus, the 360 degree assessment model emphasizes whose views (those of teachers, peer teachers, students, student mentors, administrators, parents, community members) are most predictive of valued learning outcomes.

Impact of learner-centred practices on reducing the achievement gap

To demonstrate what our research data have confirmed, in a study conducted for a major school district in the Denver, Colorado area, a set of analyses was performed on our national ALCP survey database that included students and their teachers in Grades K–3, 4–8, and 9–12 (described in detail in McCombs & Miller, 2007, 2009). School district assessment specialists were interested in looking at what a full implementation of the learner-centred model contributes to closing the achievement gap for students in Grades K–3, 4–8, and 9–12 (McCombs, 2008). A series of multiple regression analyses were computed on data sets for which there were students with complete scores on the ALCP surveys, their teachers had completed their ALCP survey, and data on classroom achievement were available. Analyses controlled for linearity of data, correlated dependent and independent variables, unequal sample sizes for ethnic and gender groups, and other known data qualities that might affect results and lead to Type I or Type II errors in interpretation. With classroom achievement as the dependent variable, low, medium, and high learner-centred teacher groups were defined for each data set (Grades K–3, 4–8, and 9–12) in our research database at that point in time (the 2006–2007 school year). Figures 11.5 to 11.10 display these results for students of different ethnic groups and genders with classroom achievement as the dependent variable.

Classroom achievement was defined by teacher scores of 1–100 on a measure that combined grading practices with perceived effort and conforming to a single scale within grade levels across classrooms and school contexts. The independent variables were these groups and how learner-centred they perceived their teacher's practices to be (low, medium, high) per our ALCP surveys and rubrics validated with student motivational and learning outcomes as dependent variables. Achievement score ranges differ in each of the analyses and graphs based on actual score ranges as reported by participating teachers.

The frequency analyses that defined low, medium, and high learner-centred groups involved ranking student achievement scores for each grade level sample from 1 to 100 (the teacher's grading practices converted to standardized achievement scores) and defining these achievement groups as close to distribution thirds as possible (McCombs & Quiat, 2002) – we use SPSS frequencies to enter score distributions into an ordered chart from 1 to 100 for achievement scores. We define cut-off scores as close to thirds as the data allow. With achievement scores as the dependent variable, independent variable groups are correlated but form a meaningful picture of what happens to gender or ethnic group achievement gaps as students progress in their schooling years with more or less learner-centred teachers. This methodology combines qualitative and quantitative data in ways researchers and practitioners can make sense of and in ways that are meaningful to them.

The rubric or empirically derived cut-off score for determining low, medium, and high learner-centred groups was derived empirically in multiple-method analyses (e.g. factor analysis, hierarchical linear analyses), and causal modelling in a variety of content areas in each grade level range (cf. Meece et al., 2003; Vanchu-Orosco & McCombs, 2007; McCombs et al., 2008). This learner-centred rubric is the result of analyses that have identified the mean score range for those teacher practices perceived by students to be most supportive of their highest levels of classroom achievement (and overall standardized test scores for samples that also had these scores at the individual student level) in core content areas (reading, mathematics, social studies, science, art, and music). Table 11.4 summarizes our findings in establishing the learner-centred rubric for Grades 4–8.

In Figs. 11.5 and 11.6 for Grades K–3, young children in various ethnic groups had the highest levels of classroom achievement with medium and high learner-centred teachers, although none of these differences were significant. It is clear, however, that for Black children in our sample, they are lagging behind their peers and performed best with medium learner-centred teachers whose practices were more teacher-directed. Gender groups were not significantly different with

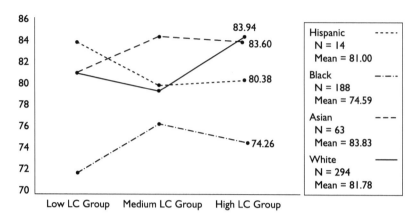

Figure 11.5 Classroom achievement by learning-centred groups and ethnicity (Grades K–3).

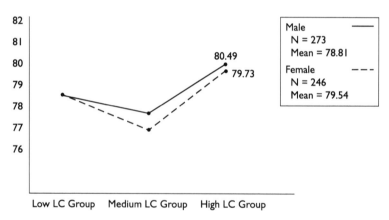

Figure 11.6 Classroom achievement by learning-centred groups and gender (Grades K–3).

low and medium learner-centred teachers but had their highest levels of perform-ance with high learner-centred teachers. By the middle school years, Figs. 11.7 and 11.8 show classroom achievement differences are more pronounced for all ethnic groups with low and medium learner-centred teachers, and while White students achieved best with all learner-centred teacher groups, the results were not significantly different with high learner-centred teachers. In the middle grades, girls consistently performed better than boys except with high learner-centred teachers, where the differences were not significant. By high school, Figs. 11.9 and 11.10 show that with high learner-centred teachers, classroom achieve-ment score gaps are not significant for ethnic or gender groups, the most impres-sive score gains being found for Asian students. Black and Hispanic students also achieved at significantly higher levels with high learner-centred teachers than low or medium learner-centred teachers.

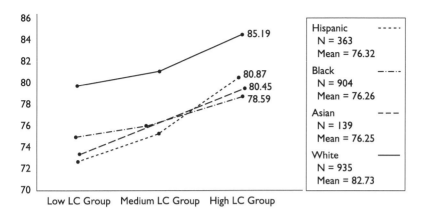

Figure 11.7 Classroom achievement by learning-centred groups and ethnicity (Grades 4–8).

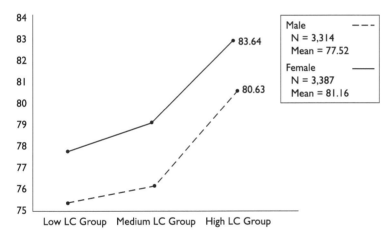

Figure 11.8 Classroom achievement by learning-centred groups and gender (Grades 4–8).

Figures 11.5 to 11.10 reveal that as schooling continues, children move from perceiving more learner-centred practices in early elementary years where ethnic and gender classroom achievement differences are relatively small between more and less learner-centred teachers from the children's perspectives. For Grades K–3, Figs. 11.5 and 11.6 show that young children in various ethnic groups had the highest levels of classroom achievement with medium and high learner-centred teachers, although none of these differences were significant. It is clear, however, that for Black children in our sample, they are lagging behind their peers and performed best with medium learner-centred teachers whose practices were more teacher-directed. Gender groups were not significantly different with low and medium learner-centred teachers but had their highest levels of performance with high learner-centred teachers.

By the middle school years, Figs. 11.7 and 11.8 show classroom achievement differences are more pronounced for all ethnic groups with low and medium learner-centred teachers, and while White students achieved best with all learner-centred teacher groups, the results were not significantly different with high learner-centred teachers. In the middle grades, girls consistently performed better than boys except with high learner-centred teachers where the differences were not significant.

The findings were similar for middle school and high school students. By high school, Figs. 11.9 and 11.10 show that with high learner-centred teachers, classroom achievement score gaps are not significant for ethnic or

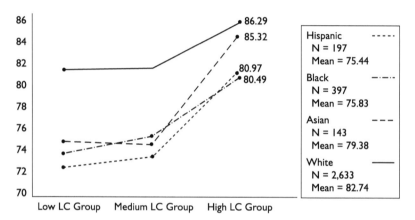

Figure 11.9 Classroom achievement by learning-centred groups and ethnicity (Grades 9–12).

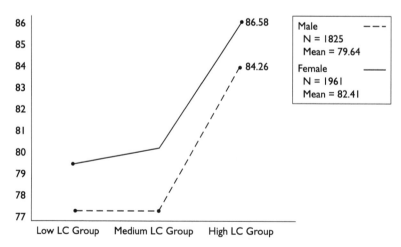

Figure 11.10 Classroom achievement by learning-centred groups and gender (Grades 9–12).

gender groups, the most impressive score gains being found for Asian students. Black and Hispanic students also achieved at significantly higher levels with high learner-centred teachers than low or medium learner-centred teachers.

Implications are that simple but highly reliable and valid student self-assessment surveys capture the type of 360 degree evaluation and assessment data for informing a twenty-first-century assessment and accountability system. The data demonstrate that all learners desire to learn in an environment of caring and feeling personally safe (at intellectual, social, emotional, and physical levels) while also being challenged to perform at their highest levels.

What it will take to get to the ideal 360 system

In a world with growing concerns about school safety, knowing what students are actually experiencing is becoming more important as a research and evaluation focus (e.g. ETS, 2011a, 2011b; Federation of Children, 2012; Rogers, 2012). Our data show that for more than four in five of the approximately 40% of students who leave school or lose their love for learning, their perspective is clear: the reason is they know that what they are learning and how they are learning it is not valued or relevant to them (McCombs, 2013a, 2013b). In talking with students from elementary to college school levels, we have learned that too many students (over 60%) express concerns that their personal and individual dreams, aspirations, and hopes for the future are being ignored (McCombs, 2001, 2012; McCombs & Quiat, 2002).

To meet these basic student needs, we are looking more closely at what relational issues and school climate and classroom context concerns are not being met. Our collaborative research projects with a learner-centred, whole-person framework has resulted in powerful evidence that as much as 80% of the variance in student learning outcomes can be accounted for with learner and person-centred approaches (cf. Cornelius-White, 2007; Klein & Cornell, 2010). Recent national and international studies also confirm that person-centred principles and practices provide the best theoretical model and framework for school change and educational transformation (Gilbos & Schmeidler, 2011; Hout & Elliott, 2011; Harter, 2012; Lyon, 2013; Rogers et al., 2013).

Reflection and analysis of our findings led to the development of an overarching framework (see Fig. 11.1). This figure displays the essential domains of all living systems (see Wheatley & Frieze, 2011), and educational systems that function to promote individual learning (see Hargreaves, 2011) must include personal, technical, and organizational domains (McCombs, 2001, 2010; McCombs & Miller, 2007, 2009) that account for varying degrees of the non-random and significant variance in individual differences in learner performance. The variance accounted for is between 20% and 45% in specific recent studies (Daniels et al., 2001; Meece et al., 2003; Vanchu-Orosco et al., 2007, 2010; Daniels & Clarkson, 2010), indicating that some of the most powerful student and teacher variables assessed by the ALCP surveys have been identified. Many researchers in the USA have argued that teacher development and training be learner-centred (e.g. Darling-Hammond, 2006; Rothstein, 2010), so that assessment and accountability systems consider student views in 360 degree models. In the context of learning to learn, all learners need to be empowered with the skills and competencies that allow them to be agents in their own learning. When students are empowered with voice and choice, they become self-regulated regardless of the context or how learner-centred the environment is through the perceptions of the student learners.

In the summary of our main findings, it is important to highlight a meta-finding:

> *When researchers, educators, and policy-makers focus on the big picture of individual learning and change, the ALCP 360 degree assessment methodologies supported and built individual and system capacity for engaging in collaborative and integrated approaches to both research and evaluation of successes and failures and areas needing further refinement.*
>
> (Cornelius-White et al., 2013; McCombs, 2013a, 2013b)

These approaches considered the views of all learners in our educational systems from a 360 degree person-centred perspective and provided meaningful feedback to all with access to the ALCP data at different levels of system responsibility (e.g. individual teachers, students, administrators, researchers). In the area of self-development, the overall learner-centred model includes research transparency and an invitational as opposed to a mandated approach, so that threats to self of being evaluated are minimized and willingness to learn and change is maximized (Harter, 2012).

Implementing a learner-centred 360 degree assessment system

The 360 degree self-assessment and multi-method evaluation methods for looking at school culture and climate are a major innovation – particularly if they give a bigger role to student voice and participation in an ongoing and evolving way through the development, planning, implementation, and evaluation phases of the school reform and transformation process (e.g. Greene & Azevedo, 2010; Gilbos & Schmeidler, 2011; Liu, 2012). The concept of a 360 degree assessment is not new and has been in use by business and industry as a tool to motivate employees to higher degrees of job satisfaction and productivity (McCombs, 2008). In education, fears about whether people can accurately describe the extent to which practices are meeting their learning needs are dispelled when using an evidence-based holistic learner-centred model that focuses on fostering learning partnerships and relationships, as shown in Figs. 11.1 to 11.4. These figures reflect the research support from neurological and psychological research for these claims (cf. Caine & Caine, 2011) and the processes researchers find to be vital to system change and transformation, including dialogue and collaboration to implement a 360 degree assessment and evaluation system (e.g. Spady, 2006,

2007; Schwahn & Spady, 2010; Fullan, 2011; Hargreaves, 2011; Wheatley & Frieze, 2011; Senge, 2012). To examine how a 360 degree assessment system was implemented in real school contexts, the next section looks at two studies by Vanchu-Orosco et al. (2007, 2010) with middle school students, and three studies by Daniels and Clarkson (2010), Daniels et al. (2001), and McCombs et al. (2008) with Grades K–3 students.

Using the ALCP surveys with pre-adolescent students

The studies in Table 11.2 examined the effects of learner-centred practices on pre-adolescent academic engagement and achievement via profile analysis using multidimensional scaling and latent profile analyses respectively. Using a national sample of fourth (n = 686) and fifth (n = 727) grade students, relationships between student motivational characteristics, perceived teaching practices, and goal orientation were examined. Multiple regression analysis identified the portion of observed student achievement score accounted for by latent student profiles. Analyses revealed two profiles accounted for approximately 33% of variance in achievement, supporting previous research and theory. As shown in Table 11.3, the studies by Vanchu-Orosco et al. (2007, 2010) revealed that positive perceptions of learner-centred practices were significantly related to mastery goal orientation and performance goal orientation. These two variables accounted for between 11% and 13% of the variance in the prediction of student motivation for the sample of middle school students studied. In total, the findings in Table 11.3 were significant at the $P < .05$ level in documenting that students who believe their teacher provides a learner-centred environment are more likely to be self-efficacious, task mastery-oriented, and less likely to avoid work or require extrinsic rewards. Studies with Grades 4–8, 9–12, and college students are ongoing (see McCombs, 2007, 2009, 2012; McCombs & Miller, 2007, 2009).

Using the ALCP surveys with young students

In studies by Daniels and Clarkson (2010), Daniels et al. (2001), and McCombs et al. (2008), a total of 2097 students and 124 teachers from seven states (California, Florida, Texas, Michigan, South Dakota, Washington, and Minnesota) were included in the analyses. The grade-level student breakdowns were as follows: kindergarten 21%, first grade 32%, second grade 23%, and third grade 24% – the sample was composed of 51% females and 49% males. The K–3 Assessment of Learner-Centred Practices surveys were used to examine children's and teachers' perceptions of practices to create positive interpersonal relations, provide motivational support, and facilitate learning. Children's perceptions of these practices being utilized in the classroom, based on 22 baseline practices, significantly predicted their perceptions of competence and interest in school learning at all grade levels.

Specifically, factor analysis (principal components) with a varimax rotation was conducted on the student survey data. This analysis yielded three significant factors (eigenvalue greater than 1; 38.9% variance explained by all three factors;

27.5% for factor 1; 6.5% for factor 2; and 4.9% for factor 3). Factor 1 mapped to 'creates positive interpersonal relationships/climate'; factor 2 mapped to 'provides motivational support for learning'; and factor 3 mapped to 'facilitates thinking and learning'. The significance of this result was that there was an immediate mapping from these factors to learner-centred practices domains shown in Table 11.1: for young children, these results are consistent with their ability to discriminate fewer independent categories of practices than older students while still being able to perceive the most significant domains of practice defined by these three factors.

Research considerations in creating 360 degree assessment systems

As educators, researchers, and policy-makers consider 360 assessment and accountability systems, the 'value-added' 360 degree model is proposed and found to demonstrate to various constituencies that students, teachers, and schools are performing at high levels and up to both expectations and standards set at local, state or national levels (Noell et al., 2009). A variety of models have been developed to measure the extent to which various reforms are working by rigorously studying what the system looks like with and without various evidence-based practices and for different groups of learners, cultures or contexts (e.g. Bracey, 2004; Goe, 2008; Braun et al., 2010; Goldhaber, 2010; Chamberlin, 2011; Marx, 2012). The value-added self-report approach gives voice to students' experiences and data show significant benefits of 360 degree assessments in higher learning outcomes while providing the rigour and value supporting learning and the emergence of learning to learn skills (e.g. Hanushek & Rivkin, 2010; Friedman et al., 2011; Hargreaves, 2011; Wheatley & Frieze, 2011; Scharmer, 2012).

One-size models no longer fit twenty-first-century global learning needs

Person-centred theorists and researchers (Cornelius-White et al., 2013) argue that the educational system must be viewed as organic and in service to the natural learning of students, teachers, administrators, and parents alike. When grounded on a core belief in the inherent tendency of all people to learn for a lifetime, person-centred educational systems start with the value that:

> schooling and education are the fundamental means to develop each learner's unique potential to contribute in a way that is meaningful and relevant to him or her.

As collaborators in our transformation approach (cf. McCombs, 2013a, 2013b), this value-based assumption reflects all learners as naturally self-regulated and self-motivated agents of their own learning. Our data (McCombs & Miller, 2007, 2009; McCombs, 2012) confirm findings that giving students and teachers choices and agency underlies their ability to develop, learn, and demonstrate self-regulation and responsibility regardless of their age or stage of development, as argued by Walls and Little (2005) and Zimmerman and Schunk (2001).

Using research and evaluation methodologies as collaboration tools

The successful implementation of transformative 360 degree models requires dialogue and collaboration processes that consider learners' developmental levels and teachers' abilities to create learner-centred cultures of collaboration and respectful dialogue. For example, Quinn (2012) studied models to capture personalized and whole-person learning experiences needed in twenty-first-century learning and accountability systems. Among these are ways to make content accessible at varying times and locations, using job aides, and helping individual learners gain advanced skills and competencies over time that are sustained learning to learn skills. This integrated smart system model uses simple categories of learner variables to assess the essence of what it takes to personalize instruction and allow for students to learn effective dialogue and collaboration skills in an ongoing learning process with others anytime and anywhere. It is an emergent learning model that is proactive in promoting learning and whose data can be easily captured for quality improvement and accountability purposes.

According to Gilbos and Schmeidler (2011), simple rules can reliably and validly be used for data management and decisions about data reduction. This methodology uses inductive conclusions derived from existing databases that apply consistency rules and similarity-weighted aggregation to estimate a similarity function from the data. This rule-based approach is an example of the heuristic nature of research designs guiding studies of the learner-centred model and 360 degree assessment with ALCP classroom and school level measures.

Understanding participants' developmental levels of dialogue and collaboration skills

Twenty-first-century learning systems must include understanding not only of intellectual developmental levels, but also developmental levels as clarified in the Learner-Centred Psychological Principles that take us to the whole-person level (e.g. McCombs et al., 2008; Fullan, 2011; Hargreaves, 2011; Dweck, 2012; Harter, 2012; Scharmer, 2012). Differences in developmental levels include the categories in the Learner-Centred Psychologiical Principles that holistically consider cognitive and metacognitive, affective and social, learning to learn skills, and content knowledge and skills. Building these skills into a school culture requires an understanding of how a culture of dialogue and collaboration is created and how changes in thinking and motivation emerge when higher-order learning skills are successfully mastered (Deakin-Crick, 2012).

Creating learner-centred cultures for dialogue and collaboration

In our research (McCombs & Miller, 2007, 2009; McCombs, 2012), when opportunities for dialogue and collaboration are part of a school and classroom culture, learners naturally evolve in their desire for finding the time and ways to work together on learning projects. Human needs for positive learning and personal relationships are the lever for propelling learners of all ages or backgrounds to talk with and collaborate on learning projects. Such relational activities have been shown to make learning more fun, interesting, and deeper in terms of retaining required concepts and skills over time (e.g. Spady, 2006, 2007; Schwahn & Spady, 2010; Caine & Caine, 2011).

Putting the human learner at the centre of 360 degree systems

Enhanced organizational functioning (functioning that supports meaningful learning and engages all learners in lifelong learning processes) *requires* a supportive environment that gives teachers and all school leaders time to reflect, discuss, and share experiences, as well as receive social and emotional support (McCombs, 2004a, 2004b; Deakin-Crick et al., 2007). This allows teachers to deal with aversive, non-learner-centred school policies and requirements and negative student reactions to these policies (McCombs & Miller, 2007, 2009).

Frick and Frick (2010) support the need for ethics and principles of connectedness that lead to the creation by people, via interpersonal processes and social networks, of moral school leadership programmes of solid research quality. As shown in this chapter, the ALCP 360 degree assessment system provides evidence-based and personally meaningful data that are easily obtained in a timely and clear manner. The learner-centred principles and model is a meta-framework guiding all instructional decisions with little or no disruption of other programmes or assessment systems in use by specific schools and school systems. Using 360 degree ongoing learner assessments of the climate and culture of their classrooms and schools therefore becomes a viable and morally appropriate option.

The ALCP data presented in this chapter show that what students perceive and self-report about their classroom and school practices provide reliable and valid evidence that they are engaged learners in a climate and culture of learner-centred practices (cf. McCombs & Miller, 2007, 2009). Students reported and were observed to love the ways they are learning and love to come to school when the context and culture met their individual learning needs. Sometimes these needs were best met with teacher-directed practices and in other cases they were met with more freedom to make choices in how they learn. The main finding of our quantitative research is:

> *What counts and what leads to positive growth and development from pre-kindergarten to Grade 12 and beyond is caring relationships and supportive learning rigour.*

When students have at least one multi-year relationship of caring and support in a culture of caring and learning rigour, they acquire learning to learn skills that prepare them for the less than ideal teachers they may encounter in their overall schooling (cf. McCombs, 2004a, 2004b, 2013a, 2013b; Deakin-Crick, 2012).

Conclusions

This chapter has presented the case for the 360 degree learner-centred assessment framework as a simple solution to understanding students' views of the quality of their educational experiences and environments. These 360 degree assessment tools suggest they may be useful complements to data about student achievement of valued outcomes from high-stakes testing approaches to accountability. The feedback provided in the learner-centred model of consultation, training, guided reflection, and ongoing assessment and mentoring in a culture of collaboration is a central factor in the sustainability and cost-efficiency of this model (McCombs & Miller, 2007, 2009). Individual feedback is a process teachers learn initially through the learner-centred model consultation and capacity-building processes that focus on self-reflection on their beliefs and practices through the eyes of their students. Feedback that fosters learning to learn and a lifelong love of learning in our learner-centred model is data-driven with levels of 'need to know' information confidential to the learner. Learner self-reporting also provides educators and parents with information they can use to help individual students develop learning to learn skills.

The complexity to be captured by the vast number of variables influencing learning at individual and collective levels requires a data-driven look at how complex human systems can be shaped by research-validated principles of engagement in lifelong dispositions (McCombs, 2012). The simplicity suggested by our findings lies in (a) a focus on whose perspective matters most in an empirical sense (i.e. the learner's), (b) the learning and change methodologies that support desired sustainability, and (c) lack of system disturbance with a framework that is independent of particular content programmes or other assessment approaches that are required for accountability. The road to a 360 degree transformative assessment and accountability system with a learner-centred framework has been demonstrated in our ongoing research to be straightforward and cost-effective compared with similar models commercially available (McCombs, 2012, 2013a, 2013b). We encourage others in the research and policy worlds, along with their collaborative education partners, to consider this in their contexts.

References

Adams, J., Khan, H.T.A., Raeside, R., & White, D. (2009) *Research methods for graduate business and social science students.* New Delhi, India/Thousand Oaks, CA: Response Books/Sage.

American Psychological Association (APA) (1993) *Learner-centered psychological principles: Guidelines for school redesign and reform.* APA Task Force on Psychology in Education. Washington, DC: American Psychological Association and Mid-Continent Regional Educational Laboratory.

American Psychological Association (APA) (1997) *Learner-centered psychological principles: A framework for school reform and redesign.* APA Work Group of the Board of Educational Affairs. Washington, DC: American Psychological Association.

Barton, P.E., & Coley, R.J. (2010) *The black–white achievement gap: When progress stopped.* Princeton, NJ: Educational Testing Service, Policy Information Center. Available at: http://www.ets.org/Media/Research/pdf/PICBWGAP.pdf [accessed 4 February 2012].

Bracey, G.W. (2004) RESEARCH: Serious questions about the Tennessee value-added assessment system, *Phi Delta Kappan, 85*(9), 12–14.

Braun, H., Chudowsky, N., & Koenig, J. (Eds.) (2010) *Getting value out of value-added: Report of a workshop.* Washington, DC: National Academy Press.

Caine, R.N., & Caine, G. (2011) *Natural learning for a connected world: Education, technology, and the human brain.* New York: Teachers College Press.

Chamberlin, J. (2011) 'Why can't some children manage stress?', *Monitor on Psychology, 42*(2), 77.

Clay, R.A. (2010) 'More than one way to measure', *Monitor on Psychology, 41*(10), 52–55.

Cornelius-White, J. (2007) 'Learner-centered teacher–student relationships are effective: A meta-analysis', *Review of Educational Research, 77*(1), 113–143.

Cornelius-White, J., Motschnig-Pitrik, R., & Lux M. (Eds.) (2013) *Interdisciplinary handbook of the person centered approach: Connections beyond psychotherapy.* New York: Springer.

Daniels, D., & Clarkson, P. (2010) *A developmental approach to educating young children.* Thousand Oaks, CA: Corwin Press.

Daniels, D.H., Kalkman, D.L., & McCombs, B.L. (2001) 'Young children's perspectives on learning and teacher practices in different classroom contexts: Implications for motivation', *Early Education and Development, 12*(2), 253–273.

Darling-Hammond, L. (2006) 'Constructing 21st-century teacher education', *Journal of Teacher Education, 57*(X), 1–15.

Deakin-Crick, R. (2012) 'Deep engagement as a complex system: Identity, learning power and authentic enquiry', in S. Christenson, A. Reschly, & C. Wylie (Eds.) *The handbook of research on student engagement* (pp. 675–694). New York: Springer.

Deakin-Crick, R., McCombs, B., Haddon, A., Broadfoot, P., & Tew, M. (2007) 'The ecology of learning: Factors contributing to learner-centred classroom cultures', *Research Papers in Education, 22*(3), 267–307.

Duffy, F.M. (2011) 'The revolutionaries: A directory of informed critics, creative innovators, and system "architects" and "builders" who are advocates for the transformation of education systems and their component school systems'. Available at: www.thefmduffygroup.com.

Duffy, T.M., & Kirkley, J. R. (2004) *Learner-centered theory and practice in distance education.* Mahwah, NJ: Erlbaum.

Dweck, C.S. (2012) 'Changing mindsets, motivating students', Live Rebroadcast, 14 August. Available at: https://event.on24.com/eventRegistration/EventLobby Servlet?target=registration.jsp&eventid=387466&sessionid=1&key=33BEAFA36 605A9BE3EADA9EBDA44882E&partnerref=EW-PD+&sourcepage=register.

Educational Testing Service (ETS) (2011a) *A strong start: Positioning young Black boys for educational success.* ETS's Addressing Achievement Gaps Symposium,

Washington, DC, 14 June. Available at: http://www.ets.org/s/achievement_gap/conferences/strong_start/overview.html[accessed 15 February 2012].

Educational Testing Service (ETS) (2011b) 'View a statistical profile' (PDF), in *A strong start: Positioning young Black boys for educational success.* ETS's Addressing Achievement Gaps Symposium, Washington, DC, 14 June. Available at: http://www.ets.org/s/achievement_gap/conferences/strong_start/overview.html [accessed 15 February 2012].

Federation for Children (2012) *Parents know best.* Available at: http://www.parentsknowbest.com.

Frick, J.E., & Frick, W.C. (2010) 'An ethic of connectedness: Enacting moral school leadership through people and programs', *Education, Citizenship and Social Justice*, 5(2), 117–130.

Friedman, J.N., Rockoff, J.E., Altonji, J., Angrist, J., Card, D., Chamberlain, G. et al. (2011) 'Evaluating teachers: The important role of value-added', The National Bureau of Economic Research. Available at: http://www.immagic.com/eLibrary/ARCHIVES/GENERAL/NBER_US/N111231C.pdf.

Fullan, M. (2010a) *The moral imperative realized.* Thousand Oaks, CA: Corwin Press.

Fullan, M. (2010b) *All systems go: The change imperative for whole system reform.* Thousand Oaks, CA: Corwin Press.

Fullan, M. (2011) *Change leader: Learning to do what matters most.* San Francisco, CA: Corwin Press.

Gilbos, R., & Schmeidler, D, (2011) *Case-based predictions.* World Scientific Series in Economic Theory. London: Imperial College Press.

Goe, L. (2008) 'Key issue : Using value-added models to identify and support highly effective teachers', *NNC for Teacher Quality.* Available at: http://www2.tqsource.org/strategies/het/usingvalueaddedmodels.pdf.

Goldhaber, D. (2010) 'When the stakes are high, can we rely on value-added?', *American Progress* (December). Available at: http://www.americanprogress.org/wp-content/uploads/issues/2010/12/pdf/vam.pdf.

Greene, J.A., & Azevedo, R. (2010) 'The measurement of learners' self-regulated cognitive and metacognitive processes while using computer-based learning environments', *Educational Psychologist*, 45(4), 203–209.

Hanushek, E.A., & Rivkin, S.G. (2010) 'Generalizations about using value-added measures of teacher quality', *American Economic Review*, 100(2), 267–271.

Hargreaves, A. (2011) 'A *festschrift* for Andy Hargreaves: 11 papers by leading and emerging scholars celebrating and concentrating on the life work of Andy Hargreaves', *Journal of Educational Change*, 12(2), 131–139.

Harter, S. (2012) *The construction of the self: Developmental and sociocultural foundations.* New York: Guilford Press.

Hout, M., & Elliott, S.W. (Eds.) (2011) *Incentives and test-based accountability in education.* Committee on Incentives and Test-Based Accountability in Public Education. Washington, DC: The National Academies Press.

Klein, J., & Cornell, D. (2010) 'Is the link between large high schools and student victimization an illusion?', *Journal of Educational Psychology*, 102(4), 933–946.

Lambert, N., & McCombs, B.L. (Eds.) (1998) *How students learn: Reforming schools through learner-centered education.* Washington, DC: APA Books.

Law, B. (2005) 'Creating moral schools: The enabling potential of critical friends groups', *Educational Horizons*, 84(1), 53–57.

Lee, J., & Shute, V.J. (2010) 'Personal and social-contextual factors in K–12 academic performance: An integrative perspective on student learning', *Educational Psychologist*, 45(3), 185–202.

Liu, O.L. (2012) 'Student evaluation of instruction: In the new paradigm of distance education', *Research in Higher Education*, 53(4), 471–486.

Lyon, H. (2013) 'Rogers' man of tomorrow is the effective teacher of today', in C.R. Rogers, H.C. Lyon, Jr., & R. Tausch (Eds.) *On becoming an effective teacher: Person-centered teaching, psychology, philosophy, and dialogues with Carl R. Rogers*. London: Routledge.

Marx, R. (2012) 'Promoting quality: Federal regulatory efforts in teacher education and beyond', Presentation to the American Psychological Association (APA) Educational Leadership Conference, Washington, DC, 7 September.

McCombs, B.L. (1991) 'Computer-based technology (CBT): Its current and future state', in T.M. Shlecter (Ed.) *Problems and promises of computer-based training*. Norwood, NJ: Ablex.

McCombs, B.L. (1994) *Development and validation of the Learner-centered Psychological Principles*, Draft Report, March. Aurora, CO: Mid-Continent Regional Educational Laboratory.

McCombs, B.L. (2001) 'Self-regulated learning and academic achievement: A phenomenological view', in B.J. Zimmerman & D.H. Schunk (Eds.) *Self-regulated learning and academic achievement: Theory, research, and practice* (2nd edn., pp. 67–123). Mahwah, NJ: Erlbaum.

McCombs, B.L. (2004a) 'The case for learner-centered practices: Introduction and rationale for session', Paper presented to the Annual Meeting of the American Educational Research Association, San Diego, CA.

McCombs, B.L. (2004b) 'The Learner-Centered Psychological Principles: A framework for balancing a focus on academic achievement with a focus on social and emotional learning needs', in J.E. Zins, R.P. Weissberg, M.C. Wang, & H.J. Walberg (Eds.) *Building academic success on social and emotional learning: What does the research say?* (pp. 23–39). New York: Teachers College Press.

McCombs, B.L. (2007) 'Balancing accountability demands with research-validated, learner-centered teaching and learning practices', in C.E. Sleeter (Ed.) *Educating for democracy and equity in an era of accountability* (pp. 41–60). New York: Teachers College Press.

McCombs, B.L. (2008) 'From one-size-fits-all to personalized learner-centered learning: The evidence', *The F.M. Duffy Reports*, 13(2), 1–12.

McCombs, B.L. (2009) 'Commentary: What can we learn from a synthesis of research on teaching, learning, and motivation?', in K.R. Wentzel & A. Wigfield (Eds.) *Handbook of motivation at school* (pp. 655–670). New York: Routledge.

McCombs, B.L. (2010) 'Learner-centered practices as a comprehensive theoretical model for enhancing college student success: A longitudinal study from 2006 to 2009 at San Antonio College', Paper presented to the Annual Meeting of the American Educational Research Association, Denver, CO, April.

McCombs, B.L. (2011) 'Learner-centered practices: Providing the context for positive learner development, motivation, and achievement', in J. Meece & J. Eccles (Eds.) *Handbook of research on schools, schooling, and human development*. Mahwah, NJ: Erlbaum.

McCombs, B.L. (2012) 'Educational psychology and educational transformation', in W.M. Reynolds & G.E. Miller (Eds.) *Comprehensive handbook of psychology, Vol. 7: Educational psychology* (2nd edn., pp. 493–533), New York: Wiley.

McCombs, B.L. (2013a) 'The learner-centered model: Implications for research approaches', in J.H.D. Cornelius-White, R. Motschnig-Pitrik, & M. Lux (Eds.) *Interdisciplinary handbook of the person-centered approach: Connections beyond psychotherapy*. New York: Springer.

McCombs, B. L. (2013b) 'The learner-centered model: From the vision to the future', in J.H.D. Cornelius-White, R. Motschnig-Pitrik, & M. Lux (Eds.) *Interdisciplinary handbook of the person-centered approach: Connections beyond psychotherapy*. New York: Springer.

McCombs, B.L., Daniels, D., & Perry, K.E. (2008) 'Children's and teachers' perceptions of learner-centered practices, and student motivation: Implications for early schooling', *Elementary School Journal, 109*(1), 16–35.

McCombs, B.L., & Miller, L. (2007) *Learner-centered classroom practices and assessments: Maximizing student motivation, learning, and achievement*. Thousand Oaks, CA: Corwin Press.

McCombs, B.L., & Miller, L. (2009) *The school leader's guide to learner-centered education: From complexity to simplicity*. Thousand Oaks, CA: Corwin Press.

McCombs, B.L., & Quiat, M.A. (2002) What makes a comprehensive school reform model learner-centered?, *Urban Education, 37*(4), 476–496.

McCombs, B.L., & Whisler, J.S. (1997) *The learner-centered classroom and school: Strategies for enhancing student motivation and achievement*. San Francisco, CA: Jossey-Bass.

Meece, J.L., Herman, P., & McCombs, B.L. (2003) Relations of learner-centered teaching practices to adolescents' achievement goals, *International Journal of Educational Research, 39*(4/5), 457–475.

Patall, E., Cooper, H., & Wynn, S.P. (2010) 'The effectiveness and relative importance of choice in the classroom', *Journal of Educational Psychology, 102*(4), 896–915.

Quinn, C. (2012) 'Learning wisdom', ITForum article available at: http://www.quinnovation.com/LearningWisdom.html [accessed 29 September 2012].

Rogers, C.R., Lyon, H.C., Jr., & Tausch, R. (2013) *On becoming an effective teacher*. London: Routledge.

Rogers, T. (2012) *Inside the bully economy*. Available at: http://www.salon.com/2012/03/04/inside_the_bully_economy/singleton/.

Rothstein, J. (2010) 'Teacher quality in educational production: Tracking, decay, and student achievement', *Quarterly Journal of Economics*, February, pp. 175–214.

Scharmer, O. (2011) 'Leading from the emerging future: Minds for change – future of global development', Paper prepared for ceremony to mark the 50th anniversary of the BMZ Federal Ministry for Economic Cooperation and Development, Berlin, Germany, November.

Scharmer, O. (2012) *Theory U: Chapter 21*. Available at: http://www.theoryu.com/documents/TU-ch21.pdf or http://www.presencing.com.

Schwahn, C.J., & Spady, W.G. (2010) *Total leaders 2.0: Leading in the age of empowerment*. Landham, MD: Rowan & Littlefield.

Senge, P. (2011) *Collaborative culture: Insights from Peter Senge on the foundations of organizational learning*. Available at: http://sourcepov.com/2011/01/11/collaborative-culture/ [accessed 22 January 2011].

Senge, P. (2012) 'The necessary revolution: How we got into this predicament', *Reflections: The SoL Journal, 9*(2), 20–33. Available at: http://c.ymcdn.com/sites/www.solonline.org/resource/resmgr/Docs/Senge_9.2.pdf.

Spady, W. (2006) *Fundamental unity leadership percepts*. Unpublished document by author.

Spady, W. (2007) *Are we looking for reform re-form, or transform education?* Unpublished working paper, Keystone, CO.

Vanchu-Orosco, M., & McCombs, B.L. (2007) 'The relationship of learner-centered practices to adolescent achievement goals: A proposed use of hierarchical linear modeling methods', Paper presented to the Annual Meeting of the American Educational Research Association, Chicago, IL.

Vanchu-Orosco, M., McCombs, B.L., & Culpepper, S.A. (2010) 'Understanding relationships between learner-centered practices and adolescent achievement: Theory building with latent profile analysis', Paper presented to the Annual Meeting of the American Educational Research Association, Denver, CO, April.

Vasquez Heilig, J., & Nichols, S. (2013) 'A quandary for school leaders: Equity, high-stakes testing and accountability', in L.C. Tillman & J.J. Scheurich (Eds.) *Handbook of research on educational leadership for diversity and equity*. New York: Routledge.

Walls, T.A., & Little, T.D. (2005) 'Relations among personal agency, motivation, and school adjustment in early adolescence', *Journal of Educational Psychology*, *97*(1), 23–31.

Wheatley, M., & Frieze, D. (2007) 'Beyond networking: How large-scale change really happens: Working with emergence', *School Administrator*, Spring. Available at: http://www.margaretwheatley.com/articles/largescalechange.html.

Wheatley, M., & Frieze, D. (2011) *Walk out, walk on: A learning journey into communities daring to live the future now*. San Francisco, CA: Berrett-Koehler.

Whisler, J.S., & McCombs, B.L. (1989) *CORE: A middle school self-development advisement program*. Aurora, CO: Mid-Continent Regional Educational Laboratory.

Zimmerman, B.J., & Schunk, D.H. (Eds.) (2001) *Self-regulated learning and academic achievement: Theoretical perspectives* (2nd edn.). Mahwah, NJ: Erlbaum.

Chapter 12

Learning to learn in practice in non-formal education

Paul Kloosterman

Abstract

This chapter focuses on the implications of learning to learn on the roles of learners and educators, drawing on two projects in the field of European non-formal educational programmes. Learners have to take new roles and develop new competences involving planning learning, learning with others, and reflection on the learning outcomes and process. This is a quite challenging step for many adult learners. Often their experience in traditional education leaves them with a negative perception of learning and a negative image of themselves as learners. To (re)gain the confidence in your own ability to become an independent learner takes time, reflection, and the support of others. The main challenge for educators is having the belief and trust that learners are best placed to know their own learning needs, and being able to facilitate the path that the learner has chosen. Creating a good social climate and the ability to support the individual learning process of learners are, among others, crucial roles for the 'new' facilitator. Still many new challenges are ahead of us when it comes to learning and supporting learners in the future. The real sea change will be the shift from an educational system that has as its main objective the transmission of knowledge and skills within a given time-frame into a system that is able to facilitate the generation and development of self-directed learners.

Key words: facilitator's role, learner's role, ability, support, development.

Introduction

Learning to learn has profound implications for the role and competences of both learners and educators. Competence in learning to learn requires the individual learner to take responsibility for his or her own learning, both the process of learning – or the journey – as well as the outcome. Taking up that responsibility is a big step for many learners, while handing over that responsibility is an enormous step for many educators. In this chapter, I focus on the crucial aspects of this change of roles in which responsibility for what is learned and how it is learned is progressively handed over to the learner. The chapter draws on two projects in the field of European non-formal educational programmes for adult education and youth work.

The Learning to Learn research and practice project

From 2008 to 2010, a European network of seven organizations undertook the Learning to Learn research and practice project (Grundtvig Multilateral Project, 2008). These organizations' aim was to collaborate to develop, implement, and analyse innovative approaches to teaching and learning in the field of non-formal adult education to help support learners in planning, organizing, implementing, and assessing their own learning. Initially, the project undertook an extensive literature review on learning to learn in order to explore related concepts, theories, and practices. Six literature reviews in different language domains were produced (Chisholm et al., 2010). On the basis of these, the project team developed approaches to learning and teaching designed to support learners to develop the skills, knowledge, and attitudes to plan, implement, organize, and assess their own learning.

Thirteen countries were involved in the project – Austria, Belgium, Croatia, Germany, Hungary, Iceland, Ireland, Italy, Lithuania, Portugal, Romania, Slovenia, and Spain – and the teaching staff of the institutions involved were trained in the proposed approaches prior to the start of the project. In the initial analysis phase, 27 educational activities all over Europe were followed and analysed, partly through on-the-spot interviews and observations and partly through online questionnaires.

Two categories of projects contributed data to the analysis:

- Practice projects – adult education activities organized by the core partners of the project consortium, which were analysed through on-site observation, learning diaries, and online surveys of learners and educators.
- Satellite projects – adult education activities organized by associated partners of the project consortium, which were analysed exclusively through online surveys of learners and educators.

The analysis, together with the outcome of the literature reviews resulted in a research synthesis report (Chisholm et al., 2010) that also provided a foundation for a handbook (Kloosterman & Taylor, 2012) to inspire learning facilitators to introduce these methodologies and approaches in their own practice. The project benefited from financial support from the Grundtvig Programme, a part of the Lifelong Learning Programme of the European Commission.

European Youth in Action Programme

The other project that provides material for this chapter is the Training of Trainers for European Youth in Action Projects. The author is a member of the team of this long-term training course that takes place every year within the framework of the Youth in Action Programme of the European Commission. The course, which consists of three residential seminars, online learning and a practice phase, trains trainers from all over Europe to contribute to the improvement of the quality of projects within the Youth in Action Programme. In the last six years, learning to learn has become a crucial focus in the course, although the term 'self-directed learning' was used to describe the learning to learn competence. The learning to learn competence is seen as an essential competence for trainers, both for themselves as learners as well as in their role as a facilitator of learning for other people. Thanks to the long-term character of the course and to the fact that it takes place every year, the team has the opportunity to experiment with and to develop their approach to learning to learn together with the participants.

Why learning to learn?

The competence to plan and organize your own learning is a necessary and vital competence for engaging with our rapidly changing world. For this reason, it fits well as one of the key competences in the Life Long Learning strategy of the European Commission. In the world we live in now, it is no longer viable for people to engage in formal learning until the age of 18 or 25 and then assume that this will be enough for the rest of their life. To understand and deal with the constant change, we need to be able to learn throughout the life span and, to do this successfully, we need to be able to take responsibility for our own learning purposes and pathways.

Alongside this 'practical' reason for the need for self-directed learners, learning to learn is part of the worldwide debate about the reform of education into a process in which the learner is at the centre and where the needs, talents, passions, and wishes of learners are the starting point for engagement in learning. This is not a new concept but the introduction of learning to learn as a key competence for lifelong learning revitalized the discussion about how education can adapt to the needs of a global, interconnected world.

Self-directed learning and learning to learn

There is a strong link between learning to learn and the concept of self-directed learning. This concept was developed during the 1970s, by people such as Tough, Knowles, and Hiemstra, as part of the framework of adult education in the United States (http://www-distance.syr.edu/distancenew.html). Guglielmino, who developed the Self-Directed Learning Readiness Scale (SDLRS) in 1977, identified a self-directed learner as:

> one who exhibits initiative, independence, and persistence in learning; one who accepts responsibility for his or her own learning and views problems as challenges, not obstacles; one who is capable of self-discipline and has a high degree of curiosity; one who has a strong desire to learn or change and is self confident; one who is able to use basic study skills, organize his or her time, set an appropriate pace for learning, and develop a plan for completing work; one who enjoys learning and has a tendency to be goal-oriented.
>
> (Guglielmino, 1977: 73)

Findings from the two projects: Four fields of competence

The findings emerging from our projects identified four main fields of competence in learning to learn, or self-directed learning:

- Awareness of self as a learner
- Organizing and planning one's learning
- Learning with others
- Reflection, reviewing, and self-assessment.

Awareness of self as a learner

The projects included exercises and guidance for learners to reflect on their learning by looking back on how they have learned. Often participants revealed that this was the first time that they had done this sort of reflection. Their reflection and evaluation on their learning was primarily built on how successful they were in school and for some of them on learning style inventories they once did. The exercises provided in these projects, however, invited them to look at learning in a much broader lifewide way and often this revealed surprises for the individual.

What became clear was that people who scored badly in tests and examinations at school often saw themselves as bad learners. Learning becomes something negative, something to avoid. This was a sad finding since, as Rogers (1969) argues, all human beings have a natural potentiality for learning.

Our shared view as adult educators was that the problem lies much more in an educational system that is not capable of recognizing, following or adjusting to the unique ways that individual people learn. As Robinson says:

> Current approaches to education and training are hobbled by assumptions about intelligence and creativity that have squandered the talents and stifled the creative confidence of untold numbers of people. . . . Mass systems of public education were developed primarily to meet the needs of the Industrial Revolution and, in many ways, mirror the principles of industrial production. They emphasize linearity, conformity and standardization. One of the reasons they are not working now is that real life is organic, adaptable and diverse'.
>
> (Robinson, 2011: 8)

This leaves a lot of adults with a negative self-image in relation to their ability to learn, which can lead to self-doubts when they are faced with the invitation to take responsibility for their own learning. A prerequisite for learning to learn, to be able to organize and plan your own learning, is the need to have the confidence in your own ability to become an independent learner. This requires the space to explore your own learning identity and broader understanding of what learning is, and how we engage in it. For many adult learners, this is a big step, which takes time, reflection, and trust in sharing with others.

Learning style tests and inventories are often used to identify learning style preferences. There is real doubt about the scientific basis of the concept of learning styles and there is a real risk that putting people into a specific learning styles 'box' might actually limit their learning. As the Research Synthesis Report of the Learning to Learn Project (Chisholm et al., 2010: 50) states:

> The experience of this project demonstrates that simplistic assumptions about learning styles of people are misleading. Learning differences do not exist between people, but rather between contexts and these go far beyond the modality of the content matter: they have to do with the learner and their current state of mind and mood, their level of exhaustion, the timing, the content, the educator, the relation and level of trust between the actors, the environment, the spoken and unspoken expectations and many more and equally relevant aspects.

Despite this, it is important that adult learners who take learning into their own hands are aware of and reflect on their own way of learning. This requires a step beyond looking at 'how did I learn until now?' Reflecting and analysing how they learned to date does not offer the possibility of exploring the wide variety of other strategies that might lead to selected learning outcomes. As well as the question 'how did I learn until now?', other questions such as 'how do I like to learn?', 'which ways of learning better fit my passions and needs?', 'what are other ways of learning I'm not aware of?', and 'how do I want to challenge myself in learning?' can open new interesting perspectives. Being competent in learning to learn requires a constant reflection on and evaluation of one's learning by oneself and with others, looking backwards, assessing the present context, and looking forward to new goals and purposes

Organizing and planning one's learning

Initially, the Training of Trainers programme provided participants with different kinds of tools to plan their learning. The thinking behind this was simple: after filling in a self-assessment questionnaire on different trainers' competences, participants defined their learning objectives and then filled in a form in which they wrote down how, when, and with whom they wanted to work on these objectives. It was called a Personal Development Plan and it was the instrument to come back to, to check and when necessary to adapt to, during the course. For most participants, it did not work. Some of them became seriously confused when having to set their learning objectives. They were simply not ready for that and felt quite unsure about setting directions that would guide them for the coming year. The majority of the participants managed to set learning objectives and even completed the 'how', 'when', and 'with whom' but discovered, sometimes after a few days, sometimes after some weeks, that they could not keep up with their own plan. This led to feelings of guilt and inadequacy, not desirable emotions for sustaining self-directed learning.

In discussion with these participants, several things became clear:

- Not sticking with their plan did not mean they were not learning. They were just learning other things.
- Setting objectives for the whole course (almost a year) was too demanding and too much of a responsibility.
- The learning objectives set at a given time were valid for that moment. New experiences and insights that occurred during the course raised new and often more interesting questions for participants.
- The learning plan seemed to become more of an obstacle than a stimulus for their learning – something you have to do simply because it is written down.

Merriam and Caffarella (1999), referring to the work of Tough (1971) and Knowles (1975), described the process of self-directed learning as follows:

> Tough's list of thirteen steps represents key decision-making points about choosing what, where, and how to learn:
>
> 1. Deciding what detailed knowledge and skill to learn
> 2. Deciding the specific activities, methods, resources, or equipment for learning
> 3. Deciding where to learn
> 4. Setting specific deadlines or intermediate targets
> 5. Deciding when to begin a learning episode
> 6. Deciding the place at which to proceed during a learning episode
> 7. Estimating the current level of one's knowledge and skill or one's progress in gaining the desired knowledge and skill
> 8. Detecting any factor that has been hindering learning or discovering an efficiency aspect of the current procedures
> 9. Obtaining the desired resources or equipment or reaching the desired place or resource
> 10. Preparing or adapting a room for learning or arranging certain other physical conditions in preparation for learning
> 11. Saving or obtaining the money necessary for the use of certain human or nonhuman resources
> 12. Finding time for the learning
> 13. Taking steps to increase the motivation for certain learning episode

Tough assumed that adults have a wide range of abilities for planning and guiding their own learning activities. Meanwhile, Knowles's (1975) five-step model of self-directed learning consists of:

1. Diagnosing learning needs
2. Formulating learning goals
3. Identifying human and material resources for learning

4.   Choosing and implementing appropriate learning strategy
5.   Evaluating learning outcomes

The steps of Tough and Knowles are quite similar and follow 'normal procedures' of project management. As with project management, this often bears no resemblance to reality in which people quite often plan a project in a non-linear way. There are many situations where a project was planned and implemented collaboratively and informally and only later were the aims and objectives, critical path, and success criteria formulated and added. Nevertheless, these were well-managed projects.

Spear and Mocker (1984: 5–9) provide a different explanation for how adult learners organize their own learning. They explain the process as follows:

a.   The triggering event for a learning project stems from a change in life circumstances.
b.   The changed circumstance provides an opportunity for learning.
c.   The structure, method, resources, and condition for learning are directed by the circumstances.
d.   Learning sequences progress as the circumstances created in one episode become the circumstances for the next logical step.

It shows the risk of translating rigid processes and frameworks from a quasi-scientific background into a learning context. As Ken Robinson (2010) says:

> We have to go from what is essentially an industrial model of education which is based on linearity and conformity to a model that is based more on principles of agriculture. We have to recognise that human flourishing is not a mechanical process; it's an organic process.

It can be argued that learning according to a predefined project management model does not work for most people. People have different ways and preferences for organizing and planning. This does not mean that learners should stop thinking about what they want to learn. Rather, that it is more important to define the directions and develop the capacity to be flexible when it comes to different roads, strategies, and options that can be used on the journey in such a way that it meets the learners' changing needs and interests, and makes it an enjoyable trip. For example, one of the participants of the Training of Trainers said:

> The learning plan I made in the first seminar is on the wall above my desk. I look at it every morning. During the first weeks it only scared me. I felt guilty about having done nothing yet, and I didn't know where to start. But now I even add new points and to my surprise discover all the time that I already did parts of my learning plan, yet not according to the plan – they just happen in unexpected moments.

Learning with others

Although individual responsibility is an important element in learning to learn, communication and cooperation with others are crucial in the journey of becoming a self-directed learner. Experience from the project demonstrates that learning relationships with others can help people to broaden their views of themselves and extend their aspirations. This is especially so when it comes to the topic of learning, in which people might have a limited view of their own capacities and possibilities based on experiences in the past. Many people have the tendency to focus on those things they feel they are not good at and seem to have blind spots when it comes to their talents and potential. Communication with others in a context of trust can help people to widen their self-perception. At the same time, peers can help each other on the content of learning by sharing their questions, ideas, and expertise. Indeed, sharing and discussion are essential when it comes to learning: 'For most learners involved in this project, joint discussions of shared experiences were the most powerful catalyser for reflection' (Chisholm et al., 2010: 49).

A relatively new dimension to 'learning with others' has emerged with the number of online learners growing on a daily basis. More and more e-learning platforms and applications are offered to accompany learning activities and at the same time the number of learners using social media to communicate is increasing. In the Training of Trainers, different online tools are offered to participants in order to facilitate their learning. However, the success of these tools is variable. Some participants flourish in this kind of environment and use all the potential that is there to explore, share, and discuss. Some participants try for a while but then acknowledge it is 'simply not their thing'. A third group visits the site regularly, follows what is happening, and contributes every now and then. In fact, the use of online tools is strongly related to the participants' relationship with the Internet in their daily lives. Nevertheless, like many online activities, educational strategies to enhance learning and performance are still 'under construction'.

Reflection, reviewing, and self-assessment

Being able to look back at what one has been doing, understand what one learned from it, and decide where to go from there is probably the most crucial competence in learning to learn. Learning from reflection comes very naturally to human beings. We have a natural need to change and to develop. We tend to reflect and improve, but often in formal learning our experience is different. In traditional education systems, we were not encouraged to reflect on our learning; instead, others would tell us if we had learnt something successfully or not. Our natural capacity to reflect was not sufficiently used for learning in school. Of course, we used that capacity in other parts of our life where we were learning as well, but not planned or in a conscious, structured way.

In non-formal education, the practice of reflection is often well established. In our project, the daily reflection groups consisting of five to eight participants sharing their impressions and learning at the end of the day were regarded as of significant value and were most appreciated by the participants. In fact, learning to learn places greater emphasis on the value of reflection and makes it clear that more differentiated methods are needed to support learners in self-reflection. Thus the dimension of reflecting on learning became an added element in our model: reflecting on what I learned and how I learned it. There was also the challenge to find an appropriate balance between individual and group reflections. Reflection groups functioned as a safe place to come back to at the end of the day and to share experiences but at the same time they limited what was reflected on. Participants also welcomed time for individual reflection, as well as spaces for conversations with just one other.

There were a wide variety of preferences on how to reflect. Some people liked to write about their experiences in their learning diary, while others participated in intensive talks or preferred to reflect in more creative ways or in silent meditation. For many people, these planned reflection moments were new and they needed to discover which suited them best or what combination of methods helped them the most.

When the element of assessment is involved in self-reflection, many learners became unsure and express that they did not feel able to assess themselves: 'How do I know if I have learned enough?', 'What is the value of my own assessment?', 'How can I be objective about myself?' They understood 'assessment' as a final, summative judgement on them or their learning, just like assessment in an exam, and this led to performance anxiety. However, successful learning to learn requires self-assessment to be seen as a time when the learner harvests the results and outcomes of their learning in order to decide where to go next, or to follow up. The idea that you can tick that a certain topic has been 'done' is valid in very few cases. It would mean that there is nothing left to learn on that topic. Self-assessment also requires the support of others. The 'self' here does not necessarily mean that the learner does it alone, but means that the learner is, ultimately, the one who is responsible for the assessment. Others can be of great value in assisting in the process.

Discussions of findings: Educators becoming facilitators of learning

Educators may be inspired by self-directed learning and committed to enabling their learners to take responsibility for their own learning. However, participants may not be willing, ready or able to do so. They may like the notion but have no idea how to proceed. Many of them have never learned how to be self-directed in their learning or, worse, they have 'unlearned' it. As Heron (1999: 11) argues:

> This leads to the classical dilemma of all educational reform. Students have the need and the right to be released from oppressive forms of education and should be encouraged to participate in educational decision-making. But they are conditioned and disempowered by these forms,

and may not have the motivation, or the personal, interpersonal and self-directing skills required, to break out of them. So they may be neither satisfied nor effective when encouraged to co-operate with you and to be participative.

Supporting learners in a process in which they walk their own unique learning path, deciding themselves what and how to learn, means a radically new role for educators. Instead of walking in front of the group and directing them through the different landscapes, the 'new' educator ensures that the different paths that learners take are pleasant, motivating, and challenging. The 'new' educator also helps facilitate each individual learner to negotiate their chosen path. This is probably the biggest change engendered by the need for learning to learn, namely, the educator becoming a facilitator of another person's learning.

Apart from practical strategies, the most crucial implication of this change is at the level of the attitude of the educator. It requests a genuine trust that learners know best their own needs and an authentic willingness to support learners on their way (L2L Project Learning to Learn, 2009: 4) .

The word 'facilitate' originates from French *faciliter* and Italian *facilitare*, where *facile* means 'easy' or 'accommodating'. The facilitator accommodates the learning journey of the learner. The opposite of a facilitator of learning is somebody who directs the learning for the learner – a person who decides what should be learned, how it should be learned, and when it is finished. The traditional teacher takes this role. They see themselves as the one responsible for the learning process. In contrast, a facilitator does not take that responsibility but leaves it to the learner. The role of the facilitator is first of all to support the learners to take that responsibility and plan and organize their own learning.

Creating a social climate for learning

What makes a good social climate for learning? What is it that creates the conditions that encourage people to be open to change, for something 'new', for 'challenge' and for taking initiative and getting active? Certainly there is no standard recipe for this. As people learn in different ways, different circumstances and contexts will stimulate their learning. Hence a social climate for learning should facilitate different styles and needs.

The Learning to Learn Research Synthesis Report suggests some indicators of what constitutes a social climate for learning. After the initial review of the qualitative analysis of all practice projects, the research team formulated a set of hypotheses about aspects of the environment that support the development of learning to learn as follows (Chisholm et al., 2010: 54):

Learning to learn is supported by:

1. a diverse group of learners
2. transparency of learning objectives, planned methodology and learning process

3. confidentiality that learners can take trust in
4. safe learning spaces allowing for trial and error and learning without fear
5. trust, respect and appreciation between and among educators and learners
6. educators pro-actively accepting, while not abusing, their function as role models
7. a mutual rewarding reciprocal partnership between educators and learners
8. clearly defined roles of educators and learners
9. a supportive and empowering role of educators
10. group norms that are openly negotiable, but also binding once negotiated
11. structures and relations allowing educators and learners to intervene and engage without feeling restrained by time pressure, group size or programme setting
12. openness about and appreciation for questioning and changing roles, functions, hierarchies and power relations, allowing for and facilitating responsibility shifts.

Diversity, openness, safety, and mutual support are crucial elements here. Learners should be able to show themselves in their differences and this diversity needs to be appreciated. Human expression on all dimensions – intellectual, creative, emotional, and spiritual – should be encouraged and appreciated as a contribution to the learning process. Openness is essential to create a climate in which learners can ask the questions they have, express their doubts, ask for support, and offer their support to others. Meanwhile, to try out new things, to make mistakes, and to be vulnerable requires a high level of safety in a group. Awareness is also essential of the importance of mutual support in order to learn in a group.

A facilitator cannot create a social climate on his or her own but needs the cooperation of the group to do so. It should be a shared responsibility of learners and the facilitator to create and maintain a social climate that supports learning. The role of the facilitator is to initiate the conversation and to emphasize the importance of having a climate in the group that allows all members to learn. By introducing the different elements that contribute to a social climate, it is possible to raise the awareness and motivation of the learners to build on this together.

The most important point, however, is that the social climate genuinely contributes to learning. A group atmosphere that does not create openness, safety, and mutual support will ruin any educational group activity. Acknowledging the importance of this means giving appropriate time and space to build group relationships and identity, to allow learners to get to know each other and to show themselves in all their diversity using methods and exercises that involve different human dimensions and senses.

Learning on the agenda

To be successful in facilitating learning to learn means that the process of learning should be on the agenda for discussion during any educational activity. Learners who are responsible for their own learning should not only reflect on what they learn but also on how they learn. Awareness of one's own learning preferences and styles can help learners to better plan their learning and at the same time can motivate them to try new ways of learning. Exercises that allow learners to reflect on how they learned something often have remarkable results. Many learners realize that they never thought about their ways of learning before but just followed what was offered to them, sometimes successfully, sometimes unsuccessfully. Looking back at important learning moments in their life, including those outside education, and talking about them together with other people gives adult learners new insights.

The learning interview

During the Learning to Learn Project, a method was developed called 'the learning interview'. In this exercise, participants interviewed each other with the help of an interview guide about their learning. The interview guide contains around 60 questions but participants are invited to come up with their own questions as well. The guide functions mainly as a framework to help the interviewer. Questions centre around 'planning learning', 'seeing yourself as a learner', 'learning moments', 'learning with others', 'ways of learning', and 'the impact of learning'. The learning interview is undertaken in pairs, with both participants taking the role of interviewer and interviewee. This exercise always results in intensive and personal dialogue. During the evaluation, participants often mention how they appreciate talking about their learning to somebody else. Expressing doubts, questions, and frustrations, as well as the enjoyable side of learning opens the way for ongoing sharing and discussion about different strategies for learning.

In contrast to learning styles inventories, which carry the risk of people putting themselves into boxes, open sharing of the purposes, processes, and strategies for learning invites learners to explore and broaden their learning options. Reflecting on one's learning also leads to an awareness about how one has learned up to the present, as well as presenting new possibilities for learning in the future.

Big groups and small groups

Most educational programmes are designed for a group of learners who are supposed to follow a shared programme and to profit from it. However, if learners are viewed as people with individual learning needs and preferences, a common and equal group process is not appropriate. What is required is a radical review of how to design educational programmes. This does not mean implementing individual programmes for each and every learner. But we do need to offer space for learners to follow their own learning needs while at the same time emphasizing and creating possibilities for peer learning. The risk of self-directed learning is that learners just follow their own way, making learning a solo activity. It is important to stress the significant power of learning together. Learning on one's own is a limited process in which the individual misses the opportunities offered by cooperation, support, and feedback. In the Learning to Learn Project, many learners considered their peers the most important resource for their learning. It was not about the whole group learning together but about small groups with common interests and needs, people who identify with each through certain topics and/or specific ways of working.

For the facilitator, the task is to structure the programme in such a way that individuals have the opportunity to get to know each other's interests and needs. Subsequently, the programme should offer sufficient space and time for people to work together. This does not mean a ban on whole-group work in an educational programme; there will still be common topics and interests and a need to share the results of smaller groups. These smaller groups change after a while and new groups with new interests are formed. The 'big' group still remains an important reference point and safe place to come back to. The challenge for the facilitator is to construct a programme in which there is the right balance between letting participants work in the whole group and providing space for smaller groups and individuals to work on their own topics in their own way. The tendency of many educators is to focus too much on the whole group in order to maintain control of what is happening. This may be understandable but it is counter-productive when the ultimate aim is that learners progressively take control of their own learning.

Facilitation of individual learning

Accompanying self-directed learners means the facilitator needs to pay attention to individual learners. The role is not so much about providing answers to the learners but about asking those questions that help the individual learner to achieve more clarity about their own needs, passions and goals, and the steps they need to take on the learning journey. The self-directed learner has a lot to reflect on and many choices to make. The 'right' questions can be very important in supporting this process.

Observing and listening are crucial competences for facilitators of learning. Many learners, especially at the beginning of the process, are used to listening to the facilitator talk. The critical element for the facilitator, however, is to listen carefully to and observe attentively what learners say and do, in order to discover and recognize the specific needs, blocks, and passions of the learners. As an observer of the learning process, the facilitator is often in a good position to provide feedback to the learner to help them broaden their self-perception. Feedback can only be given on those aspects that can be observed, although learners sometimes have the false impression that facilitators are able to provide 'complete feedback' on their whole life.

All people have needs and passions, though many of these needs and passions are hidden, not spoken about. Passions are often not recognized or taken seriously in our education system because they are seen as strange, silly or to be consigned to 'the box of dreams'. However, passions are probably the most important drive for learning. A facilitator that can recognize and awaken these passions and help the learner to reconnect to them is touching the source of self-directed learning journeys.

Confidence-building

To be a self-directed learner requires a certain level of self-confidence. To decide for oneself, to make one's own plan, to relate to others for support, and to assess one's own learning process requires a belief in one's own capacities and competences. The level of confidence and reasons for lack of confidence can be very diverse and it is therefore quite difficult to say something in general about this. Nevertheless, within the field of youth work and social work, there is a lot of experience regarding confidence and motivation-building, and guiding principles' from the domains of social and youth work transfer well into the educational field.

Learning facilitator showing involvement

The first steps on the road of self-directed learning can feel insecure and lonely ones, so to have somebody who follows the learner, listens to and supports them can be of great value. Although in the end it is the responsibility of the learner to decide when and why they need support, a facilitator should take a much more active and initiating role at the beginning of the programme. Since for most learners this role of the facilitator will be new, it might be difficult for the facilitator to initiate and build the relationship. Therefore, simple, regular initiatives taken by the facilitator to show their involvement and interest can have a motivating effect on the learners. Similarly, the learning facilitator may consider taking a 'grandmother' role, as Sugata Mitra (2010) describes in his 'Hole in the Wall Project' with children in the slums of New Delhi:

> Use the grandmother model; Stand behind the kids and admire them all the time. Just say to them: 'That's cool, that's fantastic, what is that, can you do that again, can you show me some more!'

Making change explicit

Taking time to explicitly look at and reflect on a learner's successful progress contributes to their self-esteem. Sometimes it helps to emphasize such success and change. Many people have the tendency to see their behaviour as 'not that important' or even negative – in these cases, it is good to re-label observations that people make and to emphasize and express the relevance of the steps that have been accomplished.

Assisting in structuring wishes, needs, and aims

To express one's needs and to formulate one's aims in learning is one of the most difficult things for any learner. Placing too much emphasis on encouraging learners to define their learning objectives also carries a risk – many learners simply do not function in a linear way. However, it is important to take some steps here, to define a direction, to have some idea about where one is going. For many learners, it will not help to ask them directly what their learning objectives are. Better to have a more general exchange about their future, their passions, their wishes and needs to help set a direction and an overall goal. The role of the facilitator here should be to ask questions and to suggest possible paths.

It may be difficult for a learner to set realistic learning objectives for themselves. People often set goals for themselves that are unrealistic or only reachable in the long term. This risks disappointment and loss of motivation. It is better to set short-term and reachable aims, and a facilitator can assist the learner to break down over-ambitious or unrealistic goals.

Linking to others and confronting self-limiting perceptions

The value of peers in self-directed learning cannot be overestimated. The facilitator can try to link people in as many ways as possible, and the reasons for bringing learners together are varied: similar topics, similar questions and doubts, contradictory perceptions, different styles of learning, and so on.

People can hold very fixed ideas about themselves. Often these self-perceptions limit their learning because negative perceptions close down options. Offering feedback, reinforcing success, and pointing out the potential that a facilitator observes can invite people to develop a broader view of themselves as learners and their possible options. This is relevant not only for one-to-one contact between the facilitator and the learner but also for creating an appropriate atmosphere for this kind of behaviour in a group. This is because a group that develops an attitude that allows members to express in words the potential and strengths they see in others will contribute to the broadening of the potential of the whole group. Once this is established, the next step is to create enough safety for group members to challenge each other and to ask critical questions.

Challenges ahead

The challenges for education in the future include how to support learners and facilitators into their new roles. However, beyond this the real sea change will be the shift from an educational system that has as its main objective the transmission of knowledge and skills to individual learners within a given time frame, into a system that has the expertise to facilitate and accompany the generation and development of self-directed learners. If we accept and recognize that learning never stops and ongoing learning is necessary for people to deal with the challenges of a fast changing world, we have to acknowledge that our understanding of how we structure the provision of education has to be revisited.

A helpful metaphor – educational gas stations

From the perspective of lifelong learning, one could question if it still makes sense to develop educational activities as 'closed' programmes in which a set of learning objectives are planned that have to be reached by the end of the activity. A metaphor, which may be more helpful, is to see educational activities as the gas stations that one finds along motorways. A gas station is a place where a person takes the opportunity, on their own and with other travellers they meet there, to look back on the journey they have taken so far, on those things they discovered while travelling and on how they chose to travel; a place where they meet other travellers who are going in the same direction as them. It also is a place where they find information and inspiration for alternative ways to travel. They might also find people who would like to accompany them on the next part of their journey. Last but not least, it is the place to fill up on gas to provide energy for the rest of the journey.

An educational gas station should be a place where learners can, if they wish, meet other learners to whom they can relate, sharing both the content and the 'how' of their learning. A moment to share what they learned and the way they learned. The educational activity is thus transformed from learning about a chosen topic into a space where one reflects on one's learning to date and makes plans for future learning. The big question here is what services the educational gas station should provide so that this process can take place.

In 2011 a series of three- to six-day residential courses took place in the European non-formal education field, these explored how the ideas about the educational gas station related to European non-formal education. The trainers identified several key issues and challenges. First, there was the task of creating the right atmosphere and environment in which to invite people to join this process of informal learning. Expecting the group to 'do their own thing' was not considered a viable option by the facilitators, but offering a full programme on the first day was seen as counter-productive to enabling individuals to engage in self-directed learning. It was considered essential to create the conditions for an appropriate learning environment, within the group, before going into the core programme. There was no single formula but transparency about the purpose and the role of the facilitation team was essential.

For some participants, creating their own learning programme was considered too much because it was at odds with what they had experienced in other educational programmes. This was partly to do with the social dimension of collaborating with others, having the courage to approach other learners in the group, being open to questions, and ready to trust oneself and one's fellow learners in being able to make this a meaningful experience. It is essential that these learners are assisted in such a way that they can find their places, just like at some gas stations there are service points for fixing cars.

On the other hand, some participants flourished in this kind of learning environment and were extremely motivated, yet it was difficult to find the right balance between the interests of the whole group and the interests of the individual or small group. It was hard for the facilitators to know how to act in these situations, especially because in non-formal education 'group-learning' has always been a priority and a highly valued element of pedagogy.

Conclusion: Towards non-linear learning

Educational programmes often assume a linear way of thinking. Many educational programmes are developed according to five or seven steps that promise to deliver a particular outcome or competence. When the power and responsibility for designing the learning process are in the hands of educators, one could argue for this approach. However, most people do not learn in a linear fashion. Learners go up and down, around in circles, and backwards and forwards. Unexpected learning moments emerge all the time and people frequently change their plans and focus.

As self-directed lifelong learners plan and structure their own learning, they will be challenged by the absence of linear, logical programmes. Stepping away from the safe structure of linear programmes brings new challenges and ambiguity to learners as well as educators: How can we structure and scaffold such learning in a way that enables self-direction but ensures a positive learning outcome? This kind of 'natural' learning does not take place in formal educational programmes but in people's real lives, where there are few linear structures and programmes. With 'natural learning', we learn at certain moments, sometimes falling back, making big strides again, before things suddenly come together; some situations help a lot, and sometimes certain emotions block or stimulate us. It is chaotic, unpredictable, and full of surprises.

Dealing with ambiguity and change is a key competence for everybody to develop, since it is closely related to self-directed learning. In our daily lives, we are all confronted with ongoing change, an unpredictable future, and lack of clear answers to questions. This uncertainty can easily lead to feelings of anxiety and fear, which are precisely those feelings that stifle creativity, growth, innovation, and learning. To be able to cope with today's challenges, the competence to deal with ambiguity and change is crucial and at the heart of this is self-directed learning and learning to learn. Education should play a central role in assisting people to develop these competences and enabling them to respond constructively to ambiguity and change, which should be embedded in the curriculum. It is an ambiguous time for society and for education. The crucial point is for educators to take up the opportunity to create learning contexts in which all learners can flourish and grow and become self-directed lifelong learners.

References

Chisholm, L., Fennes, H., Karsten, A., & Reich, K. (2010) *Learning to Learn – A method in action. Literature review – Research Synthesis Report.* Innsbruck: Institute of Educational Sciences. Available at: http://learning2learn.eu/.

Grundtvig Multilateral Project (2008) *Learning to Learn: Progress report.* Available at: http://eacea.ec.europa.eu/llp/project_reports/documents/grundtvig/multilateral_projects_2008/grundtvig_gmp_141973_learning_to_learn.pdf.

Guglielmino, L.M. (1977) 'Development of the Self-Directed Learning Readiness Scale', Doctoral dissertation, University of Georgia, Athens, GA.

Heron, J. (1999) *The complete facilitator's handbook.* London: Stylus.

Hiemstra, R. (various) Available at: http://roghiemstra.com/.

Kloosterman, P., & Taylor, M. (2012) *Handbook for facilitators: Learning to learn in practice.* Vilnius: Fridas.

Knowles, M. (1975) *Self-directed learning: A guide for learners and teachers.* New York: Association Press.

L2L Project Learning to Learn (2009) *A key competence for all adults?!* Available at: http://learning2learn.eu/.

Merriam, S.B., & Caffarella, R.S. (1999) *Learning in adulthood: A comprehensive guide.* New York: Wiley.

Mitra, S. (2010) *The child-driven education,* TED talk. Available at: http://www.ted.com/talks/sugata_mitra_the_child_driven_education.html.

Robinson, K. (2010) *Bring on the learning revolution!,* TED talk. Available at: http://www.ted.com/talks/sir_ken_robinson_bring_on_the_revolution.html.

Robinson, K. (2011) *Out of our minds: Learning to be creative.* Chichester: Capstone Publishing.

Rogers, C. (1969) *Freedom to learn.* Columbus, OH: Charles E. Merrill.

Spear, G.E., & Mocker, D.W. (1984) 'The organizing circumstance: Environmental determinants in self-directed learning', *Adult Education Quarterly, 35*(1), 1–10.

Tough, A. (1971) *The Adult Learning Project.* Toronto: OISE.

Chapter 13

Learning to learn, lifewide and lifelong learning

Reflections on the New Zealand experience

Rosemary Hipkins and Bronwen Cowie

Abstract

The chapter uses the idea of 'transfer' to explore relationships between learning to learn, lifelong and lifewide learning. Their portrayal in the New Zealand Curriculum is discussed. We outline how they have been understood by school professionals, drawing in particular on research of the implementation of key competencies. Our synthesis rests on an expansion of focus from acts of learning *per se* to include the learner *as a whole person*. From the learner's perspective, learning to learn is about learning to do and be, not just to know. We argue that students cannot leverage the potential for lifelong or lifewide learning in the absence of a strategic awareness of how to develop, access, and activate resources and practices that support their learning. There are implications here for what the teacher does to support students, mindful of the rich life experiences learners bring and of the fluidity of their possible futures.

Key words: lifewide learning, lifelong learning, transfer, support.

Introduction

'Learning to learn' and 'lifelong learning' are often conflated in practice. In this chapter, we argue that these twin terms, while obviously related, are differently focused, and each is deserving of explicit attention. *Learning* to learn implies that there are aspects of learning process to which attention should be directed in the moment. There is an assumption that changing understandings of the aspects of specific interest (i.e. the *learning about learning* that transpires) will enhance the likelihood of future successful learning. Lifelong learning, on the other hand, directs attention to the capacity to learn over the longer term and by implication to go on learning, in contexts and for purposes which cannot immediately be specified, or even fully anticipated. To this we add a third idea: 'lifewide' learning recognizes that learners belong to, and that learning takes place in, multiple contexts and communities (Hay & Penney, 2013). While school is an important context for learning about learning, it is not the only possible setting from which insights about learning might be drawn. In this chapter, we use the notion of 'transfer' as a generative connector of these three ideas.

The New Zealand Curriculum offers a vision for students who are 'lifelong learners'. By implication this vision encompasses learning to learn *and* lifelong and lifewide learning. Arguably, you cannot leverage the full potential for lifelong or lifewide learning in the absence of a strategic awareness of how to develop, access, and activate resources and practices that support your learning. There are implications here for what the teacher does to support students, mindful of the rich life experiences learners bring and of the fluidity of their possible futures. In this chapter, we illustrate and amplify these ideas, with the New Zealand schooling context as our point of reference.

The nebulous positioning of learning to learn in the New Zealand Curriculum

The New Zealand Curriculum (NZC; Ministry of Education, 2007) provides a national framework that points to important outcomes for learning but does not specify precisely how those outcomes ought to be achieved. Based on this framework, every school must design a local curriculum to build on existing strengths and meet their learners' needs. This section outlines where and how learning to learn is positioned within this 'bare bones' policy framework. It makes the case that, while clearly signalled by NZC as important, learning to learn as a construct central to the development of the capacity for lifelong and lifewide learning remains somewhat nebulous. It is hinted at in many places, yet can remain elusive in the absence of explicit exemplification of what it could look like in action. Schools need to build their own interpretations of what it *means* to learn to learn and what might be involved in fostering this capacity via school-based learning experiences.

The front half of NZC is aspirational and was immediately well received (Cowie et al., 2009). It provides: a vision for young people to be and become 'confident, connected, actively involved, lifelong learners' (Ministry of Education, 2007: 8); ten principles to act as 'foundations for curriculum decision-making' (p. 9); a set of eight broad value-sets to be 'encouraged, modelled and explored' (p. 10); and five key competencies, defined as 'capabilities for living and lifelong learning' (pp. 12–13).[1] The front half also provides high-level guidance about the role of each of eight learning areas in contributing to a 'broad, general education' (p. 16), a section of advice on 'effective pedagogy' (pp. 34–36), and advice on designing a local curriculum (pp. 37–44). The back half of NZC is more traditional in its specification of curriculum content, packaged as high-level progressions of learning outcomes at eight levels across eight learning areas.

In the NZC vision statement, lifelong learners are defined as being: 'literate and numerate; critical and creative thinkers; active seekers, users and creators of knowledge; and informed decision-makers' (p. 8). While all worthy aspects of a learner profile, nothing here explicitly links these aims to the practicalities of what it might mean to learn to learn in the various learning areas[2] or in a range of contexts and settings across the life span. Learning to learn is explicitly named as one of the set of ten principles but its nature *as a principle* is sketched only in the broadest possible, indeed somewhat circular, terms:

> **Learning to learn:** *The curriculum encourages all students to reflect on their own learning processes and to learn how to learn.*
>
> (Ministry of Education, 2007: 9)

The principles are positioned within the NZC framework as 'foundations for curriculum decision-making', so there is a clear signal here that specific attention to learning to learn should be happening during teacher's curriculum decision-making in the moment, as well as over time. It is their responsibility to set up appropriate learning opportunities for their students. The key competencies give clear signals about what these learning opportunities might need to *add* to traditional learning goals. Key competencies are defined as 'capabilities for living and lifelong learning', but little in the general preamble about them, or in the definitions of the five named key competencies, has anything *specific* to add in the way of propositions about the intended scope and reach of learning to learn. An oblique reference in the definition provided for Thinking as a key competency illustrates the challenges schools face when determining what learning to learn might mean for their practice:

> Students who are competent thinkers and problem-solvers actively seek, use and create knowledge. They *reflect on their own learning*, draw on personal knowledge and intuitions, ask questions, *and challenge the basis of assumptions and perceptions.*
>
> (Ministry of Education, 2007: 12, emphasis added)

A metacognitive/reflective dimension that strengthens thinking capabilities is signalled by the first phrase in italics, and an epistemic dimension by the second. A similar oblique but reasonably clear signal can be found in the statement that outlines the role played by languages additional to the language of instruction (i.e. English, which has its own Learning Area statement):

> As they learn a language, students develop their understanding of the power of language. They *discover new ways of learning, new ways of knowing, and more about their own capabilities.* Learning a language provides students with the cognitive tools and strategies to learn further languages and to increase their understanding of their own language(s) and culture(s).
>
> (Ministry of Education, 2007: 24, emphasis added)

One implication here is that students will be learning more about their *learning* capabilities. Furthermore, to the idea of reflecting on learning *per se*, this statement adds *ways of knowing* as a dimension of learning. However, the reflective, ontological sensibility implied here could easily pass school professionals by if they cannot personally bring to mind specific examples of how ways of knowing might differ (for example, across cultures or across different discipline areas).

Overall, then, the general sense in NZC is that learning to learn and lifelong learning were taken by the curriculum developers as self-evident constructs, and that naming them in the front half of NZC might be sufficient to stimulate relevant changes to teaching and learning.[3] Implementation research has revealed similar challenges in determining meaning for key competencies and what their enactment in a school-based curriculum could and should look like. In the next section, we review these challenges, and draw parallels with issues of meaning-making in relation to learning to learn and lifelong and lifewide learning.

Learning from the challenges of implementing the key competencies

Across three years of a research project called Curriculum Implementation Exploratory Studies (CIES), we tracked recursive spirals of deepening insights into the *nature* of key competencies and the role they could play in implementing NZC's visionary intent (Hipkins & Boyd, 2011; Hipkins et al., 2011). The school professionals who took part in the CIES Project wrestled with these matters during successive cycles of making curriculum changes and reflecting on what transpired. As a consequence, their thinking about key competencies shifted over the three years of the study, at which time understandings began to plateau. This happened at the point where schools were seeking to explicitly integrate key competencies into the learning areas. By now key competencies were well understood as important enablers of active engagement and participation in wider school contexts but their possible impact on traditional 'academic' outcomes was still rather unfocused (Cowie et al., 2011).

In response to this finding from CIES, the Ministry of Education commissioned applied research that enabled us to work with leading teachers to develop rich illustrations of the reciprocal relationship between key competencies and each of the eight learning areas.[4] We wished to show how opportunities to explicitly strengthen an aspect of competency would simultaneously play out as rich opportunities to develop an aspect of more traditional learning in the relevant subject. We found that our own insights into the nature of the key competencies continued to deepen during this project, as did those of the teachers with whom we worked. Typically, these inspirational professionals could do more than they could explicitly articulate. Working with us often showed them further reciprocal potential in co-fostering subject learning and key competencies.[5] We (the researchers) had expected to find different dimensions to the individual competencies when integrated into the different learning areas. What we found instead were some deep dimensions of competency that spanned the learning areas but played out differently in specific learning contexts.

Table 13.1 gives a very brief flavour of some illustrative professional learning trajectories typical of those that unfolded across these four to five intensive years of researcher–practitioner partnerships. The middle column illustrates how teachers understood the key competencies with their existing practical wisdom as a reference point. The right-hand column illustrates a still-evolving trajectory of

Table 13.1 Examples of deepening understandings of key competencies

NZC name for key competency	Illustrative early understandings	Still evolving insights
Managing Self	Being on time, being organized, setting goals, and planning how to meet them Exercising some choice	Importance of fostering resilience/risk-taking in learning Thinking about oneself as a capable learner
Relating to Others	Demonstrating appropriate interpersonal behaviours Use and receipt of supportive peer feedback, peer mentoring, etc.	Fostering empathy Valuing diversity in experiences and ideas as a resource for learning
Thinking	Deploying specific thinking strategies Reflecting on own thinking	Finding and framing problems, as well as problem-solving Exploring ideas *as ideas* (Bereiter & Scardamalia, 2006) Epistemic thinking
Using Language, Symbols and Texts	Identification of new words/terminology and symbols Decoding and making meaning of specialist texts	Growing awareness of constructed nature of texts and the acts of interpretation required to 'read' and 'author' them
Participating and Contributing	Taking part in traditional group work with assigned roles Playing an active part in teacher-led conversations, etc.	Exercising autonomy while engaging with learning of personal, immediate learning group, and societal importance Exercising agency as a responsible and engaged participant in collective learning contexts

expanded understandings as deeper dimensions of competency emerge. Space in this chapter does not permit for an exhaustive discussion of these changing insights. In the following paragraphs, we have selected just three examples to illustrate the nature and complexity of the learning challenges entailed, beginning with the key competency Managing Self.

The aspects of competency listed as illustrative early understandings of Managing Self have an important characteristic in common. All of them are behaviours that can be supported and scaffolded within a classroom environment (or indeed in any context where a more experienced learner provides prompts and/or supervision to keep the 'self manager' on an already marked out track). This is akin to learning to drive in a dual-controlled car. The learner is demonstrably managing an aspect of their learning, but how might they fare when the support is withdrawn and they now need to go it alone, with all the decisions and actions that entails? Strengthening resilience illustrates this challenge well. To dust oneself off and try again after failing in a first attempt at learning something requires a number of aspects of self-management that no-one else can do for you. For example, feelings of frustration, disappointment, even shame may need to be put aside. The courage to try again must be marshalled and serious self-disciplined attention paid to the nature of the learning shortcoming that caused the lack of success in the first place. All of these things the learner must be *willing* to do – no-one else can coerce them. A whole chapter could be written about the dispositional challenges inherent in managing oneself, or indeed any of the key competencies (see, for example, Carr et al., 2008).

Similarly, encouraging students to use different thinking strategies in the classroom can be prompted and supported with specific models,[6] as can metacognitive reflection on how well these strategies were used (e.g. using specific journaling formats). However, thinking *beyond* the given parameters of learning tasks (as in problem-finding and -framing, not just problem-solving) requires an independence of thought and considerably greater intellectual effort. Again the learner cannot be coerced – they have to be disposed to do such thinking, and to recognize instances when it is appropriate to do so. The latter requires a sensitivity to context that can only develop with time and practice, and may not develop at all if learners are not given sufficient opportunities to see modelled, and then to practise, genuine independence of thought (Alexander et al., 2011, for example, describe characteristics of such learning opportunities).

As well as thinking about thinking *per se* (i.e. metacognition), it is important that, as students begin to mature, they experience increased opportunities to think about the nature of knowledge and of knowing – so-called epistemic thinking. Thinking about their own knowing cues some reflective dimensions of Managing Self, as already discussed. Thinking about other ways of knowing points towards strengthening capacities for empathy and respect for difference, which are dimensions of the key competency Relating to Others. Yet another challenge is suggested by research on likely trajectories of epistemological development (Elby & Hammer, 2001). If students are to grow in awareness of different ways of knowing, yet not get stuck with highly relativist impressions that 'anything goes and nothing matters',[7] they also need to develop awareness that defensible knowledge-building demands discipline-based thinking. By this we mean that students need to experience 'junior versions' of the actual knowledge-building practices employed in different discipline areas (Perkins, 2009).

When NZC was being developed, the key competency titled Using Language, Symbols and Texts was, for a time, titled 'Meaning Making'. With hindsight it is a pity this title was found unconvincing by some teachers and school leaders who saw meaning-making as the core business of students' day-to-day learning. Their traditional interpretation of meaning-making puts the focus on the meaning that *students* make, i.e. their personal understanding. A much more expansive interpretation of Using Language, Symbols and Texts cues how meaning is made *in the world*, in different ways, in different contexts, in different knowledge-building disciplines, or via the semiotics of communication technologies, including language itself. An illustrative shift here is from 'literacy' as entailing the reading skills that are a necessary (but not sufficient) enabler of learning, to a focus on scientific literacy, say, or historical thinking,[8] as specific practices of making and expressing meaning in the world, about which there is much to learn (see, for example, Kress, 2003).

The shifts just illustrated point to several important dimensions of competency/ capability that also have particular salience for considerations of learning to learn. The focus on dispositions, for example, directs attention to the *active* role the learner must play: ultimately, no-one else can do your learning for you, or demonstrate your capabilities for you. This is not to say that others have no role to play – the right sorts of support can make a difference and we will have more to say about this shortly. The focus on contexts directs attention to the *situated* nature of learning and the importance of having access to learning opportunities that really do afford equitable chances to demonstrate competency.[9] The focus on specific ways of knowing, with associated thinking challenges, directs attention to the importance of offering *substantive* learning opportunities. What students learn about, and for what purpose, can impact for good (or not) on learners' motivation and willingness to really stretch their competencies (Hipkins, 2012).

Parallels between evolving understandings of key competencies and learning to learn

The learning to learn principle was a well-received element of NZC, and tended to be aligned with the key competencies quite early in the implementation process. This is what we observed during the final stage of the CIES Project:

> A powerful cycle of iterative learning takes place when schools connect their further exploration of the nature of the key competencies to this earlier professional learning. [Whole school programmes that had taken place before NZC was released.] For example key competencies have now been connected to ideas about lifelong, 21st Century, or self-regulated learning, including Guy Claxton's ideas about learning power. In consequence schools might next consider how the key competencies are related to, and might transform, existing practices in areas such as inquiry learning, student goal setting, self-management approaches, or formative assessment. School leaders have been strategic in making these connections to ensure that teachers see how key competencies sit alongside, as well as stem from, developments related to professional learning contracts such as ICT, AToL [Assess to Learn], or literacy PD.
>
> (Hipkins et al., 2011: 35)

A recent report from New Zealand's Education Review Office (ERO) addressed the extent to which the NZC principles were evident in the curricula of the schools they visited. This report described learning to learn (along with the principles of high expectations and inclusion) as entailing 'what has traditionally been regarded as good pedagogy' (Education Review Office, 2012: 14). In the absence of explicit criteria for what this good pedagogy might look like, it is only possible to infer what ERO had in mind from the examples they gave in their report. For them, enacting learning to learn would appear to entail a degree of learner choice and independence (e.g. via 'inquiry learning'), combined with some structured goal-setting and opportunities for the learner to evaluate their own progress towards those goals.

The weaving together of key competencies and learning to learn, as outlined in both the CIES and ERO reports, arguably aligns more closely with the 'Illustrative early understandings' column of Table 13.1 above. There appears to be an assumption that students will be ready, willing, and able to use these self-regulation behaviours (goal-setting, etc.) in other contexts. However, the right-hand column of Table 13.1 illustrates the substantive shifts that can occur over time in understanding of the nature of key competencies, especially when there are opportunities to bring practice knowledge and research knowledge together. What else might we be missing in our learning to learn insights? Could we achieve the same degree of shift in ideas about learning to learn as we have seen in our ongoing key competencies work? If the association of strong traditional, pedagogical approaches with students 'learning how to learn' does indeed rest on an assumption that the behaviours being modelled and practised will be readily transferred to further learning (i.e. transfer is taken to be an unproblematic construct), might insights from research on transfer add to our understandings of how best to foster learning to learn?

Bringing transfer ideas to learning to learn

In the introductory section, we raised the issue of the seeming conflation of lifelong learning and learning to learn. In this section, we show how recent insights from transfer research might be used to deliberately bring them together, along with lifewide learning as a third important variant on the same theme. Our synthesis rests on an expansion of focus – from acts of learning *per se* to include the learner *as a whole person* with all the contextual specificities that entails. From the learner's perspective, learning to learn is about learning to do and be, not just to know. Our juxtaposition of learning to learn and transfer research also comes with a pedagogical frame of reference. Like key competency development, learning to learn is as much about what the teacher does as it is about the learner's actions and achievements.

Transfer research has blossomed in the early years of the twenty-first century. Bransford and Schwartz (1999) proposed that evidence of transfer should be expanded beyond *direct applications* of learning to include evidence that past learning has set up and enabled current learning. For example, when students learn to recognize broad principles at work beneath the surface of events, their learning will have left them better prepared to detect those same principles at work in future events. In this way, Bransford and Schwartz re-framed the very idea of transfer to describe it as a *preparation for future learning*. Engle (2006) contributed a further expansion in the field by forging an accommodation between transfer theory and socio-cultural views of learning. Her seminal idea of *intercontextuality* described ways of deliberately framing different learning contexts so that students come to see both the similarities and differences between them, with the potential for transfer in mind. In both these cases, transfer is supported by explicitly helping students to see how what they are learning has meaning and relevance beyond the classroom and beyond now. This action counters the assumption that a learner/student somehow will attribute the same functional value to information as the teacher does. By making the link between gaining and using knowledge explicit, both of these expansive ideas (transfer as preparation for future learning, and intercontextuality) have distinct lifewide and lifelong learning sensibilities.

Recent special issues of two journals (*Educational Psychologist* and the *Journal of the Learning Sciences*, 2012) further attest to the resurgence of interest in transfer. The journal editors attributed this resurgence to expanded views of what might count as evidence of transfer, as outlined above. Goldstone and Day (2012) also noted the generative potential in a move within scientific research to acknowledge ways in which the same broad general principles underpin the wide variety of theoretical frames now being used. Thus, from different theoretical perspectives, a number of unifying themes thread through the papers in these two collections.

We next briefly summarize several of these themes and highlight their implications for deepening insights into the pedagogical challenges of developing and strengthening students' competencies in relation to learning to learn.

- Across different theoretical framings, researchers have recognized that 'the perspective and active learning stance of the learner makes a critical difference for transfer' (Goldstone & Day, 2012: 150).
- In turn, taking an active learning stance implies that transfer has motivational/ dispositional as well as cognitive/conceptual aspects (Belenky & Nokes-Malach, 2012; Perkins & Salomon, 2012). Cognitive work and the building of a 'dictionary of experiences' (Rinaldi, 2006: 76) are both essential but students also need to be motivated to draw connections.
- Transfer is understood to involve the discernment of *both similarity and difference* across different contexts, events, and phenomena (Marton, 2006). Through experience of variation we become aware of the critical features of a phenomenon and are prepared for understanding and handling future (i.e. unknown) situations (Bowden & Marton 1998). Transfer thus involves a degree of decontextualization, including *accounting for* rather than *overlooking* contextual differences between otherwise similar activities (Wagner, 2006).
- All these challenges amount to a need for students to have multiple experiences of flexible thinking, so that they can become 'intellectual entrepreneurs' who proactively create and use opportunities to leverage their own prior knowledge in strategic and innovative ways (Goldstone & Day, 2012: 151).

The above shifts collectively imply a further important expansion in research focus to encompass an elucidation of the *conditions of learning* that allow transfer to occur (Perkins & Salomon, 2012). As we see it, the question of how teachers might design learning experiences with transfer in mind is essentially the same question as how to design for learning to learn. Table 13.2 is our attempt to draw on the above insights from research on transfer to inform ideas about how best to support students to learn to learn, both immediately (a classroom learning to learn focus) and in contexts beyond school (lifewide learning) and in the future (lifelong learning).

Table 13.2 is organized to differentiate between what students (left-hand column) and teachers (middle column) bring to learning to learn, and what they need to co-construct together during classroom learning experiences (right-hand column). The top row can be briefly characterized as highlighting the importance of *contexts*, the middle row is concerned with acts of *connection*, and the bottom row considers the student as a *whole person*.

Having elucidated recent learning from research into transfer, we are now in a position to return to the question of possible shifts in teachers' and students' understanding of what might be entailed in learning to learn. Table 13.2 begins to address the 'something more' that might be added to 'good pedagogy' (as per ERO's suggestion above) so that students do indeed develop a *strategic awareness* of how to access and activate resources and practices that support their learning. Learning that connects up knowledge and experiences from different parts of students' lives (to take just one suggestion from Table 13.2) is likely to be experienced as enjoyable and highly engaging, but to be empowering of further learning students also need to become aware of why this particular type of learning was successful for them. As David Perkins pointed out when reflecting on his own mathematical abilities, even highly strategic learners may not be aware of why they can do what they do. To find out about this strategic aspect of one's own learning is to learn to play an otherwise 'hidden game' (Perkins, 2009).

All the ways in which students might take an active learning stance, and teachers might deliberately engineer learning opportunities for them to do so, also become possible foci for *epistemic* conversations about knowledge and knowing. Students need opportunities to focus on their own knowing, for example how they know what they know, or what it feels like when some piece of important new knowledge changes the way they now 'see' many other phenomena. This has been described as having an 'epistemic experience' (Barzilai & Zohar, 2014). They need opportunities to explore how and why other people might 'know' the world in ways that they do not, which is likely to include instances where clarification of values is helpful. Students also need to experience many overt discussions of the grounds on which knowledge claims should be trusted, or not. To take just one example, Allchin (2011) discusses doing this in the context of claims made in the name of science as the important focus for 'nature of science' dimensions in contemporary science curricula.

Again, learning from the implementation of key competencies, we reiterate that simply *doing* and *experiencing* the things described in the left-hand column of Table 13.2 will be necessary but not sufficient to create rich learning to learn conversations that also have an epistemic dimension. Meta-level discussions about learning and knowing will also need to be made explicit. Thinking about how acts of learning are instances of active meaning-making needs to be seen as a

Table 13.2 Setting up conditions in which learning to learn might flourish

Insights from the transfer literature	Pedagogical capabilities needed by teachers	Conditions of learning for transfer
Students' past experiences need to be activated as learning resources: links established between their school and community-based lives are both informative and motivational (Perkins & Salomon, 2012) (*transfer-in of prior knowledge*)	**Knowing how to:** invite and build on students' existing funds of knowledge	Space and permission for playful exploration
	make explicit links between present concepts, conceptual tools and experiences, and anticipated learning topics and challenges	Frequent opportunities to practise flexible thinking
Present learning experiences need to be understood as having value for future learning; their benefits are seen to carry forward into the future (Engle, 2012) (*transfer-out to future contexts*)		Learning tasks include both familiar and novel dimensions (social setting, context, concepts, skills, etc.)
Students need to see how to connect experiences and ideas to create richer, more interconnected understandings	Engineering opportunities for recursive elaboration: learning is cumulative and becomes more nuanced over time	Rich experiences of variation increase sensitivity to salient critical features of a phenomenon (Bowden & Marton, 1998)
They need to develop or strengthen the inclination to look for similarity and differences across the various aspects of their lives as a way of making meaning and gaining power over their lives	Creating expansive links between small ideas/ experiences with the potential to coalesce into a much bigger idea	Diversity of experiences, ideas, worldviews, and contexts is positioned as a learning resource
	Supporting students to see how disparate events (in time and place) might be manifestations of the same underlying principles	Students are accountable for their learning – to themselves and to others
Students need to see themselves – and be seen – as capable of adapting knowledge to new settings	Providing scaffolded access to the knowledge-creating and legitimating practices of different disciplines, as well as tools to analyse what is the same and what is different about these practices	There are shared expectations that learning will be useful and used
They need to become confident innovators who understand how new knowledge might be made, and that they can learn to author new knowledge in some circumstances	This scaffolding has an affective dimension that builds student confidence and trust in their capacity to form their own concepts and understand ideas *as ideas*	Students have opportunities to be 'intellectual entrepreneurs'
(Transfer has identity and dispositional dimensions in addition to cognitive and metacognitive dimensions)		

valued and important dimension of learning *per se*. However, this is likely to be easier said than done. In our experience, very skilful teachers often *do* more than they can *tell*. It is feasible that some teachers who demonstrate the pedagogical skills outlined in the middle column of Table 13.2 will be largely operating with deep tacit knowledge of how to respond to learning challenges as these arise. They may make critical pedagogical choices that they cannot clearly explain to themselves, let alone be confident to discuss with students.[10] As we outline in the case study that follows, one productive way to address this challenge is for researchers with deep curriculum expertise and teachers with strong pedagogical skills to work together to build new knowledge about the challenges of shifting practice. Researchers can hold up a mirror that reflects critical dimensions of pedagogy back to skilled teachers, opening up spaces for 'indigenous invention' where new ideas about knowledge and knowing powerfully reinforce existing practice while also extending and challenging it (Heckman & Montera, 2009).

Different avenues for introducing learning to learn dimensions in classrooms

For the reasons just outlined, teachers' awareness of transfer possibilities is likely to precede and support students' growing awareness of how they might use their current learning (both about their learning and of any new knowledge of skills) in new and different contexts. However, the wide variety of teacher attributes and practices listed also suggests to us that teachers might make peda-gogical breakthroughs in their own 'learning to learn' awareness via any number of professional learning pathways. In other words, strong learning to learn opportunities for teachers might be a collateral benefit of other research that

---

Box 13.1 Teaching reading for 'lifelong literacy' (Twist & McDowell, 2010)

Two teachers from each of four primary schools worked with a small research team to explore how positioning key competencies as 'capabilities for living and lifelong learning' might transform classroom reading pro-grammes. The teachers were leaders of reading practice in their schools and most of them were active members of literary communities in their lives beyond school (e.g. in reading groups or poetry writing circles). With the encouragement of the researchers, the teachers brought their personal literary practices into their classroom programmes. Initially, they were somewhat reluctant to see these practices as appropriate pedagogy for teaching children to read. However, it soon became clear that the integra-tion of a key competency focus had transformed their reading programmes from strong but traditional skill-based practice to dynamic, shared conver-sations where *all* students enjoyed their engagement with written texts. As a consequence, most students voluntarily sought out individual reading opportunities at other times. By the end of the research, more of them than might otherwise have been the case did indeed appear to be on their way to 'lifelong literacy'.

Children were invited to bring their funds of knowledge to the *interpretive spaces* opened up during shared reading of the carefully chosen texts. For example, in one school where the goal was to foster empathy (a dimension of Relating to Others), the teachers encouraged students to put themselves into the shoes of the characters in a story about relationships. In another school, students worked as literary critics, interpreting an 'art deco' retelling of Cinderella in which the visual text told a rather different story to the written text. In these classes, Using Language, Symbols and Texts was the foregrounded key competency. The researchers found they needed to provide support so that the teachers could make explicit use of the structural and language features of English that gave such rich meaning to the chosen picture books. In every school, the interpretive space that opened up was a rich and inviting space but it was not a case of 'anything goes'. The structures and language features of the texts provided disciplined constraints to the conversations that unfolded. With the support of the researchers, the teachers developed a robust understanding of these constraints so that they could guide the conversations without unnecessarily curtailing them.

Commentary: Although the research focus was on key competencies, with a slight reframing it could just as easily have focused on learning to learn. The concepts of interpretive space (from literary theory) and intercontextuality (from transfer theory) have much in common. With the explicit invitation of the teacher, students' knowledge and experiences became deliberately deployed resources for further learning. In this example, the lifelong potential in reading programmes had multiple dimensions, including meta-conversations about how texts make meaning, and fostering disposition to be and become readers by choice, not just by necessity.

challenges and extends traditional pedagogies to focus on learning itself, and on the practices, resources, and orientations that mediate and support learning. We now test this argument out by presenting a case study that could be construed as conferring strong learning to learn benefits, although that was not the primary motivation for the research.

Where next?

In this chapter, we have made the case that learning to learn cannot be taken as a self-evident construct. If the rich potential in the concept is to be leveraged in practice, both teachers and students need opportunities for explicit conversations that 'unpack' the strategies that lead to powerful and successful learning. There is much to learn about learning to learn! As a result of the 'thought experiment' in which we used insights from transfer research as a lens for reframing and extending our own thinking about learning to learn, we now foresee a need to co-explore learning to learn with teachers in much the same way as we have recently explored the key competencies with them. Both conceptual and practical work is required to explicate the meaning and implications of the construct, how it might be fostered and activated in, for, and with both teachers and students, and to consider what it might look like in practice.

The intention that learning to learn should make a contribution to students' lifelong and lifewide learning directs attention to the whole person – who the students might be and become as a result of their learning and their learning to learn. Every student needs to experience the support that will help them develop a repertoire of practices, relationships, and places where they can experience and experiment with what is involved in generating, testing, and using knowledge that is new to them, even when this has been known to others. They need powerful experiences of authoring their own ideas – of 'intellectual entrepreneurship' – and explicit meta-conversations about these experiences of coming to know their worlds in new and enlightening ways.

The 'lifewide' idea also carries implications for forging stronger school–community links. Developing this idea is beyond the scope of this chapter but it is signalled as important in NZC: Community Engagement is one of the ten overarching principles.

> The curriculum has meaning for students, connects with their wider lives, and engages the support of their families, whānau, and communities.
> (Ministry of Education, 2007: 9)

We end this chapter by quoting the principle, both to serve as a reminder that *what* students learn needs to matter to them and others in the short term and to come with the potential for longer-term development and use. It also reminds us that the pedagogical challenges we have outlined should not be left to schools to shoulder alone. If we really are going to raise a generation of lifelong and lifewide learners, doing so needs to be a lifelong and lifewide challenge for all of those who have a vested interest in supporting students to become happy, productive members of society. Teachers, school leaders, researchers, families, whānau,[11] and communities all have something to offer and something to learn within an exploration of how to help children to learn and to learn how to learn.

Notes

1 Five are named in NZC, in contrast to the OECD's original four. They are: Thinking (not positioned as cross-cutting as in the OECD original); Using Languages, Symbols and Texts; Managing Self (a sub-set of Acting Autonomously in the OECD version); Relating to Others (a subset of Functioning in Socially Heterogeneous Groups); and Participating and Contributing.

2 NZC specifies eight learning areas: English, the arts, health and physical education, learning languages, mathematics and statistics, science, social sciences, and technology.

3 NZC was 'co-constructed' in a lengthy process during which the Ministry of Education provided leadership and structure while many education sector leaders contributed their own and their organizations' expertise. One of the authors of this chapter (Rosemary Hipkins) was a member of the high-level group that did this work and so must include herself in the implied criticism here. Hindsight is a wonderful thing! However, as this chapter will demonstrate, complex and emergent curriculum constructs can take considerable time to be fully revealed. It is likely that even the most prescient of groups would not have anticipated all the implementation challenges that have arisen, or may yet become apparent.

4 As an applied project, there is no formal report. However, 14 of these examples of leading-edge practice can be viewed as a published collection, along with notes for schools about how we carried out the work, and some generalizations about what we found, at: http://keycompetencies.tki.org.nz/Key-competencies-and-effective-pedagogy.

5 Rich descriptions of the practice of 14 of these teachers can be found at the URL in Note 4. The stories are accompanied by analysis of the reciprocal relationship between the intended subject learning and the key competency (or competencies) foregrounded for explicit attention.

6 De Bono's 'Thinking Hats' and Coster's 'Habits of Mind' are both popular in New Zealand's primary schools. The SOLO taxonomy has recently become a popular basis for structuring self-assessment tools, designed to support students to make decisions about the calibre of their thinking.

7 Deanna Kuhn has called this the 'pit of whatever' – capturing the essence of indifference towards the value of the learning/thinking on offer (Kuhn, 2008).

8 Emphasizing the intellectual effort required for historical thinking, Wineberg (2001) has famously described historical thinking as an 'unnatural act'.

9 Gee (2008) discusses the implications of placing the idea of 'opportunities to learn' in a socio-cultural context.

10 In our most recent Key Competencies project (see Notes 4 and 5 above), we found that interviewing the teachers and shaping the stories for their approval often surprised and delighted them: 'you make me sound so good'. Such comments were indicative of being unaware of just how skilled their practice actually was. It was also common that during an interview a critical detail that crystallized the whole episode might be the last thing a teacher thought to say: a throwaway line near the end of the conversation perhaps.

11 This Māori word is widely used in New Zealand as a reference to extended networks of family connections.

References

Alexander, P., Dinsmore, D., Fox, E., Grossnickle, E., Loughlin, S., Maggioni, L. et al. (2011) 'Higher order thinking and knowledge: Domain-general and domain-specific trends and future directions', in G. Schraw & D. Robinson (Eds.) *Assessment of higher order thinking skills* (pp. 47–88). Charlotte, NC: Information Age Publishing.

Allchin, D. (2011) 'Evaluating knowledge of the nature of (whole) science', *Science Education*, 95, 518–542.

Barzilai, S. & Zohar, A. (2014) Reconsidering Personal Epistemology as Metacognition: A Multifaceted Approach to the Analysis of Epistemic Thinking, *Educational Psychologist*, 49:1, 13–35, DOI: 10.1080/00461520.2013.863265

Belenky, D., & Nokes-Malach, T. (2012) 'Motivation and transfer: The role of mastery-approach goals in preparation for future learning', *Journal of the Learning Sciences*, 21(3), 399–433.

Bereiter, C., & Scardamalia, M. (2006) 'Education for the knowledge age: Design-centered models of teaching and instruction', in P. Alexander & P. Winne (Eds.) *Handbook of educational psychology* (2nd edn., pp. 695–713). Mahwah, NJ: Erlbaum.

Bowden, J., & Marton, F. (1998) *The university of learning*. London: Kogan Page.

Bransford, J., & Schwartz, D. (1999) 'Rethinking transfer: A simple proposal with multiple implications', *Review of Research in Education*, 24, 61–100.

Carr, M., Peters, S., Davis, K., Bartlett, C., Bashford, N., Berry, P. et al. (2008) *Key learning competencies across place and time: Kimihia te ara tōtika, hei oranga mō to ao*. Retrieved from: http://www.tlri.org.nz/sites/default/files/projects/9216_finalreport.pdf [accessed 2 April 2013].

Cowie, B., Hipkins, R., Boyd, S., Bull, A., Keown, P., McGee, C. et al. (2009) *Curriculum implementation exploratory studies: Final report*. Wellington: Ministry of Education. Retrieved from: http://www.educationcounts.govt.nz/publications/curriculum/57760/1 [accessed 6 April 2013].

Cowie, B., Hipkins, R., Keown, P., & Boyd, S. (2011) *The shape of curriculum change*. Wellington: Ministry of Education. Retrievd from: http://nzcurriculum.tki.org.nz/Curriculum-stories/Keynotes-and-presentations/The-shape-of-curriculum-change/Summary [accessed 6 April 2013].

Education Review Office (2012) *The New Zealand Curriculum Principles: Foundations for curriculum decision-making*. Retrieved from: http://www.ero.govt.nz/National-Reports/The-New-Zealand-Curriculum-Principles-Foundations-for-Curriculum-Decision-Making-July-2012 [accessed 3 April 2013].

Elby, A., & Hammer, D. (2001) 'On the substance of a sophisticated epistemology', *Science Education*, 85(5), 554–567.

Engle, R. (2006) 'Framing interactions to foster generative learning: A situative explanation of transfer in a community of learners classroom', *Journal of the Learning Sciences*, 15(4), 451–498.

Engle, R. (2012) 'The resurgence of research into transfer: An introduction ot the final articles of the transfer strand', *Journal of the Learning Sciences*, 21(3), 347–352.

Gee, J. (2008) 'A sociocultural perspective on opportunity to learn', in P. Moss, D. Pullin, J. Gee, E. Haertel, & L. Young (Eds.) *Assessment, equity and opportunity to learn* (pp. 76–108). Cambridge: Cambridge University Press.

Goldstone, R., & Day, S. (2012) 'Introduction to "New Conceptualizations of Transfer of Learning"', *Educational Psychologist*, 47(3), 149–152.

Hay, P., & Penney, D. (2013) *Assessment in physical education: A sociocultural perspective*. Abingdon: Routledge.

Heckman, P., & Montera, V. (2009) 'School reform: The flatworm in a flat world: From entropy to renewal through indigenous invention', *Teachers College Record*, 111(5), 1328–1351.

Hipkins, R. (2012) 'The engaging nature of teaching for competency development', in S. Christenson, A. Reschly, & C. Wylie (Eds.) *Handbook of research on student engagement* (pp. 441–456). New York: Springer.

Hipkins, R., & Boyd, S. (2011) 'The recursive elaboration of key competencies as agents of curriculum change', *Curriculum Matters*, 7, 70–86.

Hipkins, R., Cowie, B., Boyd, S., Keown, P., & McGee, C. (2011) *Curriculum implementation exploratory studies 2. Final report: February 2011*. Wellington: Ministry of Education. Retrieved from: http://www.educationcounts.govt.nz/publications/curriculum/curriculum-implementation-exploratory-studies-2 [accessed 6 April 2013].

Kress, G. (2003) *Literacy in the new media age*. London: Routledge.

Kuhn, D. (2008) *Education for thinking*. Cambridge, MA.: Harvard University Press.

Marton, F. (2006) 'Sameness and difference in transfer', *Journal of the Learning Sciences, 15*(4), 499–535.

Ministry of Education (2007) *The New Zealand Curriculum*. Wellington: Learning Media.

Perkins, D. (2009) *Making learning whole: How seven principles of teaching can transform education*. San Francisco, CA: Jossey-Bass.

Perkins, D., & Salomon, G. (2012) 'Knowledge to go: A motivational and dispostional view of transfer', *Educational Psychologist, 47*(3), 248–258.

Rinaldi, C. (2006) *Dialogue with Reggio Emilia: Listening, researching and learning*. New York: Routledge.

Twist, J., & McDowell, S. (2010) *Lifelong literacy: The integration of key competencies and reading*. Wellington: New Zealand Council for Educational Research. Retrieved from: http://www.nzcer.org.nz/research/publications/lifelong-literacy-integration-key-competencies-and-reading [accessed 6 April 2013].

Wagner, J. (2006) 'Transfer in pieces', *Cognition and Instruction, 24*(1), 1–71.

Wineberg, S. (2001) *Historical thinking and other unnatural acts: Charting the future of the past*. Philadelphia, PA: Temple University Press.

Chapter 14

Learning to learn with Indigenous Australians

Julianne Willis

Abstract

This chapter describes three case studies in learning to learn with indigenous Australians. The chapter describes how each study began with the intention of transitioning from a 'training' model of education to a 'real' or 'authentic' learning to learn model that champions a 'self-learning process'. From these studies a range of insights have evolved, including: the need to honour individual stories; to capture the 'pearls within' each individual, group, and context; to co-construct, name, define, and describe effective learning; to design and use metaphors, artistic therapies, and multi-modal/diverse strategies and activities; and the need to make quality time to do this well. Two learning design strategies – Learning Power and 4MAT – in particular supported the successful application of these ideas. Finally, these studies highlighted the need for flexibility and responsiveness in the co-construction of a learning to learn pedagogy, depending on the learning environment. The chapter concludes with an ongoing question: '*How do we rain down these words*' (Wunungmurra, 2013) about learning on the hearts, minds, and actions of our learners? While the studies offer some insights about learning to learn with Indigenous Australians, much remains to be learned.

Key words: case studies, learning to learn practice, learning to learn pedagogy, learning environment.

Introduction

This is a story about learning to learn with and from Indigenous Australians. The setting is in the Northern Territory of Australia and it begins in the 1980s in a secondary school of 600 students that offered the International Baccalaureate Diploma as a pathway for students wanting to access tertiary education. Within the Diploma there is a compulsory subject titled 'Theory of Knowledge'. Students learn about the nature of knowledge through questioning and exploring things like what is creative in mathematics? Or, how are the arts scientific? This same school also catered in a boarding environment for up to 300 Indigenous Australian students from over 40 remote communities representing 11 distinct language groups. Among these students, English literacy ranged from beginning literacy to the equivalent of Year 5 or 10 year olds.

With two colleagues, we developed and implemented a new subject titled 'Theory of Learning'. Motivated by social justice, this was an attempt at creating an equivalent metacognitive learning experience for 15–17 year old Indigenous learners boarding at the school. This group was targeted because they were most at risk of dropping out of school, they had the highest levels of English literacy of the 300 Indigenous students at the school (equivalent to the level of literacy for ages 7–10 years), they had the most potential to succeed, and they were about to enter into the Senior School Certificate course in the following year. We planned to:

- start with individual experiences of learning success and use these as a building platform for metacognitive language about learning;
- incorporate Bloom's taxonomy as a framework for structuring learning and inquiry as a process;
- include Socratic discussion circles as a strategy for exploring ideas in depth;
- teach students about Bloom's taxonomy and inquiry so that they could intentionally use these frameworks to support their learning at school, across subjects, in Years 11 and 12 and in life; and
- conclude the subject at the end of the year with visioning strategies and plans of actions applying the range of tools and behaviours students needed for success in Years 11 and 12 (16–18 year olds).

This was my first attempt at facilitating learning to learn and thinking about thinking ideas with a whole class of Indigenous students. Ideological zeal is a great motivator and we learned much over the year. Despite our enthusiasm, we were often challenged and blocked right from the beginning. For our students, learning to learn and thinking about thinking was a completely new experience. Classroom activities were dominated by significant silences and we regularly encountered a complete lack of response in some of our attempts to engage with our students. In time, we learned that our students held certain beliefs about school, which shaped their response to the initiatives. For example:

- when the timetable changed for different subjects, with different teachers, this was because the teachers had grown tired of the students and wanted to move on;
- the money for education (in particular, financing their travel and participation in a boarding school) either came from God, the Queen or the Government and this was a gift with no reciprocal expectation or shared responsibility;
- education was the least of their priorities and barely competed with football, ceremonies, relationships, family responsibilities, and grief or trauma (e.g. infant mortality, teenage death, adult premature death).

At any one point in time and in every week, the class attendance could include new students, absent students, and a handful of continuing students (often a third of each). When supporting one young woman to complete an assignment, I was personally confronted with the life challenges facing her. For this young woman, it was difficult to focus on anything at school. She had left her younger brother in the care of an alcoholic and violent mother. Every minute of every day, she feared for his safety and eventually left the school to go home to protect him. Completing her personal learning project by my established due date juxtaposed next to a fear for life and of death seemed ludicrous – both to her and to me.

Over time, my colleagues and I understood that learning to learn was a subject that we had decreed we most wanted the students to learn. When working with our students, we had not spent enough time explaining what we wanted to do and why. We had not invited them into to the deciding conversations. We had implemented this subject as if it were another teacher-imposed regime of knowledge, skills, and understanding that we had decided students needed to learn. We had implemented learning to learn as a teaching script like learning a set of lines because, even though we saw ourselves as empathic, student-centred teachers, we had not considered fully the reality of our students' lives. Over the year, we had not succeeded in convincing our students about the imperative for learning to learn in relation to their lives, in the classroom, in other subjects, across their schooling, and most importantly, outside of the classroom. Predictably, we had little evidence of any transference into other learning at school. We believed that if we had been successful in teaching our students to learn how to learn better, we should have seen our students engaging more and succeeding more in their other subjects as one indicator of success. Some of our students did upset some of the other teachers by asking them to justify the learning they had planned for their classes but their purpose was more to provoke these teachers rather than to facilitate their own learning. Attendance throughout the year did not change – again, another indicator of success would have been an increase in attendance and retention. At the same time, the students' other teachers were fighting for the time that had been allocated within the timetable for this 'subject' on the grounds that more time for literacy development *was clearly more worthwhile*. In the end, the school leadership agreed with the strong voices of these teachers and removed the subject from the timetable.

Based on this experience, we knew we had to reflect deeply about what we were doing in relation to the learning worlds of our students and the context of their schooling. In this chapter, I will first explore some commonly held assumptions about learning. I will then describe some of the characteristics and issues in Indigenous Australian contexts. Next, I will describe some work over the past five years in supporting community and individual learning to learn capabilities across three contexts, within Indigenous Australian communities in the Northern Territory of Australia. I then describe how, in 2013, we are still grappling with the paradox that Schon (1987: 93) identified all those years ago, between *education – the self learning process;* and *training – what others make you do*. Finally, I will present some conclusions about how this paradox might be addressed and, at the same time, raise some unsolved questions for further dialogue. The chapter concludes with a proposition: If we can combine learning to learn with curriculum as intentional, co-constructed, and contextualized learning design, we will have a greater chance of achieving *education*, or what Hattie (2012) describes as *visible learners* throughout life. Furthermore, we need to do this not only with students, but with teachers, school leaders, parents, and the wider community.

Common understanding about learning to learn

Learning to learn is a natural, human, hardwired process in which

> infants . . . are intrinsically inquisitive, masterful learners who learn to walk, speak and pretty much run their house holds all on their own.
>
> (Senge, 2006: 35)

The human keys to shaping 'natural' learning include: the need for meaning, or making sense of the world; purpose, or *how can I use this new meaning to benefit me?*; pleasure, or *things that give me pleasure are the things I want more of, for example, food;* and audience, or *I can see how what I do has an impact on the people around me who can also give me pleasure.* Building on this natural process, the most powerful learning occurs when learners ask their own questions and find their own answers. This means that the most powerful teaching is where the teacher activates student agency in learning to learn (Hattie, 2012). As a result, the job of teaching in the first instance is to harness these natural learning processes and work as an activator of learning.

Harnessing natural learning processes can be best achieved through ongoing negotiation (Boomer et al., 1992) and inquiry approaches to learning. Instead of being a traditional wise sage on the stage, the educator becomes an activator of learning, negotiating the focus and the process of learning with the learner to achieve desired outcomes. Through negotiation, the disengaged learner can be re-engaged and empowered. Negotiation requires more from an educator (the expert, the holder of power) than the presentation of content to a learner to memorize and repeat. It requires a willingness to include and exclude content based on consensus, where students participate in the selection of the content. Through negotiation and dialogue in pedagogy, where power is shared (Friere & Shor, 1987), the learner can be invited to make more and more of the decisions about what is being learned and how. Negotiation and dialogue in pedagogy begin to shift traditional ideas about 'the pedagogue' and develop a deeper understanding and a more participatory approach to the focus of teaching (power), the selection of content (knowledge), and the nature of the process (action). So, learning to learn not only harnesses natural learning abilities, it requires the intentional negotiation of content and process through dialogue, and this process has the power to liberate.

One of the most significant models that developed these ideas into learning sequences and practice was *action research.* Originally developed by Lewin (1946) and then further developed in the Australian context by Carr and Kemmis (1983), it was proposed that participatory emancipation and social change could be achieved through action research. Action research began to be used in education as an individual, group, whole-school, and system process for achieving major reform. The cycle of Plan, Act, Monitor, and Reflect began to dominate Australian curriculum and subject documents for educators in teaching, but also for learners in the classroom. One recent example is where learning to learn is described as a 'domain' in the South Australian Teaching for Effective Learning Framework (Government of South Australia, 2010).

Kemmis and McTaggart (1988), from Deakin University, also developed these ideas to include a broader understanding about organizations and ways in which we can analyse our work as teachers. They coached student research projects to explore these ideas in teaching contexts, in disciplines of study, such as the arts, sciences or education, in schools or across whole organizations. For example, in my own master's degree I researched the impact of action research as a change methodology for the Western Australian Department of Education. Broadly, an organization can be identified by the kinds of language or discourse, activities or practice, behaviours and systems, and social relationships or organizational structures that are in operation (Kemmis & McTaggart, 1988: 42). Furthermore, we can reflect on these descriptors of an organization to understand what has been and what is, but most importantly we can use them to describe and envision what could be. In this way, and using an action research model as a process, the language, activities, and social relationships within an organization such as a school, faculty, department or whole organization can be deliberately evolved. Learning to learn can then be integrated into planned cycles and have significant empowering impact on student learning and whole organizational learning cultures.

Hubball and Poole (2003: 11–24) draw a distinction between learner-centred and learning-centred approaches to education that is highly relevant to the development of a learning to learn approach:

> Unlike student/learner-centred education, a learning-centred approach does not necessarily imply individual learner control over issues such as content coverage, learning strategies and assessment methods. Rather, LCE [learning-centred education] requires a community of student/learners to make choices within a responsive, carefully structured, and guided learning environment . . . LCE includes both individual and collaborative learning experiences and places emphasis on the investigation and resolution of authentic problems through interactive and experiential engagement . . . Thus by calling a programme 'responsive', we mean that it responds to the diverse needs of the learners, critical teaching and learning issues in university settings, and available resources.
>
> (Hubball & Poole, 2003: 12)

The main point here is the intentional application of a diverse range of strategies that will engage a diverse cohort of learners. Another way of describing this is that an educator can choose from 'a broad repertoire of pedagogical strategies, on a continuum from teacher-centred to learner-centred' (Hubball & Poole, 2003: 13) based on student needs.

In summary, learning to learn is a natural, human, hardwired, lifelong process for learning and living 'well' in society (Senge, 2006). Learning starts with a belief that *'it' [whatever it is] is something I want – it will benefit me, my community or environment and so I need to learn about it and so I do.* Learning to learn approaches attempt to develop this basic human need by building on an individual's natural learning capacity to consciously understand learning, to name it, and then to choose what he or she needs to think, feel, and do, in order to learn something that will achieve a desired goal. This can be true for an individual learning to ride a bike or complete a mathematical task, or for a whole system of teaching professionals, learning to improve student educational outcomes.

In the twenty-first century, where knowledge is widely available through the Internet and educational curricula are increasingly available online, as predefined, measured, and standardized outcomes, learning is more than ever a social and emancipatory enterprise (Friere & Shor, 1987). Learning to learn is the capability of an individual to take conscious charge of their own learning processes in the community in an ethical and socially conscious and responsive way (Boomer et al., 1992). Learning is continuously negotiated through personal and group meaning-making where clear purpose and authentic audiences shape 'real' learning in context. To support learning to learn, teaching should be intentional, designed rather than scripted, mindfully implemented, and reflected upon (Schon, 1987). Constant feedback and use of data as evidence for diagnosis and future decision-making is a core professional skill (Hattie, 2012). Each group of learners – children, adults, teachers, school leaders, community members, parents/carers, and whole systems – has its own learning culture. Each group needs to engage in critical dialogue for themselves and with other learners to identify and understand existing learning cultures and then imagine, define, and implement new cultures that empower all members of the community to learn how to learn. The core proposition here is that, when an individual can learn explicitly how to learn and then choose to apply this capability effectively to all learning situations, they will be successful learners throughout life. This is true for the student, the teacher, the school leader, parents, tutors or coaches, and members of the wider community (Australian Council for Educational Leaders, 2010).

The context of Education for Indigenous Australians

Recently, some of my work has focused on promoting learning to learn strategies with Indigenous adults. Understanding the Australian Indigenous context is important before describing the actual work and outcomes achieved. The challenges faced by educators in Indigenous education in Australia are complex.

Historically, the day-to-day world of Australian Indigenous peoples has been invisible – and for many, continues to be invisible – in the collective consciousness of other Australians. What is often not understood is that Australia's history includes as many and as varied Indigenous groups, languages, and cultures as in

Europe or Africa. Horton (1996) suggests that Indigenous cultures reflect both traditional elements and the influence of non-Indigenous cultures.

The 2006 Australian Census reported:

- 86% of Indigenous respondents reported speaking only English at home, which is about the same as the non-Indigenous population (83%);
- 12% of Indigenous respondents reported speaking an Indigenous language at home, three-quarters of whom reported they were also fluent in English;
- many Indigenous peoples are bilingual; however, the pattern varies with geo-graphical location, with 56% of respondents living in remote areas reporting speaking an Indigenous language, compared with 1% in urban centres;
- older Indigenous peoples (over 45 years) are more likely to speak an Indigenous language than younger Indigenous peoples; of those Indigenous peoples aged 45 years and over, 13% speak an Indigenous language, compared with 10% of 0–14 year olds;
- Indigenous languages are more likely to be spoken in the centre and north of Australia than in the south.

In addition, the Australian Government reports:

> The Indigenous social surveys indicate Indigenous peoples are maintaining their links to Indigenous cultures. The 1994 National Aboriginal and Torres Strait Islander Survey (the predecessor of the NATSISS 2002) reported approximately 60% of Indigenous respondents identified with a clan, tribal or language group. The NATSISS 2002 shows a similar proportion (just over half) of Indigenous respondents continued to identify with a clan, tribal or language group despite there being a decline in the proportion (29% to 22%) of people who lived in homelands and traditional country over the period of the social surveys.
>
> (http://humanrights.gov.au/social_justice/statistics/#Heading363)

Broad mortality statistics tell another story: in short, between 2005 and 2007, the life expectancy of Indigenous Australians was approximately 15 years shorter for both females and males (healthinfonet, 2013).

Indigenous Australians are not one people or one culture. Tribal hunting-and-gathering is still within living memories and daily practices of Northern Territory Indigenous Australians. Traditional law, social structures, cultural ceremonies, customs and mores are still practised. A rich culture of art, music, dance, and sport permeates Aboriginal and Torres Strait Islander lives. There is a long history of successful and mutually beneficial interactions with peoples from other countries, including South East Asia, the Pacific Islands, and Europe. Missionary and church service and patronage have a history in many communities, with a clear perception that this has and still is a positive and constructive relationship. There is active induction into and ongoing practice in many world religions that sit alongside traditional spiritual beliefs. Many Indigenous Australians enlisted and worked in service during the two world wars for Australia. Political history includes invasion and European settlement, the stolen generations, self-determination, and recent Australian Government policy recognition (in the 1990s) that Indigenous Australians speak a language other than English. An intervention prompted by a Save the Children review that included the use of the armed forces and an apology on behalf of the nation by the Australian Prime Minister in 2008. Finally, many communities experience low employment rates and a high incidence of drug, alcohol, and physical abuse.

Education is widely understood to be a key strategy for improving health and well-being and increasing standards of living in general (http://www.abs.gov.au/AUSSTATS/abs@.nsf/Lookup/4102.0Main+Features50Mar+2011). However, as McPeake (2012) describes, in Australia today,

> A third of children living in the most disadvantaged communities start school developmentally vulnerable; around a third of Indigenous Year 5 students are below the national minimum standard for reading; Year 12 completion rates are significantly lower (56%) for students from low socio-economic backgrounds than for students from high socio-economic backgrounds (75%).
>
> (McPeake, 2012)

As these statistics illustrate, there is a wide divide in educational outcomes between Indigenous people and other people from other cultures. The moral obligation to work or walk together (Palmer, 2012), to build bridges, to make meaning, and to grow new futures is an imperative. Footprints in the sand are often used as a symbol for remembering the elders who have walked on the land before and the lessons they have to teach us, understanding 'we' are also leaving our own footprints, knowledges, and experiences in this land, and that if we walk together on this land, we can build new footprints for our children. As one Indigenous leader (Baumann, 2011) has argued: 'When we learn together, sharing and living the same language of learning, we will be empowered to create a new story for our future.'

Three projects

The following three projects describe learning to learn case studies with Indigenous Australians. The first project is with an Indigenous tertiary education institution, the second is with four urban schools and their parent communities, and the third is with one remote Indigenous community school. While in each context the student group has specifically targeted Indigenous learners, the focus of each project was different:

- curriculum, design, and development (vocational context);
- parental engagement (four urban school contexts); and
- school improvement (remote community school).

For each context, there was a deep desire to respect and work with the Indigenous cultural heritage and identity of the students and their communities. Learning cycles such as action research, appreciative inquiry or inquiry in general were perceived as more successful models for learning for students, teachers, and parents because they start with the learner's experience and story and position the learner as the 'driver or agent' of their own learning. There was also shared recognition based on evidence such as student enrolments, student retention, student success in assessment, and student course completion, that past practices and curriculum have not achieved desired student learning outcomes. In each context, the moral purposes for the projects have been similar – a deep desire to:

- improve student enrolments, attendance, and retention;
- increase student engagement in learning;
- prepare students for further learning beyond the life of the course, class or school;
- increase the number of successful assessments/course completions; and
- sustain successful practices beyond the life of the current participants (students, teachers, parents, lecturers, consultants, leaders).

Vocational and higher education institution – Batchelor Institute of Indigenous Tertiary Education

The Bachelor Institute of Indigenous Tertiary Education project focused on the review, design, development, and implementation of a course titled Preparation for Tertiary Success (PTS). This course is designed to support Indigenous adults in making the transition into tertiary education. In the first instance, the focus for the project was the development of the course content and sequencing of topics. There was also an explicit desire to include twenty-first century research findings about effective learning, especially the theory and practice of Learning Power (Deakin Crick et al., 2004; Deakin Crick, 2006). This research defined seven learning dispositions that learners need in order to be successful learners in the twenty-first century, which includes what learners need to think, feel, and do to be effective learners. Deakin Crick also developed an assessment tool – the Effective Lifelong Learning Inventory – to enable students to self-assess and as a result become aware of their *Learning Power strengths and areas for development* (Small, 2010). She argues that this is a powerful basis for self-reflection and individual learning action.

We began working with the lecturers with a priority to develop understanding about learning power so that they could implement self-assessment and coaching for learning power with their students. We assumed that we all shared a broad understanding about learning to learn and that we would be working together to implement these ideas further within the course, which had previously focused more on developing academic skills such as how to write an essay. Very quickly it became apparent that the lecturers as a group did not share the same understanding about learning to learn. There was a concern on the part of some of the lecturers about applying Learning Power ideas in this context in terms of its relevance to Indigenous learners. Within each PTS unit there was an explicit commitment to using Indigenous knowledges and cultural understanding as a major focus and core moral purpose for the course. However, in practice, this was difficult to reinforce with consistent and culturally appropriate learning to learn strategies. In reality, lecturers were often operating as individual subject teachers delivering course content and academic skills within an accredited tertiary course framework. Developing together, an explicit, recurring, embedded, and culturally responsive set of learning to learn pedagogical strategies across the course or within units of learning became an additional goal for both students and the lecturers.

At the same time, the group was working within a context of significant change and an urgent imperative to improve student learning outcomes. The client groups for whom the course was intended included both urban and remote Indigenous learners with very different learning needs and varying life experiences, including: different skills and knowledge; different levels of motivation for learning; strong personal drives about identity and purpose; some anger, frustration or despair about 'life' in general; and struggles with significant life issues and family/work responsibilities.

Time was spent listening to the lecturers' concerns and acknowledging and honouring both their individual stories and the collective contexts in which they were working. As a process for doing this, the group members were supported to explore their own experiences of learning, both personally using the Effective Lifelong Learning Inventory self-assessment and coaching process and professionally considering the teaching and learning pedagogies each lecturer was currently using to inform their own practice. Individuals and the team built bridges between lifelong personal learning experiences and research-led theory and practice, which included their institution's primary commitment to 'both-ways' development:

> a 'both-ways' philosophy which brings together Indigenous Australian traditions of knowledge and Western academic disciplinary positions and cultural contexts, and embraces values of respect, tolerance and diversity.
>
> (http://www.batchelor.edu.au, 2013/)

By naming, defining, and describing effective learning to learn, using the dimensions of Learning Power, the lecturers were enabled to connect their personal experience to an evidence base about learning. A shared language for learning to learn developed from here and this was then applied within the courses they were teaching. Throughout this journey as a team, they were able to establish explicit, recurring, and embedded learning to learn concepts and practices across the course.

The group also agreed to develop a common design process to ensure consistent pedagogy design and implementation for the new course. *4MAT* (McCarthy, 2012) was chosen as the design tool because each unit could be designed as a series of four cycles that contain different learning approaches for each quadrant. This built in variety for all learners and distinguished learn*ing* from the learn*er*. It also explicitly explored and then developed learners' strengths, making the focus for learning more relevant to them. The 4MAT design approach also engaged learners in areas they had not explored before and struck a balance between drawing on the learners' prior strengths and experiences and challenging the learners to explore new ground.

As a result, attendance, retention, and successful completion of the course improved immediately and continued to steadily improve. As a consequence of this work, Learning Power concepts have been embedded in the Principles and Practices of course delivery, as shown in a document outlining agreed principles and practices among the PTS lecturers:

PTS Principles

- Learning in PTS is about being empowered to create a new future.
- PTS is fundamentally based on principles of effective lifelong learning, Learning Power dimensions, and deep learning relationships which require close face to face interaction and learning.
- PTS incorporates 21st century learning principles, including multiple modes such as online learning.
- There will be connectedness and carry over from one unit to the next, across all of the units of the language, metaphors, key practices.
- We can all increase our Learning Power.
- Academic skills are embedded throughout all the units.

PTS Agreed Practices Brainstorm

- We will use the Spider profiles [ELLI learning power individual self-assessment feedback] as our key data collection and monitoring of learning tool.
- We will collect student narratives about how learning powers enhance their learning.
- We will develop interventions and strategies to develop the targeted areas we identify.
- We will use a 'temperature check continuum' using ELLI dimensions for student self monitoring of student learning.
- Consider think, feel, do/heart, mind, body in activities and for assignments.
- ELLI Spider profiles mentoring and coaching conversations and learning plans in every unit.
- Learning Power as an explicit framework for what we are doing.
- Metaphors from 001 are carried throughout all units – charts, wiki.

(Batchelor Institute of Indigenous Tertiary Education, 2013)

In one PTS lecturer's opinion:

> The ELLI model underpins all the PTS units and provides a common language about learning that is shared by both the students and lecturers – both groups have become more aware of their own strengths and areas needing development.

In particular, our students who have often struggled with being successful at formal learning in the past have now begun to explore what has been at the heart of those experiences and how, through understanding their own learning identity, they can change their future learning experience for the better.

A PTS graduate credited Learning Power with helping her improve her own lifelong learning skills, and particularly her resilience:

> During the past two years I've learnt to be more resilient and to keep going . . . there have been times when I wanted to give up but I told myself I have to keep going and I have, so becoming more resilient has been a big change for me.

Learning from this case study revolves around three key ideas. First, it was important to honour the individual stories of the lecturers and the students and their individual and collective contexts as learners and lecturers. Second, naming, defining, and describing effective learning power dimensions needed to involve a process whereby:

- the individual/group/community experience of successful learning is made explicit;
- this experience is then compared with twenty-first century research about effective learning;
- these are then used to build a community definition about successful learning and to develop individual and group learning identity.

Third, the use of Learning Power concepts with 4MAT principles to design and implement academic units for Indigenous students successfully catered for the diverse learning and life circumstances of the students and turned lecturer outcomes around in a positive direction. The impact of this process has enormous potential to move learning from training, or what someone does to the learner, to self-learning, or learning which is driven by the learner.

Urban schools and parent communities with the Smith Family

The Smith Family is a not-for-profit charity devoted to supporting disadvantaged children to succeed in education in Australia. It has many programmes, including experiential mentoring, literacy coaching by high school students to primary school students, family centre coordination, and Learning for Life scholarships for eligible students. The Smith Family project titled Parent Yarns – Learning Together (2012) included specific goals for Indigenous parents:

- to gain increased knowledge about their children's learning, how they can support this, and what they can do to improve progress; and

- to develop improved relationships with school staff and improved confidence to engage with staff.

Indigenous parents attending these forums in 2012 and 2013 came expecting a 'boring meeting to discuss issues'. Most parents came to the workshops because of their ongoing relationship with their school-based Aboriginal and Islander education worker, who advocated the programme and encouraged them to attend. Some parents explained that they came to sessions because they were dissatisfied with the actions of school in relation to particular incidents with their children, or they came believing they wanted to learn more about this 'mystery' called learning or schooling. The programme was built on the belief that increasing parents' understandings about learning in the twenty-first century will develop their capacity to better support their children's learning at school. Evaluation data from the Parent Yarns indicated that several individuals felt they knew nothing about schooling: that they were alone; they had low self-esteem about how to help their children; and they experienced anger either at themselves or the school. Some parents spoke about their own lack of success at school and some expressed concern about their own learning and the fact they were not able to read and write.

Ninety-minute workshops were held once a term and designed as nurturing and uplifting experiences. Families were provided with a meal and child-minding was available to give parents child-free time with each other. The sessions focused on building positive belief systems about learning and aimed to convince each individual that they and their children are hardwired to learn. The sessions were also designed to change parents' perceptions of learning from 'it's just lots of "book" learning and dense writing' to an expanded understanding about learning at school, which could include the beliefs that:

- we all have successful experiences of learning;
- we can use this success to build a vision for ourselves and our children as learners; and
- learning can be fun and can be expressed in many ways.

Parent perception data from across the four schools indicated that the main reasons for parents participating in the Parent Yarns were their desire for success for their children and their wish to get more involved with the school.

Parents' reflections on the events were positive:

It became a really fun night that got everyone involved emotionally, mentally, and physically.

I wasn't sure it was worth my precious time – but I really liked how the yarn had a schedule and everyone could have a say if they liked with no pressure if they just wanted to listen. Now my school's parent yarn has my name on their list and I feel totally empowered by this.

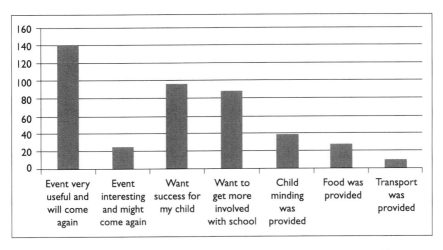

Figure 14.1 Parent perception data.

> I have been able to build confidence and respect for the teachers – I asked myself, what can I do to help not only for my daughter but the other children as well?
>
> ... all the parties that were there together – parents, staff, kids – talked together and worked together for a common cause.

This case study shows the importance of capturing the *pearls within* each individual, group, and context by facilitating workshops in which individuals and groups share their 'learning' success stories, make links between common experiences, and build shared visions for where they are headed. Through this process, parents built trust and respect, began to heal 'broken' learning journeys of the past, changed their perceptions about self as learner, and further enabled self-learning as opposed to training.

St. Francis Xavier Catholic Community School[1]

In a remote community context, Indigenous Australians live in two worlds – a traditional way of life that values kinship, totems, hunting and gathering alongside a mainstream way of life that includes formal schooling, supermarkets, houses, and business. Through school-based strategic planning discussions, the following vision emerged:

> When we learn together, sharing and living the same language for learning, we will be empowered to create a new story for our future
>
> (Baumann, 2010).

With this dream, Indigenous staff at the school were invited to discuss what they thought was good learning? Initially, there was silence. One interpretation of this silence could be the silence resulting from a group struggling to understand what this question meant (Schon, 1987). It is possible this was the first time they had been asked to think about learning as a distinct process, or if they had, they were not in an environment or a relationship with me where it was safe enough to feel that they could talk about it. Eventually, the process of thinking about learning evolved in this context with the group drawing their own personal life-learning journeys, highlighting the significant steps along the way. Discussion started when they were asked to consider the things they needed to think, feel, and do to learn successfully during significant learning experiences in their own lives.

Three years on, and after much learning together, the school is still defining learning. They have used Learning Power dimensions (Deakin Crick et al., 2004) as an overall framework for defining learning and they have shaped and re-shaped these definitions using words, symbols, songs, and explicit Learning Power weekly activity sessions. Using communications mediums other than writing has been critical in this process of making meaning about learning. Linking learning power with traditional knowledge was also important. It took 18 months to finalize the Learning Power metaphors depicted in Fig. 14.2.

Each of these metaphors has a strong Indigenous story and tradition behind it. One example involves the Golden Orb Spider as a metaphor for meaning-making. The spider and its web was chosen to represent meaning-making because

> when we watch nature it helps us to think about things. In the old days the women saw the web of the Golden Orb Spider and it gave them the idea that they could use this as a model for making string bags. In this way, weaving of many kinds was born
>
> (Baumann, 2011)

In this way, the web represents how individuals saw one thing in one context and made a link to how they could do something else in another context.

The development of these metaphors has involved a process of describing and re-describing learning. A contextual language for learning has been developed over time through a complex co-construction process. Metaphor has provided a medium through which two very different cultural understandings and traditions have come together to define learning. Metaphors and images have become a particularly significant way of building bridges between two cultures. It has involved the students, the teachers, and members of the school community in an ongoing negotiation of meaning around learning.

In feedback from staff and community members about this work (Avery et al., 2012), the idea of 'making learning real' has been repeatedly emphasized. This means:

- having real, deep listening conversations where Indigenous and non-Indigenous people deeply listen to and respect each other;

Figure 14.2 Learning power metaphors.

- understanding the real context within which people live (e.g. learning English as a Second Language and the fact that Indigenous student English literacy results in national testing are in the lowest percentile and the high staff turnover);
- being real and authentic when teaching Indigenous cultures and knowledges in the curriculum; and
- using the life experiences of the Indigenous staff and families in learning at the school.

In 2012, Elise Fenn (a teacher from the school and the project school-based facilitator) also presented the following summary about what Learning Power conversations have done at the school:

- Generated valued local knowledge
- Provided new energy and provided a force for working together and reflecting together

- Provided new ideas for teaching and learning
- Valued arts learning and engagement within the school
- Built the beginning of a shared language about learning

This case study demonstrates the importance of making time to get people to 'tell their own stories', ensuring that Indigenous Australians and non-Indigenous Australians co-construct learning definitions together as an authentic way to 'walk together' using the best of Indigenous and western knowledges and using metaphors, the arts and multi-modal strategies and activities as part of the process of co-construction. Using these and other strategies, educators can emphasize that learning is a natural, active, and shared human experience. This is especially true for learners who come from different cultures or who have had negative experiences from former learning and life experiences. Some learners, including students, teachers, and parents, need to be convinced that they can learn and have been learning all of their lives. Understanding this builds a sense of hope and creates a space for intentional positive learning action. Using these strategies, we can challenge and re-frame strongly held beliefs about 'failure' into positive learning identities.

This experience also strengthens the proposition that finding ways to co-construct shared understanding about and language for learning, where learning conversations include the life-worlds, cultures, and hearts of the learners, is critical for achieving deep community-wide discourse about learning. Time needs to be allocated for making this happen in a learning community. Co-constructing, re-constructing, and developing understanding using metaphors, images, and artistic therapies can be vehicles for building such a shared understanding. Learners, educators, leaders, and parents need to construct this together, growing a shared purpose and vision for learning in their particular cultural context.

Progress has been slow. However, the work continues and in the words of the then school Principal:

> Our Ngambara Fimityatit metaphors represent the best intentions of our two worlds. We have created a shared language for learning and a way of being that is common. It underpins and informs the decisions that we make for our school and for the children in our community. Our vision is that by walking gently together, the spirit of our metaphors will be our gift to our kids – so that they can grow strong in culture, strong in learning and strong in faith.
>
> (Jenny Cole, 2013).

Summary and conclusions

Each project began with similar explicit assumptions about learning. A 'training' delivery model of education in which knowledge is transmitted from the teacher to the student was not generating successful results. By embedding a learning to learn approach into the course, the sessions, and the school day, all learners – including students, parents, teachers, and lecturers – were supported to develop 'the self-learning process'.

In describing each project or case study, a particular finding was emphasized. Each insight was true for all projects and can be summarized as the beginning of an evidence base about learning to learn in Indigenous Australian communities that enables self-directed learning as opposed to training:

- It is important to honour the individual stories and collective contexts as learners, teachers, and lecturers. It is important to make explicit connections about learning in between individuals' personal experiences and the focus of their learning and the curriculum.
- Building a community learning identity is facilitated through naming, defining, and describing effective learning dispositions using the accumulated knowledge of a community's experience of successful learning and combining this with what twenty-first century research tells us about effective learning.
- Building trust and respect, healing some of 'broken' learning journeys of the past, and changing perceptions about self as learner is a key process. This can be described as 'capturing the *pearls within* each individual, group, and context' where individuals and groups share their 'learning' success stories, make links between common experiences, and build shared visions for where they are headed.
- The use of metaphors, images, artistic therapies, and multi-modal strategies and activities enables educators to emphasize that learning is a natural, active, and shared human experience. Despite formal learning experiences, some learners (children and adults) need to be convinced that they can learn. They have in fact been doing it all of their lives. Using a range of strategies, we can challenge and re-frame strongly held beliefs about 'failure' into positive learning identities.
- Learning conversations should include the life-worlds, cultures, and hearts of the learners, in order to co-construct shared understanding as learners negotiate the curriculum. Time needs to be allocated for making this happen in a learning community, using metaphors and artistic therapies as vehicles. Learners, educators, leaders, and parents need to find time to do this together, growing a shared purpose and vision for learning in their particular cultural curriculum context.

These case studies have also highlighted the need for flexibility and responsiveness in the delivery of learning to learn pedagogy, depending on the learning environment. When implemented in classrooms, there is potential for both educators and students to uncover a complex history, language, culture, family, social life, and political reality. This requires strong empathy and listening skills to enable the individual or group to work through these issues using a learning to learn process. When implemented in educational contexts, one main issue can be allocating enough time for teachers and learners to learn how to learn. It requires groups and individuals to commit to developing their concepts or beliefs about learning and a willingness to explore questions about how curriculum and assessment regimes are delivered.

Complexity in education has never been more clearly highlighted for me as an Anglo-Western heritage educator as when working with Indigenous Australians. Every day I learn something new about perceptions, knowledge, and connections to land, community, and tradition. The differences and the similarities of my 'world' and the 'worlds' of our Indigenous partners in education have become a focus of great significance in my work.

In addition to this, two significant frameworks supported the ongoing development of these insights: Learning Power and 4MAT. Deakin Crick (2006: 137) in championing Learning Power, contributes to this discussion by describing a need for a

> paradigm shift towards a relational and transformative model of learning, in which the creation of interdependent communities of intentional learners provides a basis for the integration of 'traditional academic' skills and outcomes with the learning dispositions, values and attitudes necessary to meet the demands of the emerging 'networked society'.

Amy Nowacki (2011: 11) discusses the impact of 4MAT:

> Problem based learning requires more than just listening; students must prepare in advance and discuss/solve problems. The 4MAT framework helps design classroom activities to support students throughout the learning process. This approach supports motivated learners to acquire, apply, generalize and reflect on new knowledge. The model, however, applies to any discipline and its flexibility allows the incorporation of various teaching techniques. We hope to inspire others to build on learning theories and to engage students. Knowledge disseminated does not equate to knowledge learned.

These case studies suggest that a merging of these two frameworks or learning design systems (Learning Power and 4MAT) has made a major contribution to learning to learn in Indigenous learning contexts. These approaches or frameworks, along with the findings described above, have enabled individuals and groups to authentically grapple with learning and learning design. Using frameworks like these in teams or across whole groups/organizations can also help us to grapple positively with how we stop delivering education as training. These frameworks or learning design systems, consistently implemented, have helped us engage critically with each new Indigenous group, consider their usefulness, and co-construct learning to learn together.

This chapter is a twenty-first century contribution to the discussion started by Schon (1987), about learning as education as opposed to learning as training. And as Perso (2012: 83) adds:

> we must better understand the belief systems and values of the primary culture of each of our students . . . teachers are willing to learn to understand their students and their needs . . . willing to become students of the cultures

in which they are entering – a willingness to engage with the heart as well as the mind.

Finally, using a question proposed by one of the parents in our Learning Together programme, this chapter explores but still asks, *how do we rain down these words about learning on the hearts, minds, and actions of our learners?* The experiences described in this chapter, using an explicit learning framework (like Learning Power) and a clear intentional design system (like 4MAT), suggest that we can combine learning to learn with curriculum as intentional, co-constructed, and contextualized learning design. Doing this, we may have a greater chance of achieving *education*, or what Hattie (2012) now describes as *visible learners* throughout life. Furthermore, we need to do this not only with the learners, but also the teachers, school leaders, parents, and the wider community. Had we done this all those years ago in our very new Theory of Learning subject, there might have been less *doing things to the learners* (or training) and more *self-directed learning, walking, learning, and designing together, in community.*

Note

1. The Ngambara Fimityatit project was developed by Catholic Education NT with funding from an Australian Smarter Schools National Partnership Project.

Acknowledgements

Miriam Rose Baumann, Imelda Palmer, Sharon Duong, Elise Fenn, Tess McPeake, Michaela Wilkes, Majella O'Neill, and Jenny Cole – all have been my colleagues, teachers, project leaders, critical friends, and editors.

Ruth Deakin Crick (Reader in Systems Learning and Leadership, University of Bristol Graduate School of Education) – my co-conspirator in the third project and academic advisor/consultant. She also met me during one of those times where life challenges you in every way. As a highly esteemed and highly regarded international educational leader, she most surprisingly believed in me.

Marilynn Willis (Consultant and Education Designer) – in two of these projects Marilynn and I have worked together to activate learning to learn. She is my partner, my inspiration, and my co-constructor in all things. This chapter is as much her work as mine.

John Pollock (husband) – my rock, my support, and my most significant life educational role model.

References

Australian Council for Educational Leaders (ACEL) (2010) *ACEL Leadership Capability Framework.* Canberra, ACT: ACEL.
Avery, M., Fenn, E., Kerinaiua, L., & Willis, J. (2012) 'An inquiry mindset, the conceptual age: Where creativity is now as important as intellectual endeavour',

Paper presented to the Australian Council for Educational Leaders Conference in Brisbane, 2012.

Baumann, M.R. (2010) Unpublished discussion with Majella O'Neill, Ruth Deakin Crick, Elise Fenn, Phillip Wilson, and Julianne Willis, Daly River, Northern Territory.

Baumann, M.R. (2011) Unpublished conversation with Julianne Willis, Daly River, Northern Territory.

Bloom, B. (1956) *Taxonomy of educational objectives*. New York: David McKay.

Boomer, G., Lester, N., Onore, C., & Cook, J. (1992) *Negotiating the curriculum*. London: Falmer Press.

Carr, W., & Kemmis, S. (1983) *Becoming critical: Education, knowledge and action research*. Geelong, VIC: Deakin University Press.

Cole, J. (2013) Unpublished conversation with Julianne Willis, Darwin, Australia.

Deakin Crick, R. (2006) *Learning power in practice: A guide for teachers*. London: Paul Chapman.

Deakin Crick, R., Broadfoot, P., & Claxton, G. (2004) 'Developing an effective lifelong learning inventory: The ELLI Project', *Assessment in Education*, *11*(3), 247–272.

Fenn E. (2012) Learning Power in Daly River School, Presentation to Catholic Education Office, Darwin.

Friere, P., & Shor, I. (1987) *A pedagogy for liberation*. New York: Macmillan.

Government of South Australia Department of Education and Children's Services (2010) *South Australian Teaching for Effective Learning Framework guide*. Adelaide, SA: Government of South Australia Department of Education and Children's Services.

Hattie, J. (2012) *Visible learning for teachers*. London: Routledge.

Horton, D. (1996) *Aboriginal Australia wall map*. Sydney, NSW: Aboriginal Studies Press, AIATSIS.

Hubball, H., & Poole, G. (2003) 'Learning-centred education to meet the diverse needs and circumstances of university faculty through an eight-month programme on teaching and learning in higher education', *International Journal for Academic Development*, *8*(2), 11–24.

Kemmis, S., & McTaggart, R. (Eds.) (1988) *The action research planner* (3rd edn.). Geelong, VIC: Deakin University Press.

Lewin, K. (1946) 'Action research and minority problems', *Journal of Social Issues*, *2*(4), 34–46.

McCarthy, B. (2012) *The learning cycle, the 21st century and millennial learners: Who they are and how to teach them*. Wauconda, IL: About Learning.

McPeake, T. (2012) 'Parent Yarns – Learning Together: Parent engagement in Australian schools', Lecture given at Bristol University, 20 December. Retrieved from http://www.slideshare.net/Ruthdeakincrick/parental-engagement-in-northern-territory-australia-tess-mc-peake

Nowacki, A. (2011) 'Using the 4MAT Framework to design a problem-based learning biostatistics course', *Journal of Statistics Education*, *19*(3), 1–24.

Perso, T. (2012) *Cultural responsiveness and school education – with particular focus on Australia's first peoples: A review and synthesis of literature*. Darwin, NT: Menzies School of Health Research, Centre for Child Development and Education.

Schon, D.A. (1987) *Educating the reflective practitioner*. San Francisco, CA: Jossey-Bass.

Senge, P. (2006) *The fifth discipline: The art and practice of the learning organization.* London: Random House.

Small, T. (2010) *Learning to achieve: A handbook of strategies for increasing learning power.* Bristol: ViTaL Partnerships.

The Smith Family (2012) *Class movie: Parent Yarns – Learning Together,* micro-documentary. Retrieved from http://learningemergence.net/2012/12/07/csll-seminar-series-parent-yarns-learning-together-parent-engagement-in-australian-schools/ accessed 26.04.14

Wunungmurra, A. (2013) 'Parent Yarns – Learning Together', workshop conversations.

Useful websites

Australian Bureau of Statistics: http://www.abs.gov.au/AUSSTATS/abs@.nsf/Lookup/4102.0Main+Features50Mar+2011

Australian Council for Educational Leaders, ACEL Leadership Capability: http://www.acelleadership.org.au/acel-leadership-capability-framework-0

Australian Indigenous Health InfoNet: http://www.healthinfonet.ecu.edu.au/health-facts/overviews/mortality

Batchelor Institute of Indigenous Tertiary Education: http://www.batchelor.edu.au

Learning Emergence: http://learningemergence.net/2012/12/07/csll-seminar-series-parent-yarns-learning-together-parent-engagement-in-australian-schools/

Index

This index uses the abbreviation L2L throughout to stand for 'learn to learn' or 'learning to learn'